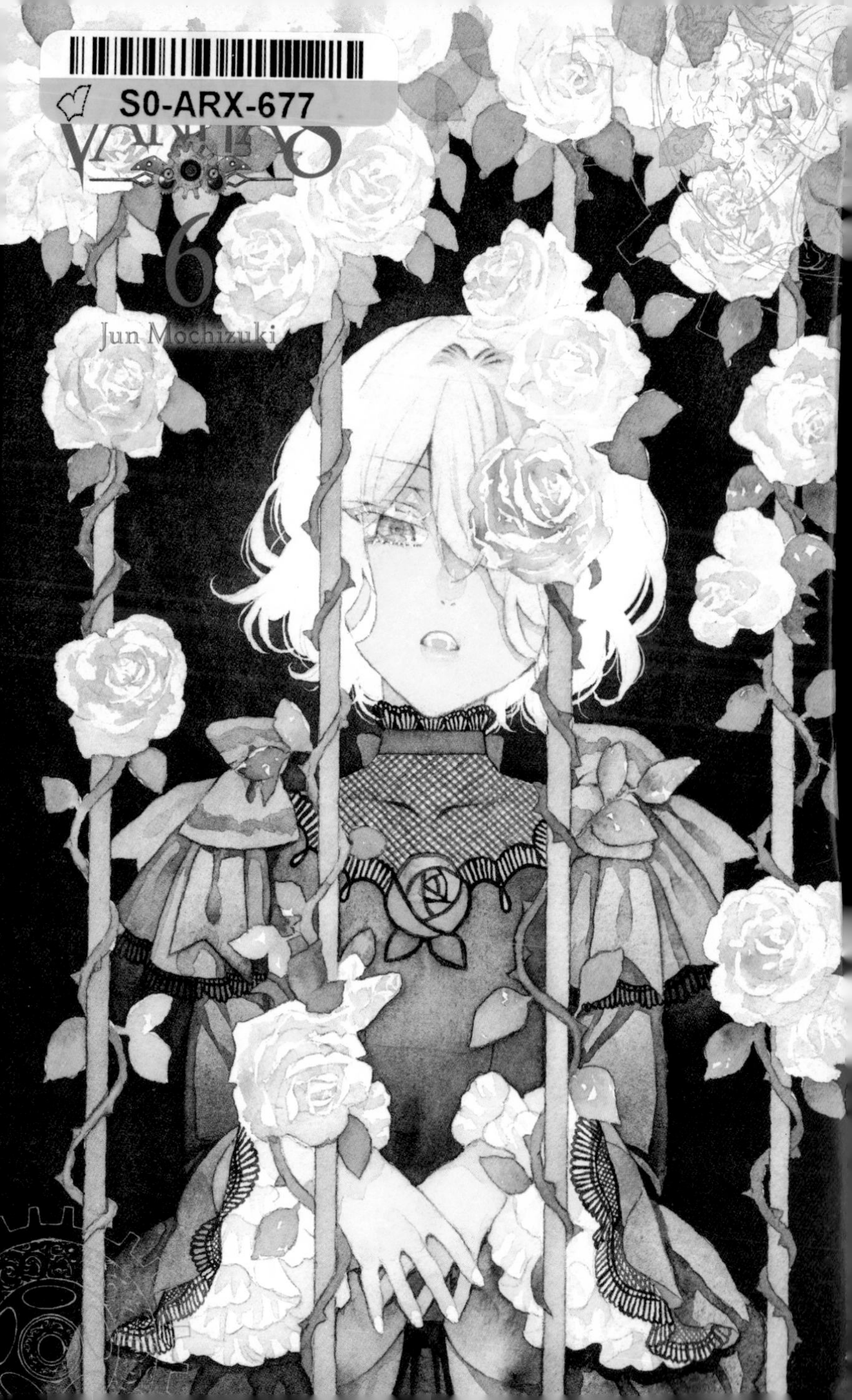
6
Jun Mochizuki

THE CASE STUDY OF VANITAS 6

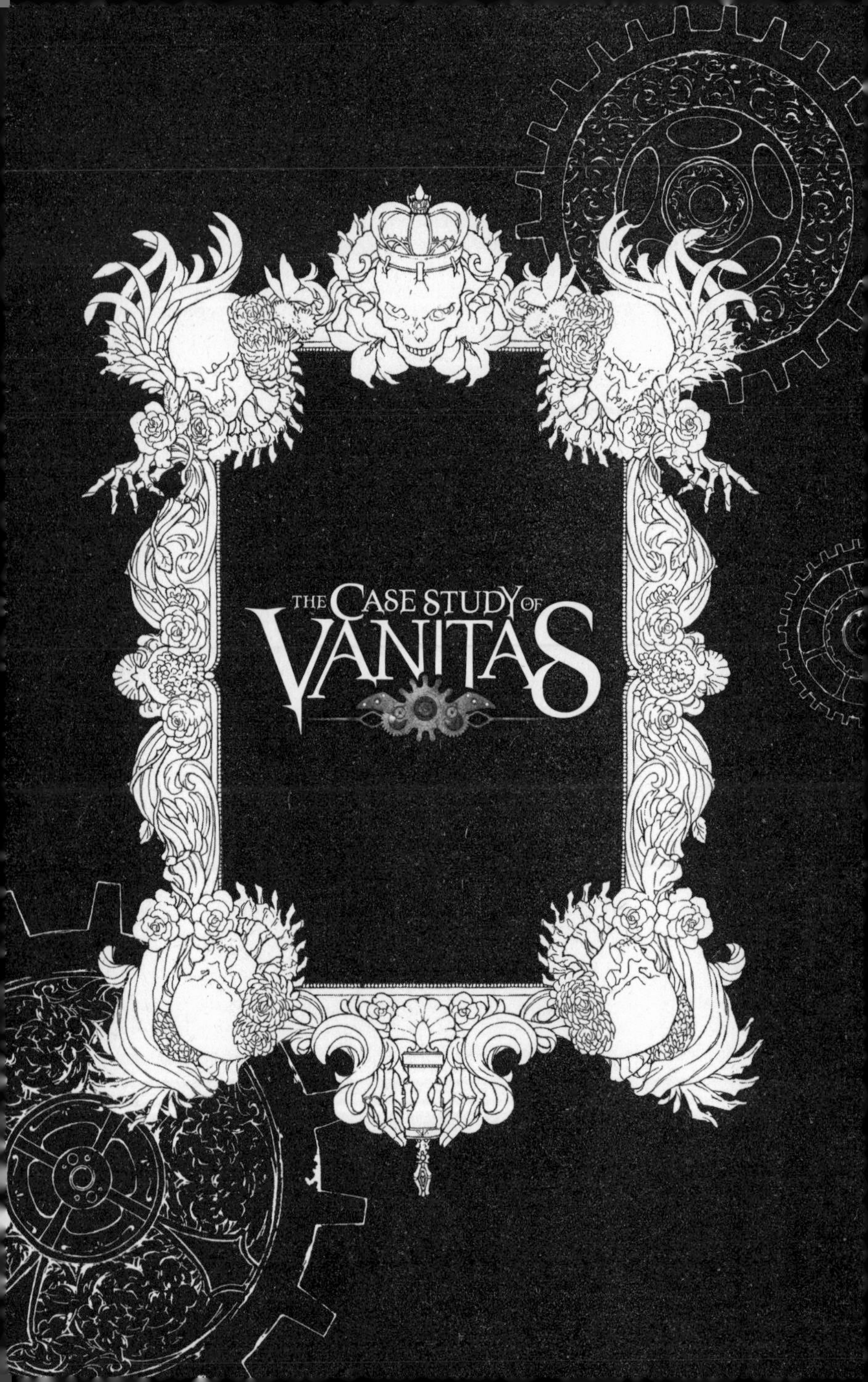
THE CASE STUDY OF VANITAS

I'M BEGINNING TO LONG FOR THE STREETS OF PARIS AGAIN.

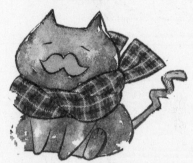

Jun Mochizuki
AUTHOR'S NOTE

I was planning to make
the material on the inside
covers more laidback this
time, but my editor said,
"Huh? There's absolutely
no need to tone it down" and
gave me the "Go" sign—
which is why it ended up
like this.

MÉMOIRE 28

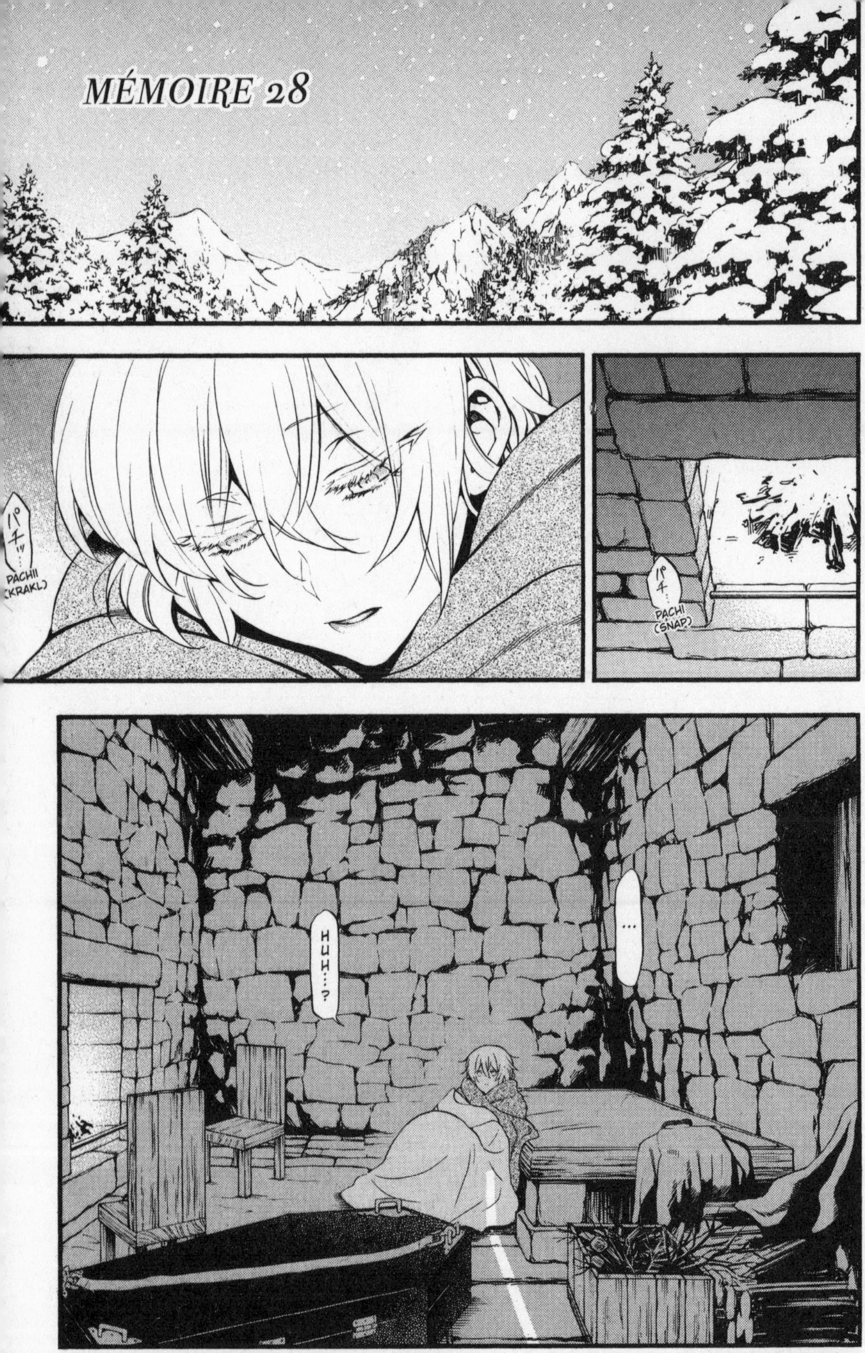
パチ…
PACHI (SNAP)
パチッ…
PACHII (KRAKL)
...
HUH...?

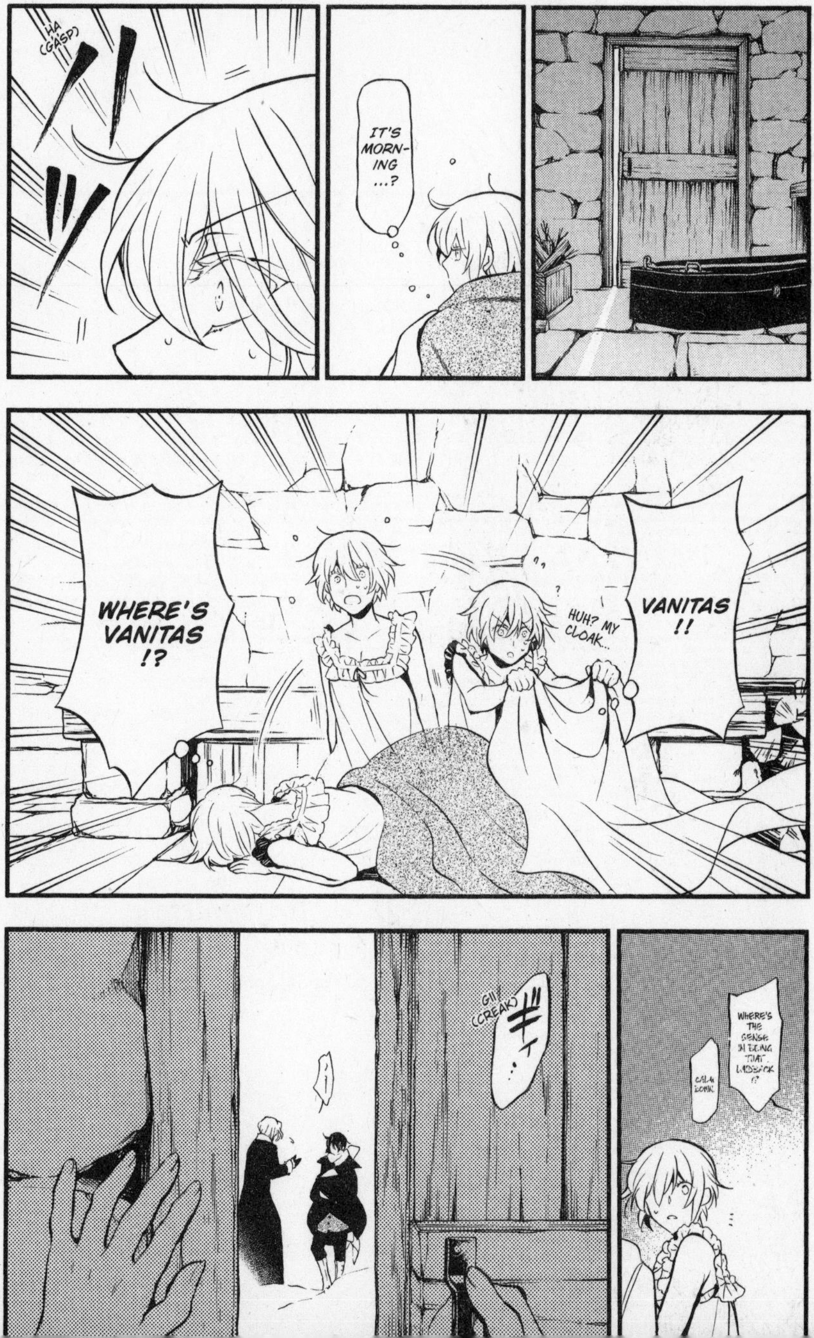
IT'S MORNING-ING...?
HA (GASP)
VANITAS!!
HUH? MY CLOAK...
WHERE'S VANITAS!?
WHERE'S THE SENSE IN BEING THAT LAIDBACK!?
CALM DOWN.
GII (CREAK)

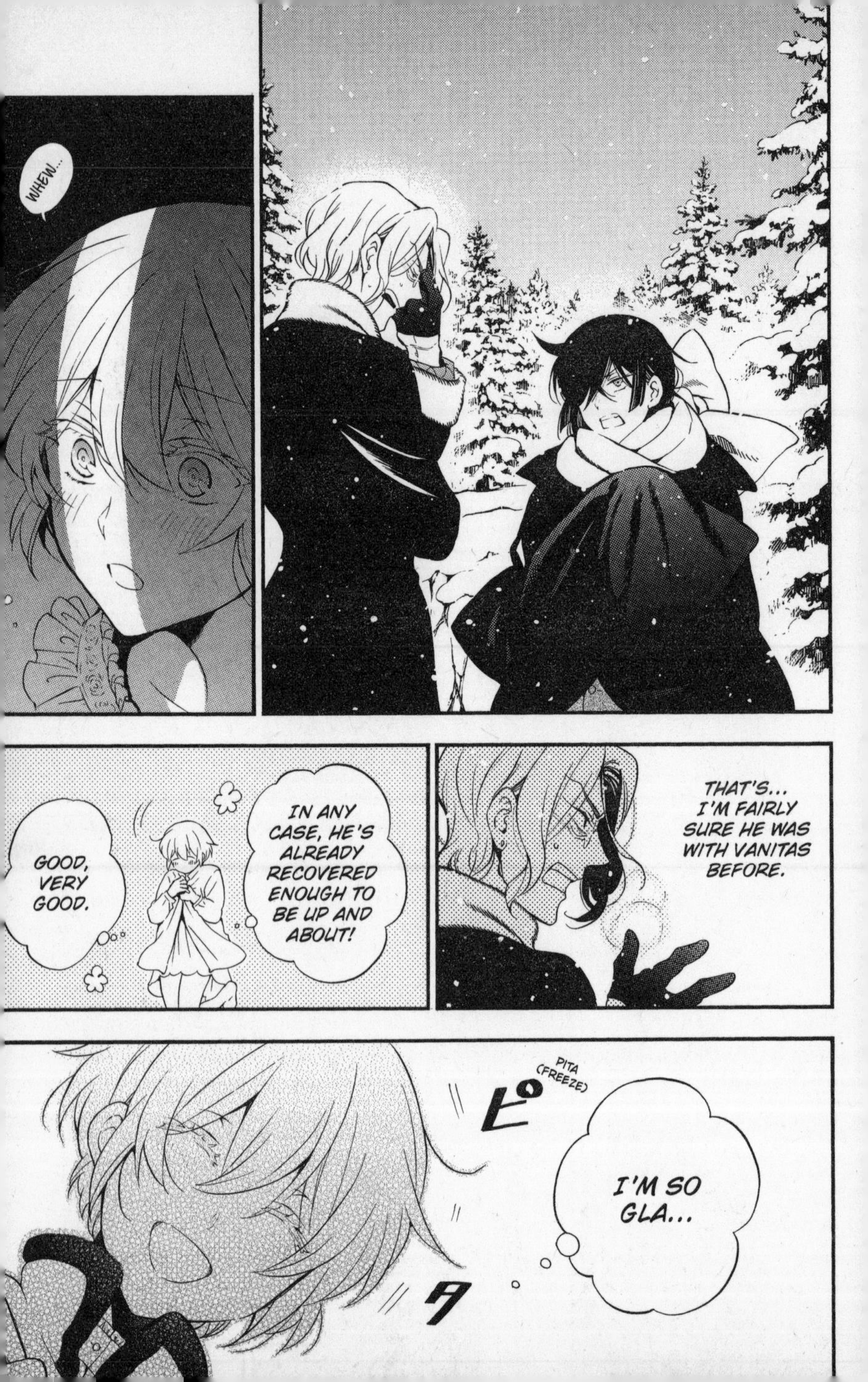
WHEW...
THAT'S... I'M FAIRLY SURE HE WAS WITH VANITAS BEFORE.
IN ANY CASE, HE'S ALREADY RECOVERED ENOUGH TO BE UP AND ABOUT!
GOOD, VERY GOOD.
ピタ
PITA (FREEZE)
I'M SO GLA...

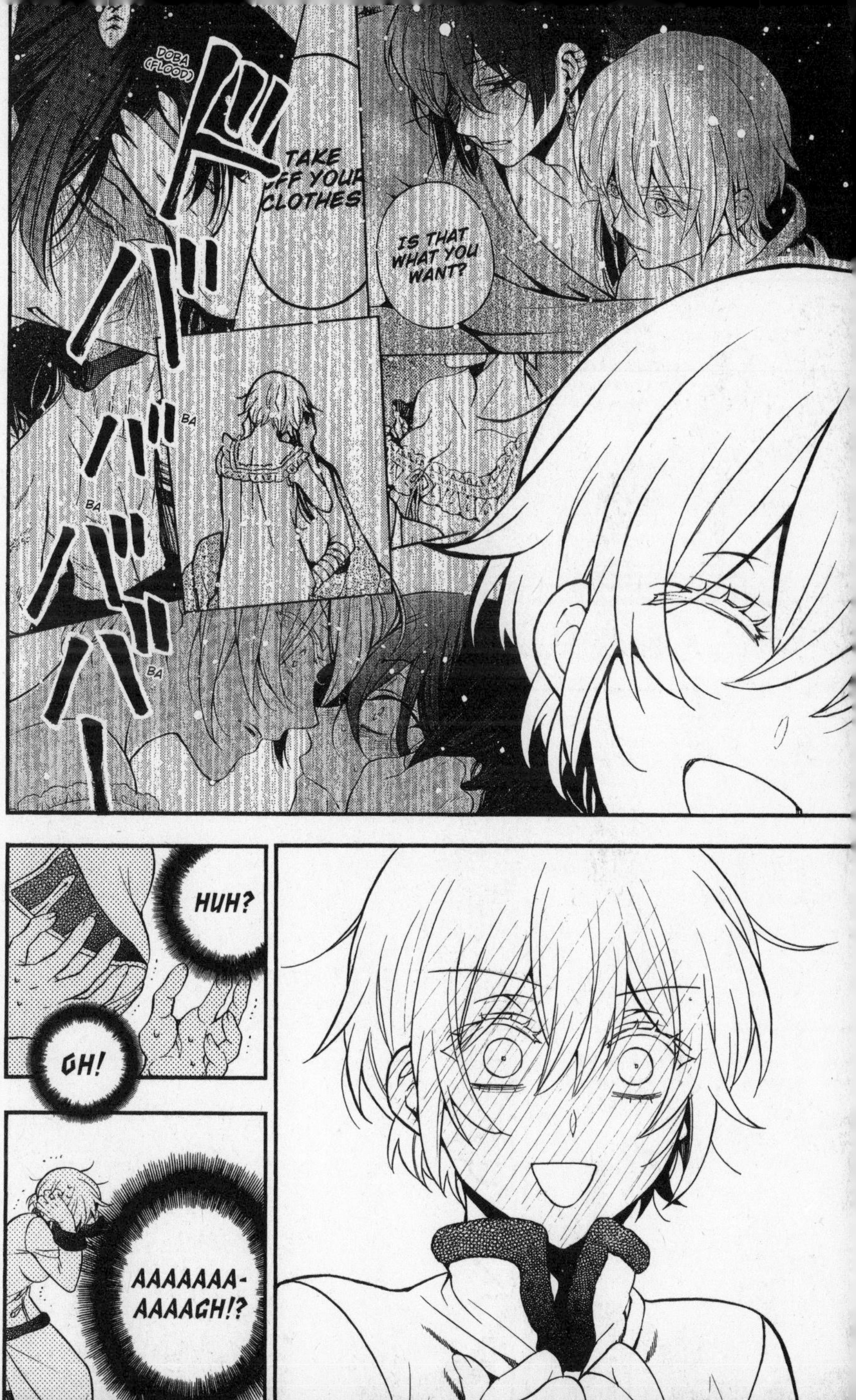
DOBA (FLOOD)
TAKE OFF YOUR CLOTHES
IS THAT WHAT YOU WANT?
BA
BA
BA
HUH?
GH!
AAAAAAA-AAAAGH!?

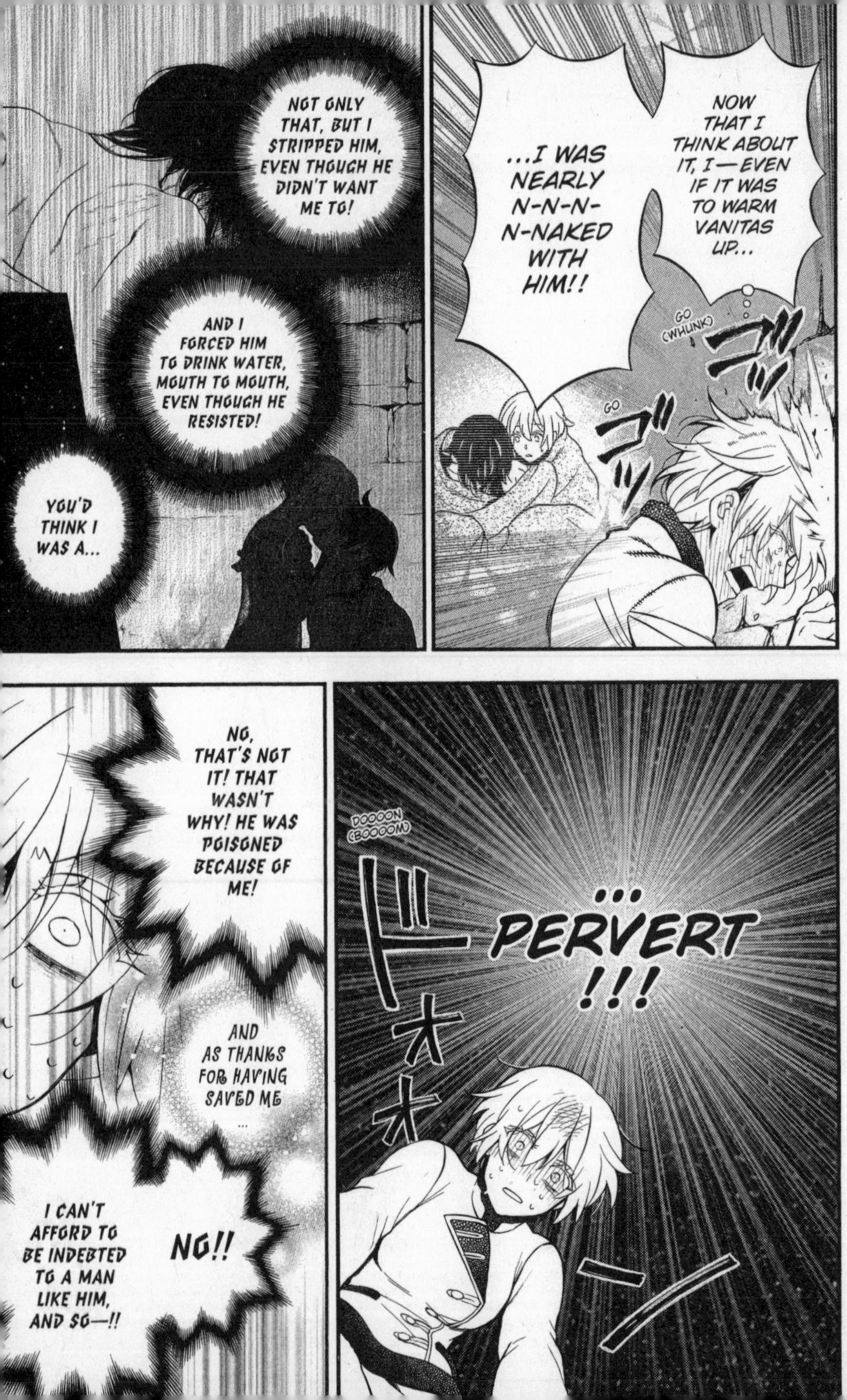
NOW THAT I THINK ABOUT IT, I—EVEN IF IT WAS TO WARM VANITAS UP...
...I WAS NEARLY N-N-N-N-NAKED WITH HIM!!
GO (WHUNK)
ゴッ
GO
ゴッ
NOT ONLY THAT, BUT I STRIPPED HIM, EVEN THOUGH HE DIDN'T WANT ME TO!
AND I FORCED HIM TO DRINK WATER, MOUTH TO MOUTH, EVEN THOUGH HE RESISTED!
YOU'D THINK I WAS A...
DOOOON (BOOOOM)
...PERVERT!!!
NO, THAT'S NOT IT! THAT WASN'T WHY! HE WAS POISONED BECAUSE OF ME!
AND AS THANKS FOR HAVING SAVED ME...
I CAN'T AFFORD TO BE INDEBTED TO A MAN LIKE HIM, AND SO—!!
NO!!

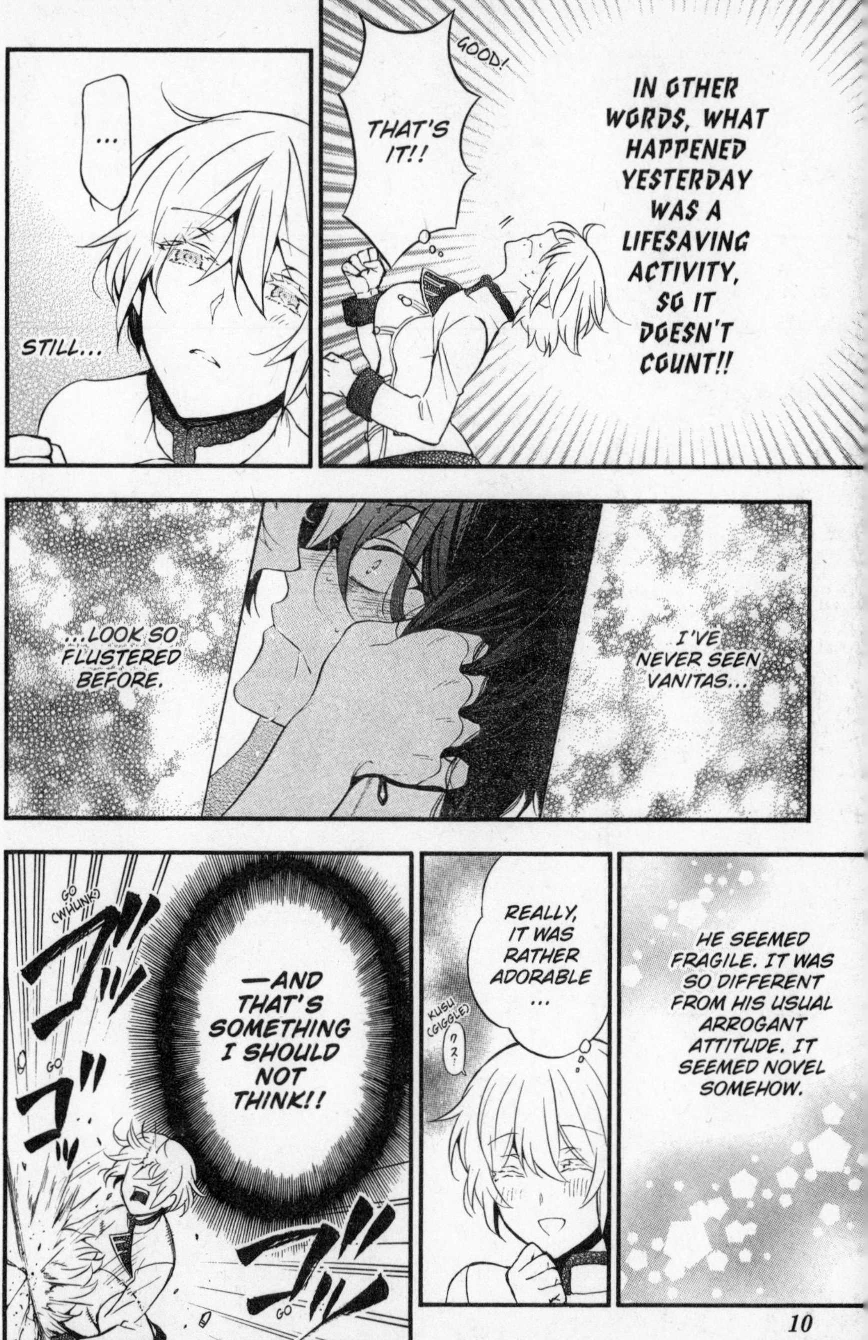
THAT'S IT!!
GOOD!
IN OTHER WORDS, WHAT HAPPENED YESTERDAY WAS A LIFESAVING ACTIVITY, SO IT DOESN'T COUNT!!
...
STILL...
I'VE NEVER SEEN VANITAS...
...LOOK SO FLUSTERED BEFORE.
HE SEEMED FRAGILE. IT WAS SO DIFFERENT FROM HIS USUAL ARROGANT ATTITUDE. IT SEEMED NOVEL SOMEHOW.
REALLY, IT WAS RATHER ADORABLE ...
KUSU (GIGGLE)
クス…
GO (WHUNK)
—AND THAT'S SOMETHING I SHOULD NOT THINK!!
GO
GO

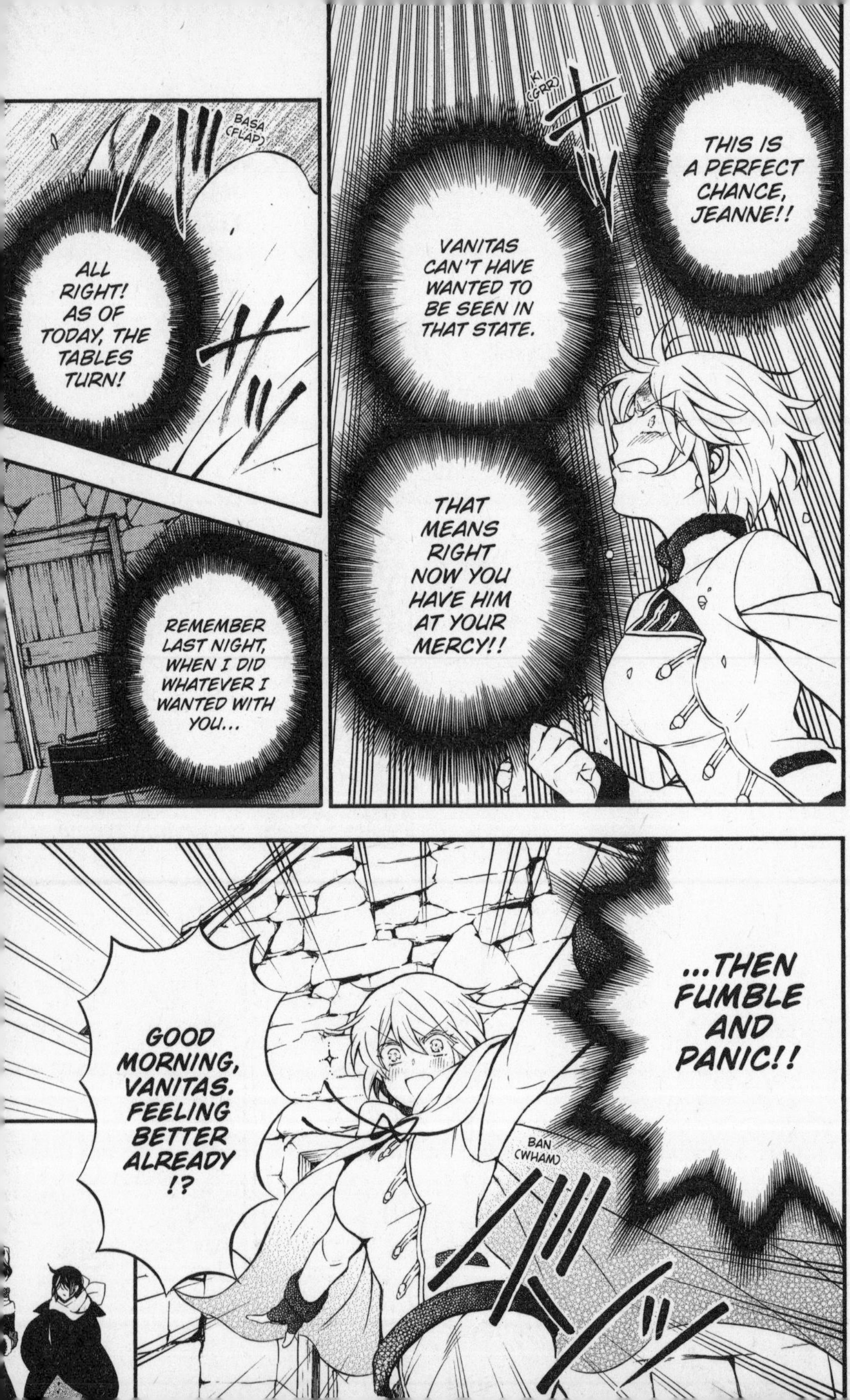
KI (GRR)
THIS IS A PERFECT CHANCE, JEANNE!!
VANITAS CAN'T HAVE WANTED TO BE SEEN IN THAT STATE.
THAT MEANS RIGHT NOW YOU HAVE HIM AT YOUR MERCY!!
BASA (FLAP)
ALL RIGHT! AS OF TODAY, THE TABLES TURN!
REMEMBER LAST NIGHT, WHEN I DID WHATEVER I WANTED WITH YOU...
...THEN FUMBLE AND PANIC!!
BAN (WHAM)
GOOD MORNING, VANITAS. FEELING BETTER ALREADY!?

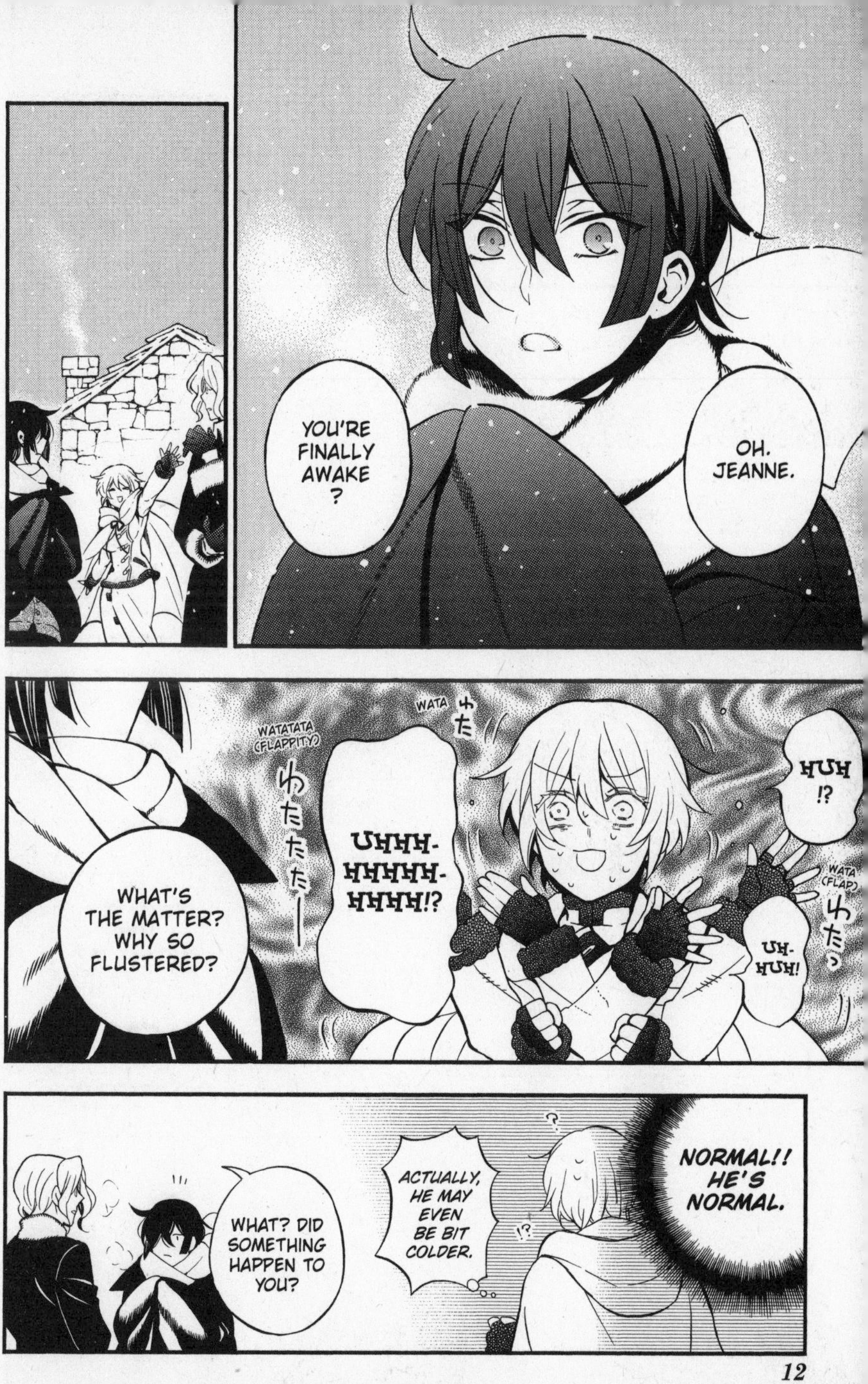
OH. JEANNE.
YOU'RE FINALLY AWAKE?
HUH!?
WATA (FLAP)
UH-HUH!
WATA
UHHH-HHHHH-HHHH!?
WATATATA (FLAPPITY)
WHAT'S THE MATTER? WHY SO FLUSTERED?
NORMAL!! HE'S NORMAL.
ACTUALLY, HE MAY EVEN BE BIT COLDER.
WHAT? DID SOMETHING HAPPEN TO YOU?

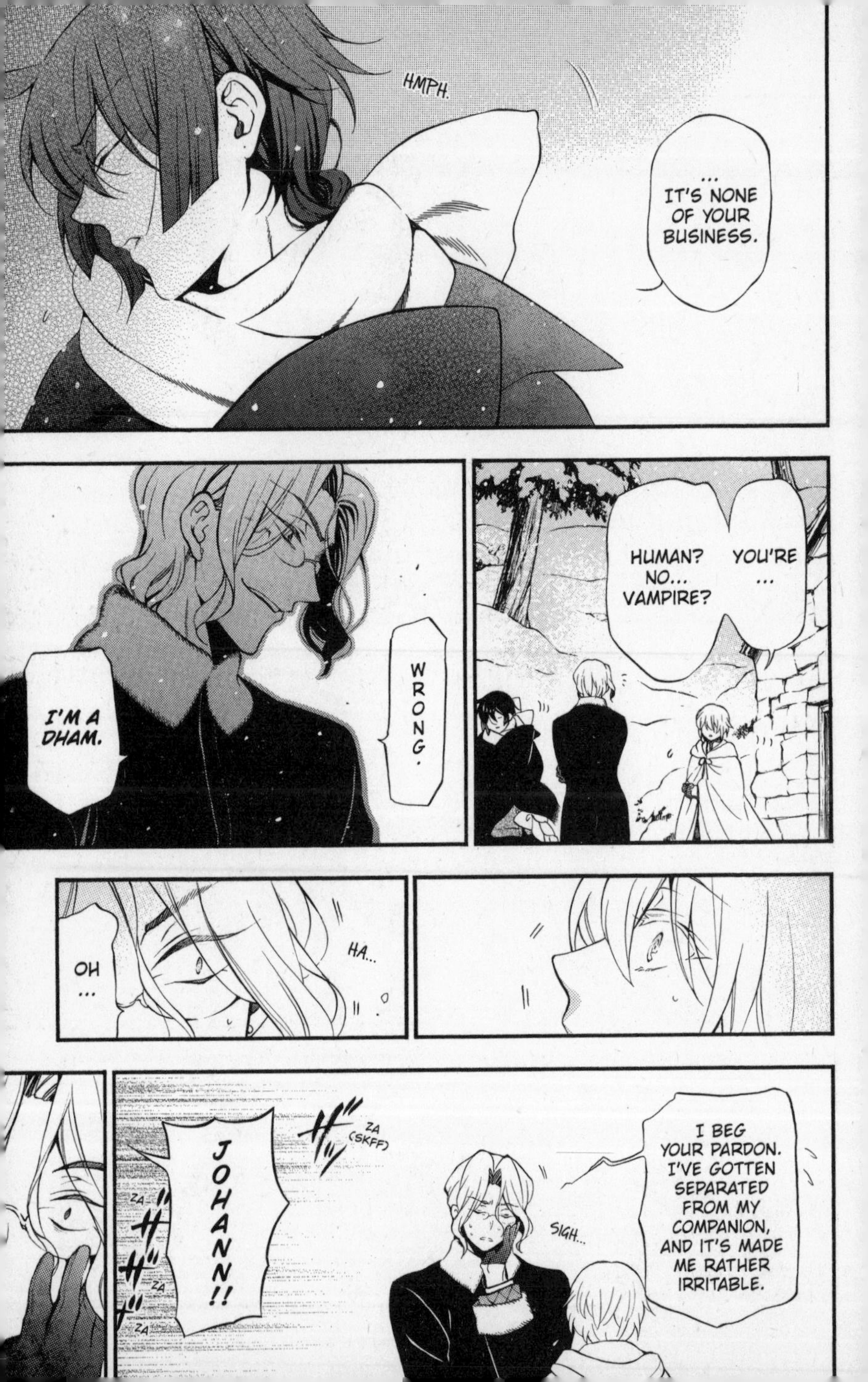
HMPH.
... IT'S NONE OF YOUR BUSINESS.
YOU'RE ...
HUMAN? NO... VAMPIRE?
WRONG.
I'M A DHAM.
HA...
OH ...
I BEG YOUR PARDON. I'VE GOTTEN SEPARATED FROM MY COMPANION, AND IT'S MADE ME RATHER IRRITABLE.
SIGH...
ZA (SKFF)
JOHANN!!
ZA
ZA
ZA

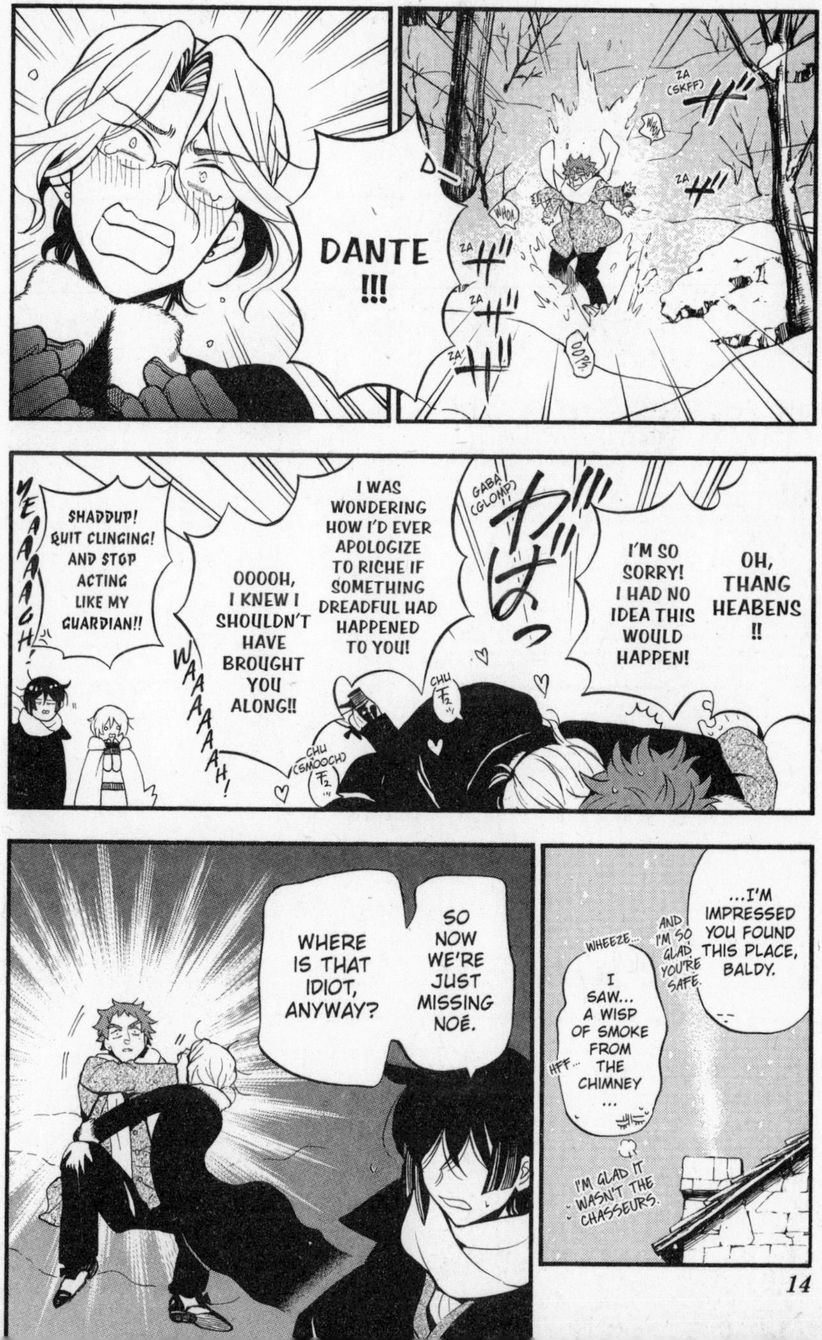
ZA (SKFF)
WHOA
ZA
WHOA
ZA
ZA
ZA
OOPS
DANTE !!!
OH, THANG HEABENS !!
I'M SO SORRY! I HAD NO IDEA THIS WOULD HAPPEN!
GABA (GLOMP)
I WAS WONDERING HOW I'D EVER APOLOGIZE TO RICHE IF SOMETHING DREADFUL HAD HAPPENED TO YOU!
OOOOH, I KNEW I SHOULDN'T HAVE BROUGHT YOU ALONG!!
WAAAAAAAH!
SHADDUP! QUIT CLINGING! AND STOP ACTING LIKE MY GUARDIAN!!
MEAAAAAGH!
CHU
CHU (SMOOCH)
...I'M IMPRESSED YOU FOUND THIS PLACE, BALDY.
AND I'M SO GLAD YOU'RE SAFE.
WHEEZE...
I SAW... A WISP OF SMOKE FROM THE CHIMNEY ...
HFF...
I'M GLAD IT WASN'T THE CHASSEURS.
SO NOW WE'RE JUST MISSING NOÉ.
WHERE IS THAT IDIOT, ANYWAY?

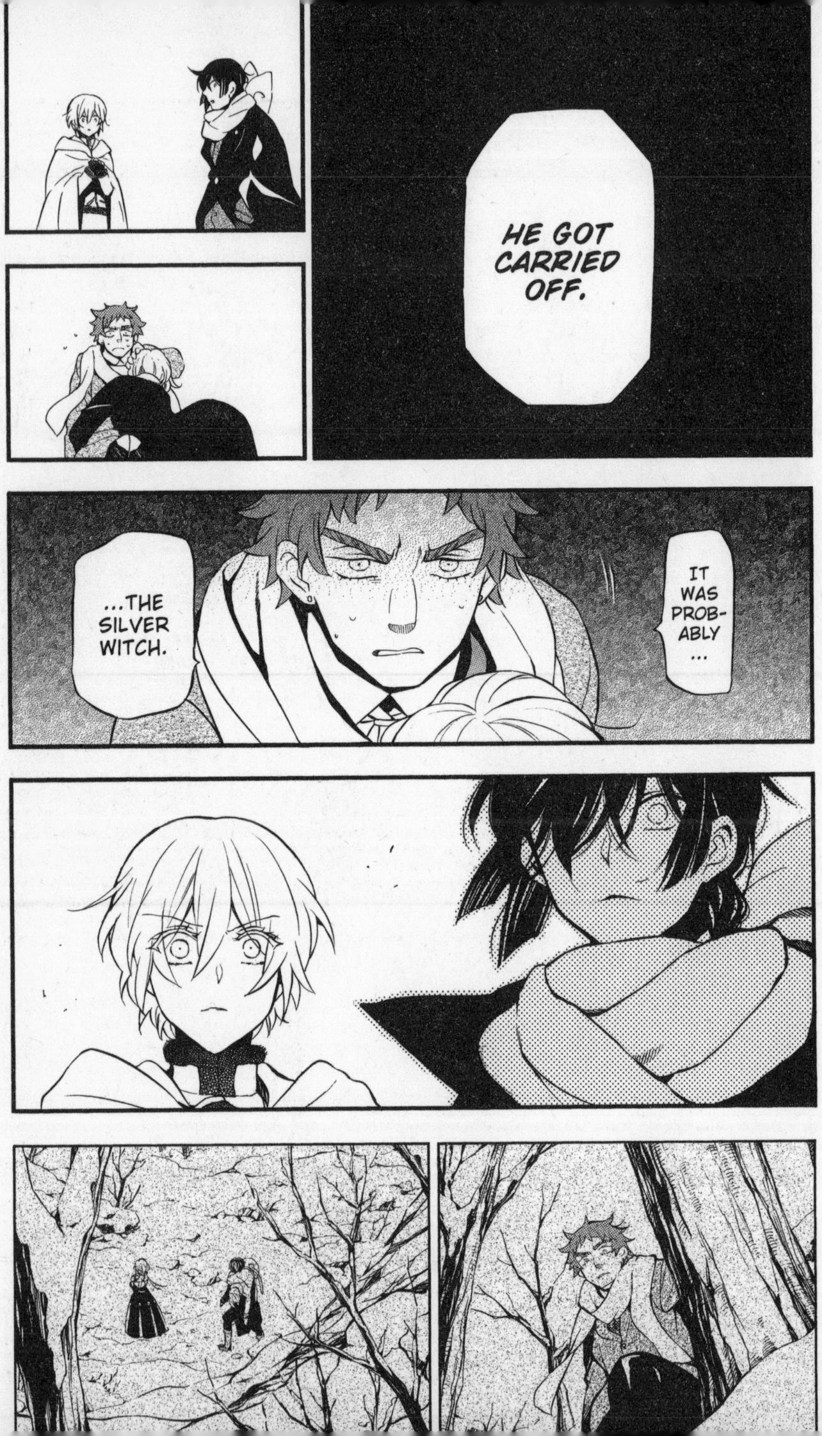
HE GOT CARRIED OFF.
IT WAS PROB-ABLY ...
...THE SILVER WITCH.

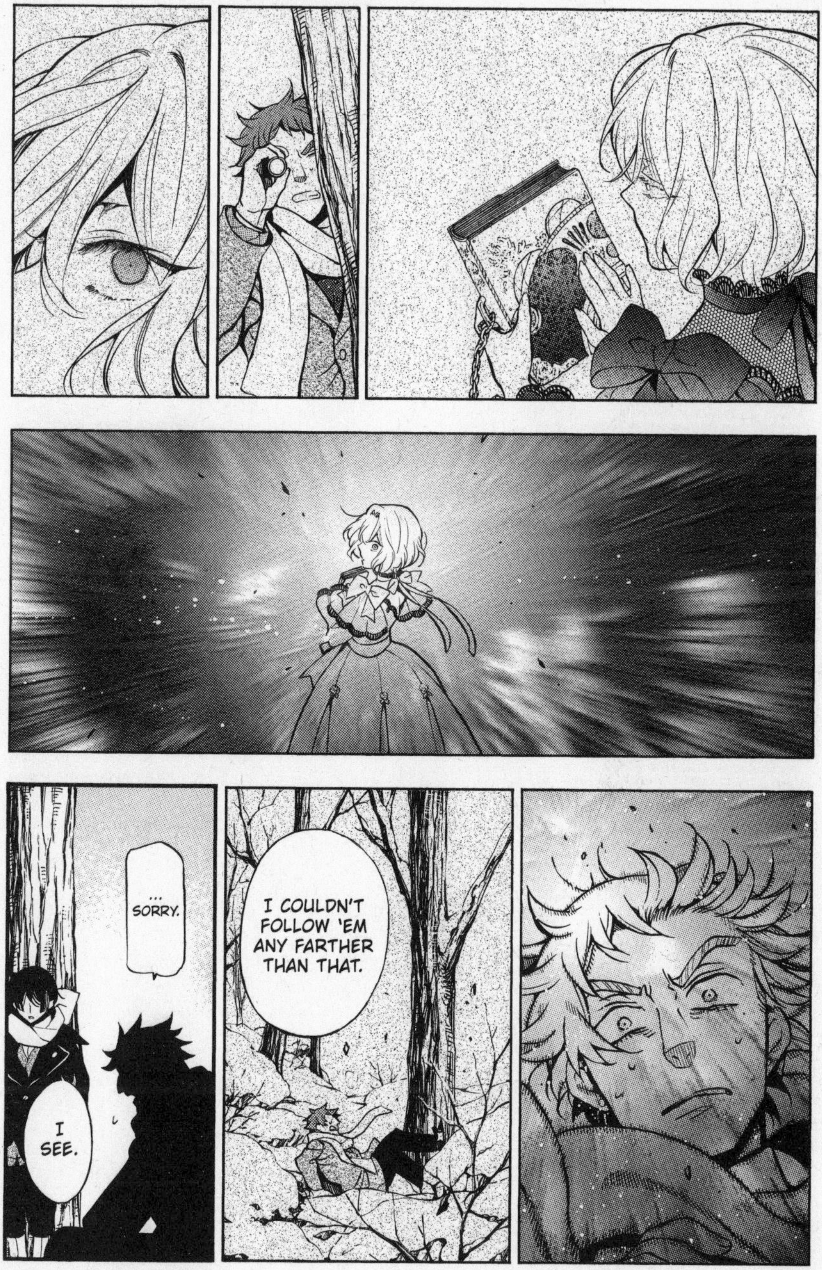
I COULDN'T FOLLOW 'EM ANY FARTHER THAN THAT.
... SORRY.
I SEE.

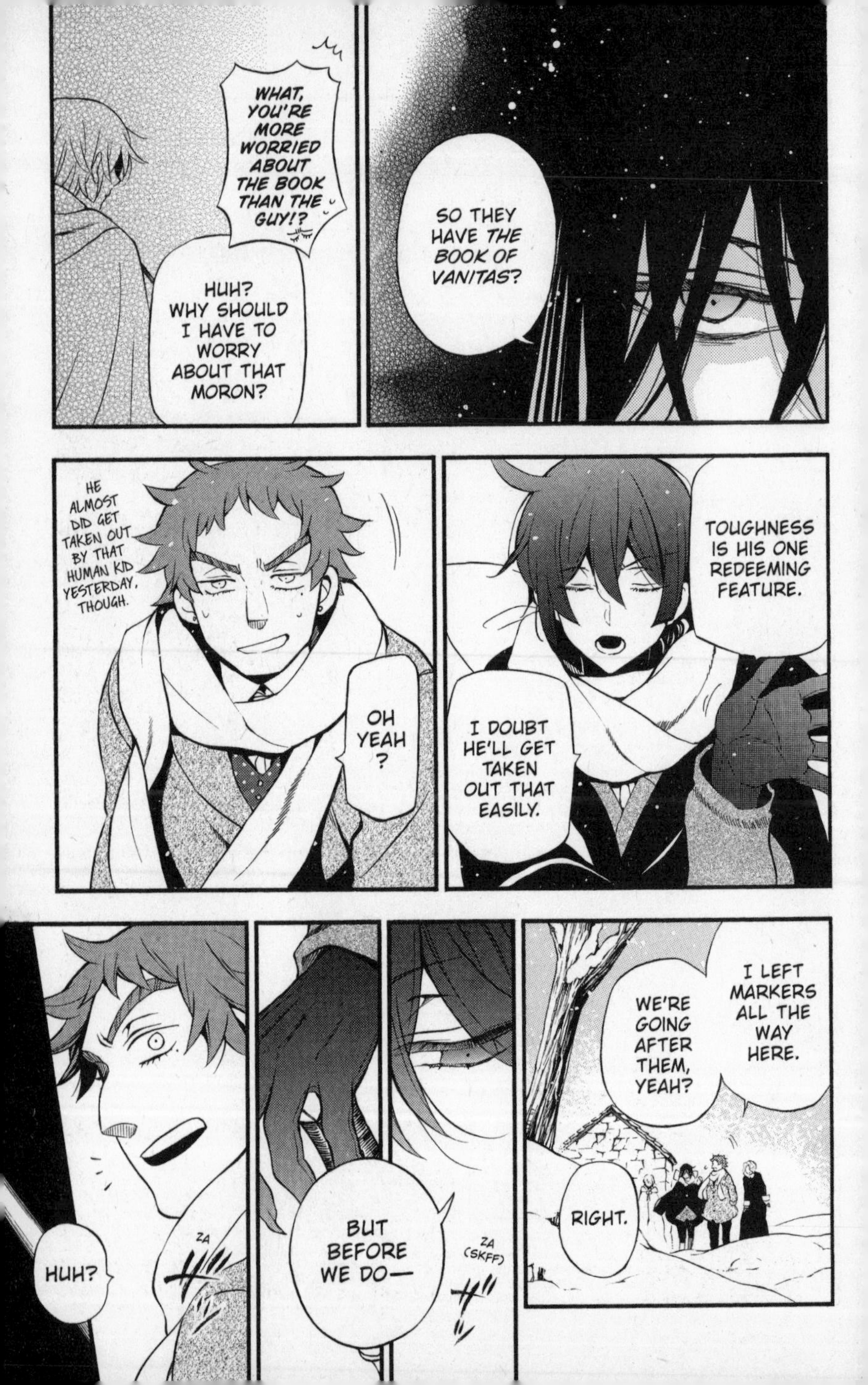
SO THEY HAVE THE BOOK OF VANITAS?
WHAT, YOU'RE MORE WORRIED ABOUT THE BOOK THAN THE GUY!?
HUH? WHY SHOULD I HAVE TO WORRY ABOUT THAT MORON?
TOUGHNESS IS HIS ONE REDEEMING FEATURE.
I DOUBT HE'LL GET TAKEN OUT THAT EASILY.
OH YEAH?
HE ALMOST DID GET TAKEN OUT BY THAT HUMAN KID YESTERDAY, THOUGH.
I LEFT MARKERS ALL THE WAY HERE.
WE'RE GOING AFTER THEM, YEAH?
RIGHT.
ZA (SKFF)
BUT BEFORE WE DO—
ZA
HUH?

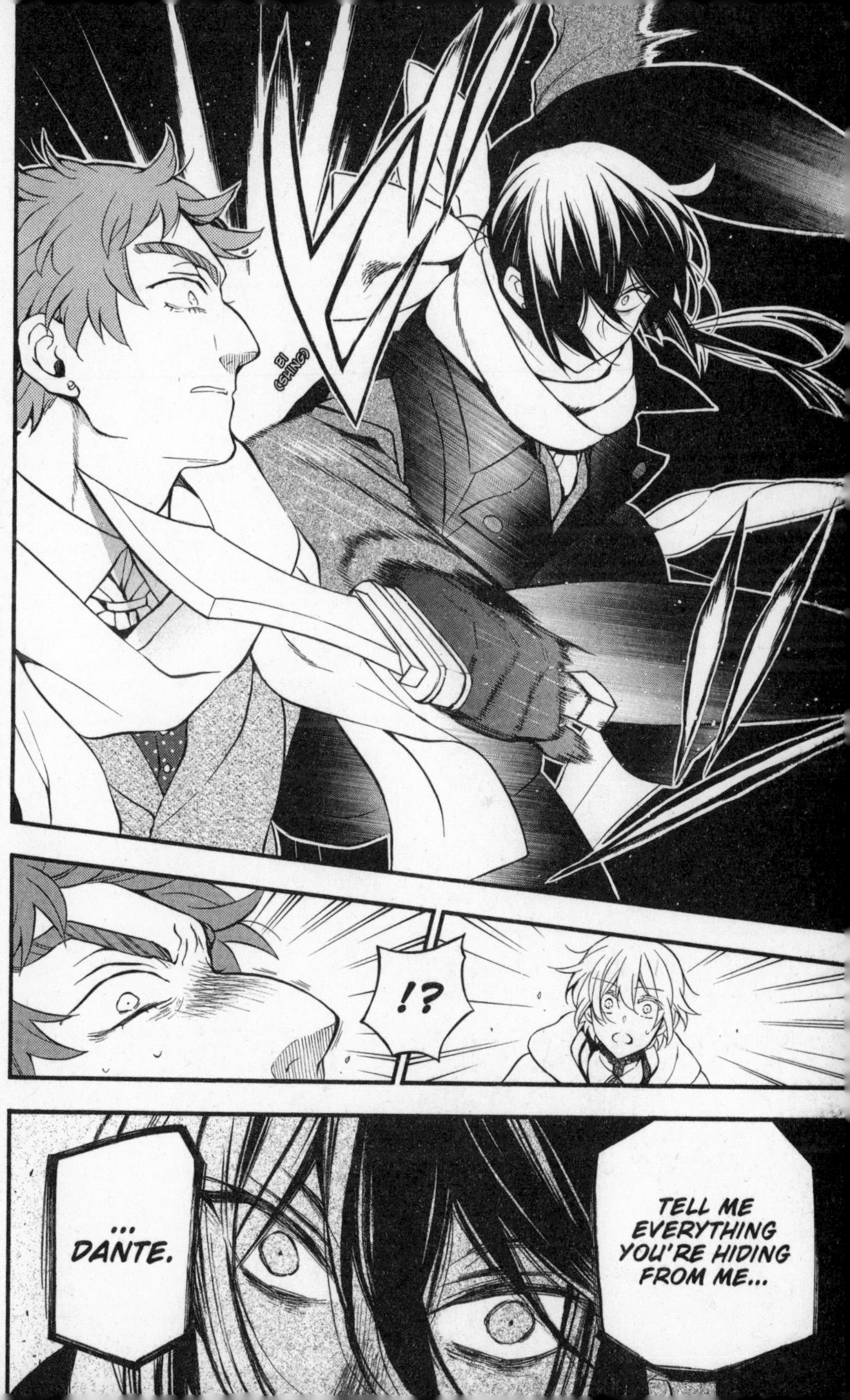
(SHING)
!?
TELL ME EVERYTHING YOU'RE HIDING FROM ME...
... DANTE.

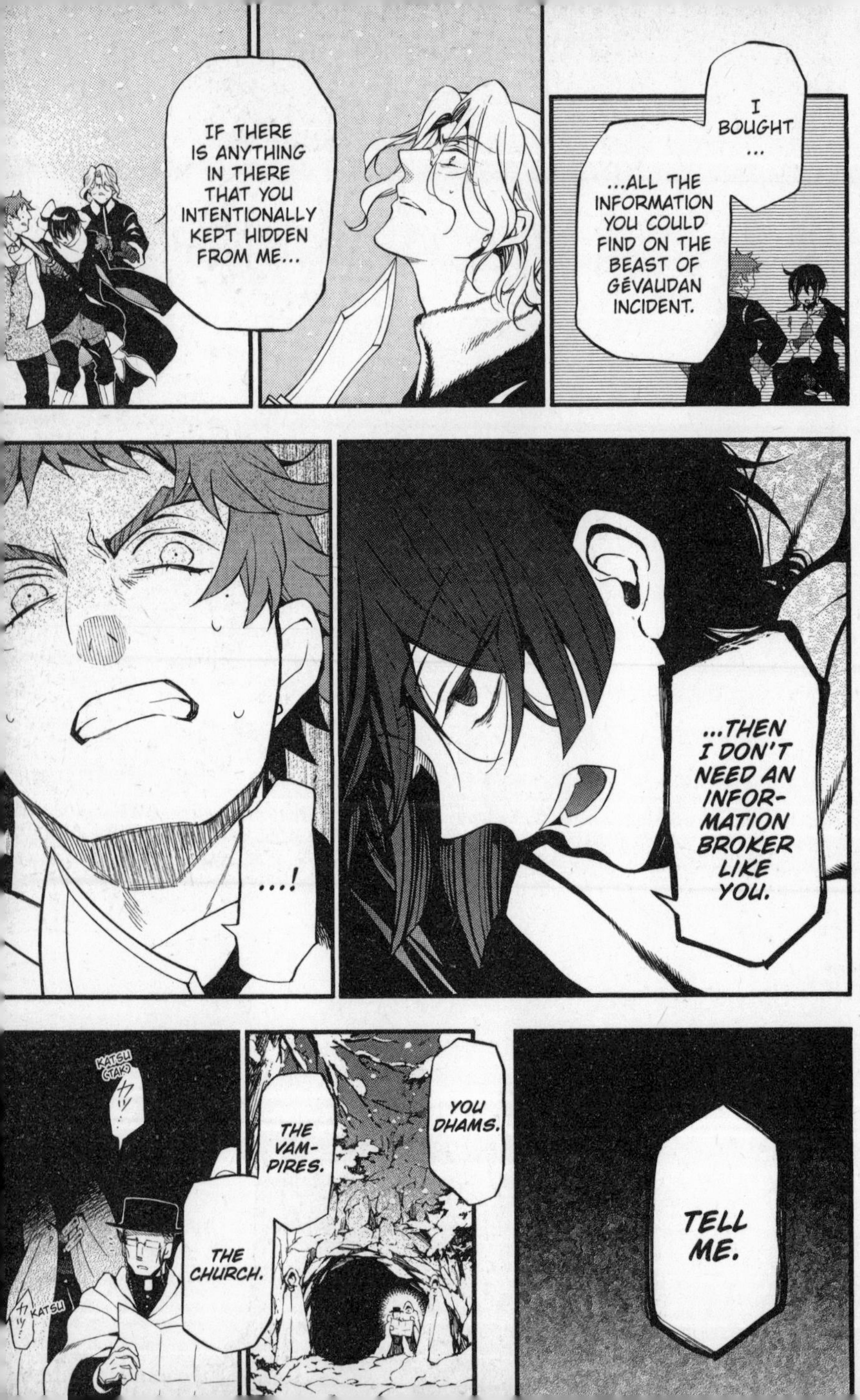
I BOUGHT ...
...ALL THE INFORMATION YOU COULD FIND ON THE BEAST OF GÉVAUDAN INCIDENT.
IF THERE IS ANYTHING IN THERE THAT YOU INTENTIONALLY KEPT HIDDEN FROM ME...
...THEN I DON'T NEED AN INFORMATION BROKER LIKE YOU.
...!
TELL ME.
YOU DHAMS.
THE VAMPIRES.
THE CHURCH.
KATSU
KATSU

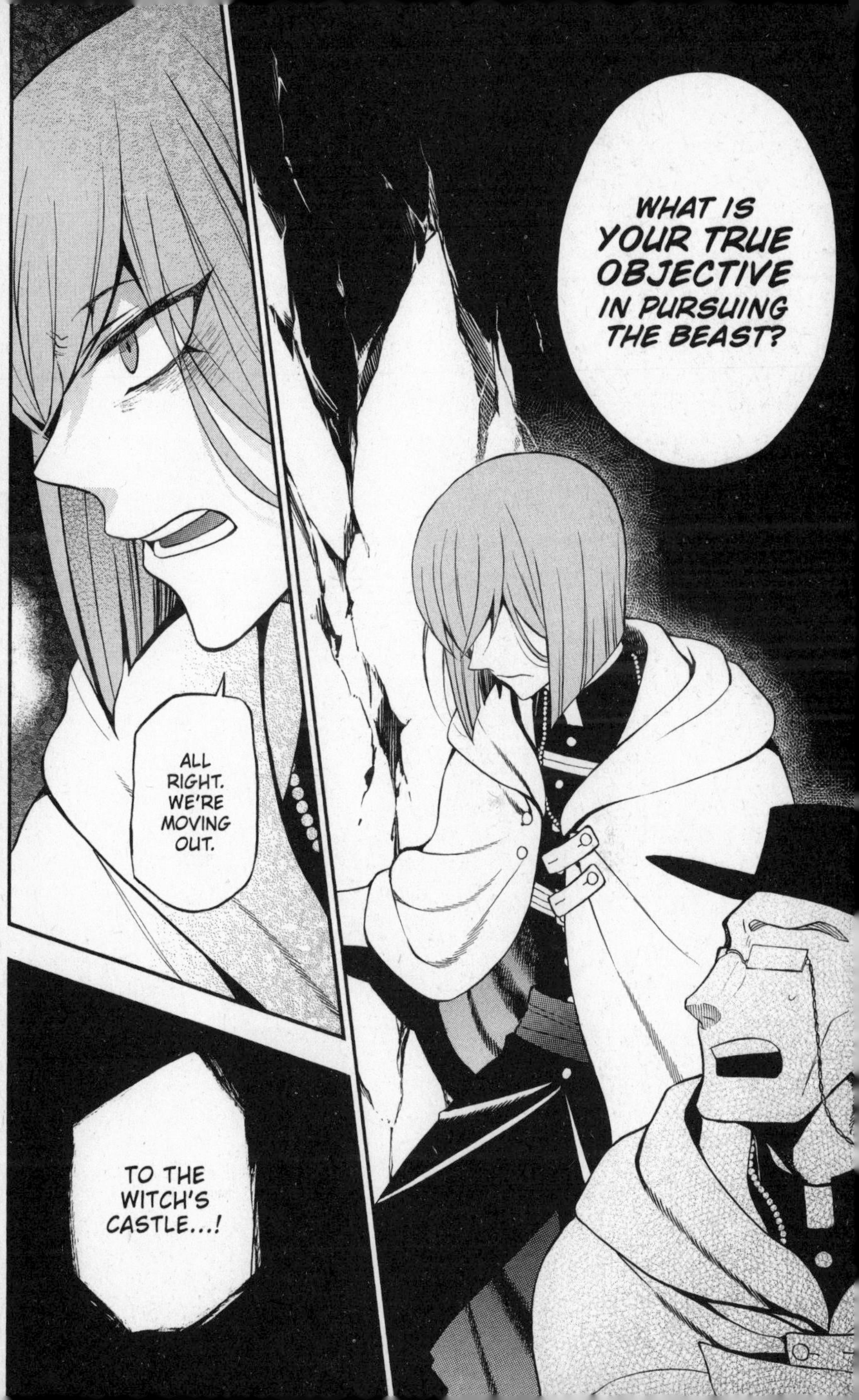
WHAT IS YOUR TRUE OBJECTIVE IN PURSUING THE BEAST?
ALL RIGHT. WE'RE MOVING OUT.
TO THE WITCH'S CASTLE...!

Mémoire 28 *Dal Segno* QUESTION MARK

Les Mémoires de Vanitas

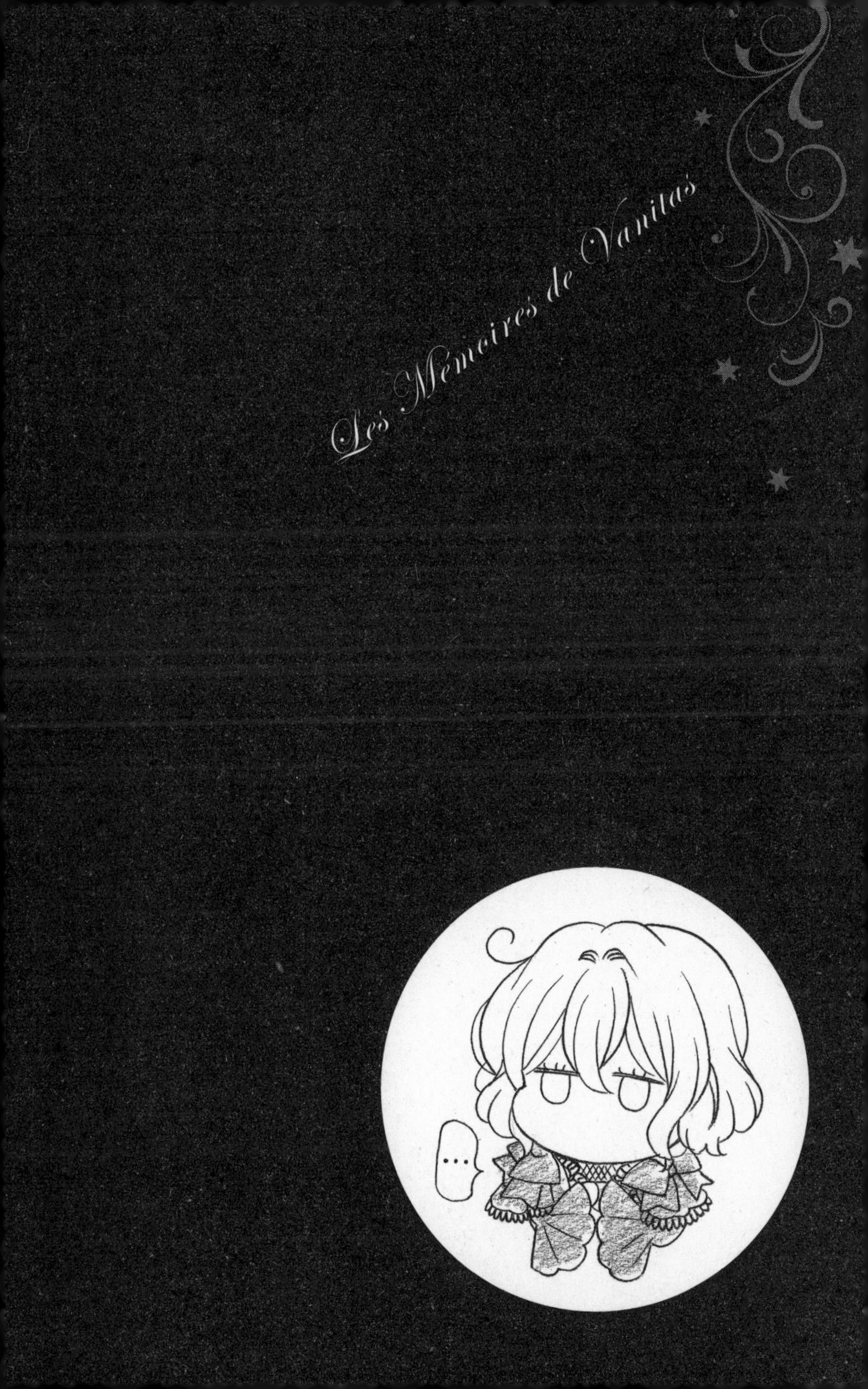
...

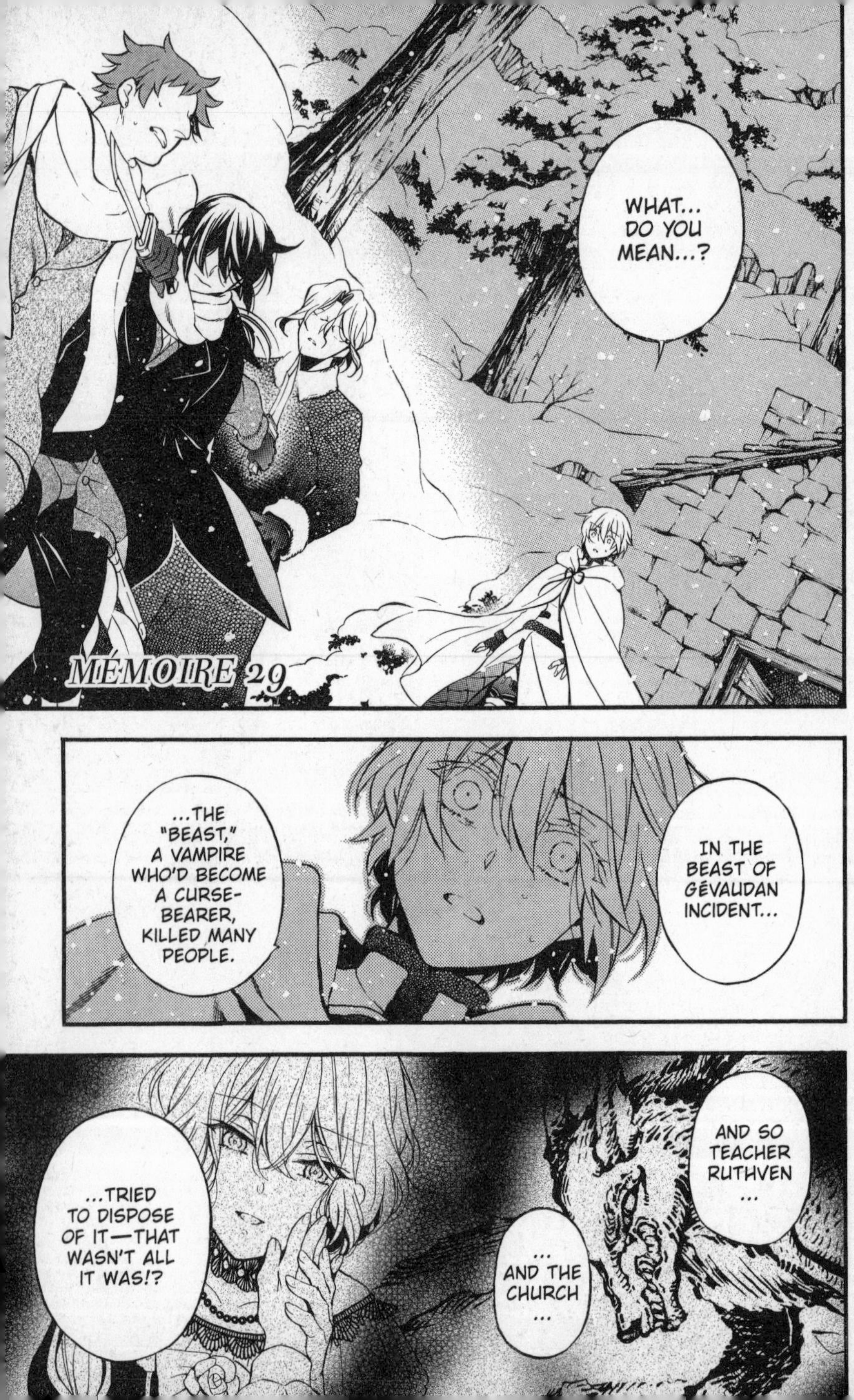
MÉMOIRE 29
WHAT... DO YOU MEAN...?
IN THE BEAST OF GÉVAUDAN INCIDENT...
...THE "BEAST," A VAMPIRE WHO'D BECOME A CURSE-BEARER, KILLED MANY PEOPLE.
AND SO TEACHER RUTHVEN...
...AND THE CHURCH...
...TRIED TO DISPOSE OF IT—THAT WASN'T ALL IT WAS!?

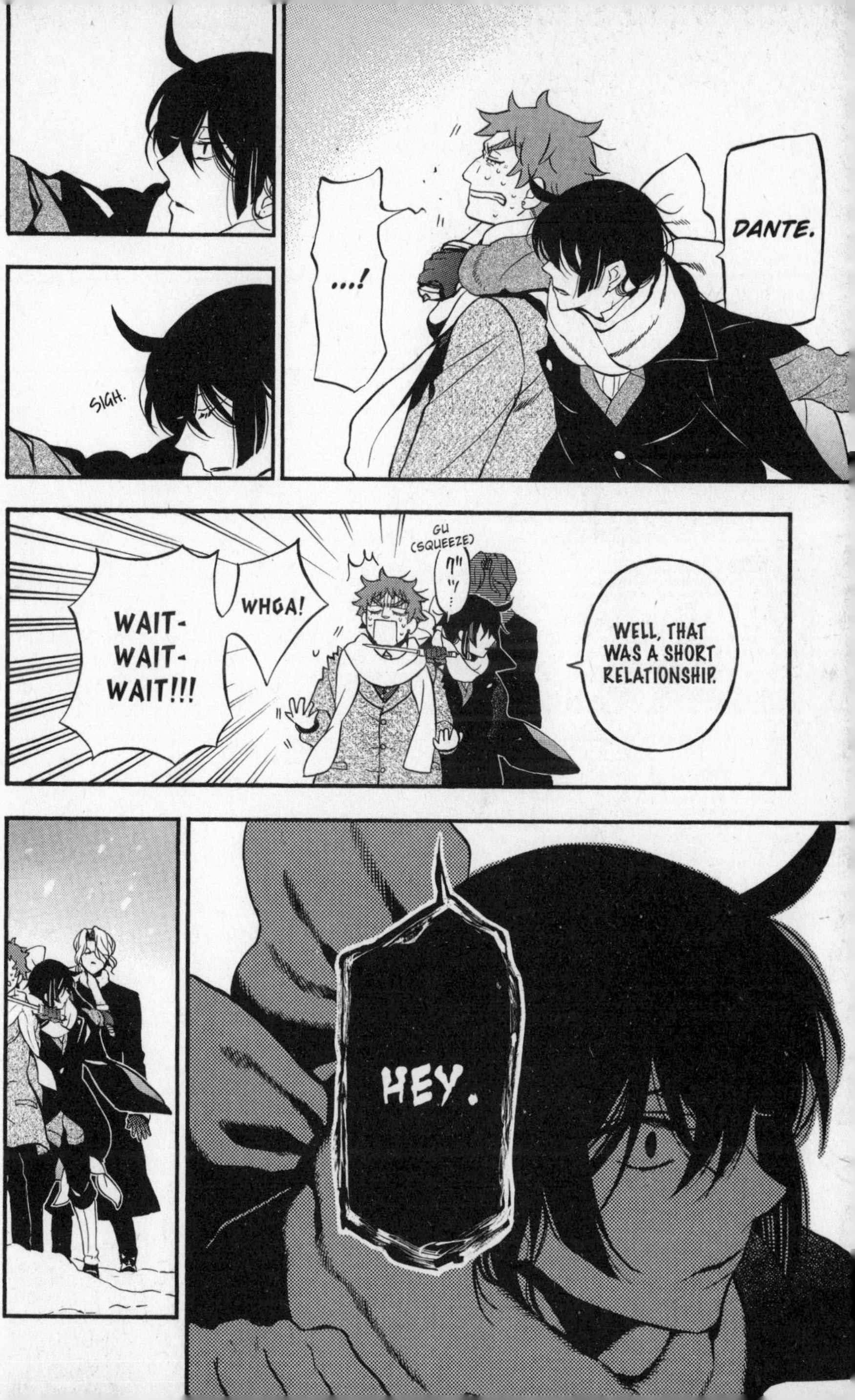
DANTE.
...!
SIGH.
WELL, THAT WAS A SHORT RELATIONSHIP.
GU (SQUEEZE)
WHGA!
WAIT-WAIT-WAIT!!!
HEY.

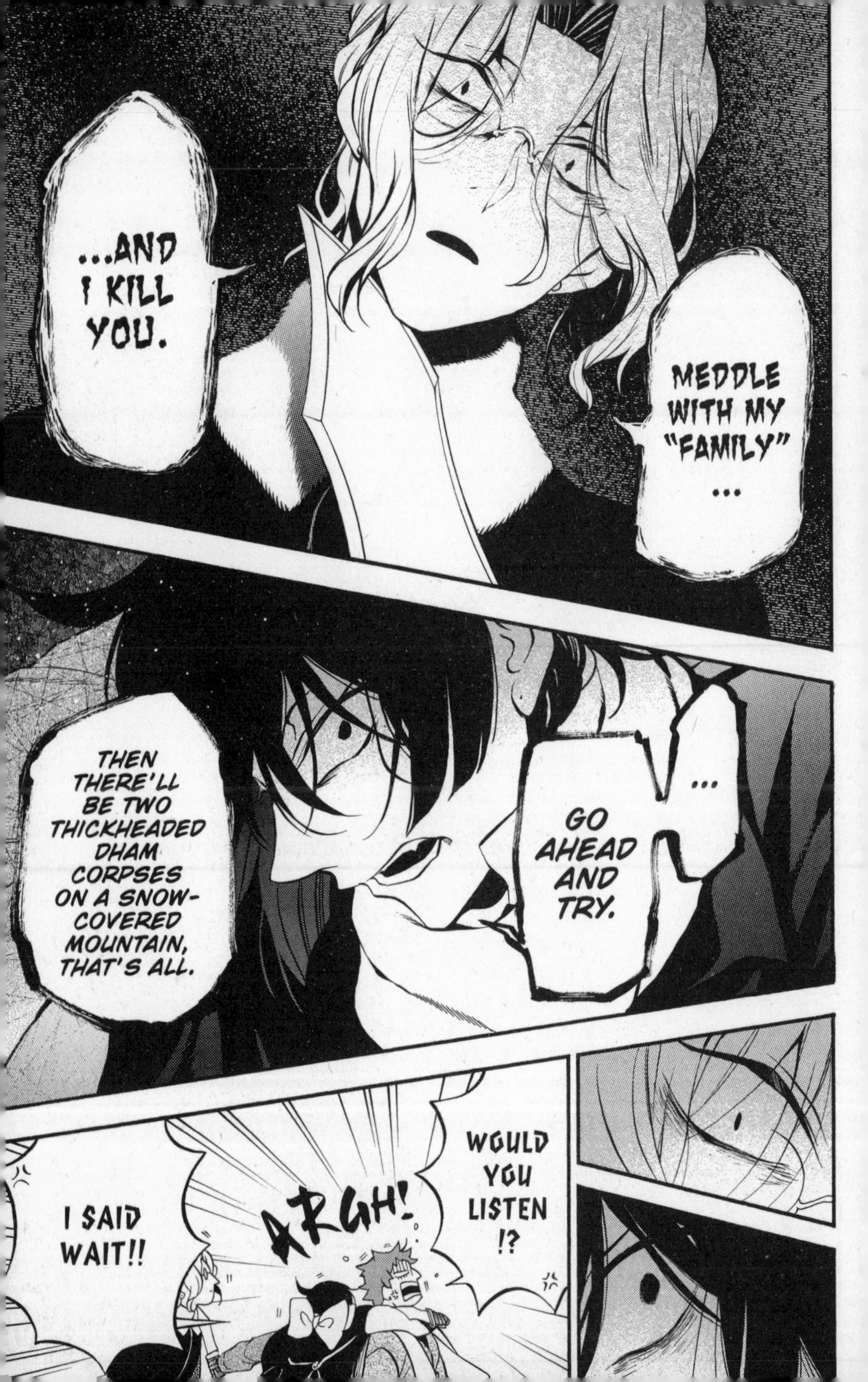
MEDDLE WITH MY "FAMILY" ...
...AND I KILL YOU.
... GO AHEAD AND TRY.
THEN THERE'LL BE TWO THICKHEADED DHAM CORPSES ON A SNOW-COVERED MOUNTAIN, THAT'S ALL.
WOULD YOU LISTEN !?
ARGH!
I SAID WAIT!!

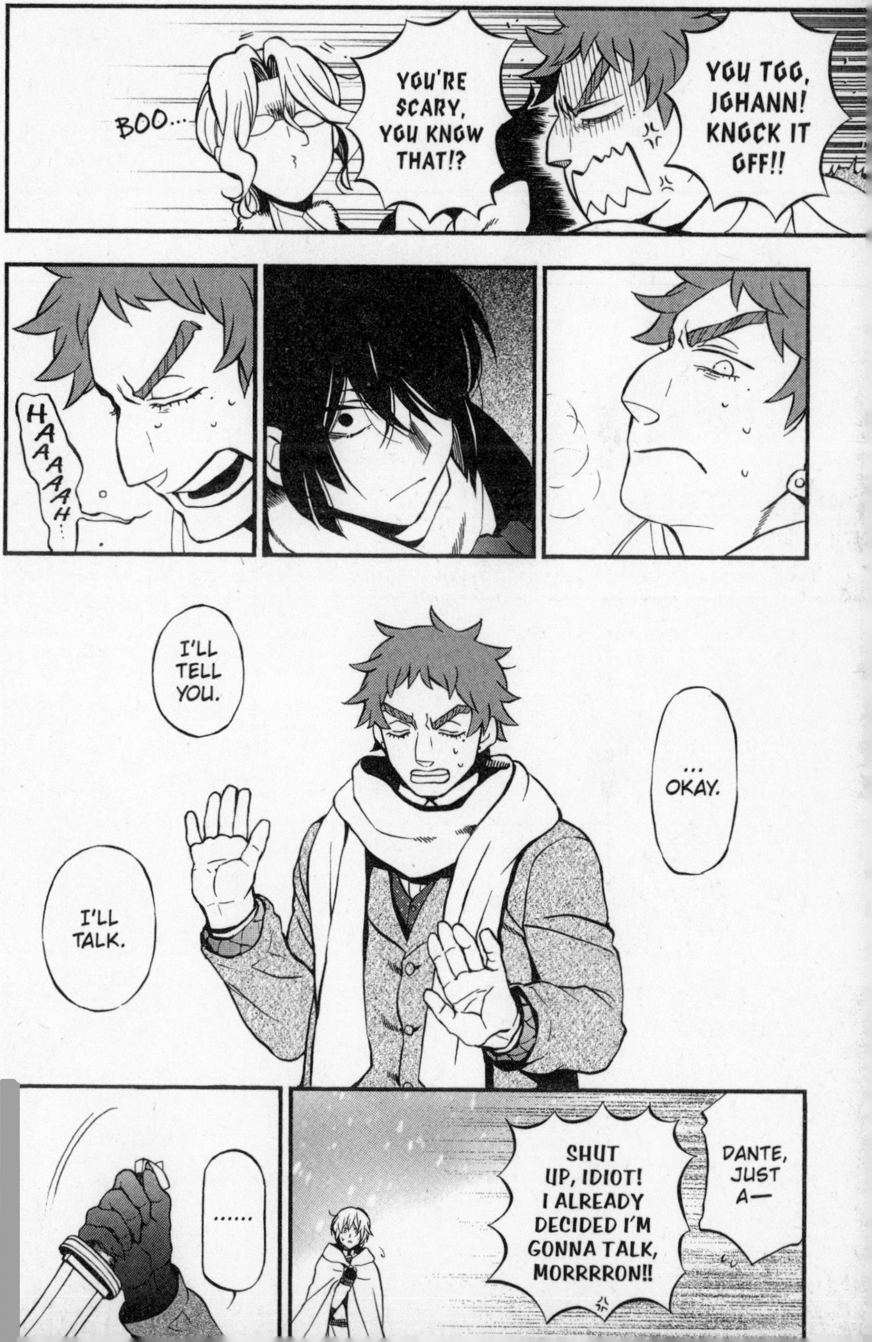
YOU TOO, JOHANN! KNOCK IT OFF!!
YOU'RE SCARY, YOU KNOW THAT!?
BOO...
HAAAAAH...
...OKAY.
I'LL TELL YOU.
I'LL TALK.
DANTE, JUST A—
SHUT UP, IDIOT! I ALREADY DECIDED I'M GONNA TALK, MORRRRON!!
......

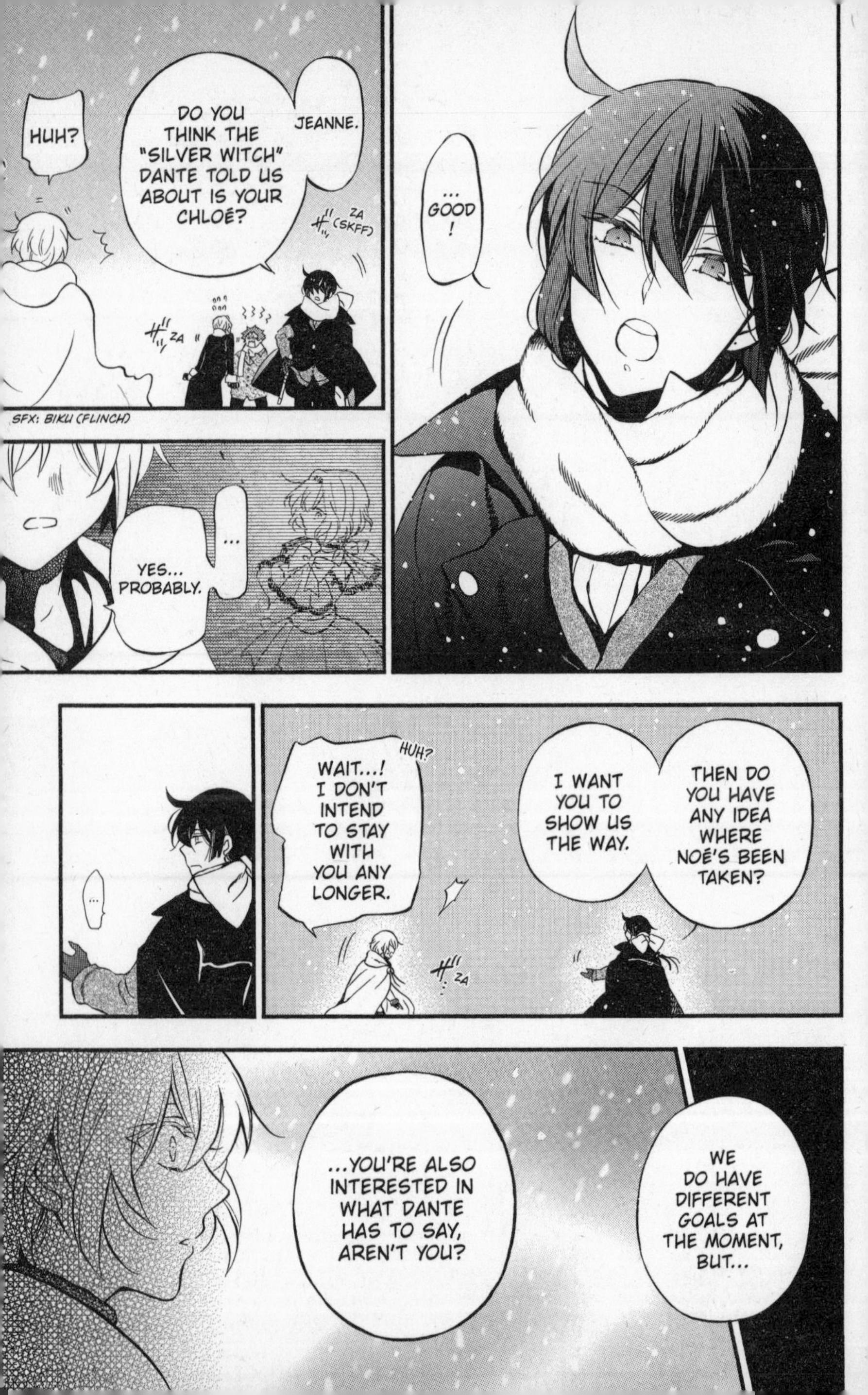
...GOOD!
JEANNE.
DO YOU THINK THE "SILVER WITCH" DANTE TOLD US ABOUT IS YOUR CHLOÉ?
HUH?
ZA (SKFF)
ZA
SFX: BIKU (FLINCH)
...
YES... PROBABLY.
THEN DO YOU HAVE ANY IDEA WHERE NOÉ'S BEEN TAKEN?
I WANT YOU TO SHOW US THE WAY.
HUH?
WAIT...! I DON'T INTEND TO STAY WITH YOU ANY LONGER.
ZA
...
WE DO HAVE DIFFERENT GOALS AT THE MOMENT, BUT...
...YOU'RE ALSO INTERESTED IN WHAT DANTE HAS TO SAY, AREN'T YOU?

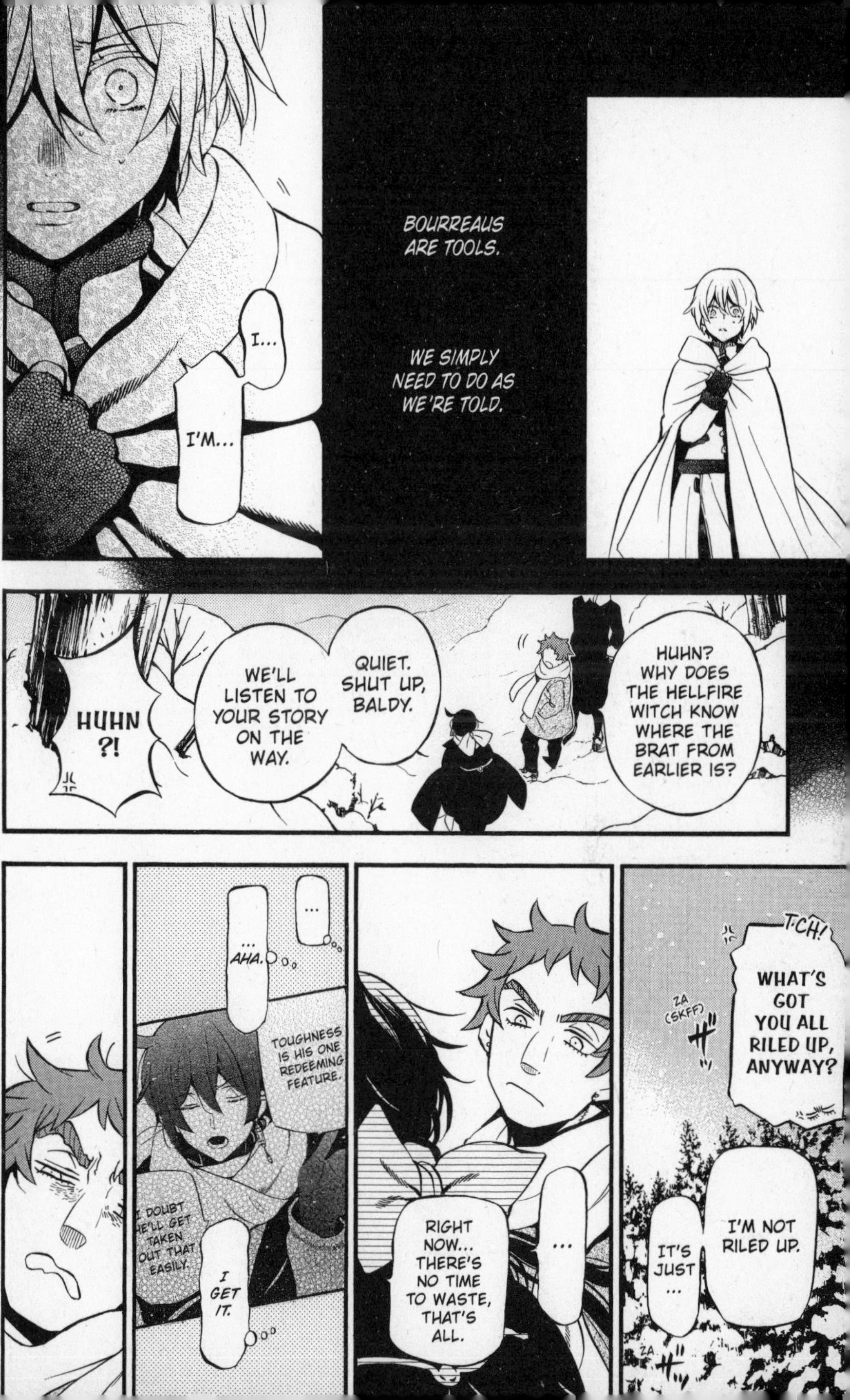
BOURREAUS ARE TOOLS.
WE SIMPLY NEED TO DO AS WE'RE TOLD.
I...
I'M...
HUHN? WHY DOES THE HELLFIRE WITCH KNOW WHERE THE BRAT FROM EARLIER IS?
QUIET. SHUT UP, BALDY.
WE'LL LISTEN TO YOUR STORY ON THE WAY.
HUHN?!
T'CH!
WHAT'S GOT YOU ALL RILED UP, ANYWAY?
ZA (SKFF)
I'M NOT RILED UP.
IT'S JUST...
ZA
...
RIGHT NOW... THERE'S NO TIME TO WASTE, THAT'S ALL.
...
...AHA.
TOUGHNESS IS HIS ONE REDEEMING FEATURE.
I DOUBT HE'LL GET TAKEN OUT THAT EASILY.
I GET IT.

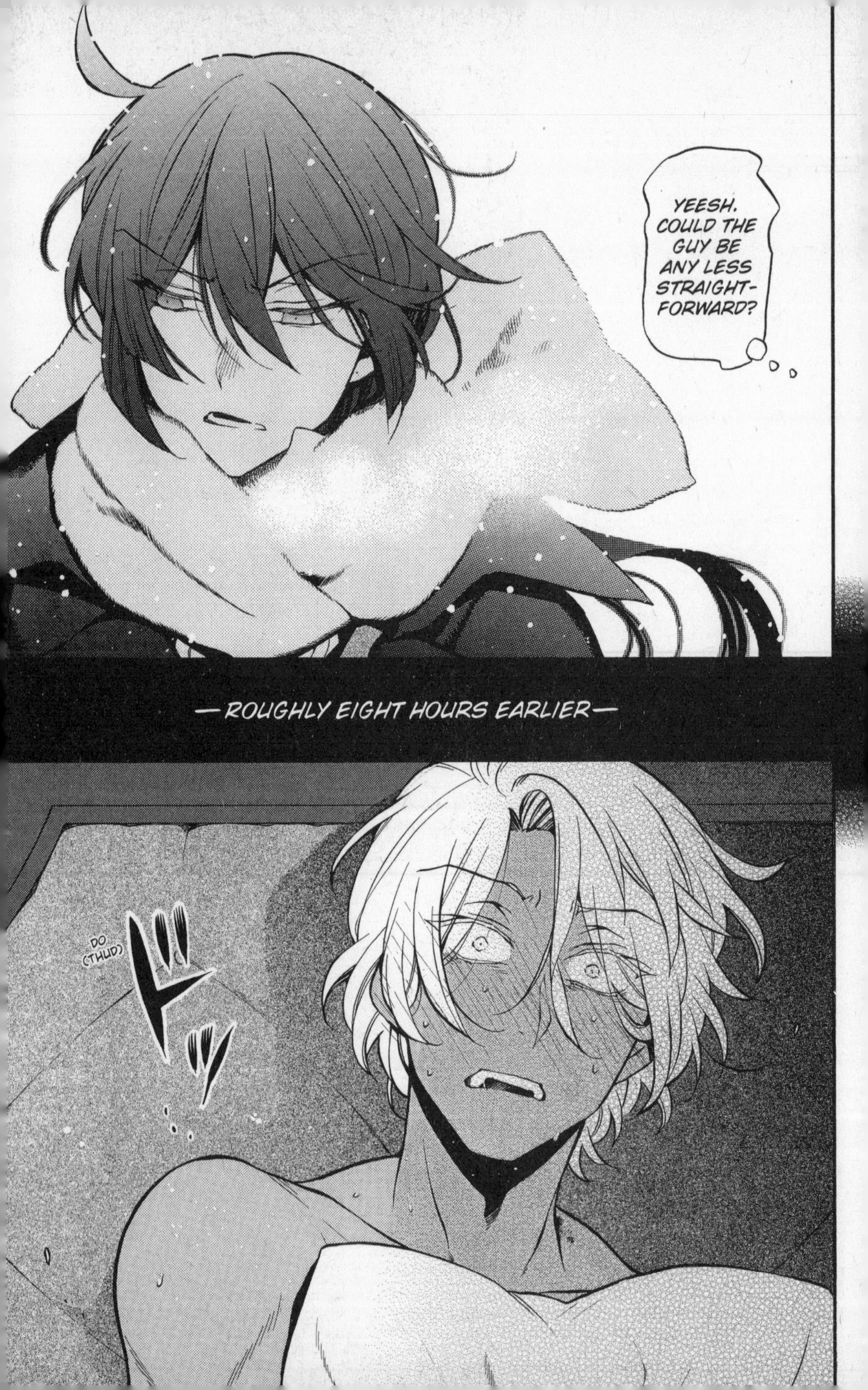
YEESH. COULD THE GUY BE ANY LESS STRAIGHT-FORWARD?
—ROUGHLY EIGHT HOURS EARLIER—
DO (THUD)

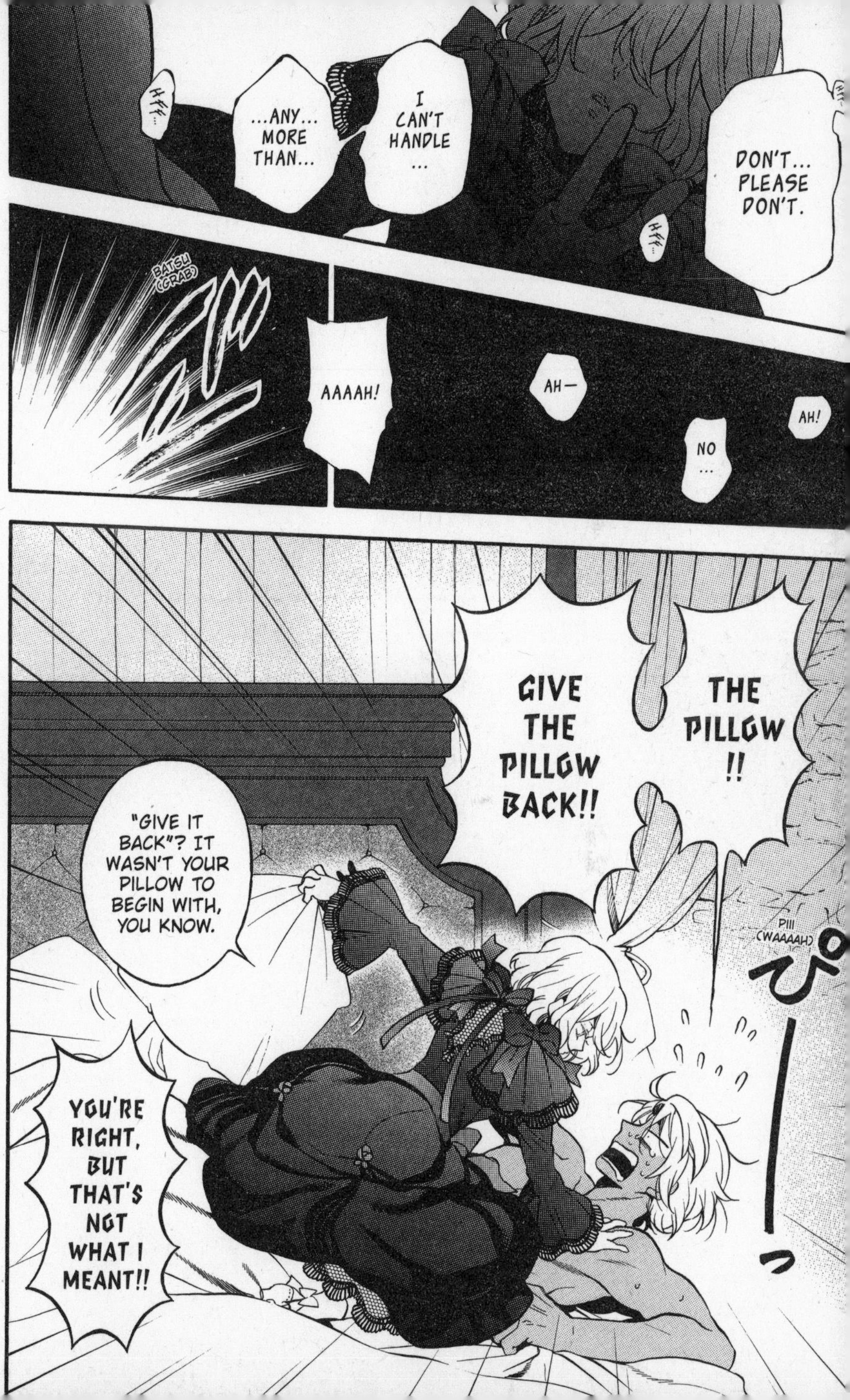
DON'T... PLEASE DON'T.
Hff...
I CAN'T HANDLE ...
...ANY... MORE THAN...
Hff...
AH!
NO ...
AH—
AAAAH!
BATSU (GRAB)
THE PILLOW!!
GIVE THE PILLOW BACK!!
PIII (WAAAAH)
"GIVE IT BACK"? IT WASN'T YOUR PILLOW TO BEGIN WITH, YOU KNOW.
YOU'RE RIGHT, BUT THAT'S NOT WHAT I MEANT!!

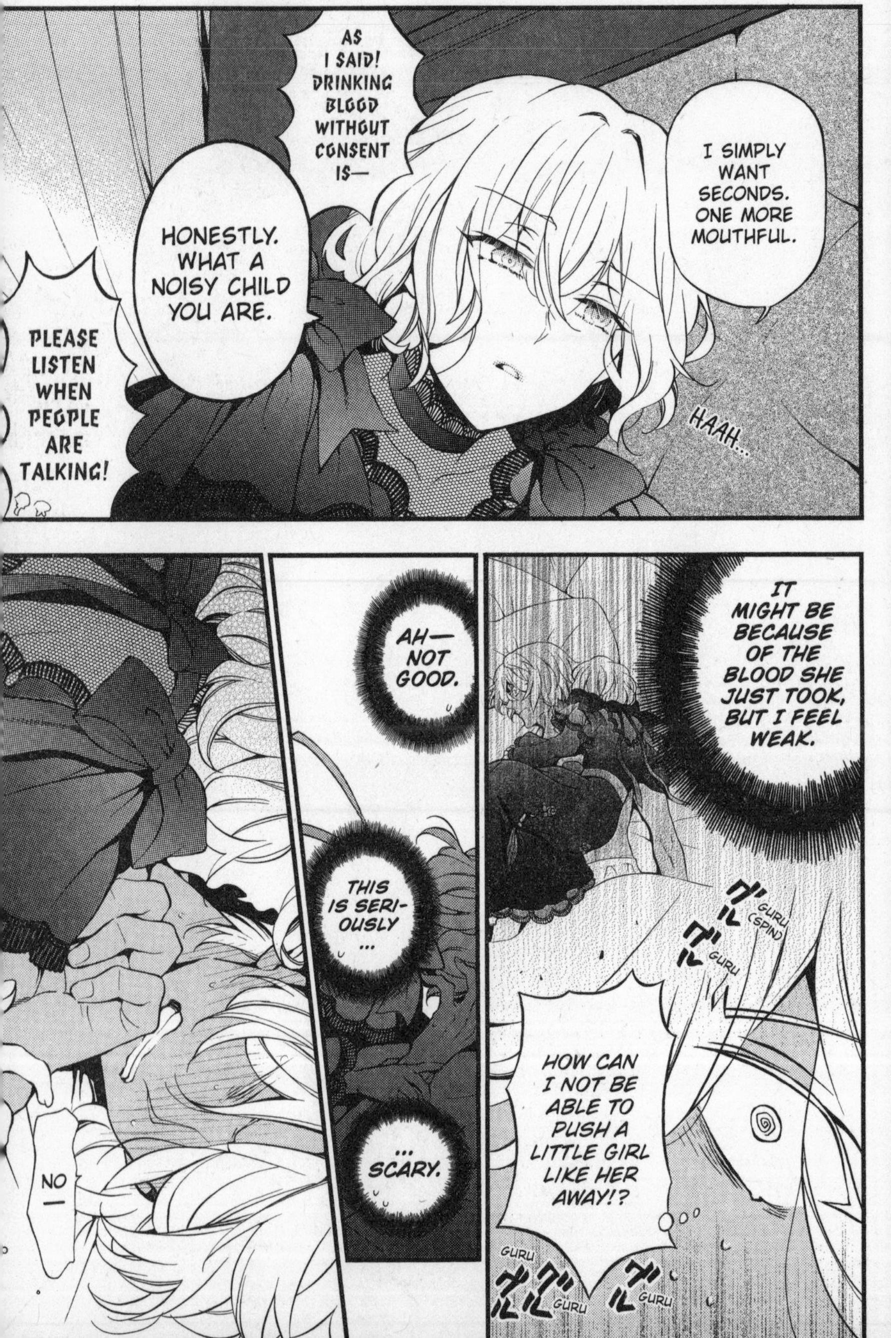
I SIMPLY WANT SECONDS. ONE MORE MOUTHFUL.
HAAH...
AS I SAID! DRINKING BLOOD WITHOUT CONSENT IS—
HONESTLY. WHAT A NOISY CHILD YOU ARE.
PLEASE LISTEN WHEN PEOPLE ARE TALKING!
IT MIGHT BE BECAUSE OF THE BLOOD SHE JUST TOOK, BUT I FEEL WEAK.
GURU (SPIN)
GURU
HOW CAN I NOT BE ABLE TO PUSH A LITTLE GIRL LIKE HER AWAY!?
GURU
GURU
GURU
AH— NOT GOOD.
THIS IS SERI-OUSLY ...
... SCARY.
NO—

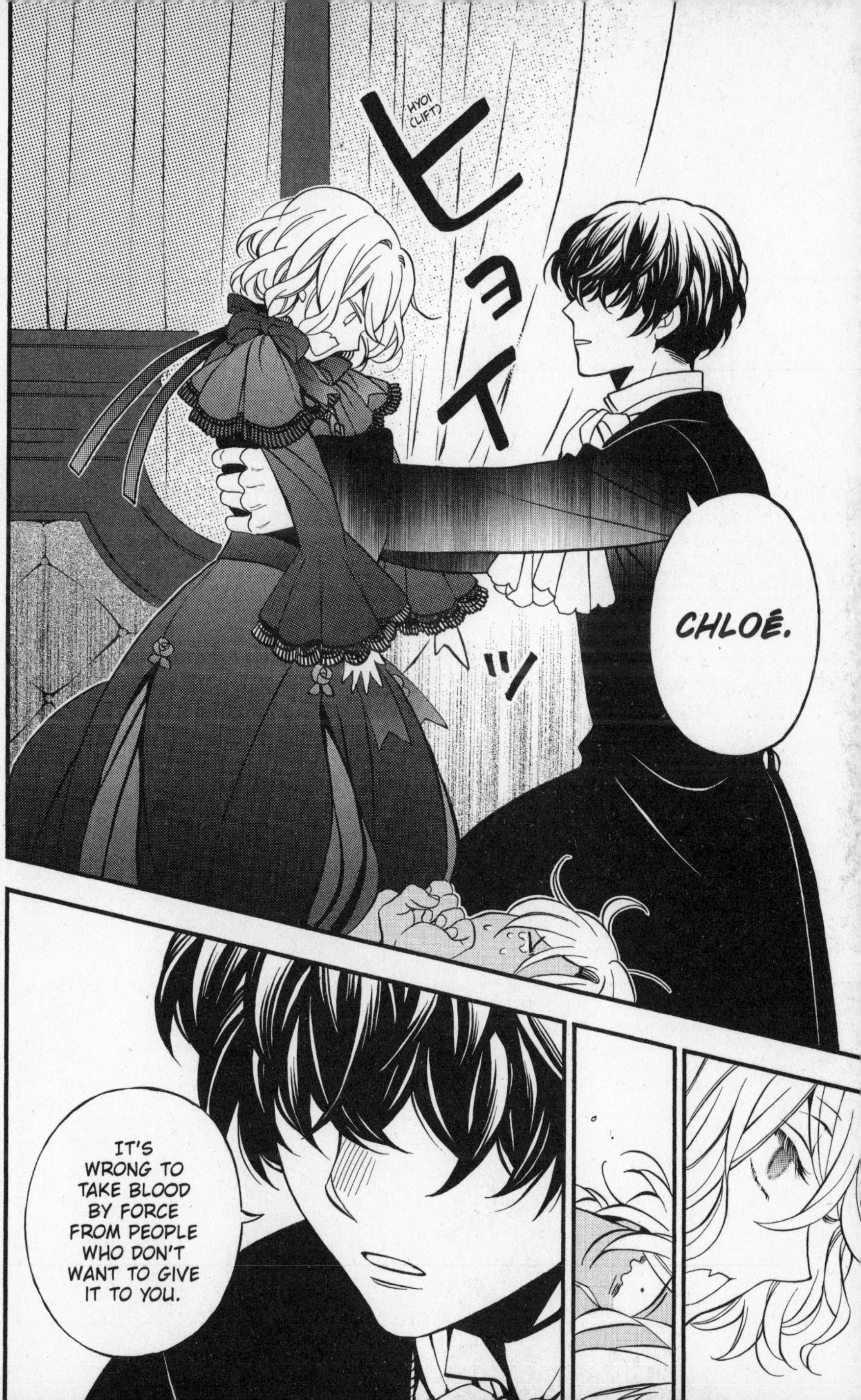
HYOI (LIFT)
ヒョイ
CHLOÉ.
ッ
IT'S WRONG TO TAKE BLOOD BY FORCE FROM PEOPLE WHO DON'T WANT TO GIVE IT TO YOU.

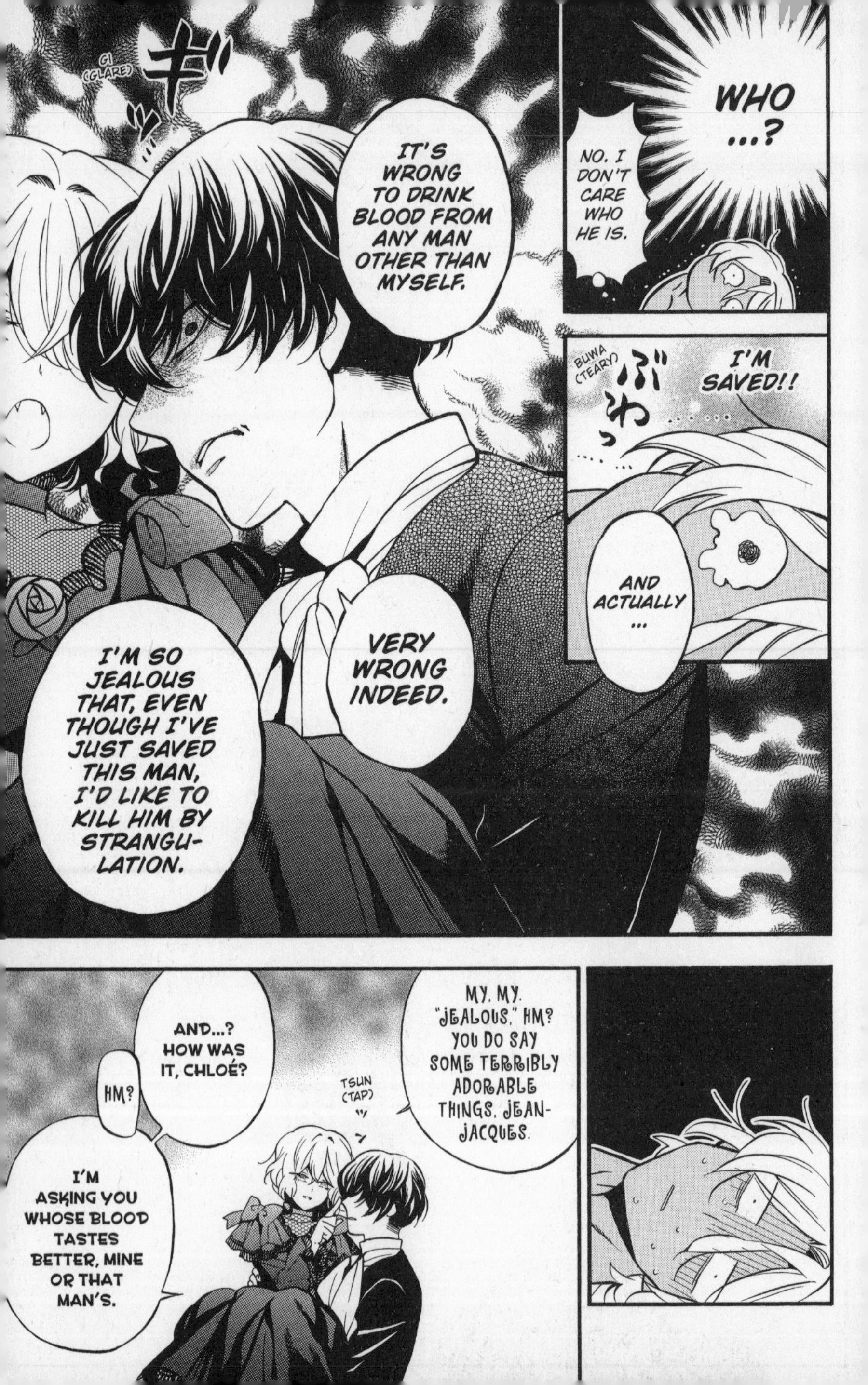
WHO ...?
NO. I DON'T CARE WHO HE IS.
BUWA (TEARY)
ぶわっ
I'M SAVED!!
AND ACTUALLY ...
GI (GLARE)
ギッ
IT'S WRONG TO DRINK BLOOD FROM ANY MAN OTHER THAN MYSELF.
VERY WRONG INDEED.
I'M SO JEALOUS THAT, EVEN THOUGH I'VE JUST SAVED THIS MAN, I'D LIKE TO KILL HIM BY STRANGU-LATION.
MY, MY. "JEALOUS," HM? YOU DO SAY SOME TERRIBLY ADORABLE THINGS, JEAN-JACQUES.
TSUN (TAP)
ツン
AND...? HOW WAS IT, CHLOÉ?
HM?
I'M ASKING YOU WHOSE BLOOD TASTES BETTER, MINE OR THAT MAN'S.

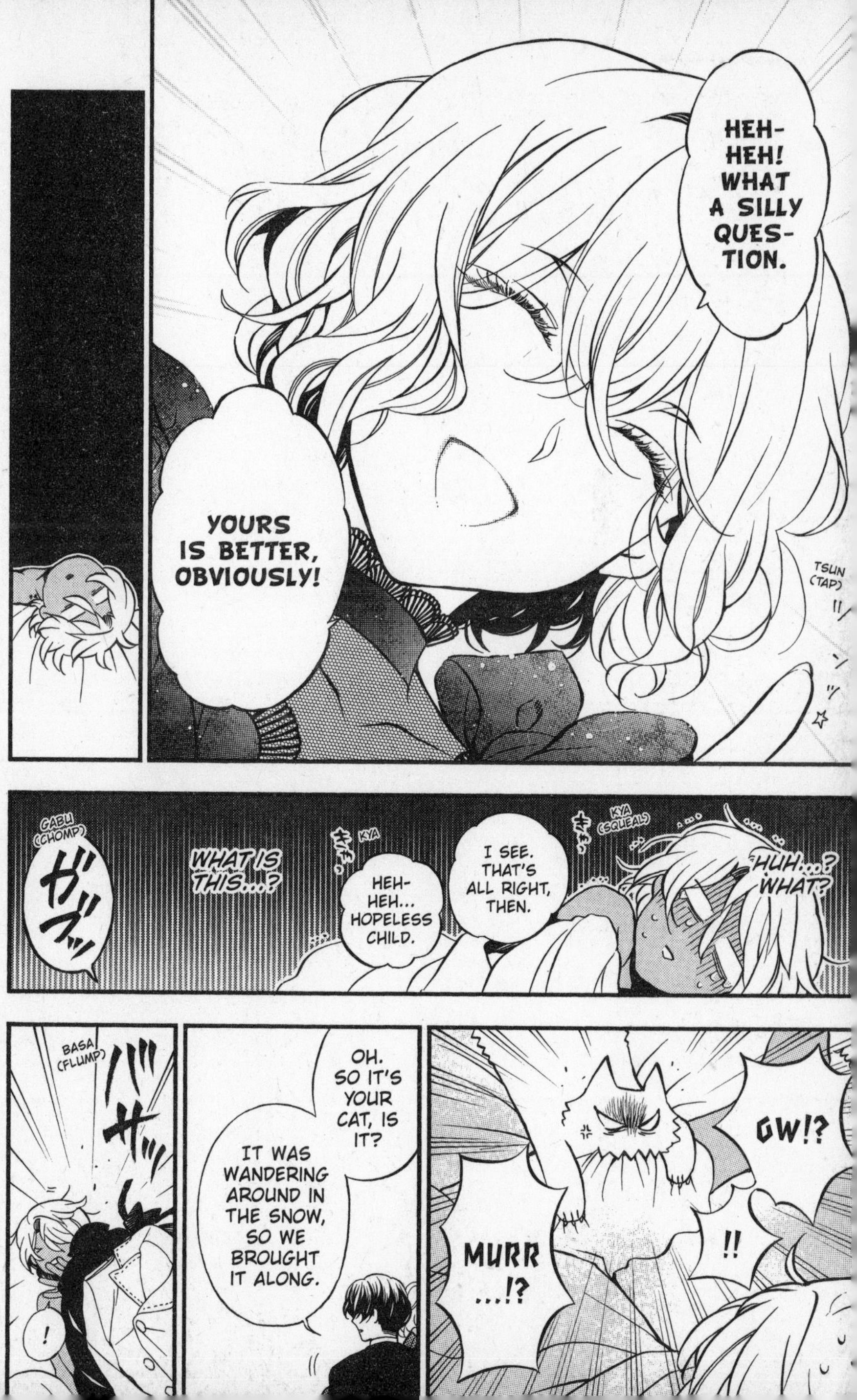
HEH-HEH! WHAT A SILLY QUESTION.
YOURS IS BETTER, OBVIOUSLY!
TSUN (TAP)
HUH...? WHAT?
KYA (SQUEAL)
I SEE. THAT'S ALL RIGHT, THEN.
HEH-HEH... HOPELESS CHILD.
KYA
WHAT IS THIS...?
GABU (CHOMP)
GW!?
!!
MURR...!?
OH. SO IT'S YOUR CAT, IS IT?
IT WAS WANDERING AROUND IN THE SNOW, SO WE BROUGHT IT ALONG.
BASA (FLUMP)
!

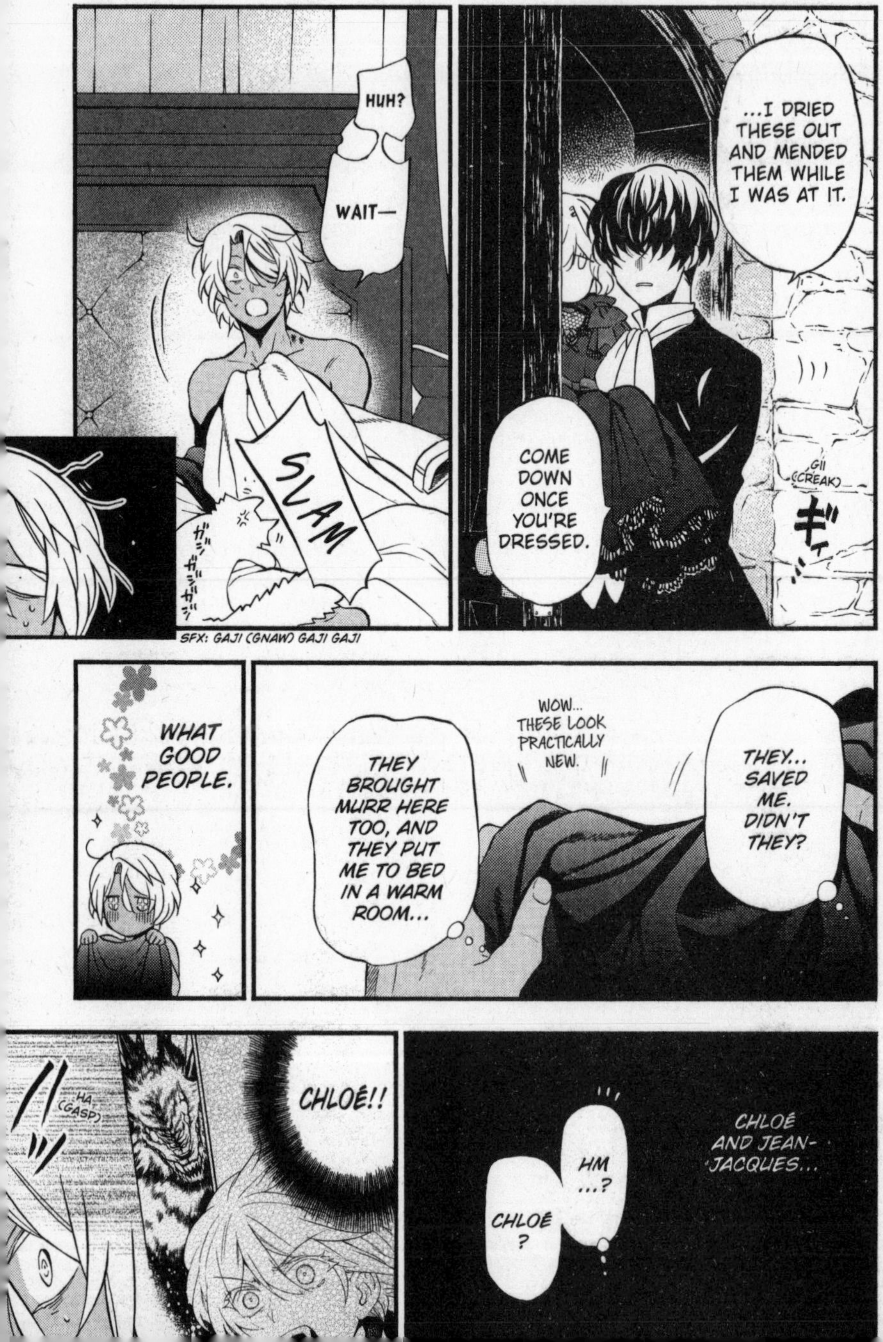
...I DRIED THESE OUT AND MENDED THEM WHILE I WAS AT IT.
COME DOWN ONCE YOU'RE DRESSED.
GII (CREAK)
HUH?
WAIT—
SLAM
SFX: GAJI (GNAW) GAJI GAJI
THEY... SAVED ME. DIDN'T THEY?
WOW... THESE LOOK PRACTICALLY NEW.
THEY BROUGHT MURR HERE TOO, AND THEY PUT ME TO BED IN A WARM ROOM...
WHAT GOOD PEOPLE.
CHLOÉ AND JEAN-JACQUES...
HM ...?
CHLOÉ ?
CHLOÉ!!
HA (GASP)

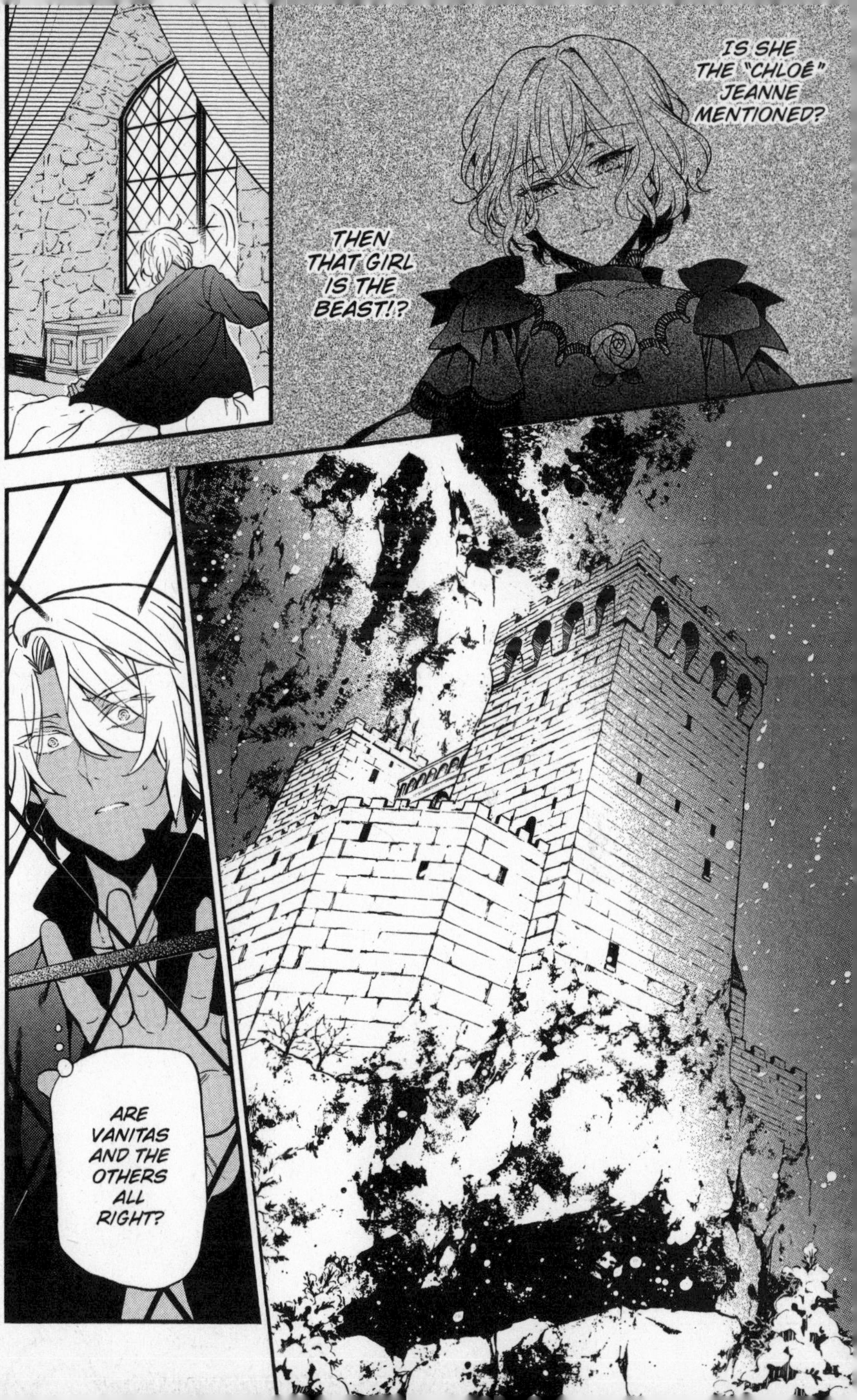
IS SHE THE "CHLOÉ" JEANNE MENTIONED?
THEN THAT GIRL IS THE BEAST!?
ARE VANITAS AND THE OTHERS ALL RIGHT?

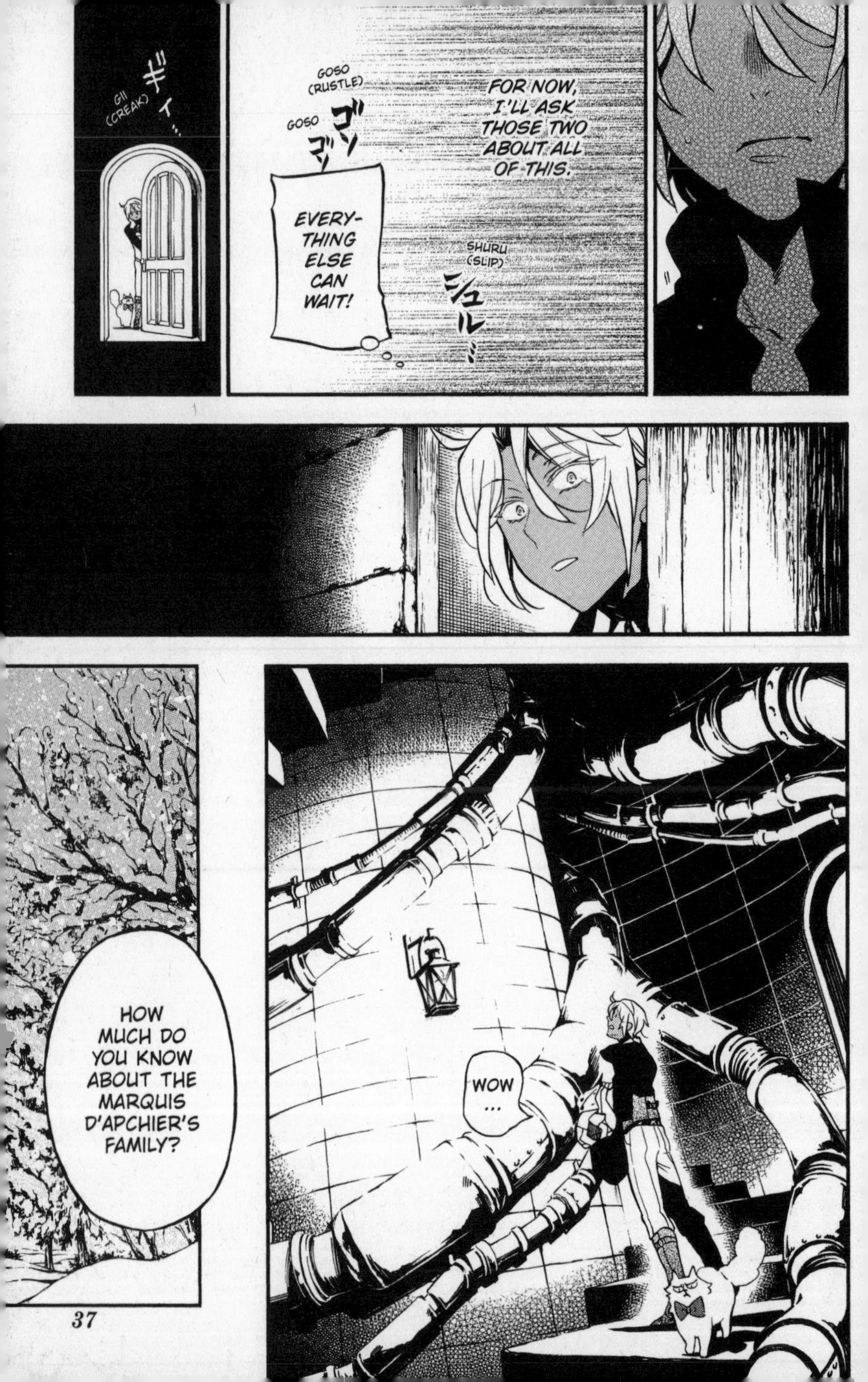
FOR NOW, I'LL ASK THOSE TWO ABOUT ALL OF THIS.
GOSO (RUSTLE)
GOSO
EVERY-THING ELSE CAN WAIT!
SHURU (SLIP)
GII (CREAK)
WOW...
HOW MUCH DO YOU KNOW ABOUT THE MARQUIS D'APCHIER'S FAMILY?

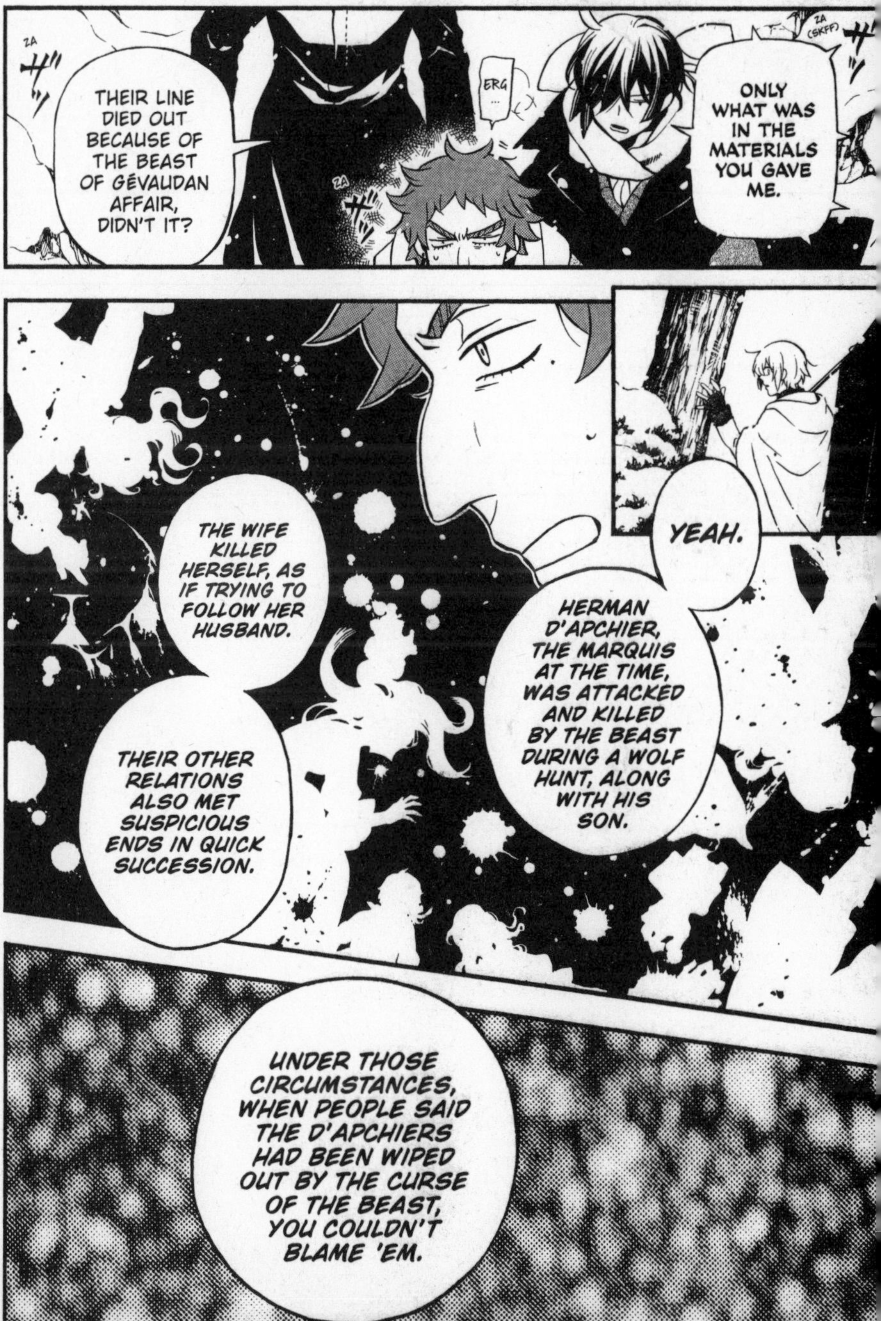
ZA (SKFF)
ONLY WHAT WAS IN THE MATERIALS YOU GAVE ME.
ERG...
THEIR LINE DIED OUT BECAUSE OF THE BEAST OF GÉVAUDAN AFFAIR, DIDN'T IT?
ZA
ZA
YEAH.
HERMAN D'APCHIER, THE MARQUIS AT THE TIME, WAS ATTACKED AND KILLED BY THE BEAST DURING A WOLF HUNT, ALONG WITH HIS SON.
THE WIFE KILLED HERSELF, AS IF TRYING TO FOLLOW HER HUSBAND.
THEIR OTHER RELATIONS ALSO MET SUSPICIOUS ENDS IN QUICK SUCCESSION.
UNDER THOSE CIRCUMSTANCES, WHEN PEOPLE SAID THE D'APCHIERS HAD BEEN WIPED OUT BY THE CURSE OF THE BEAST, YOU COULDN'T BLAME 'EM.

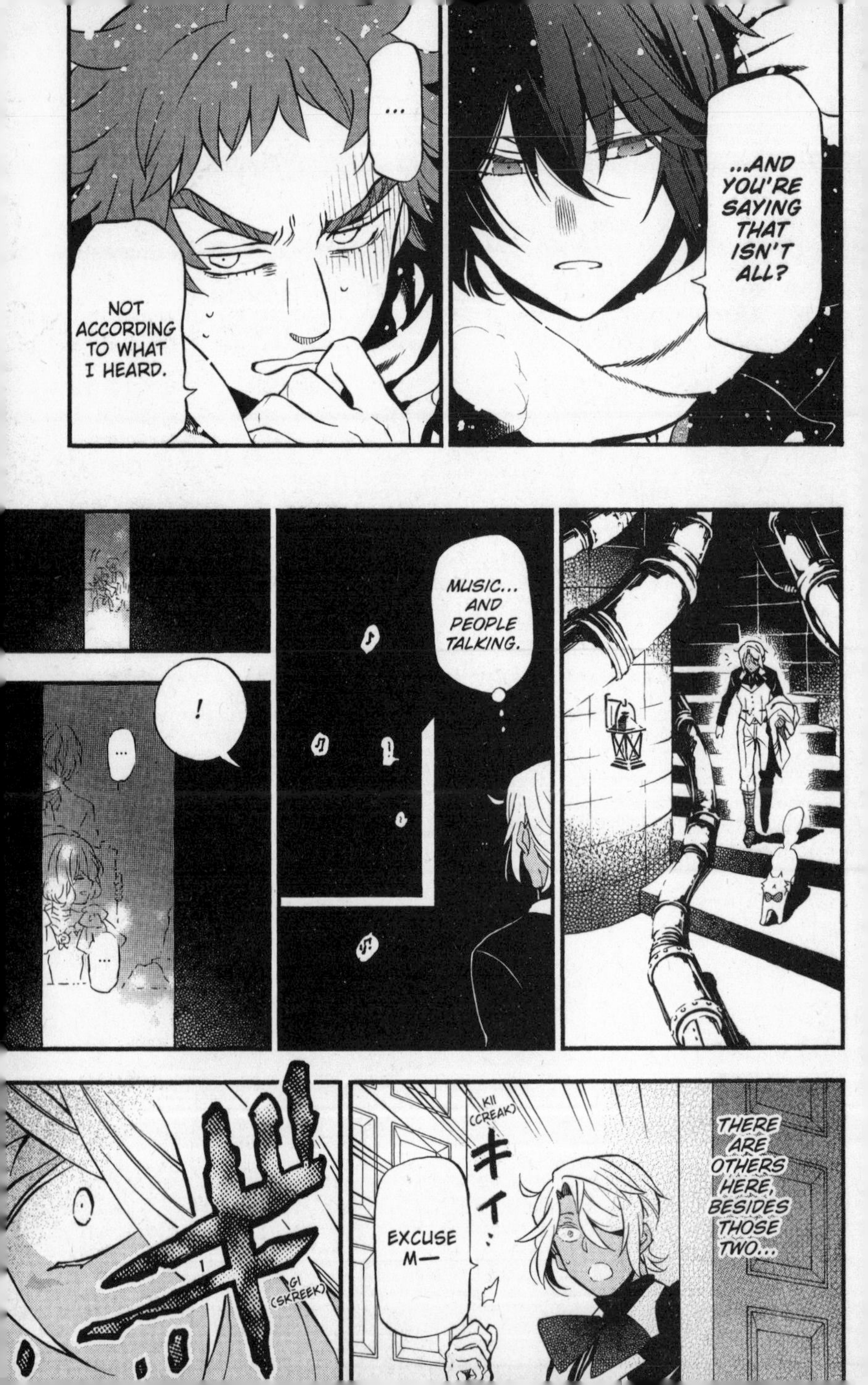
...AND YOU'RE SAYING THAT ISN'T ALL?
...
NOT ACCORDING TO WHAT I HEARD.
MUSIC... AND PEOPLE TALKING.
!
...
...
THERE ARE OTHERS HERE, BESIDES THOSE TWO...
KII (CREAK)
EXCUSE M—
GI (SKREEK)

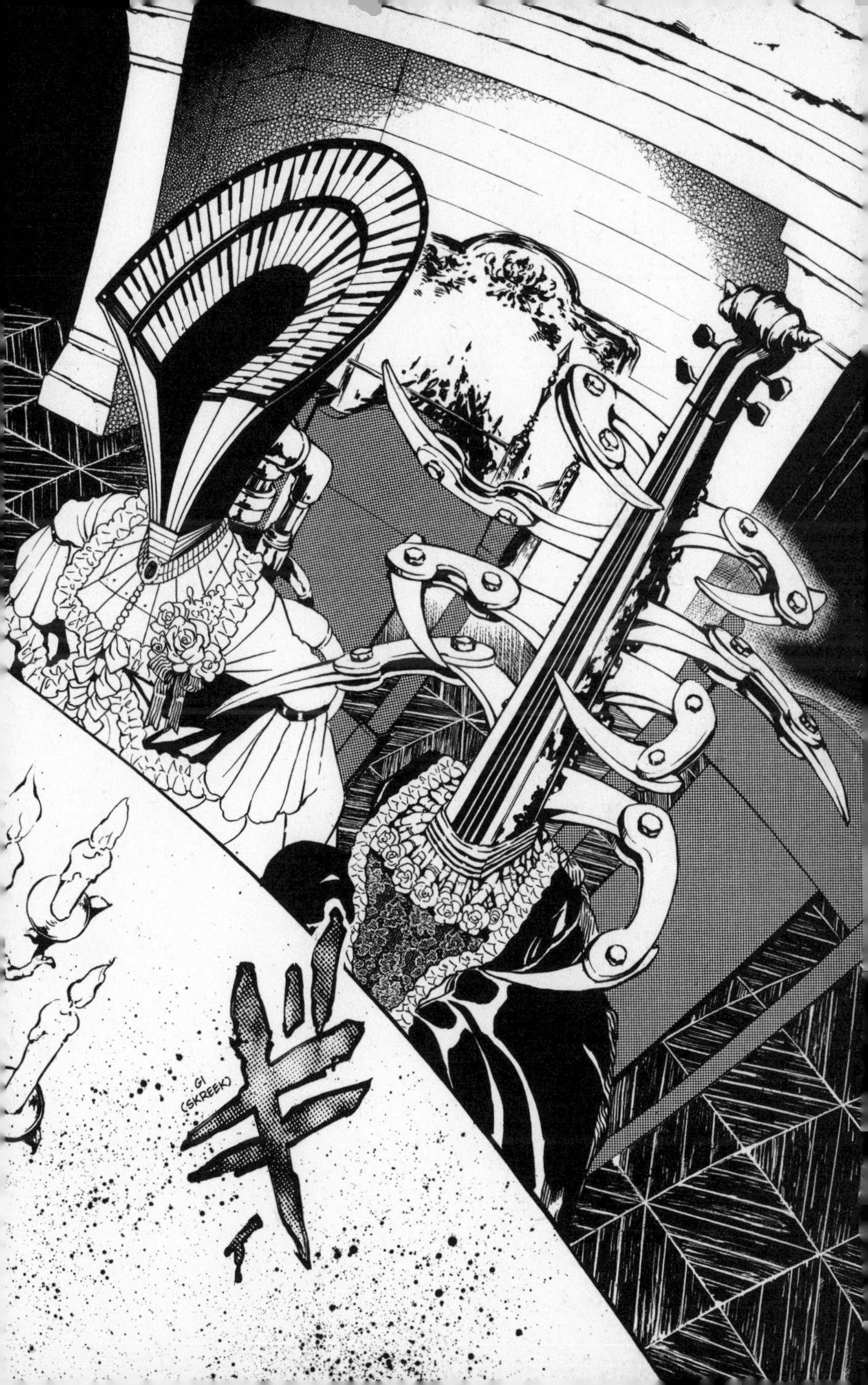
GI
(SKREEK)

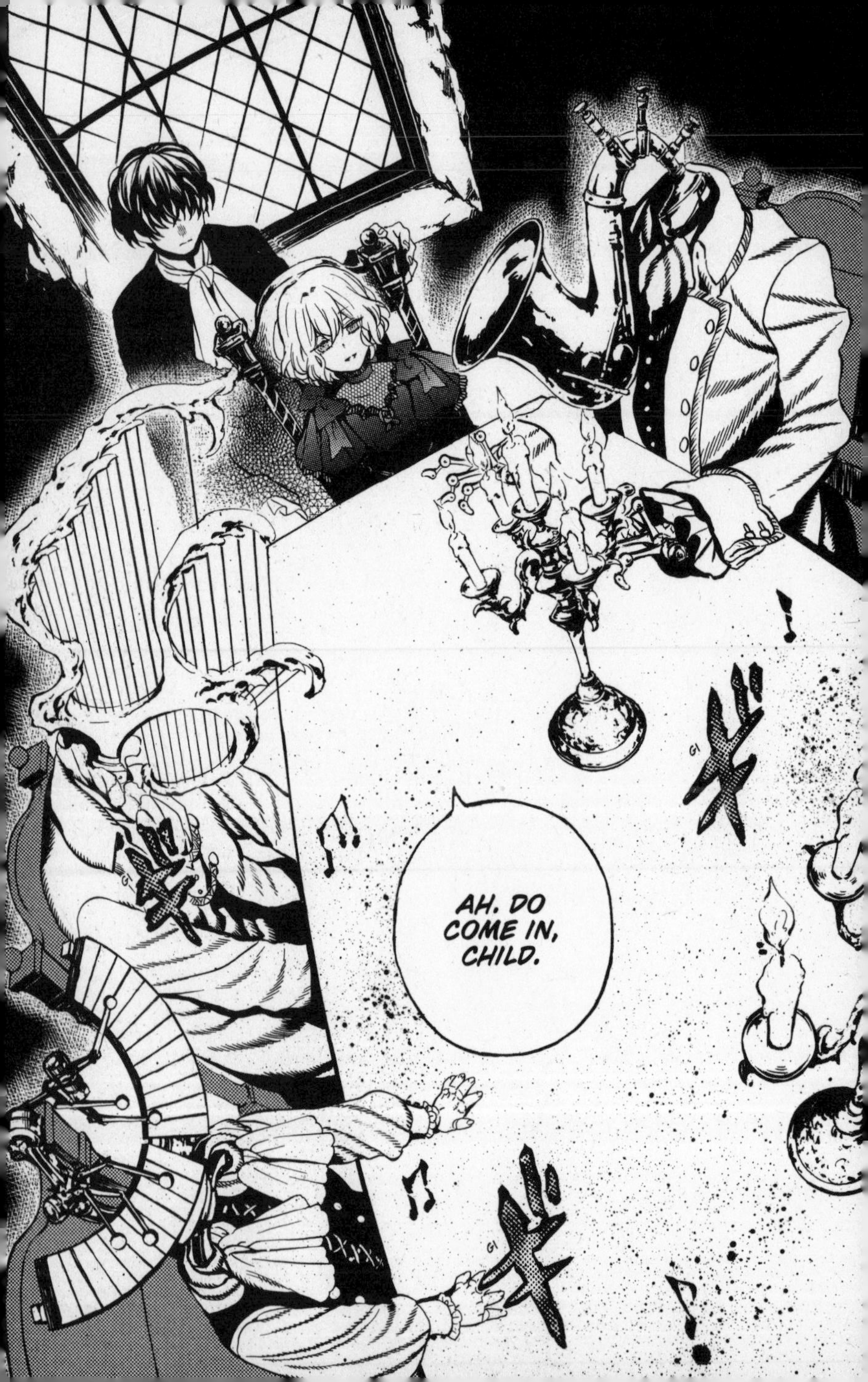
GI
AH. DO COME IN, CHILD.
GI
GI

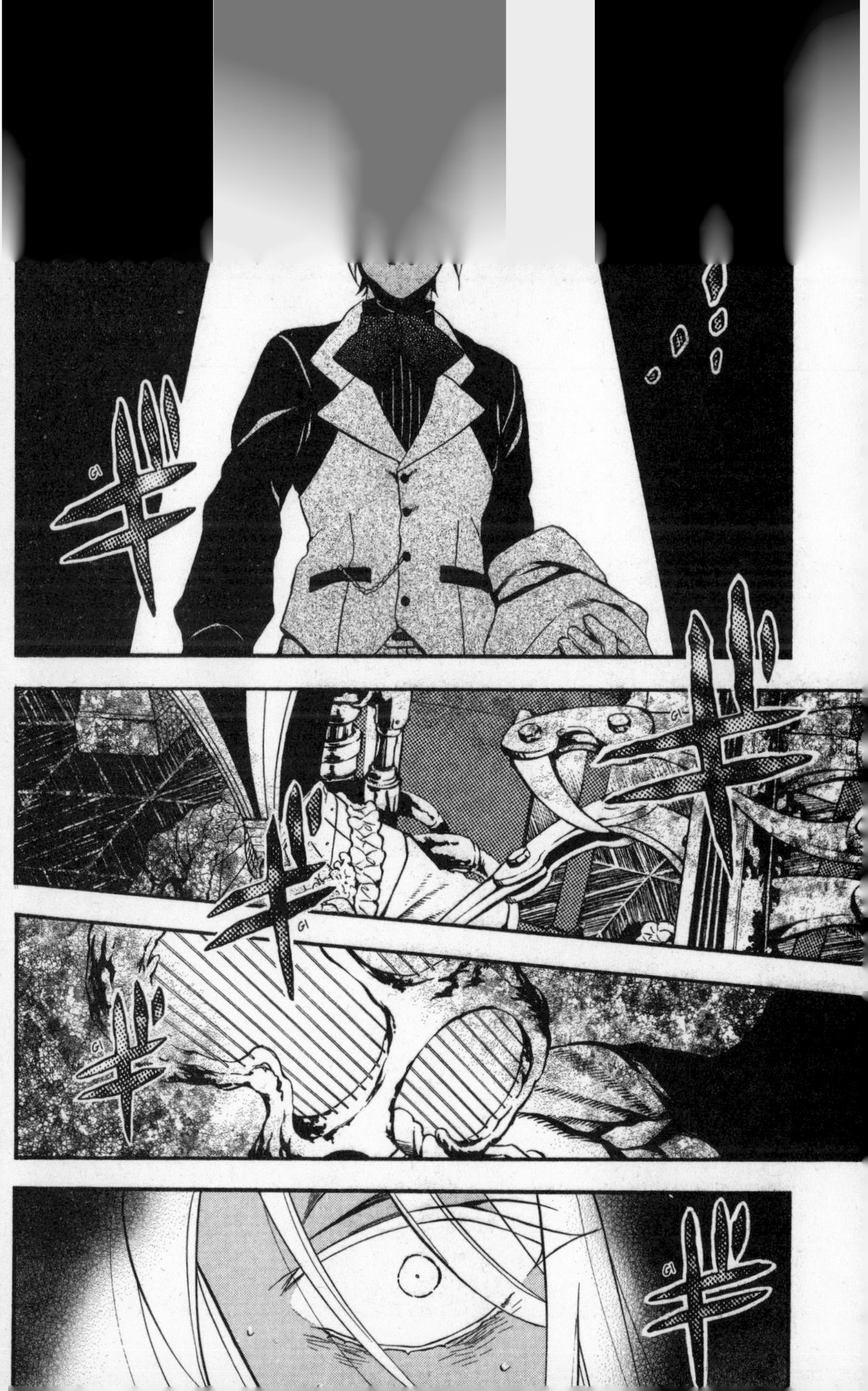
GI
GI
GI
GI
GI

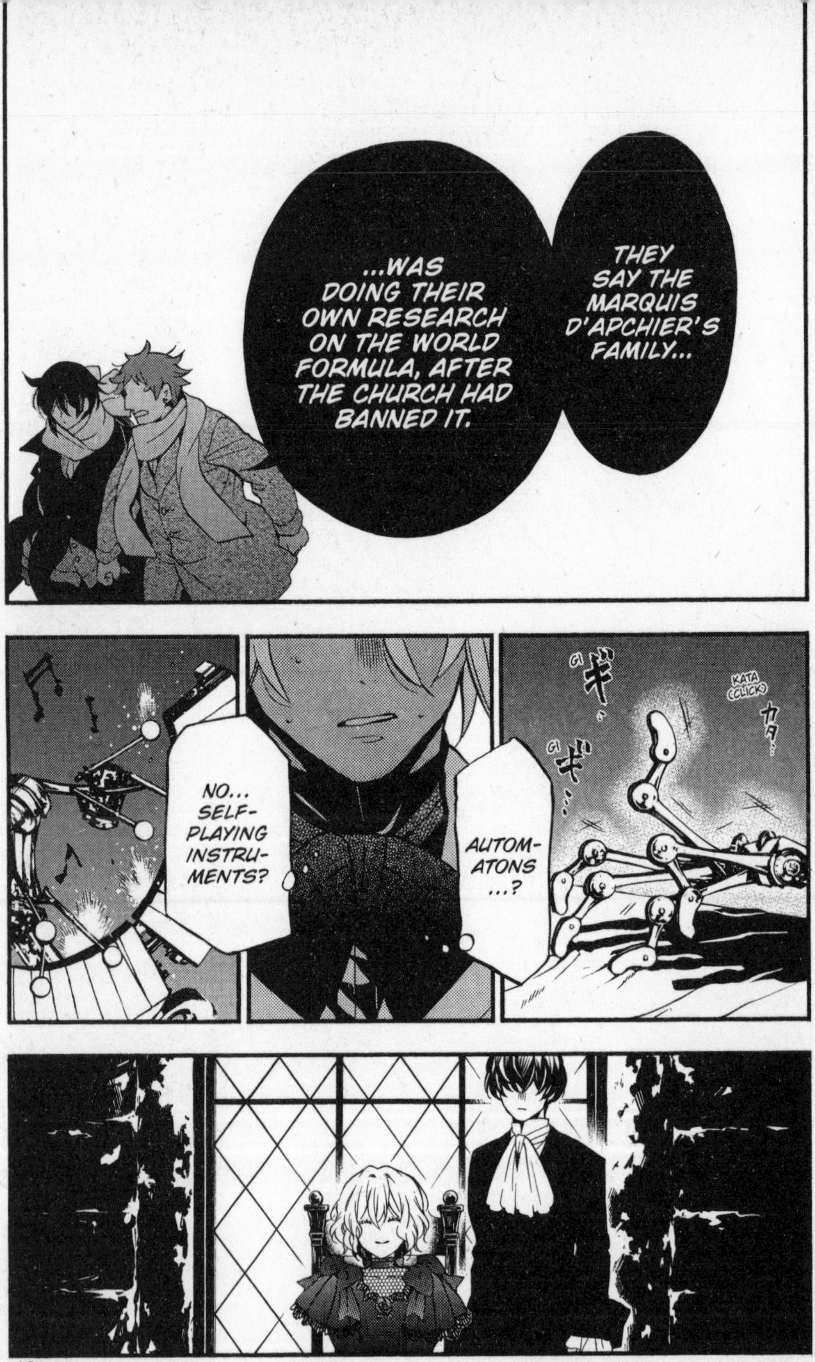
THEY SAY THE MARQUIS D'APCHIER'S FAMILY...
...WAS DOING THEIR OWN RESEARCH ON THE WORLD FORMULA, AFTER THE CHURCH HAD BANNED IT.
GI ギ
GI ギ
KATA (CLICK) カタ…
AUTOMATONS ...?
NO... SELF-PLAYING INSTRUMENTS?

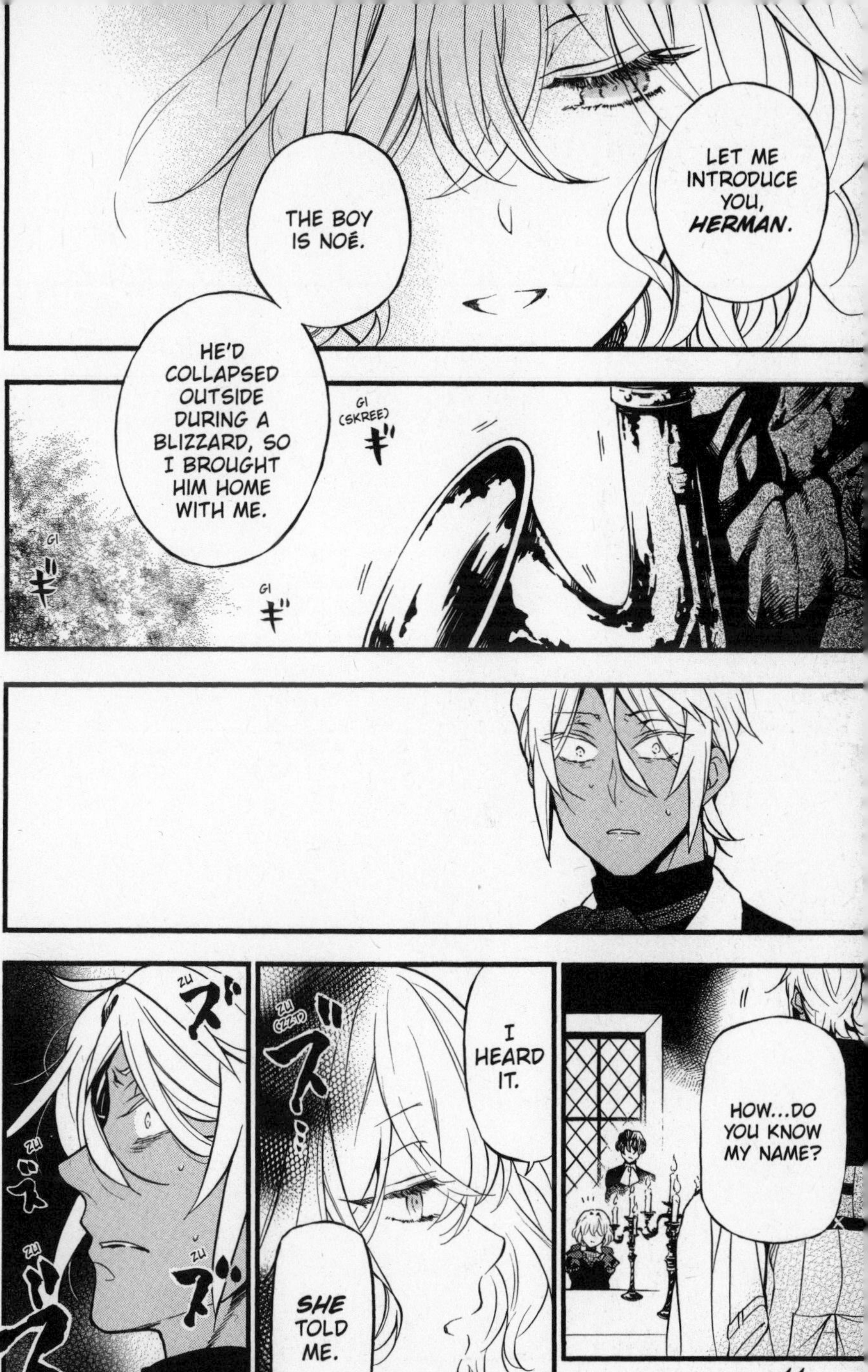
LET ME INTRODUCE YOU, HERMAN.
THE BOY IS NOÉ.
HE'D COLLAPSED OUTSIDE DURING A BLIZZARD, SO I BROUGHT HIM HOME WITH ME.
ギ GI (SKREE)
ギ GI
ギ GI
HOW...DO YOU KNOW MY NAME?
I HEARD IT.
ズ ZU (ZZZT)
SHE TOLD ME.
ズ ZU
ズ ZU
ズ ZU
ズ ZU
ズ ZU

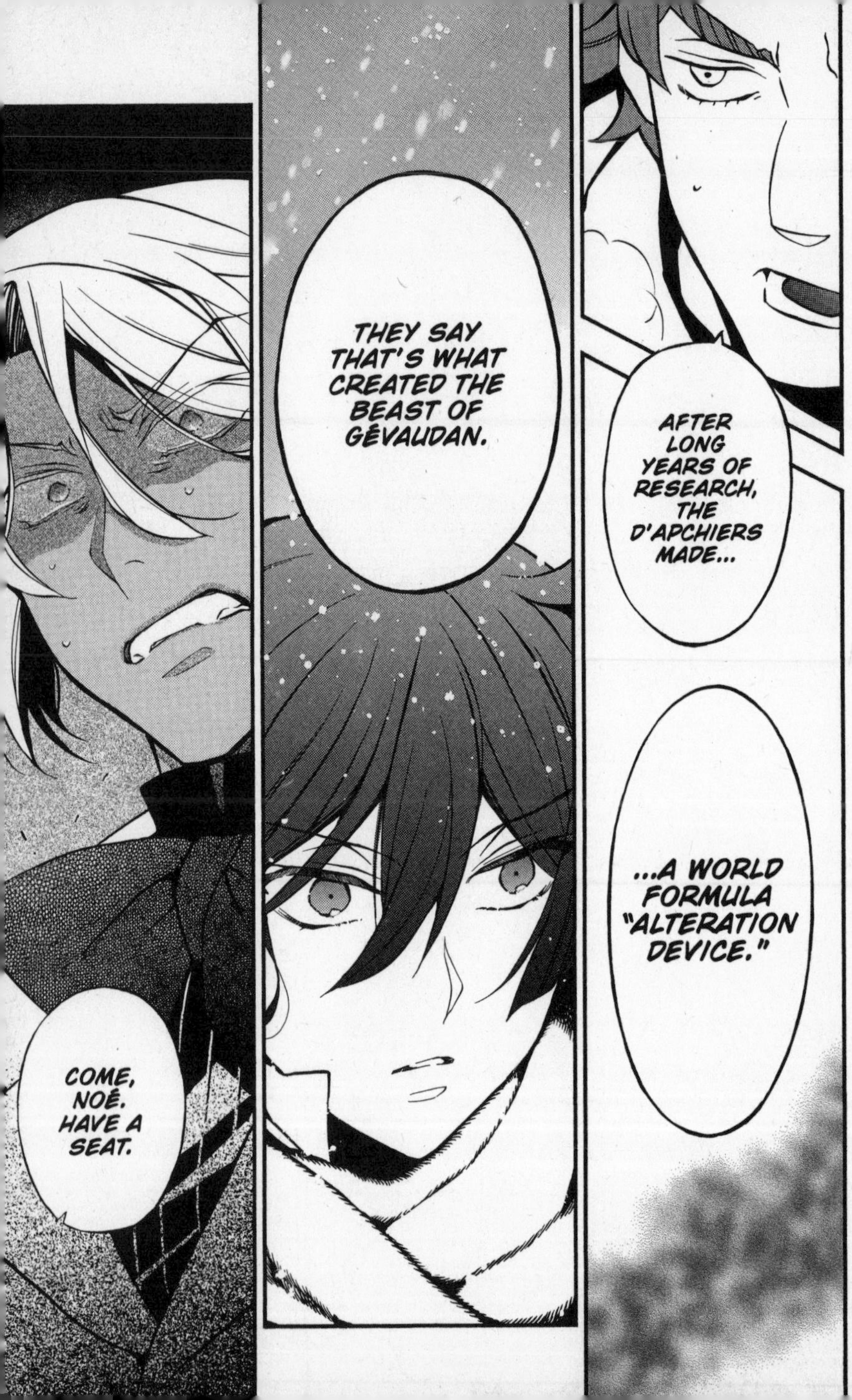
AFTER LONG YEARS OF RESEARCH, THE D'APCHIERS MADE...
...A WORLD FORMULA "ALTERATION DEVICE."
THEY SAY THAT'S WHAT CREATED THE BEAST OF GÉVAUDAN.
COME, NOÉ. HAVE A SEAT.

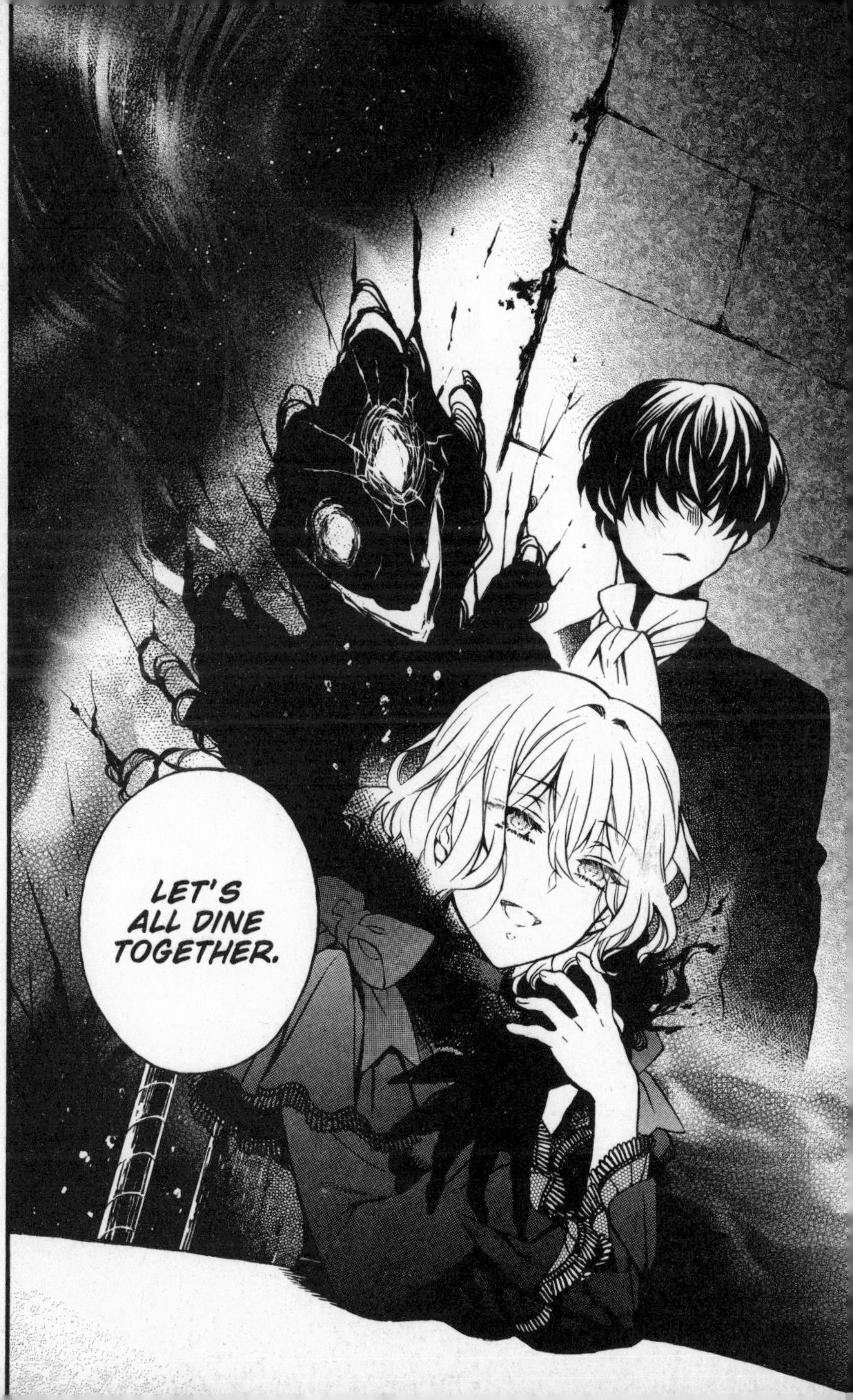
LET'S ALL DINE TOGETHER.

Mémoire 29

Château de Sorcière THE WITCH AND THE YOUTH

Les Mémoires de Vanitas

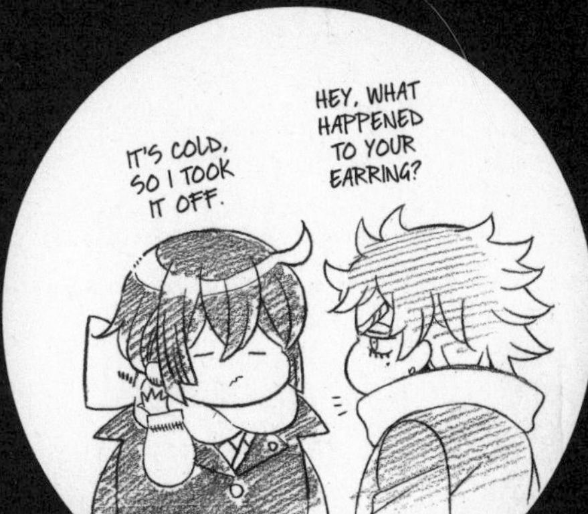
HEY, WHAT HAPPENED TO YOUR EARRING?
IT'S COLD, SO I TOOK IT OFF.

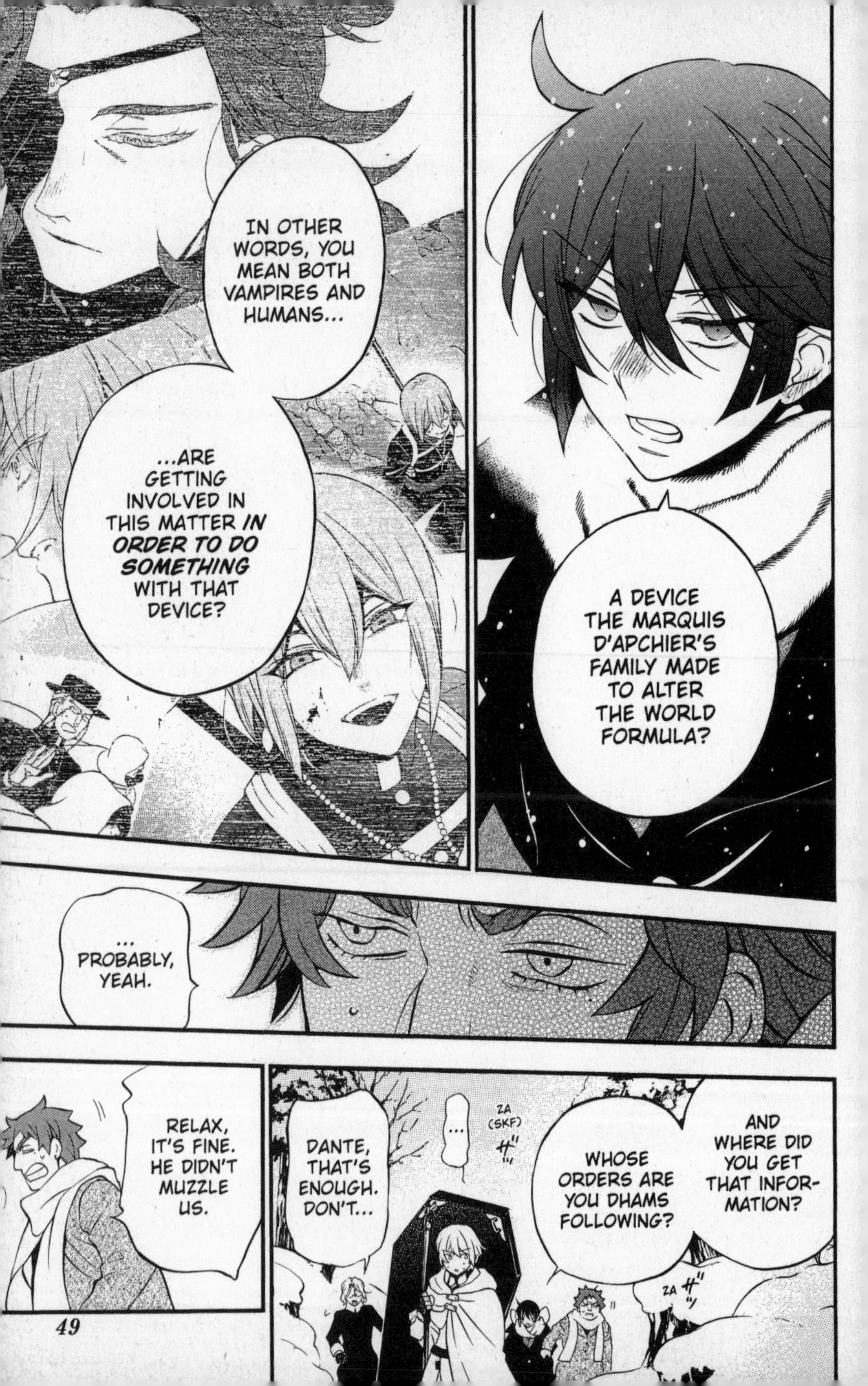
A DEVICE THE MARQUIS D'APCHIER'S FAMILY MADE TO ALTER THE WORLD FORMULA?
IN OTHER WORDS, YOU MEAN BOTH VAMPIRES AND HUMANS...
...ARE GETTING INVOLVED IN THIS MATTER *IN ORDER TO DO SOMETHING* WITH THAT DEVICE?
... PROBABLY, YEAH.
AND WHERE DID YOU GET THAT INFOR-MATION?
WHOSE ORDERS ARE YOU DHAMS FOLLOWING?
ZA (SKF)
...
DANTE, THAT'S ENOUGH. DON'T...
ZA
RELAX, IT'S FINE. HE DIDN'T MUZZLE US.

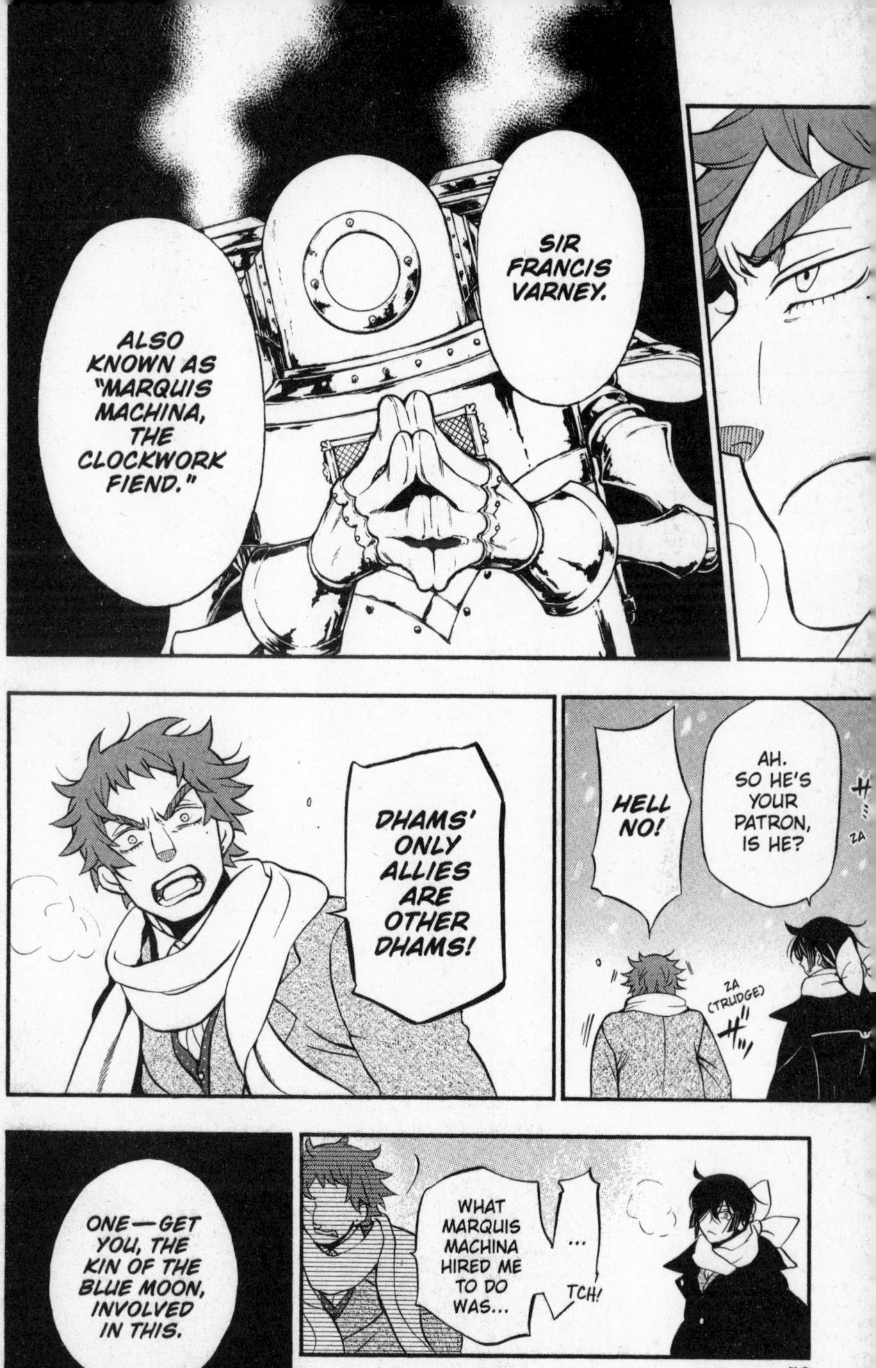
SIR FRANCIS VARNEY.
ALSO KNOWN AS "MARQUIS MACHINA, THE CLOCKWORK FIEND."
AH. SO HE'S YOUR PATRON, IS HE?
ZA
HELL NO!
ZA (TRUDGE)
DHAMS' ONLY ALLIES ARE OTHER DHAMS!
...
TCH!
WHAT MARQUIS MACHINA HIRED ME TO DO WAS...
ONE—GET YOU, THE KIN OF THE BLUE MOON, INVOLVED IN THIS.

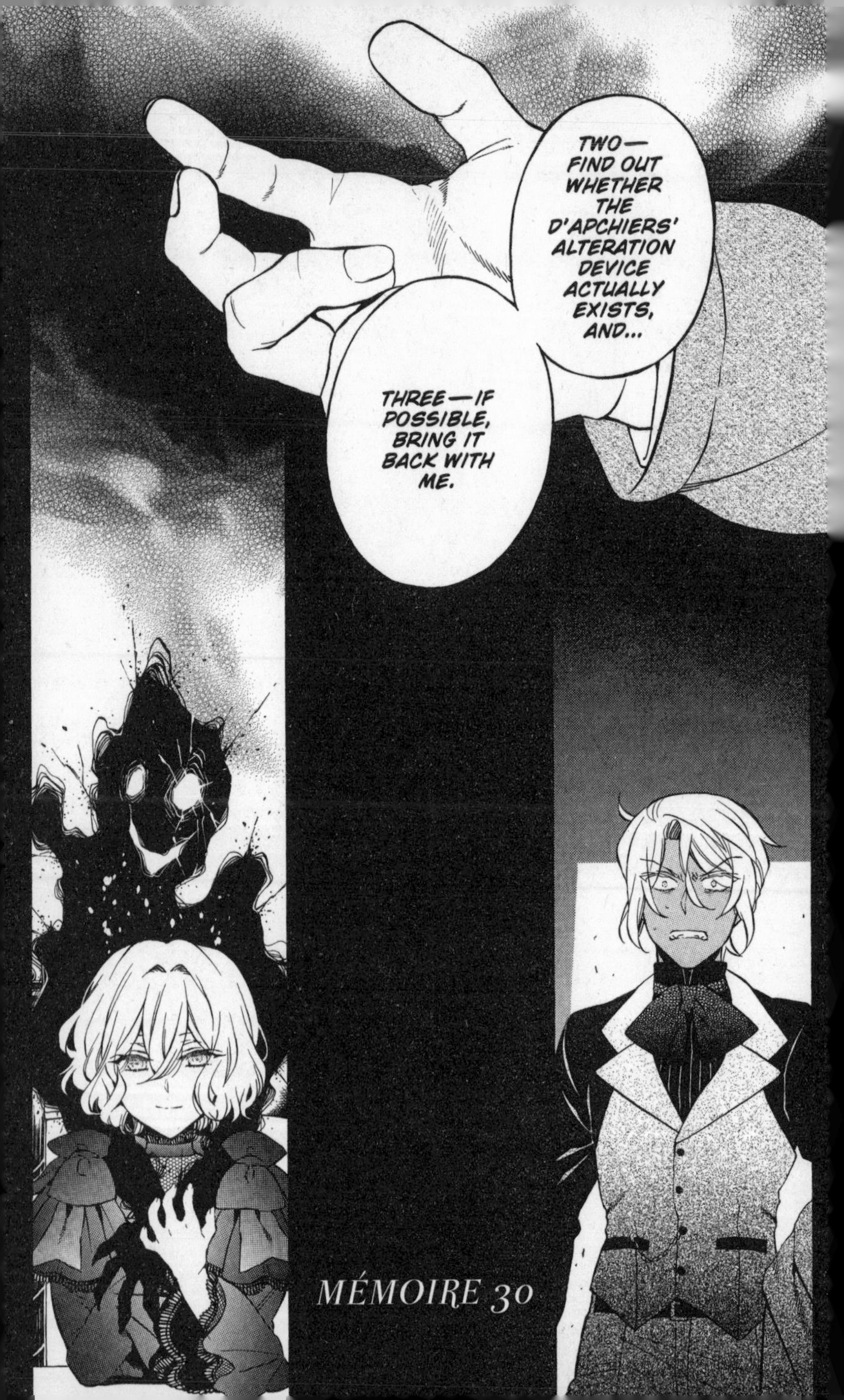
TWO—FIND OUT WHETHER THE D'APCHIERS' ALTERATION DEVICE ACTUALLY EXISTS, AND...
THREE—IF POSSIBLE, BRING IT BACK WITH ME.
MÉMOIRE 30

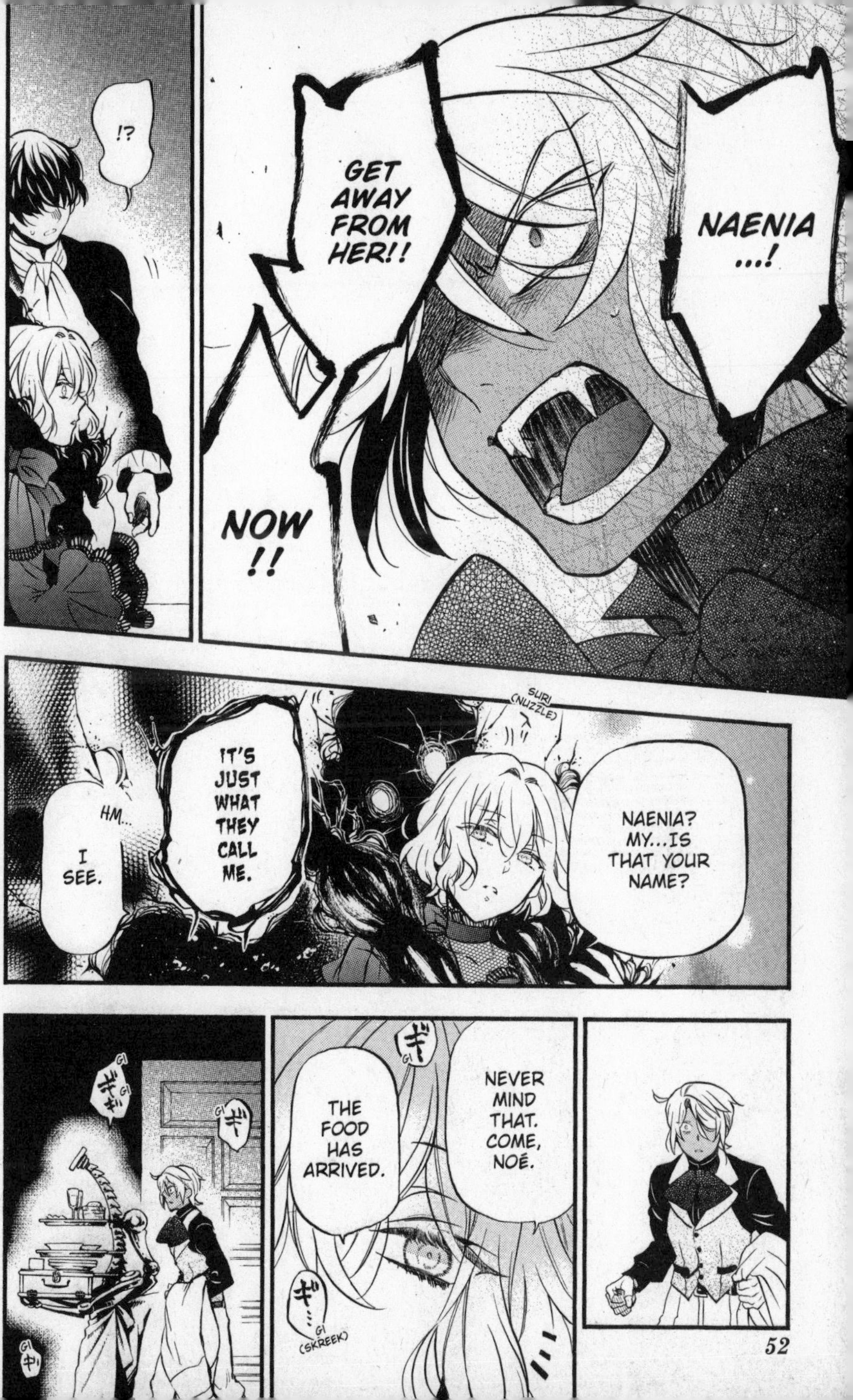
NAENIA ...!
GET AWAY FROM HER!!
NOW!!
!?
SURI (NUZZLE)
NAENIA? MY...IS THAT YOUR NAME?
IT'S JUST WHAT THEY CALL ME.
HM... I SEE.
NEVER MIND THAT. COME, NOÉ.
ギ GI
THE FOOD HAS ARRIVED.
ギ... GI (SKREEK)
ギ GI ギ GI
ギ GI
ギャ GI

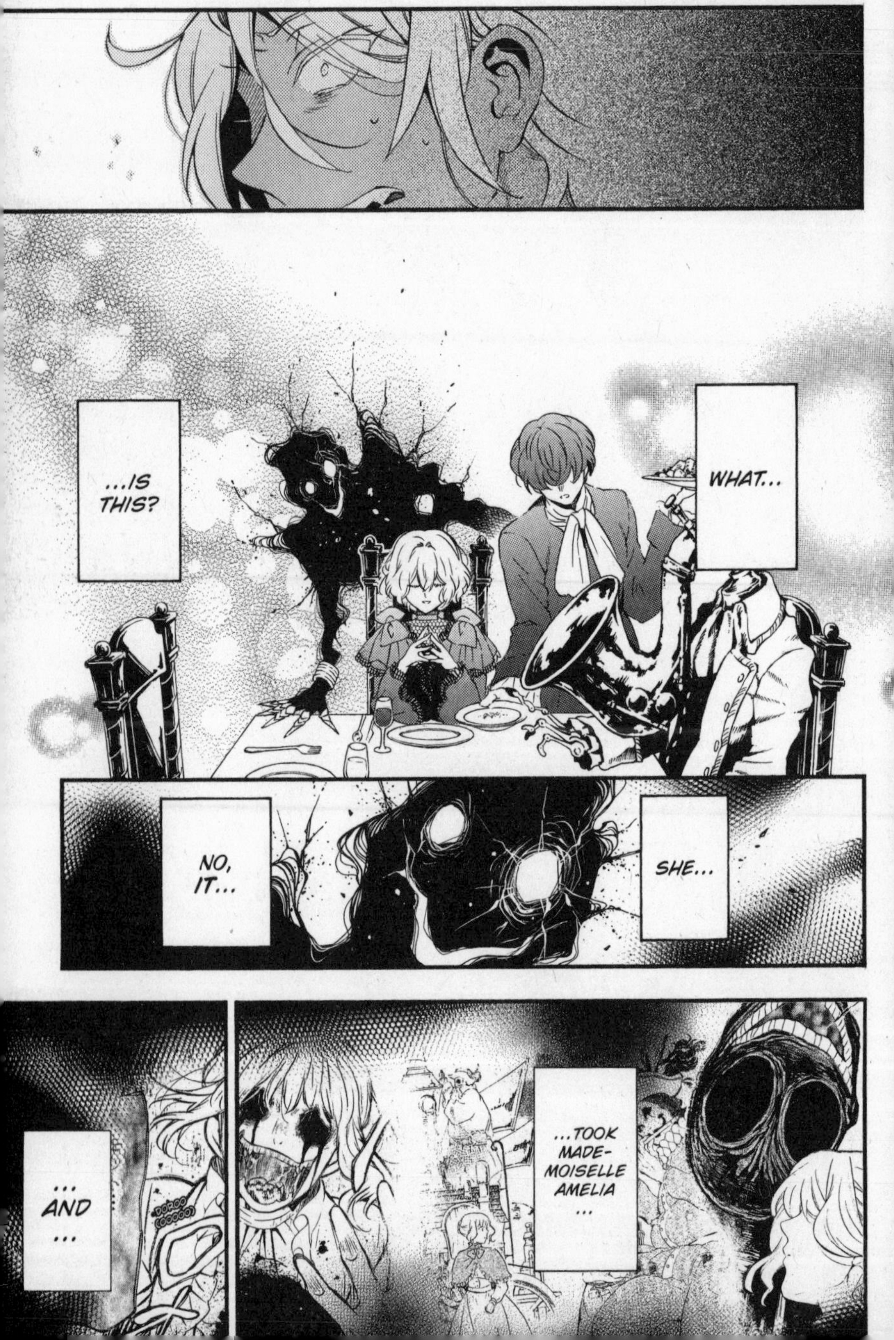
WHAT...
...IS THIS?
SHE...
NO, IT...
...TOOK MADE-MOISELLE AMELIA...
...AND...

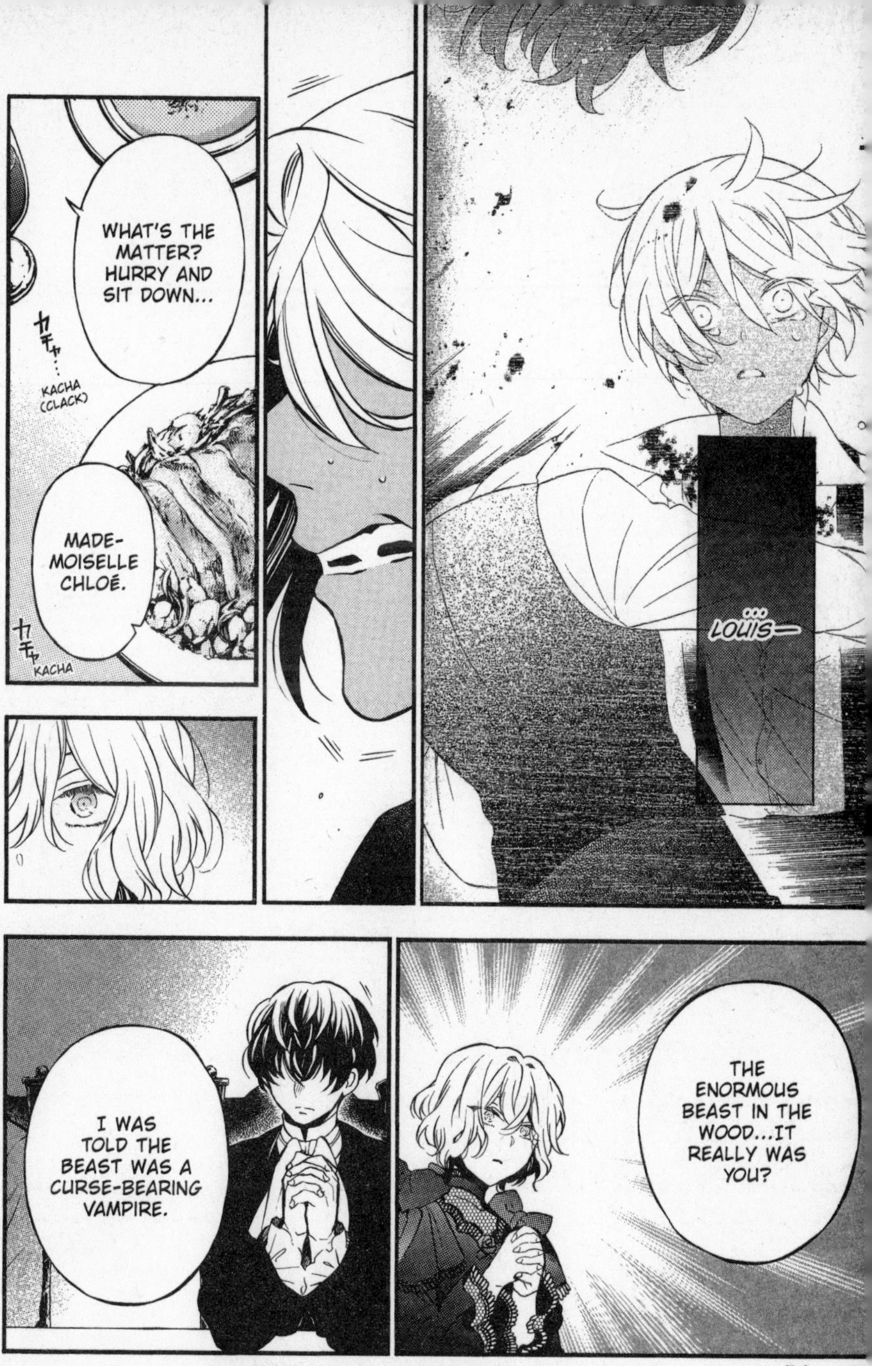
...LOUIS—
WHAT'S THE MATTER? HURRY AND SIT DOWN...
カチャ…
KACHA (CLACK)
MADE-MOISELLE CHLOÉ.
カチャ
KACHA
THE ENORMOUS BEAST IN THE WOOD...IT REALLY WAS YOU?
I WAS TOLD THE BEAST WAS A CURSE-BEARING VAMPIRE.

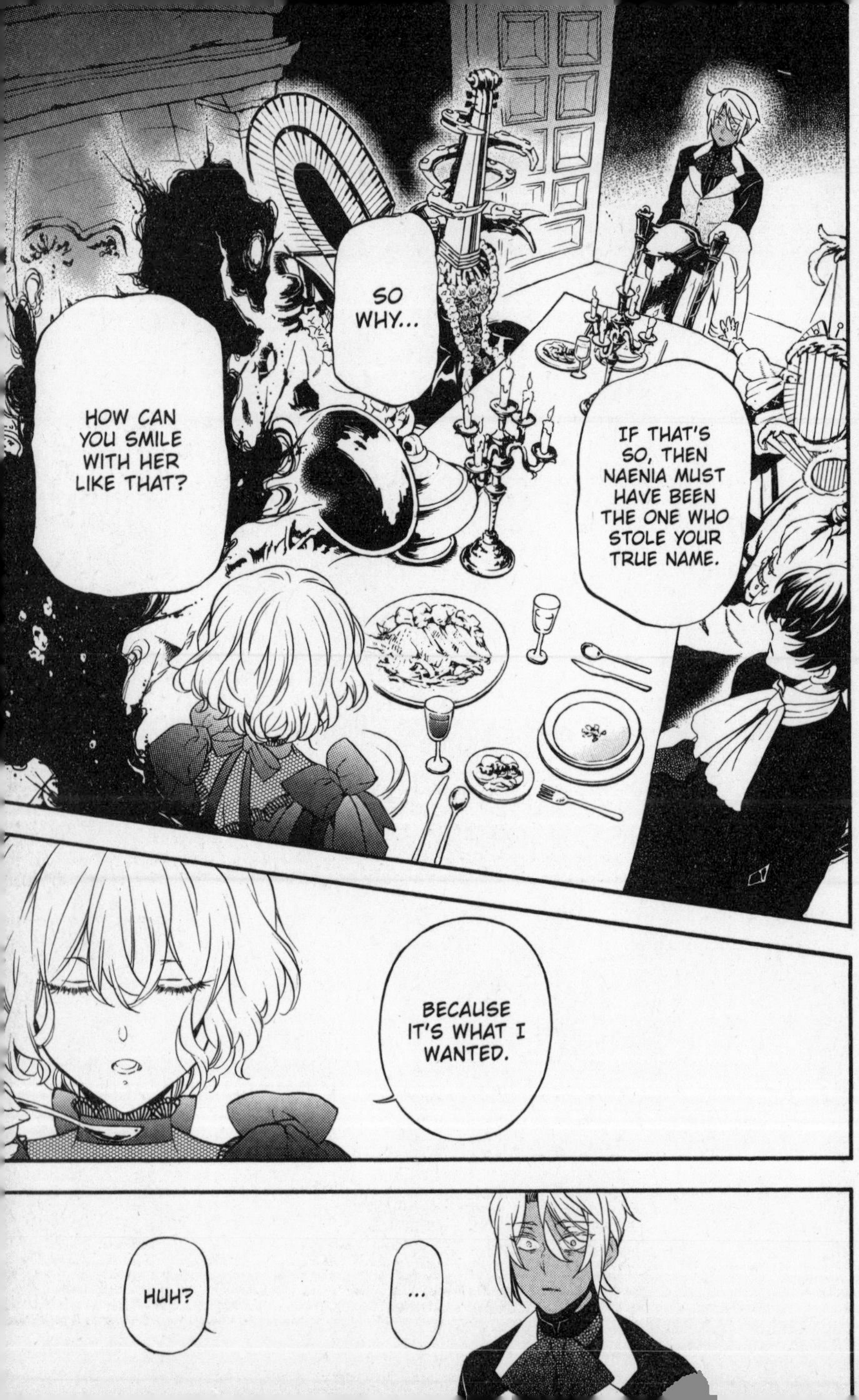
IF THAT'S SO, THEN NAENIA MUST HAVE BEEN THE ONE WHO STOLE YOUR TRUE NAME.
SO WHY...
HOW CAN YOU SMILE WITH HER LIKE THAT?
BECAUSE IT'S WHAT I WANTED.
...
HUH?

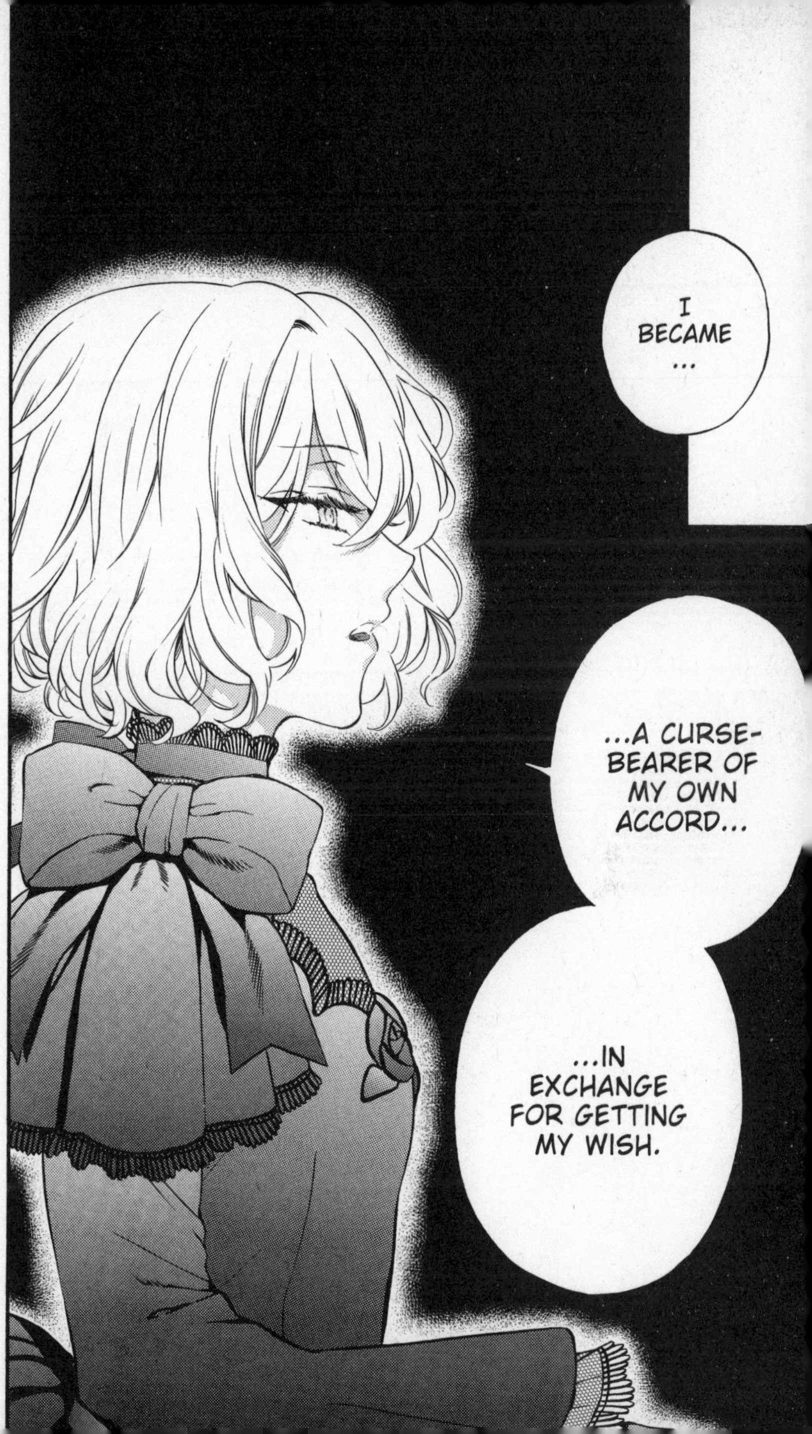
I BECAME ...
...A CURSE-BEARER OF MY OWN ACCORD...
...IN EXCHANGE FOR GETTING MY WISH.

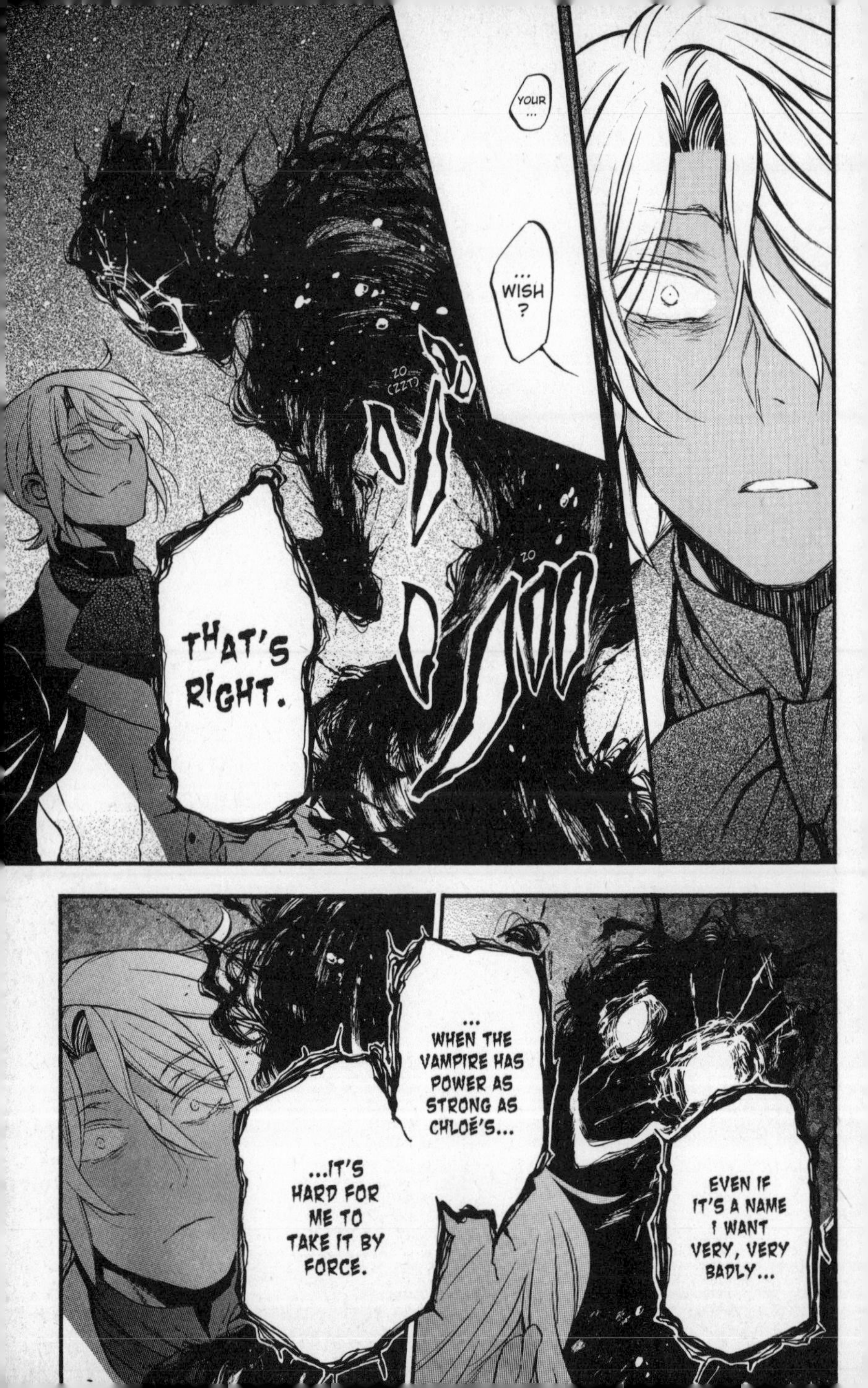

YOUR...
...WISH?
ZO (ZZZT)
ZO
THAT'S RIGHT.
EVEN IF IT'S A NAME I WANT VERY, VERY BADLY...
...WHEN THE VAMPIRE HAS POWER AS STRONG AS CHLOÉ'S...
...IT'S HARD FOR ME TO TAKE IT BY FORCE.

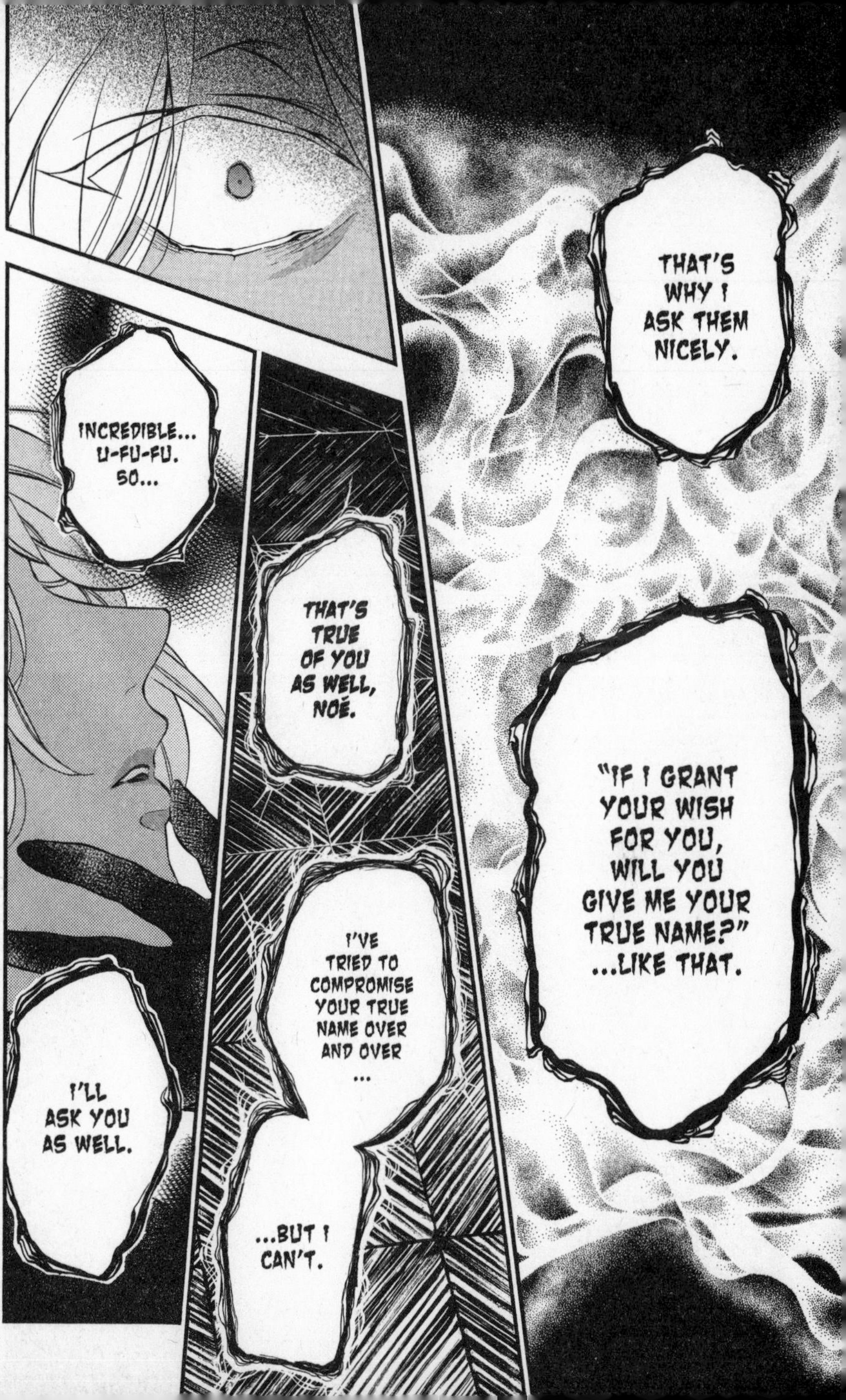
THAT'S WHY I ASK THEM NICELY.
"IF I GRANT YOUR WISH FOR YOU, WILL YOU GIVE ME YOUR TRUE NAME?" ...LIKE THAT.
THAT'S TRUE OF YOU AS WELL, NOÉ.
I'VE TRIED TO COMPROMISE YOUR TRUE NAME OVER AND OVER ...
...BUT I CAN'T.
INCREDIBLE... U-FU-FU. SO...
I'LL ASK YOU AS WELL.

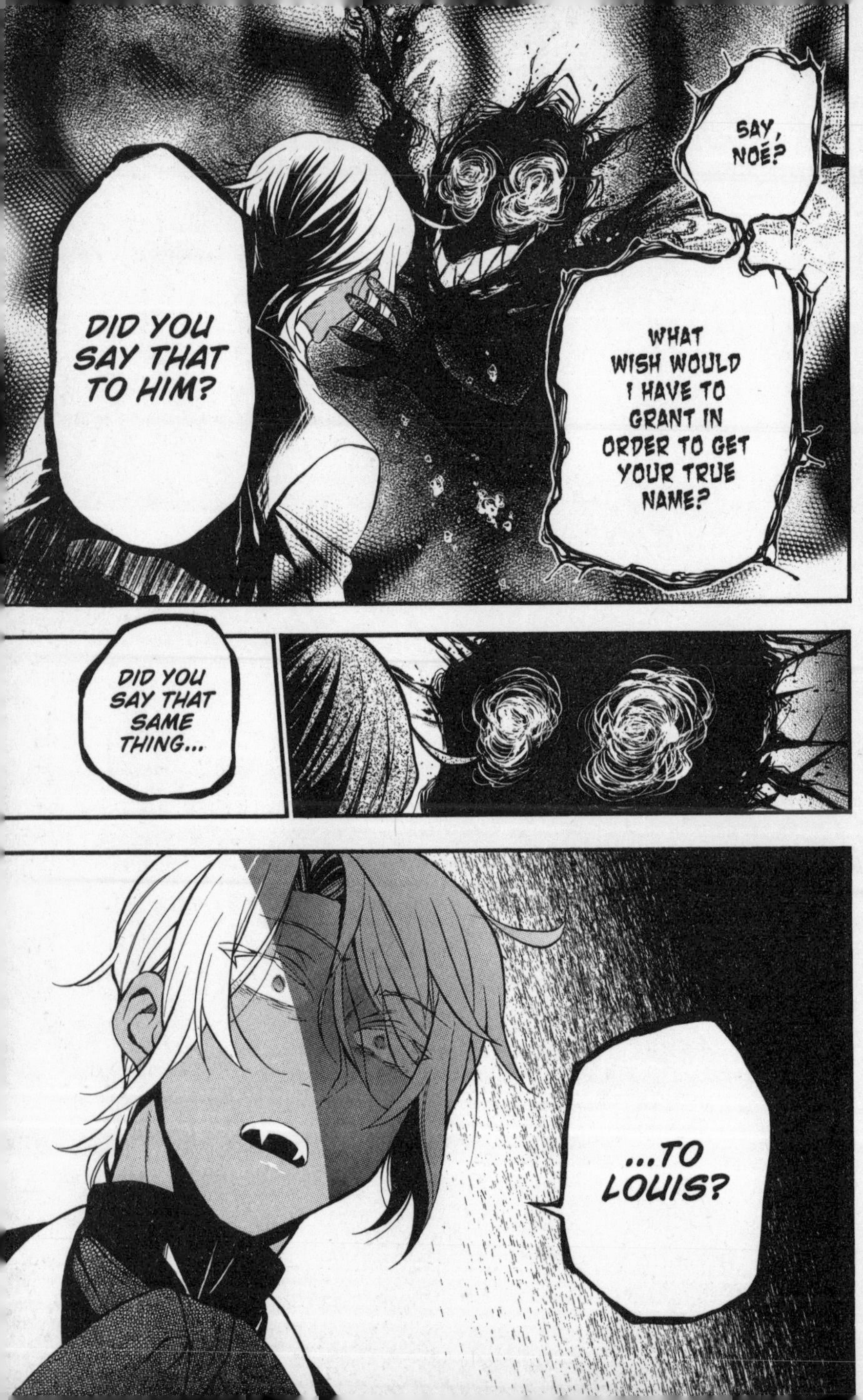
SAY, NOÉ?
WHAT WISH WOULD I HAVE TO GRANT IN ORDER TO GET YOUR TRUE NAME?
DID YOU SAY THAT TO HIM?
DID YOU SAY THAT SAME THING...
...TO LOUIS?

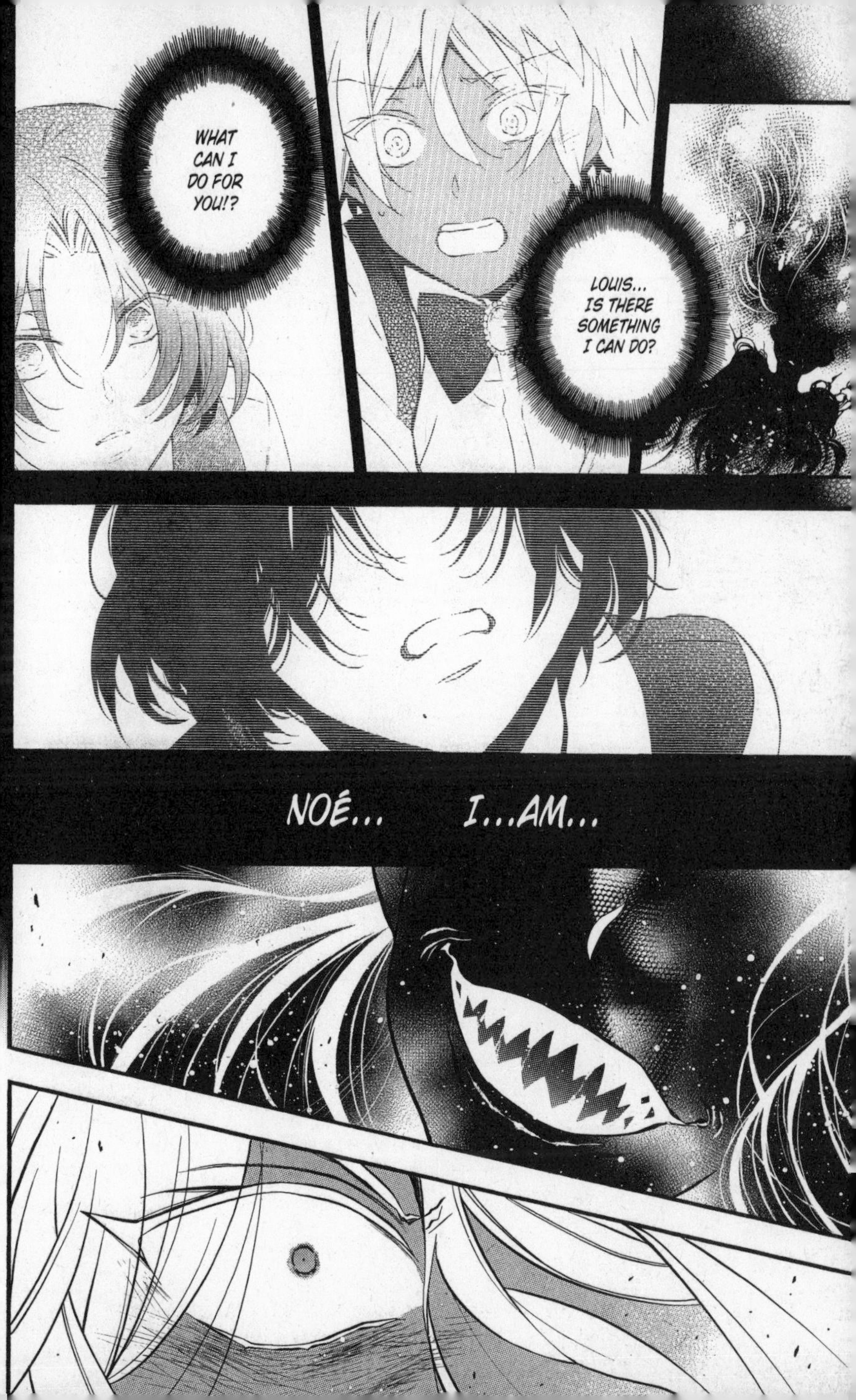
LOUIS... IS THERE SOMETHING I CAN DO?
WHAT CAN I DO FOR YOU!?
NOÉ... I...AM...

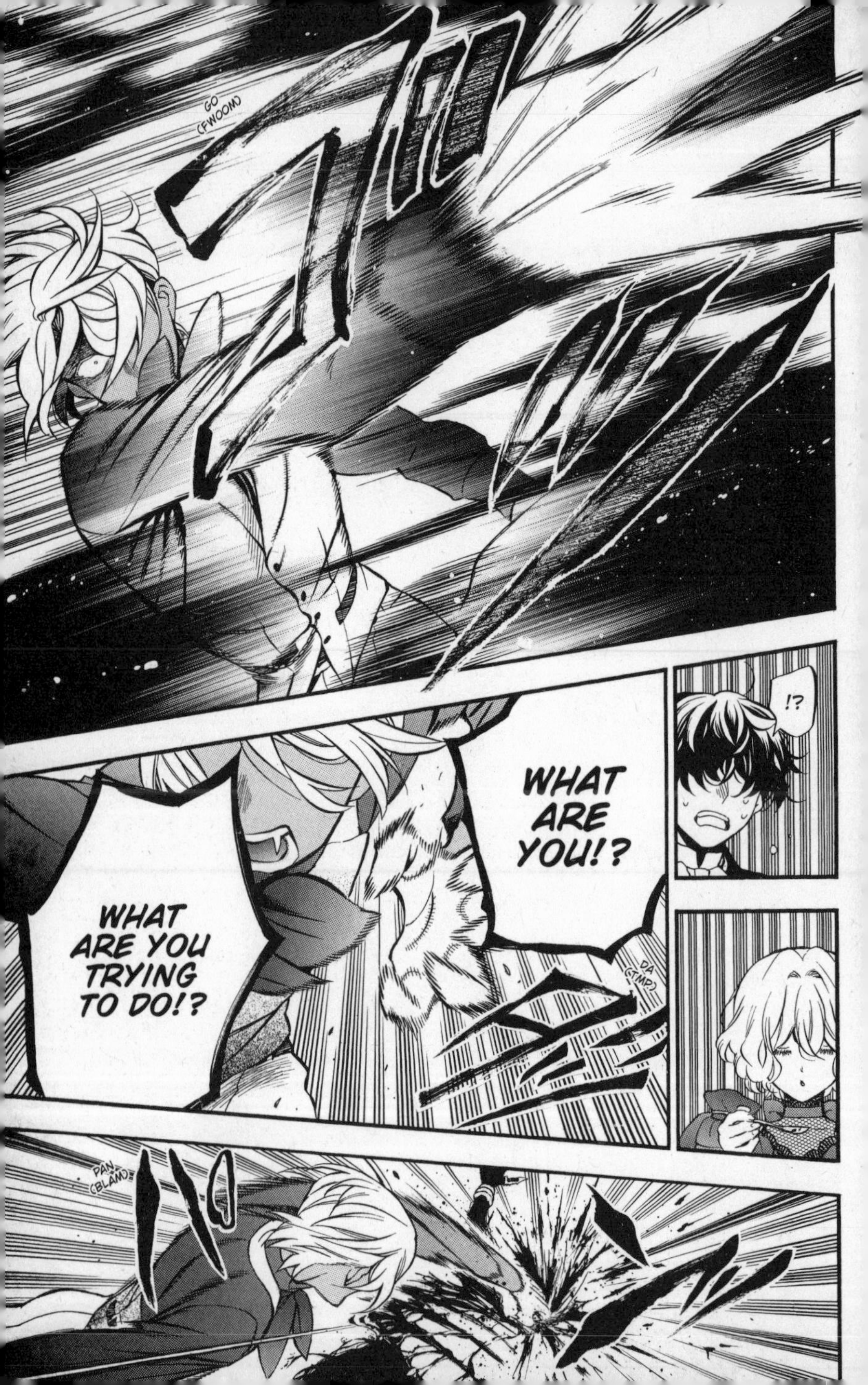
GO
(FWOOM)
!?
WHAT ARE YOU!?
DA
(TMP)
WHAT ARE YOU TRYING TO DO!?
PAN
(BLAM)

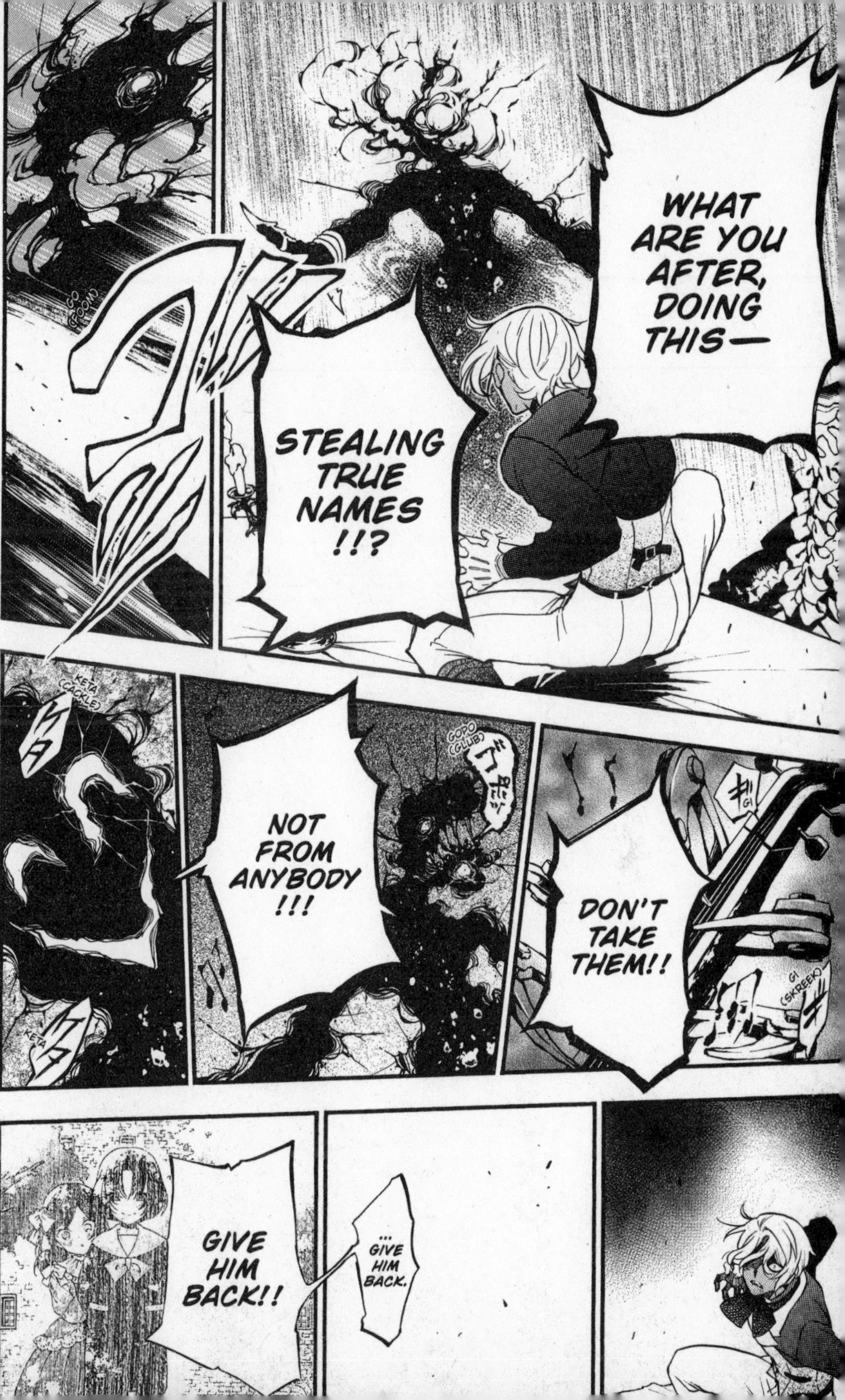
WHAT ARE YOU AFTER, DOING THIS—
STEALING TRUE NAMES!!?
GO (FOOM)
DON'T TAKE THEM!!
GI
GI (SKREEK)
NOT FROM ANYBODY!!!
GOPO (GLUB)
KETA (CACKLE)
KETA
... GIVE HIM BACK.
GIVE HIM BACK!!

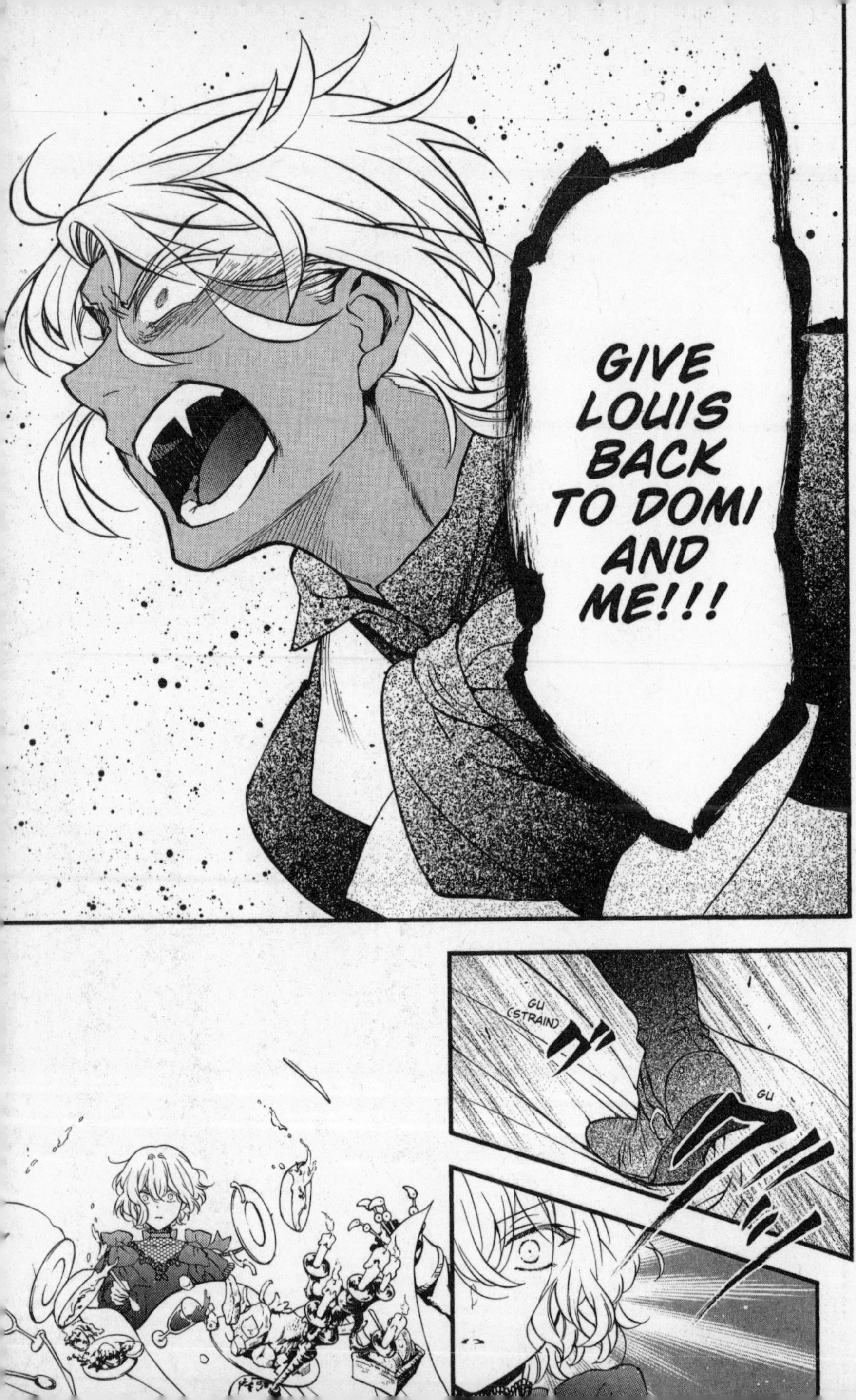
GIVE LOUIS BACK TO DOMI AND ME!!!
GU (STRAIN)
GU

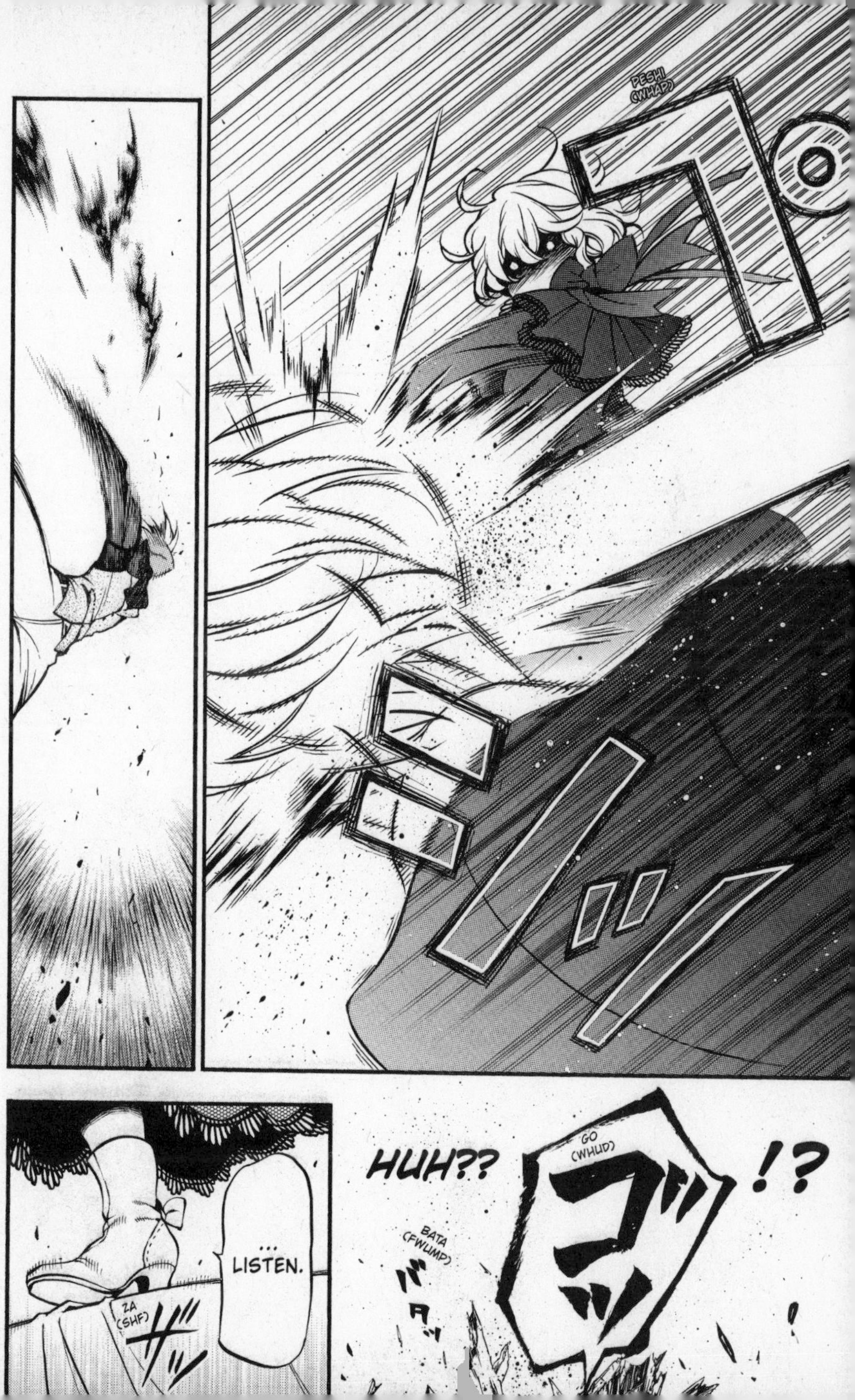
PESHI (WHAP)
!?
GO (WHUD)
HUH??
BATA (FWUMP)
... LISTEN.
ZA (SHF)

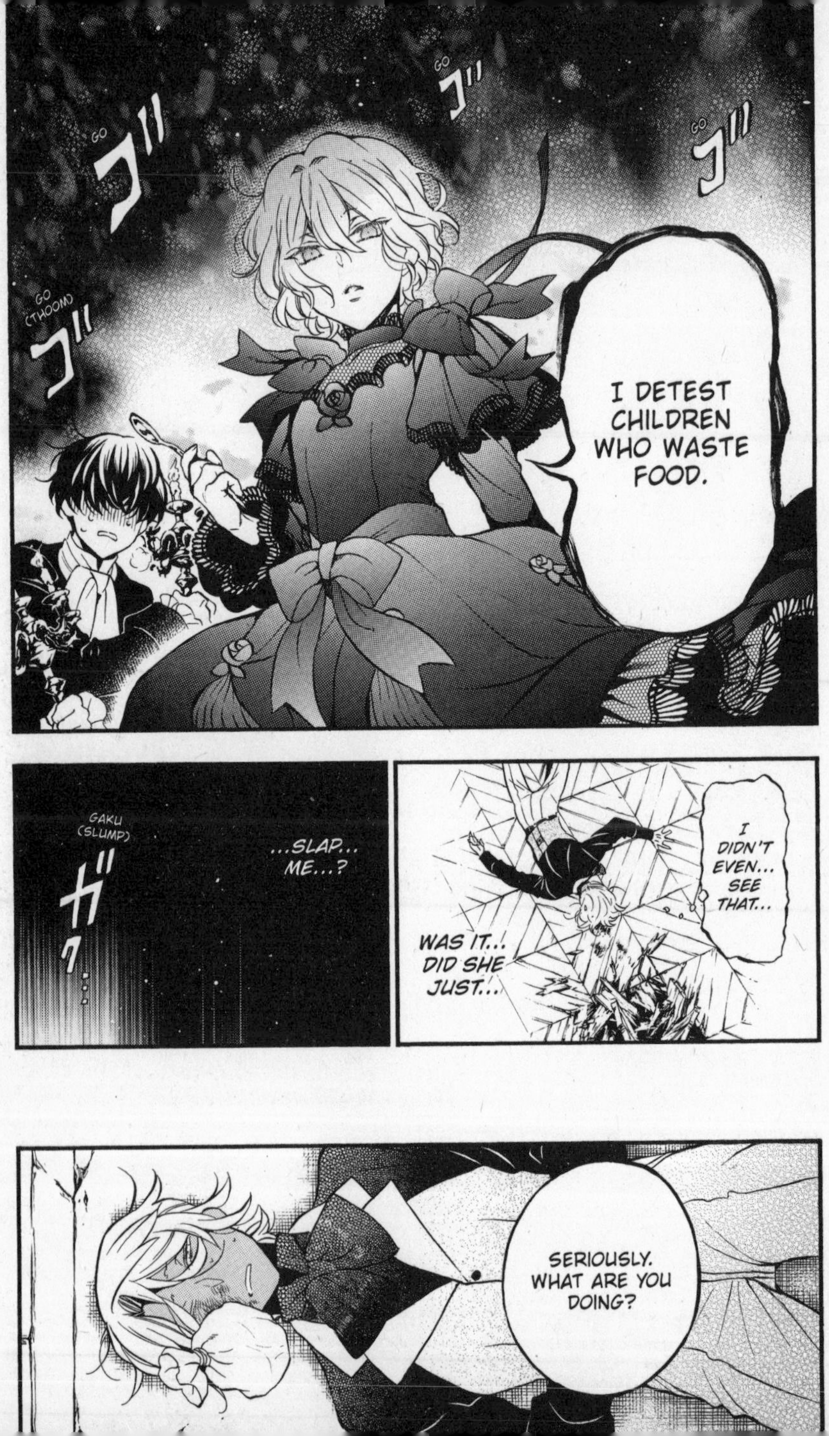
GO
GO
GO
GO (THOOM)
I DETEST CHILDREN WHO WASTE FOOD.
I DIDN'T EVEN... SEE THAT...
WAS IT... DID SHE JUST...
...SLAP... ME...?
GAKU (SLUMP)
SERIOUSLY. WHAT ARE YOU DOING?

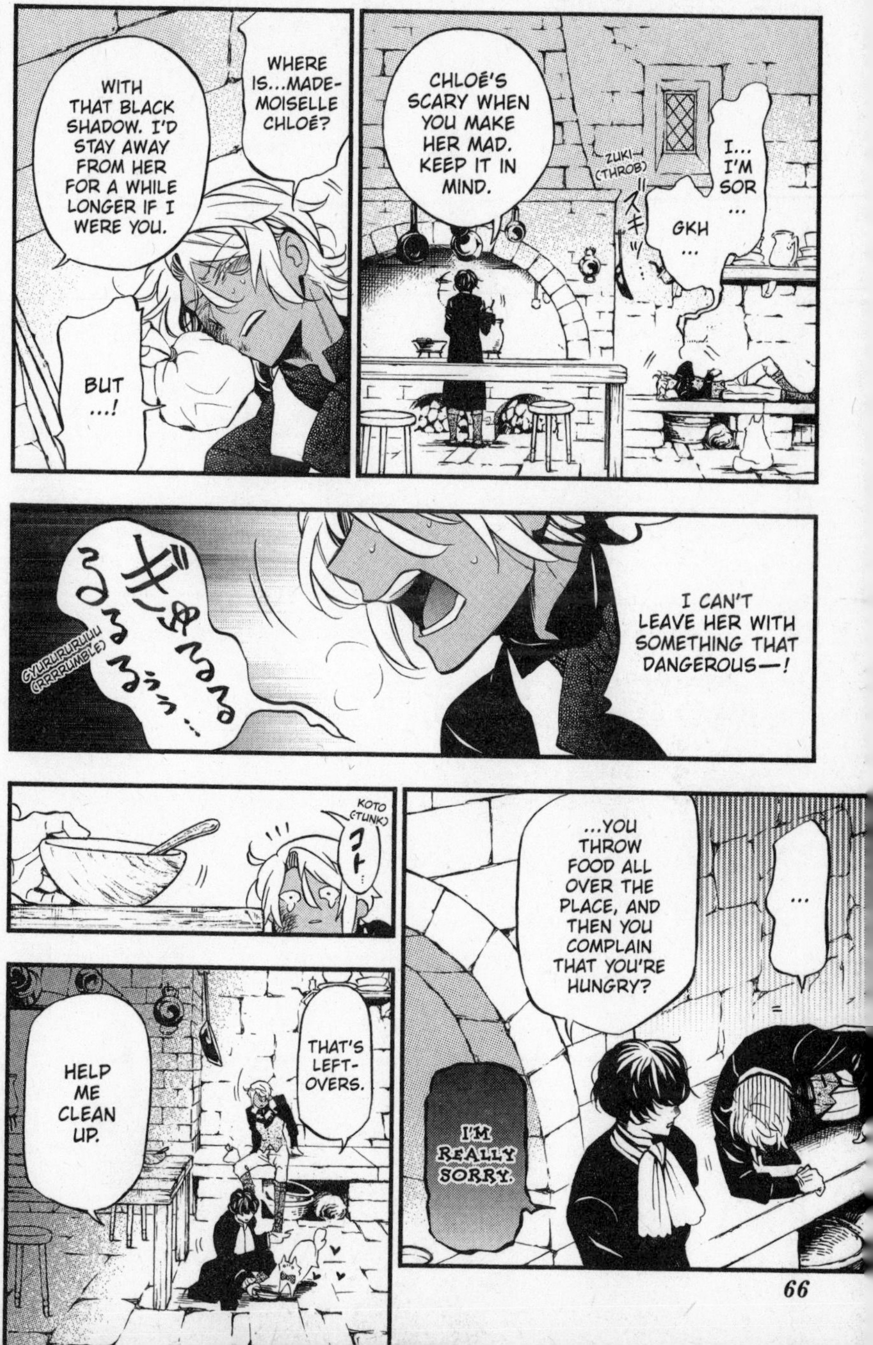
I... I'M SOR...
ZUKI (THROB)
ズキッ
GKH...
CHLOÉ'S SCARY WHEN YOU MAKE HER MAD. KEEP IT IN MIND.
WHERE IS...MADEMOISELLE CHLOÉ?
WITH THAT BLACK SHADOW. I'D STAY AWAY FROM HER FOR A WHILE LONGER IF I WERE YOU.
BUT...!
I CAN'T LEAVE HER WITH SOMETHING THAT DANGEROUS—!
ぎゅるるるるるぅぅ...
GYURURURUUU (RRRRUMBLE)
...
...YOU THROW FOOD ALL OVER THE PLACE, AND THEN YOU COMPLAIN THAT YOU'RE HUNGRY?
I'M REALLY SORRY.
KOTO (TUNK)
コト...
THAT'S LEFT-OVERS.
HELP ME CLEAN UP.

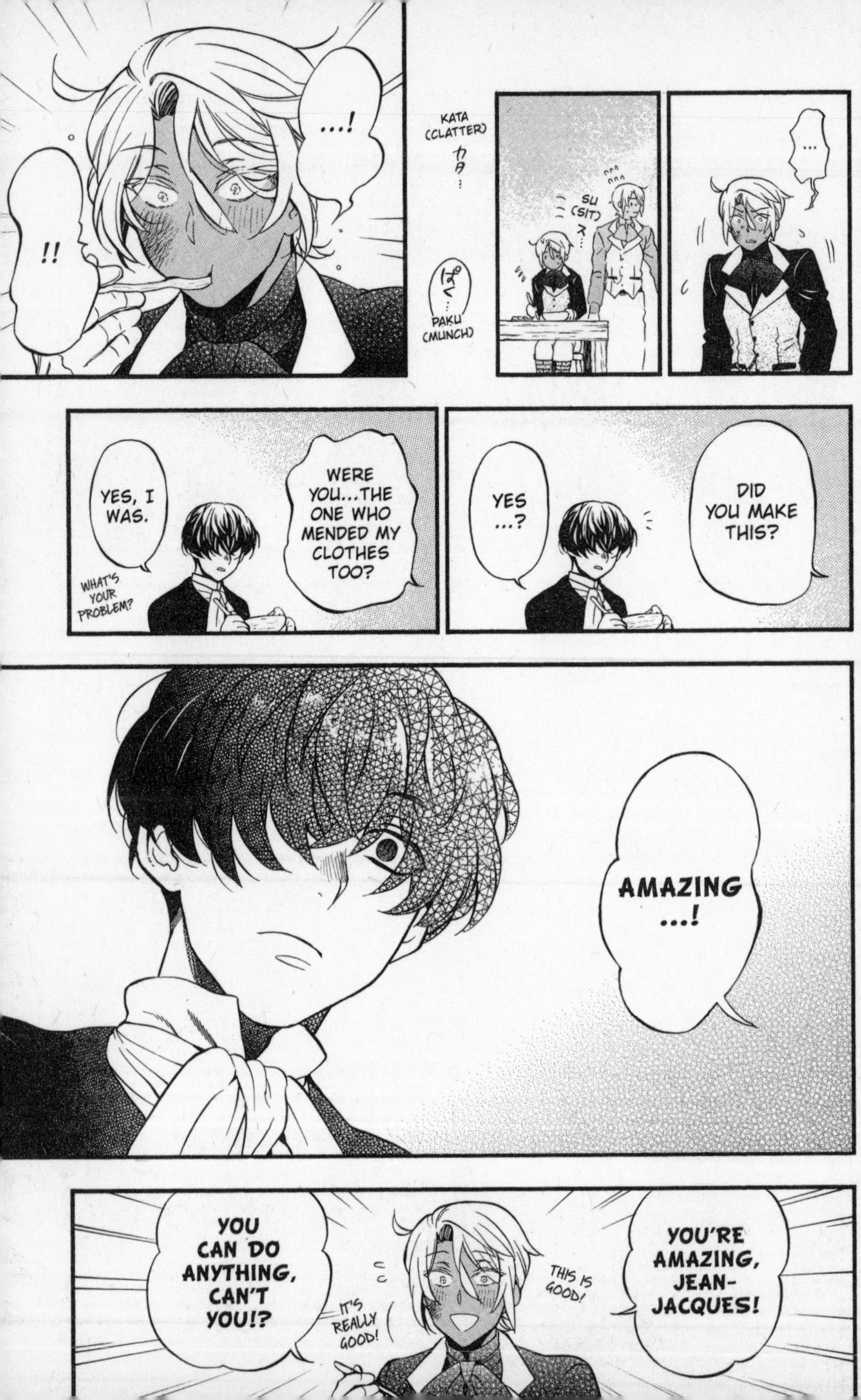
...
KATA (CLATTER)
カタ…
SU (SIT)
ス…
ぱく…
PAKU (MUNCH)
...!
!!
DID YOU MAKE THIS?
YES ...?
WERE YOU...THE ONE WHO MENDED MY CLOTHES TOO?
YES, I WAS.
WHAT'S YOUR PROBLEM?
AMAZING ...!
YOU'RE AMAZING, JEAN-JACQUES!
THIS IS GOOD!
IT'S REALLY GOOD!
YOU CAN DO ANYTHING, CAN'T YOU!?

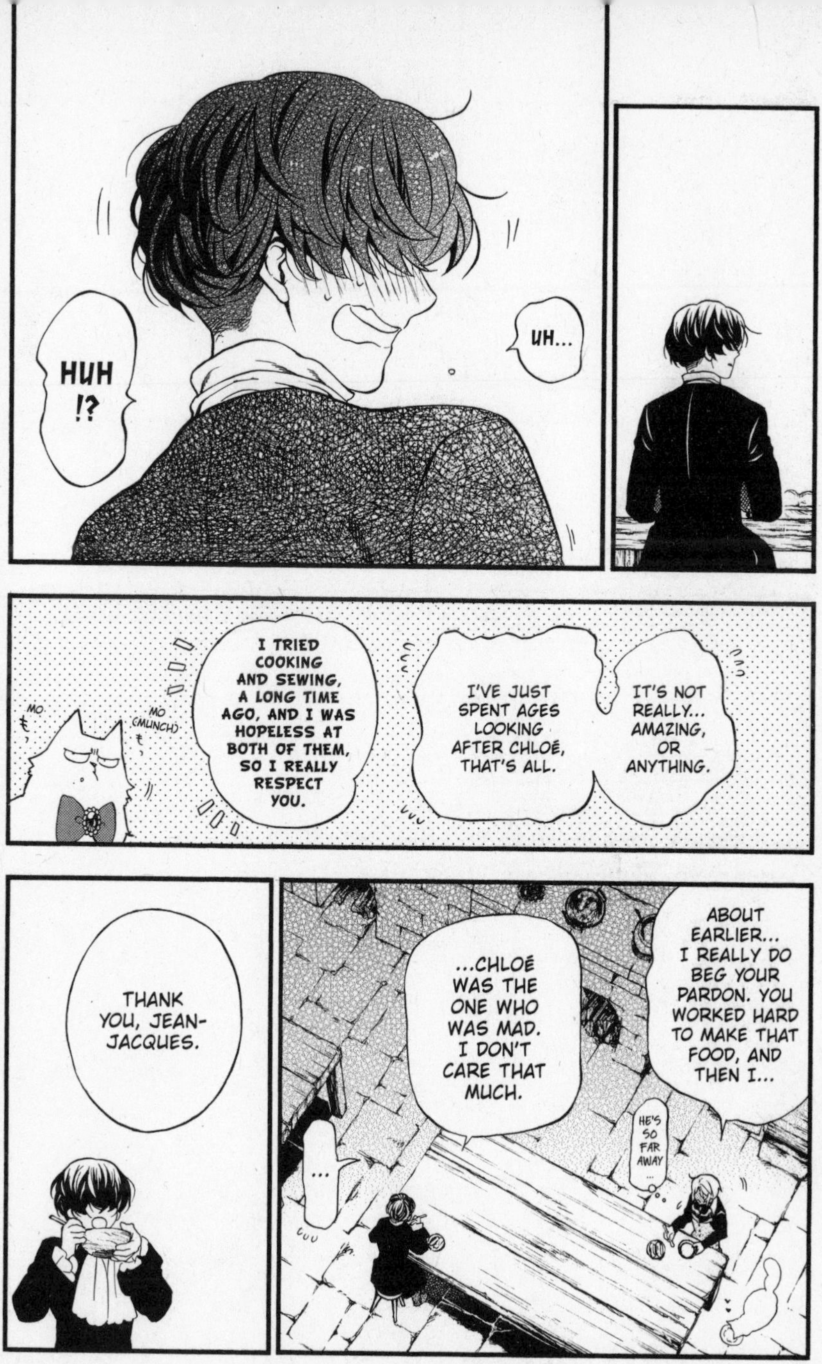
UH...
HUH!?
IT'S NOT REALLY... AMAZING, OR ANYTHING.
I'VE JUST SPENT AGES LOOKING AFTER CHLOÉ, THAT'S ALL.
I TRIED COOKING AND SEWING, A LONG TIME AGO, AND I WAS HOPELESS AT BOTH OF THEM, SO I REALLY RESPECT YOU.
MO (MUNCH) も
MO も
ABOUT EARLIER... I REALLY DO BEG YOUR PARDON. YOU WORKED HARD TO MAKE THAT FOOD, AND THEN I...
...CHLOÉ WAS THE ONE WHO WAS MAD. I DON'T CARE THAT MUCH.
HE'S SO FAR AWAY...
...
THANK YOU, JEAN-JACQUES.

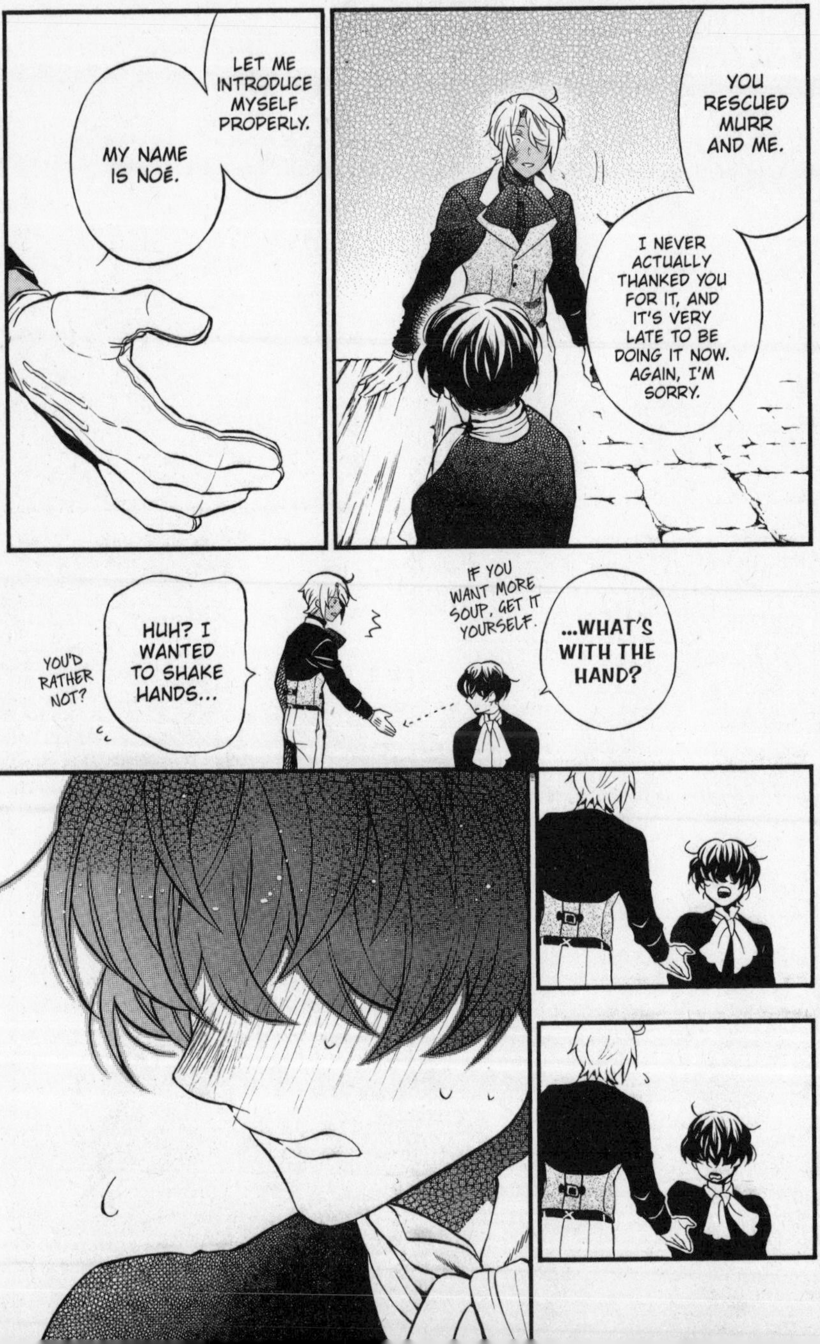
YOU RESCUED MURR AND ME.
I NEVER ACTUALLY THANKED YOU FOR IT, AND IT'S VERY LATE TO BE DOING IT NOW. AGAIN, I'M SORRY.
LET ME INTRODUCE MYSELF PROPERLY.
MY NAME IS NOÉ.
...WHAT'S WITH THE HAND?
IF YOU WANT MORE SOUP, GET IT YOURSELF.
HUH? I WANTED TO SHAKE HANDS...
YOU'D RATHER NOT?

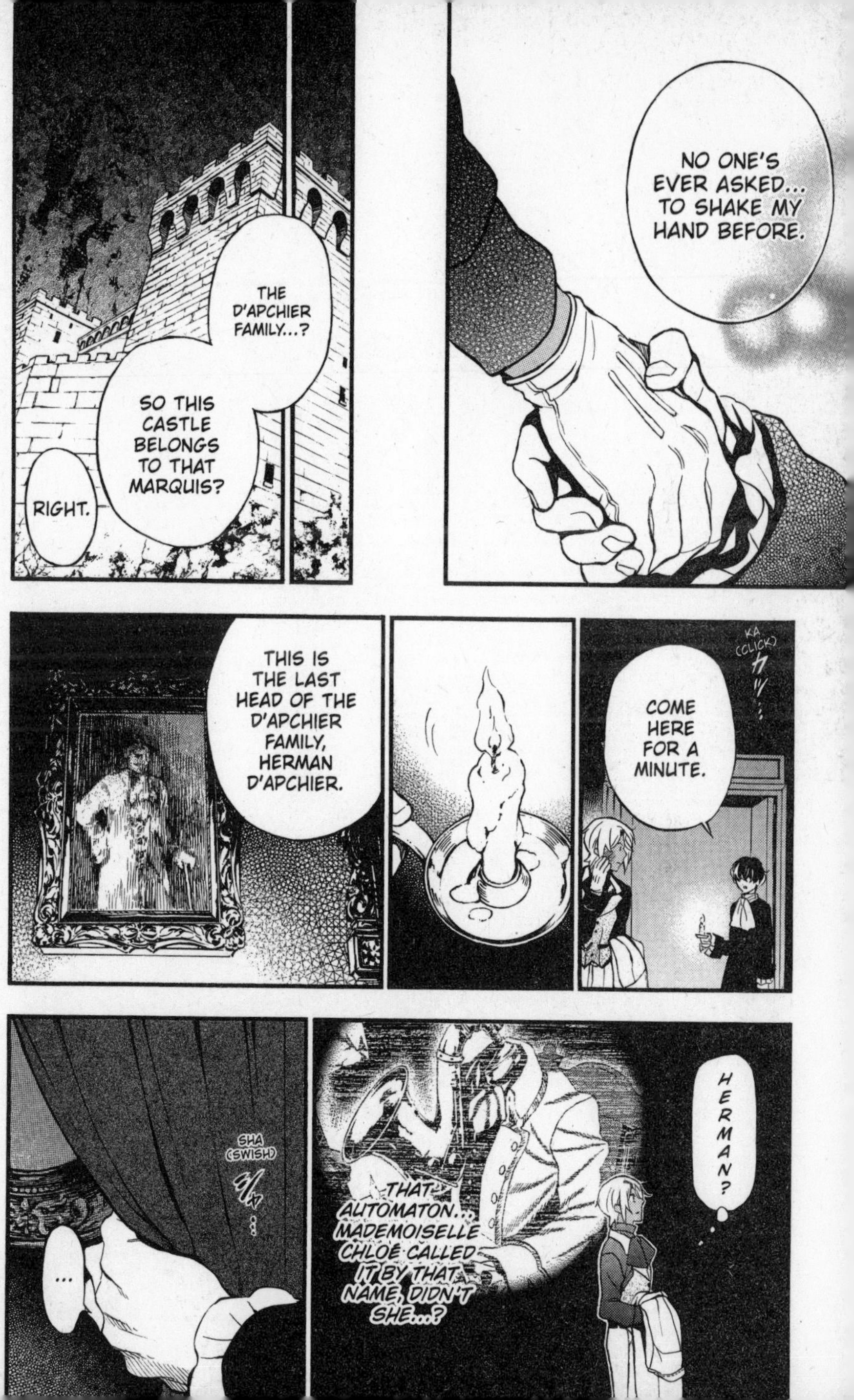
NO ONE'S EVER ASKED... TO SHAKE MY HAND BEFORE.
THE D'APCHIER FAMILY...?
SO THIS CASTLE BELONGS TO THAT MARQUIS?
RIGHT.
KA (CLICK)
COME HERE FOR A MINUTE.
THIS IS THE LAST HEAD OF THE D'APCHIER FAMILY, HERMAN D'APCHIER.
HERMAN?
THAT AUTOMATON... MADEMOISELLE CHLOE CALLED IT BY THAT NAME, DIDN'T SHE...?
SHA (SWISH)
...

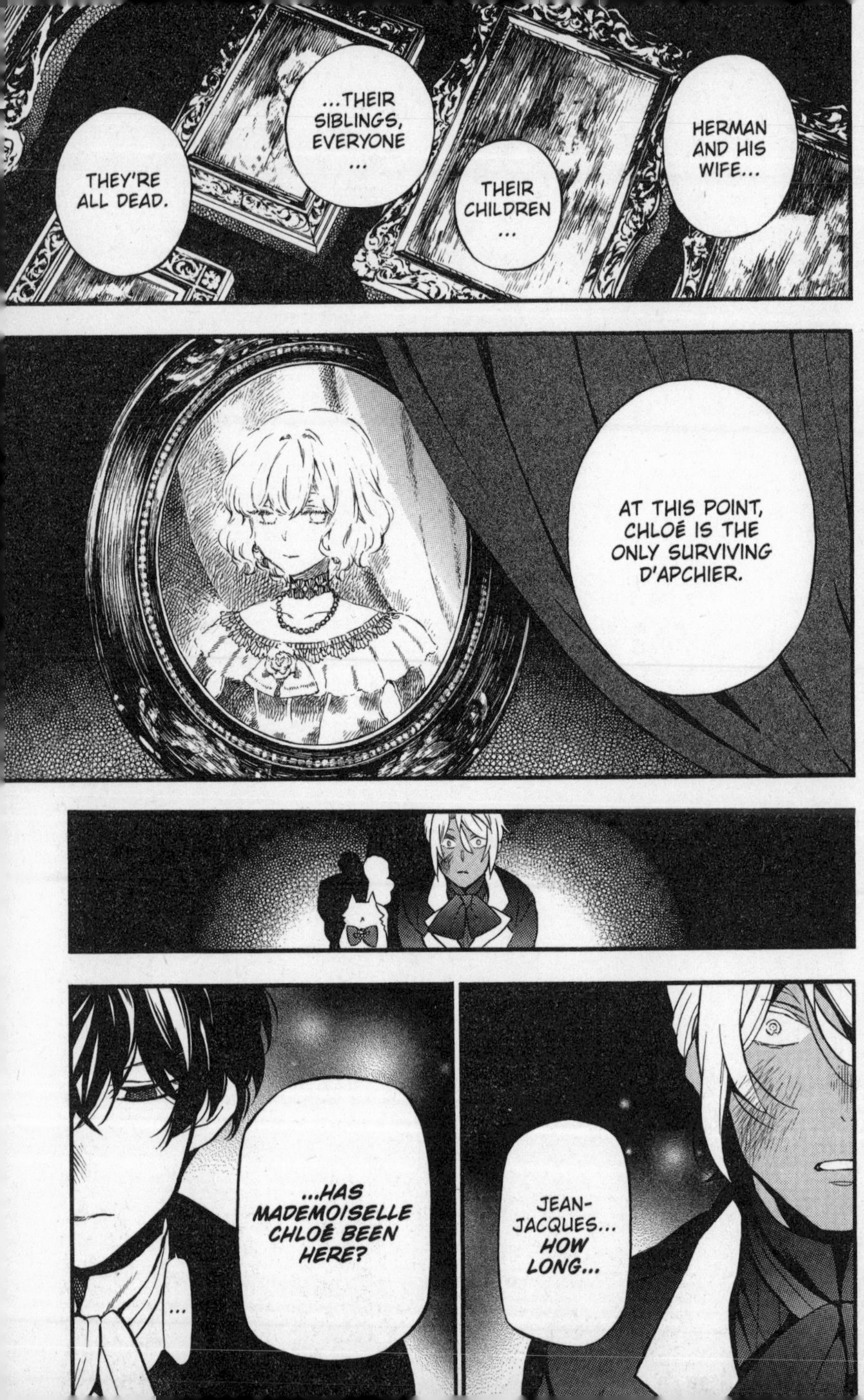
HERMAN AND HIS WIFE...
THEIR CHILDREN ...
...THEIR SIBLINGS, EVERYONE ...
THEY'RE ALL DEAD.
AT THIS POINT, CHLOÉ IS THE ONLY SURVIVING D'APCHIER.
JEAN-JACQUES... HOW LONG...
...HAS MADEMOISELLE CHLOÉ BEEN HERE?
...

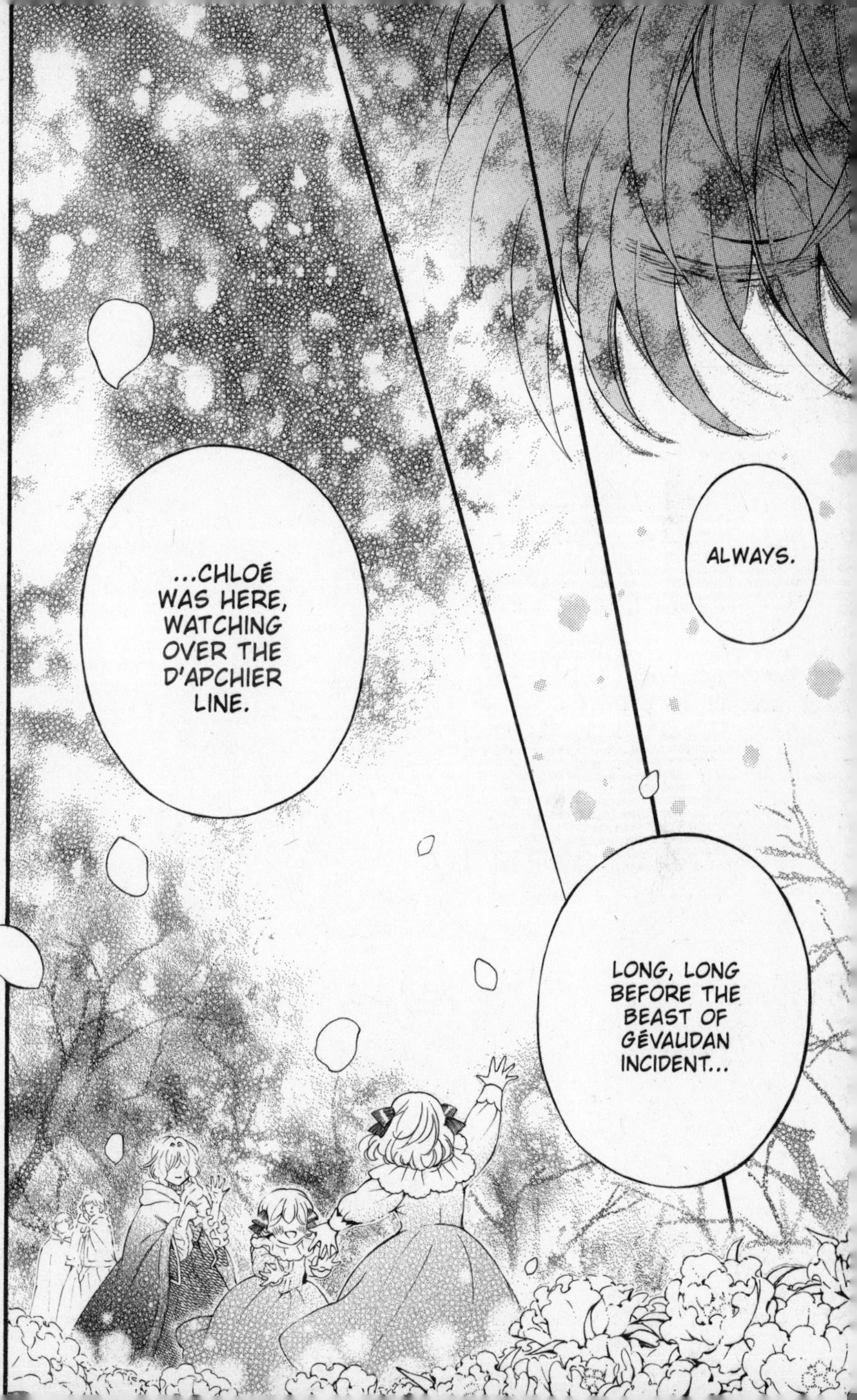
...CHLOÉ WAS HERE, WATCHING OVER THE D'APCHIER LINE.
ALWAYS.
LONG, LONG BEFORE THE BEAST OF GÉVAUDAN INCIDENT...

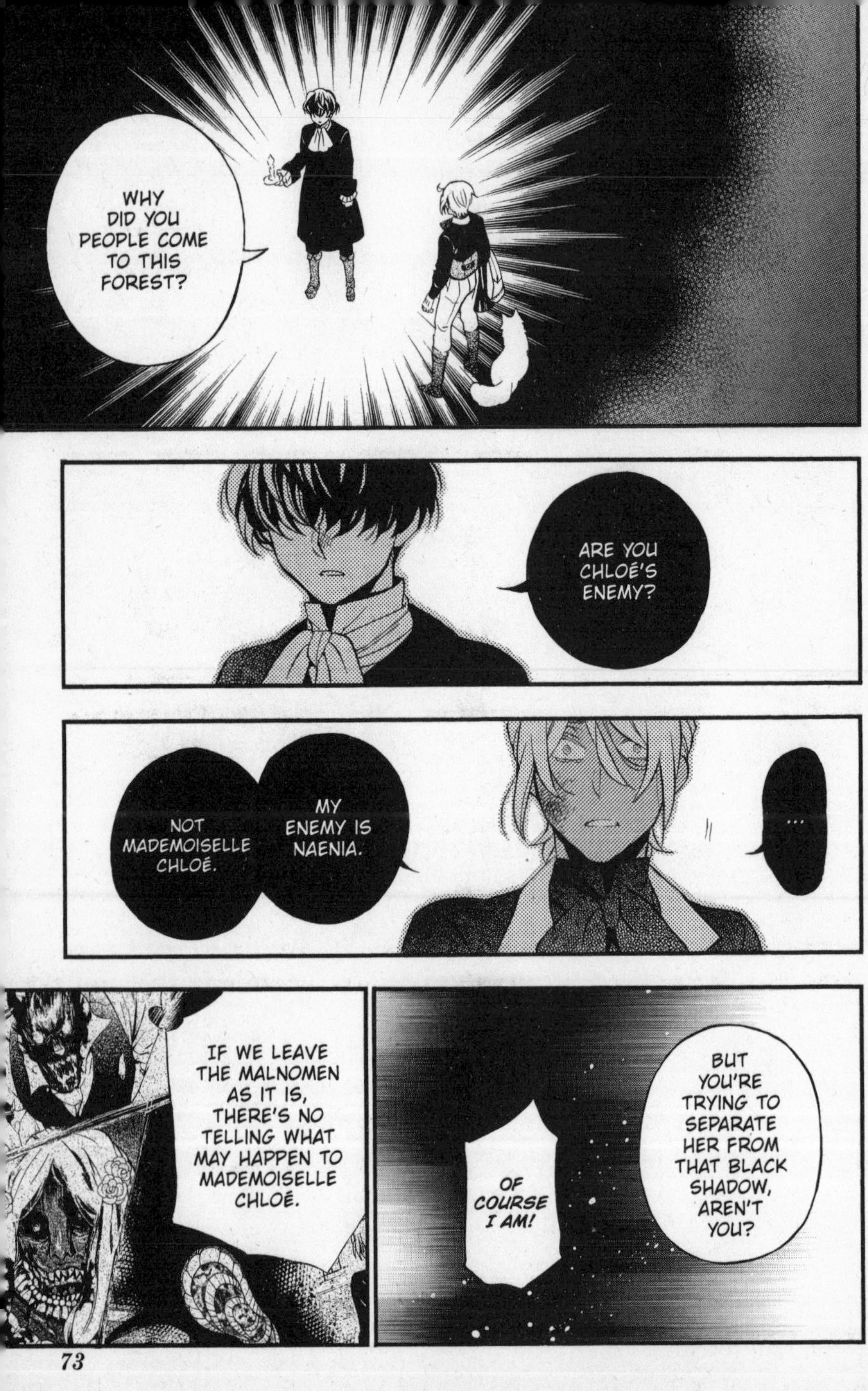
WHY DID YOU PEOPLE COME TO THIS FOREST?
ARE YOU CHLOÉ'S ENEMY?
...
MY ENEMY IS NAENIA.
NOT MADEMOISELLE CHLOÉ.
BUT YOU'RE TRYING TO SEPARATE HER FROM THAT BLACK SHADOW, AREN'T YOU?
OF COURSE I AM!
IF WE LEAVE THE MALNOMEN AS IT IS, THERE'S NO TELLING WHAT MAY HAPPEN TO MADEMOISELLE CHLOÉ.

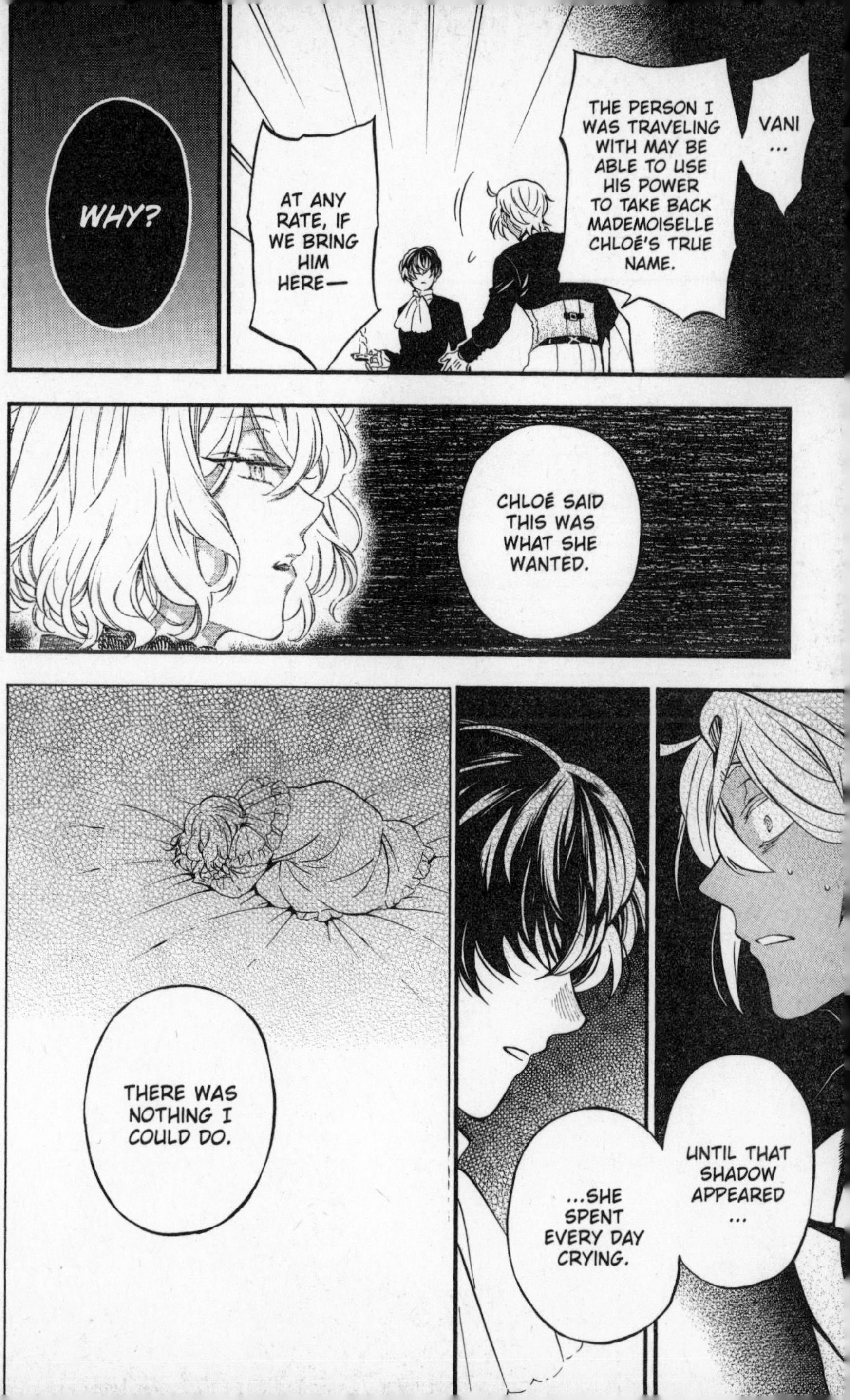
VANI...
THE PERSON I WAS TRAVELING WITH MAY BE ABLE TO USE HIS POWER TO TAKE BACK MADEMOISELLE CHLOÉ'S TRUE NAME.
AT ANY RATE, IF WE BRING HIM HERE—
WHY?
CHLOÉ SAID THIS WAS WHAT SHE WANTED.
UNTIL THAT SHADOW APPEARED...
...SHE SPENT EVERY DAY CRYING.
THERE WAS NOTHING I COULD DO.

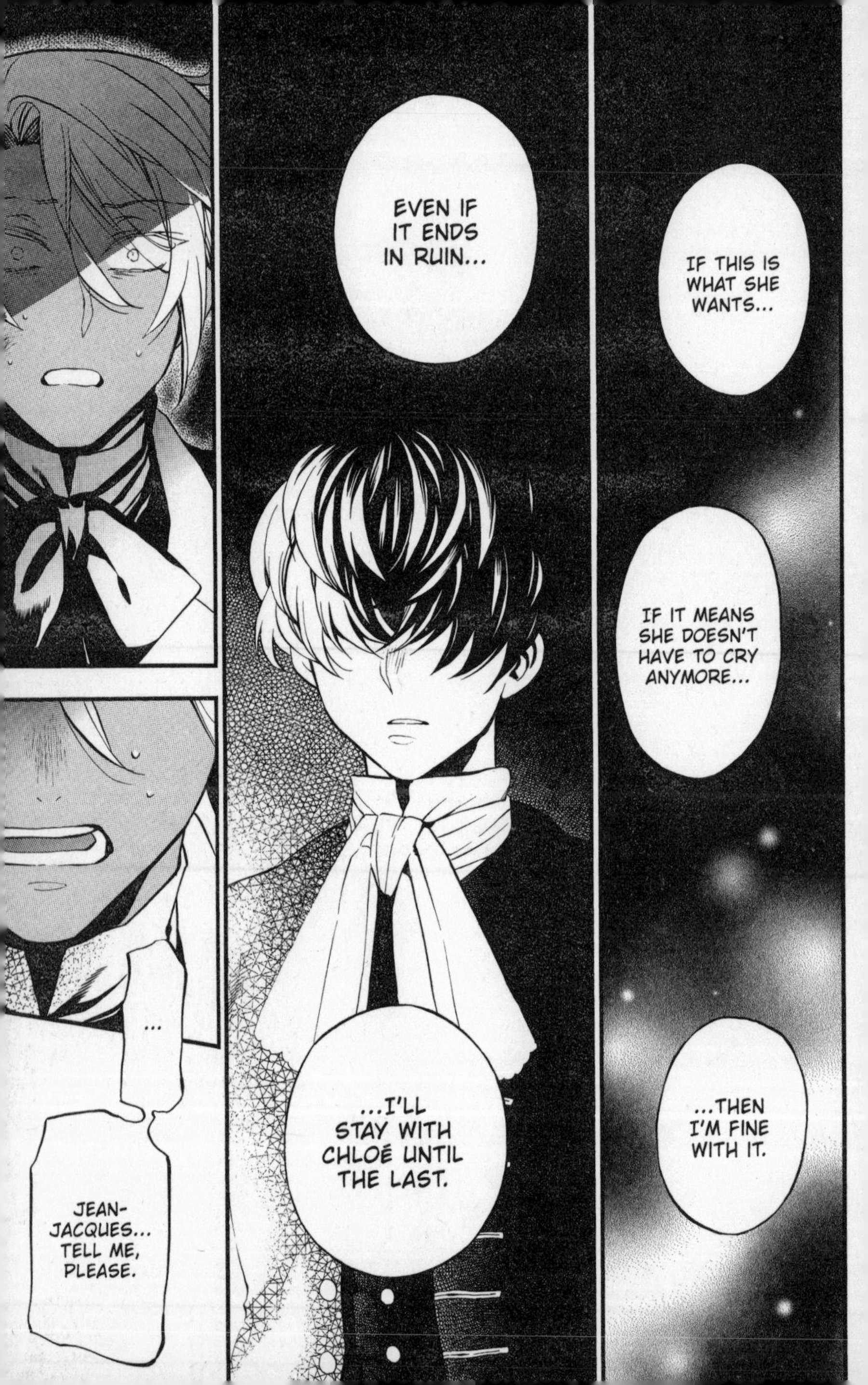
IF THIS IS WHAT SHE WANTS...
IF IT MEANS SHE DOESN'T HAVE TO CRY ANYMORE...
...THEN I'M FINE WITH IT.
EVEN IF IT ENDS IN RUIN...
...I'LL STAY WITH CHLOÉ UNTIL THE LAST.
...
JEAN-JACQUES... TELL ME, PLEASE.

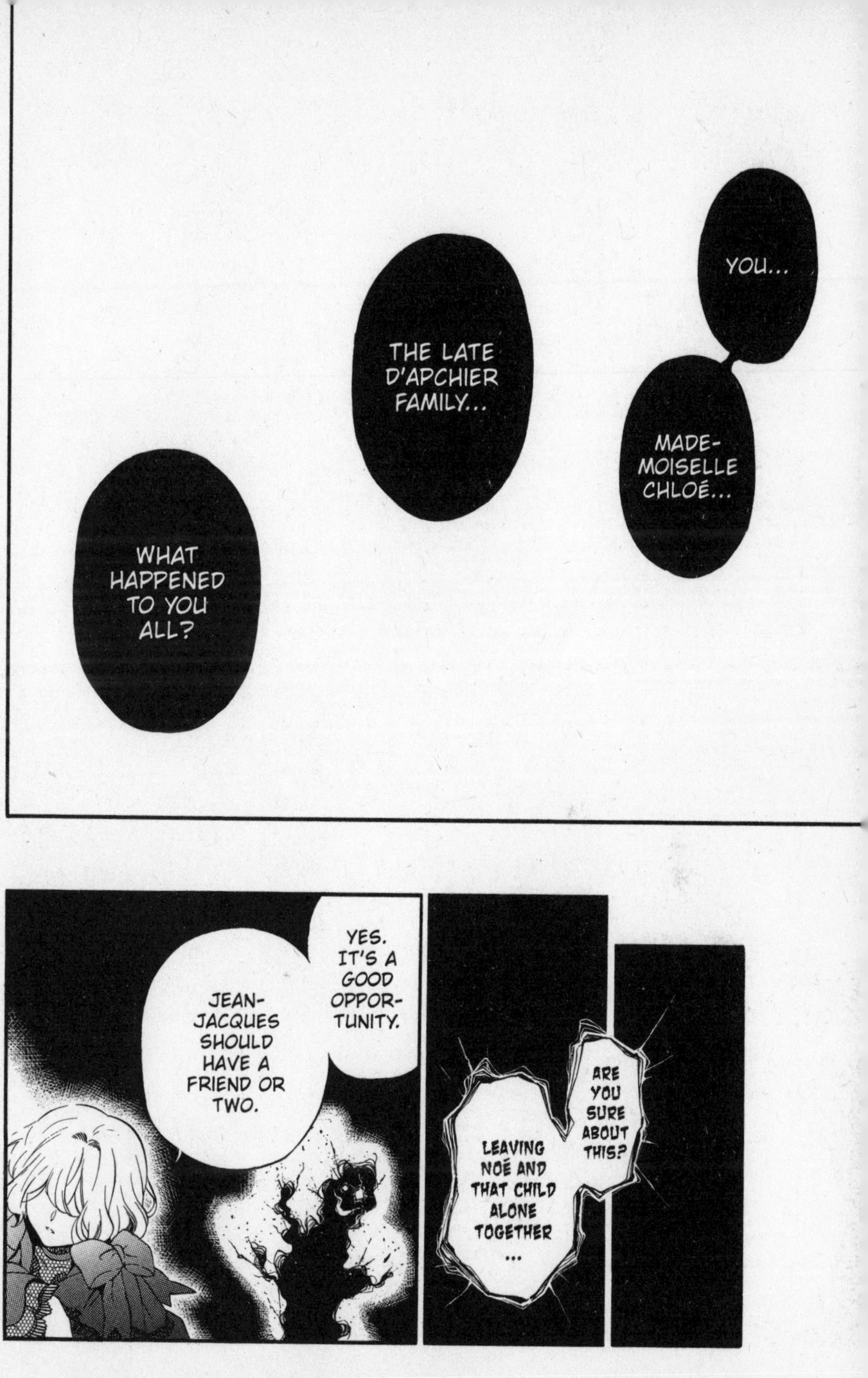
YOU...
MADE-MOISELLE CHLOÉ...
THE LATE D'APCHIER FAMILY...
WHAT HAPPENED TO YOU ALL?
ARE YOU SURE ABOUT THIS?
LEAVING NOÉ AND THAT CHILD ALONE TOGETHER...
YES. IT'S A GOOD OPPORTUNITY.
JEAN-JACQUES SHOULD HAVE A FRIEND OR TWO.

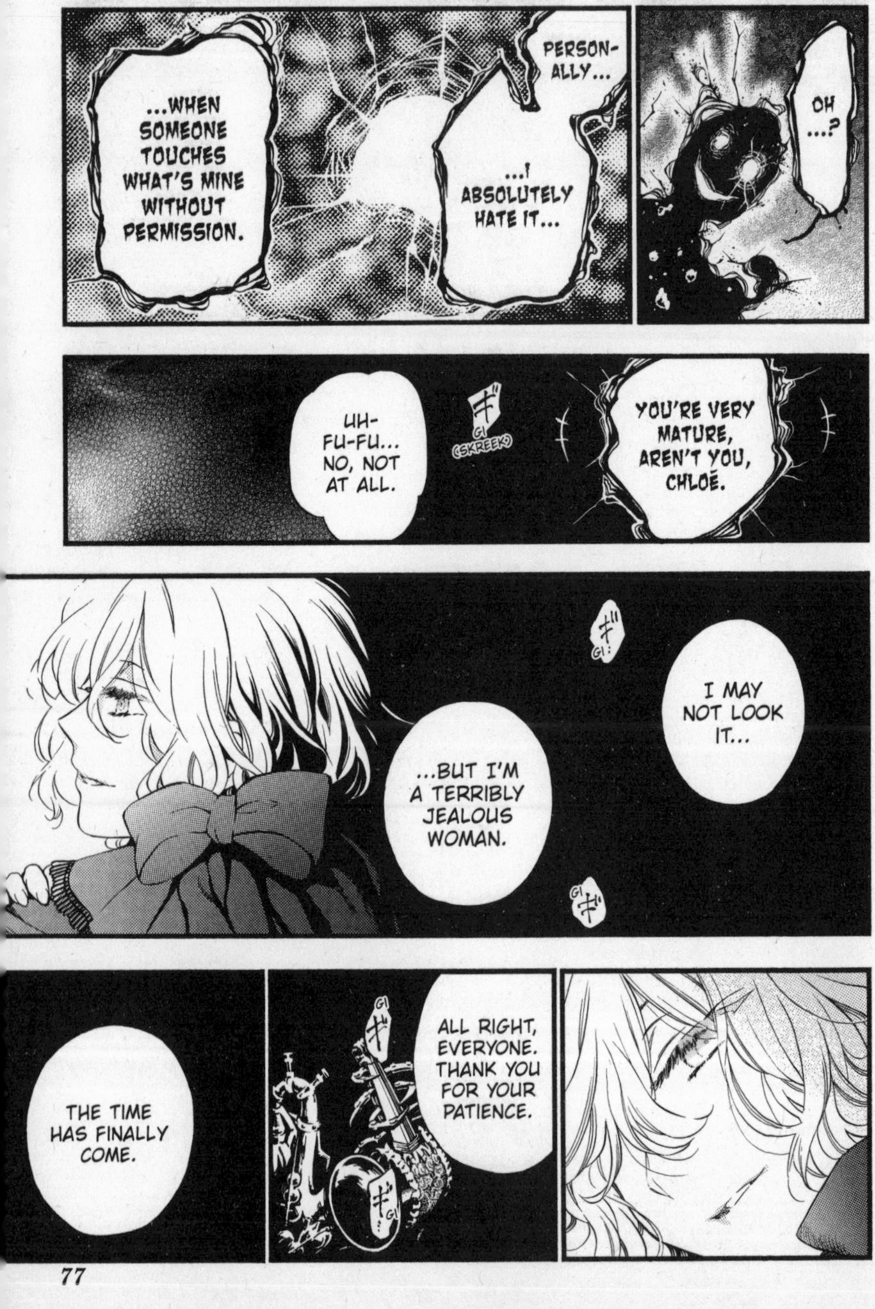
OH ...?
PERSON-ALLY...
...I ABSOLUTELY HATE IT...
...WHEN SOMEONE TOUCHES WHAT'S MINE WITHOUT PERMISSION.
YOU'RE VERY MATURE, AREN'T YOU, CHLOÉ.
ギ GI (SKREEK)
UH-FU-FU... NO, NOT AT ALL.
ギ GI
I MAY NOT LOOK IT...
...BUT I'M A TERRIBLY JEALOUS WOMAN.
GI ギ
ALL RIGHT, EVERYONE. THANK YOU FOR YOUR PATIENCE.
GI ギ
ギ GI
THE TIME HAS FINALLY COME.

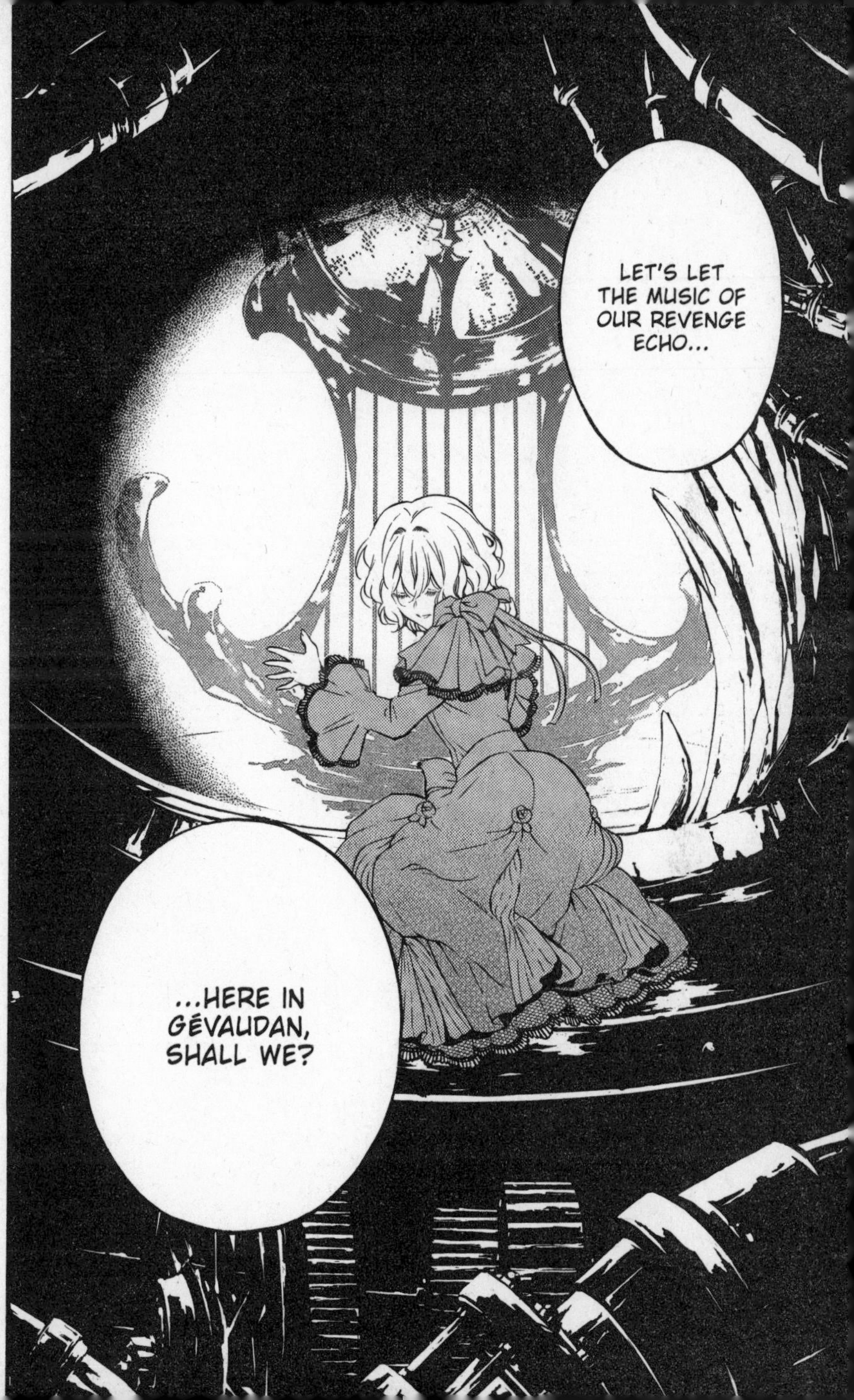
LET'S LET THE MUSIC OF OUR REVENGE ECHO...
...HERE IN GÉVAUDAN, SHALL WE?

Mémoire 30 Strascinando TREMOLO

Les Mémoires de Vanitas

THE CASE STUDY OF
VANITAS

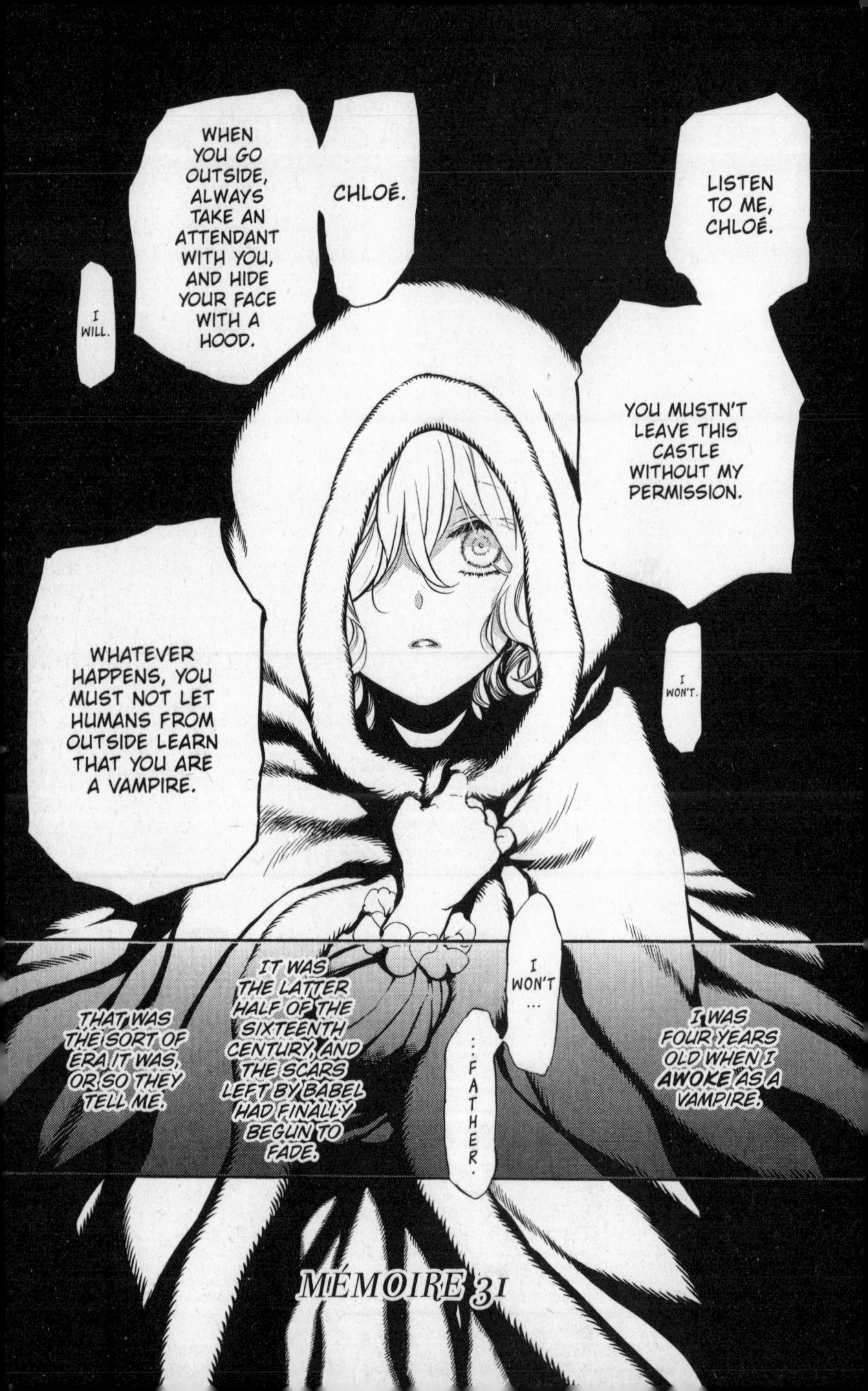
LISTEN TO ME, CHLOÉ.
CHLOÉ.
WHEN YOU GO OUTSIDE, ALWAYS TAKE AN ATTENDANT WITH YOU, AND HIDE YOUR FACE WITH A HOOD.
I WILL.
YOU MUSTN'T LEAVE THIS CASTLE WITHOUT MY PERMISSION.
I WON'T.
WHATEVER HAPPENS, YOU MUST NOT LET HUMANS FROM OUTSIDE LEARN THAT YOU ARE A VAMPIRE.
I WON'T...
...FATHER.
I WAS FOUR YEARS OLD WHEN I AWOKE AS A VAMPIRE.
IT WAS THE LATTER HALF OF THE SIXTEENTH CENTURY, AND THE SCARS LEFT BY BABEL HAD FINALLY BEGUN TO FADE.
THAT WAS THE SORT OF ERA IT WAS, OR SO THEY TELL ME.
MÉMOIRE 31

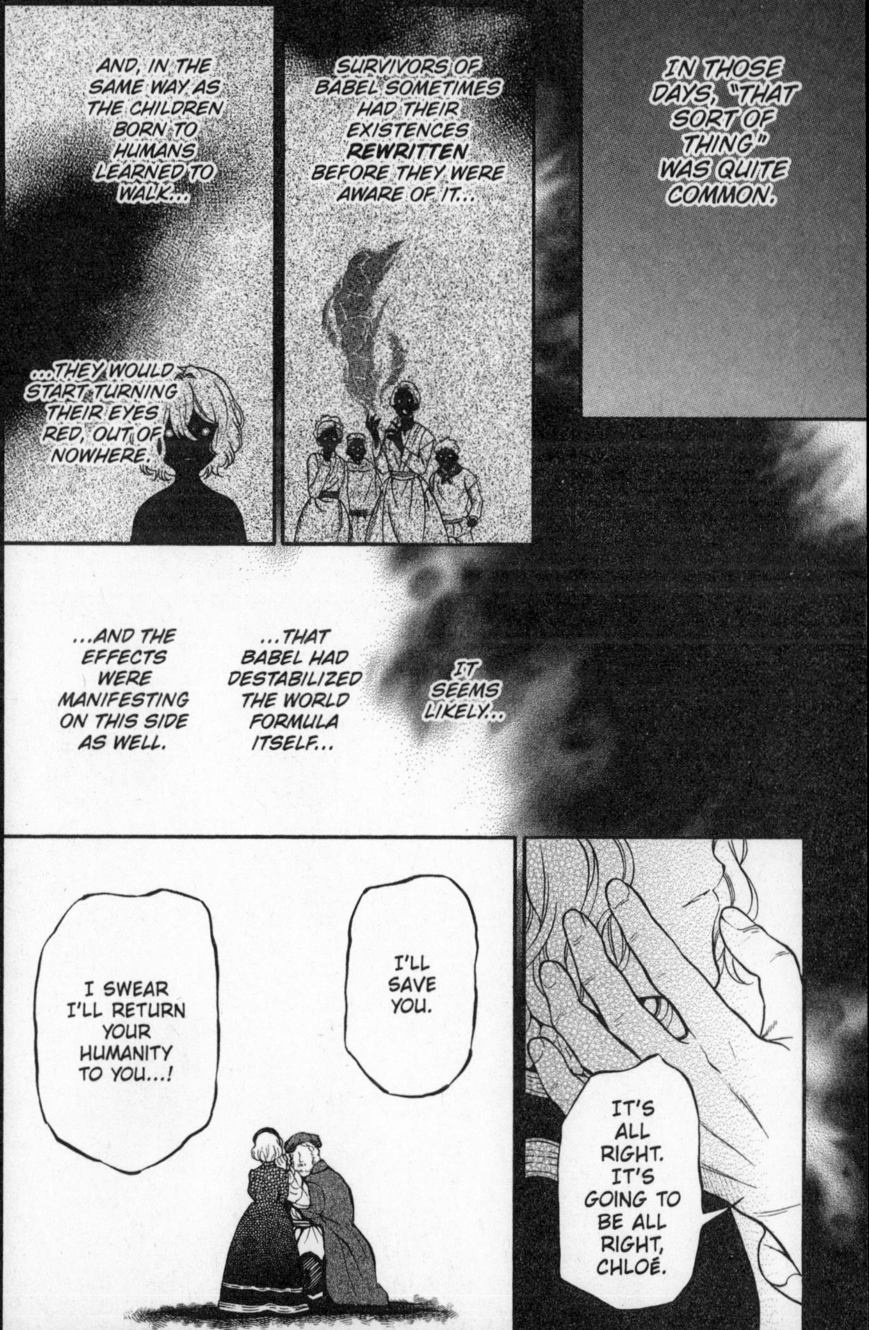
IN THOSE DAYS, "THAT SORT OF THING" WAS QUITE COMMON.
SURVIVORS OF BABEL SOMETIMES HAD THEIR EXISTENCES **REWRITTEN** BEFORE THEY WERE AWARE OF IT...
AND, IN THE SAME WAY AS THE CHILDREN BORN TO HUMANS LEARNED TO WALK...
...THEY WOULD START TURNING THEIR EYES RED, OUT OF NOWHERE.
IT SEEMS LIKELY...
...THAT BABEL HAD DESTABILIZED THE WORLD FORMULA ITSELF...
...AND THE EFFECTS WERE MANIFESTING ON THIS SIDE AS WELL.
IT'S ALL RIGHT. IT'S GOING TO BE ALL RIGHT, CHLOÉ.
I'LL SAVE YOU.
I SWEAR I'LL RETURN YOUR HUMANITY TO YOU...!

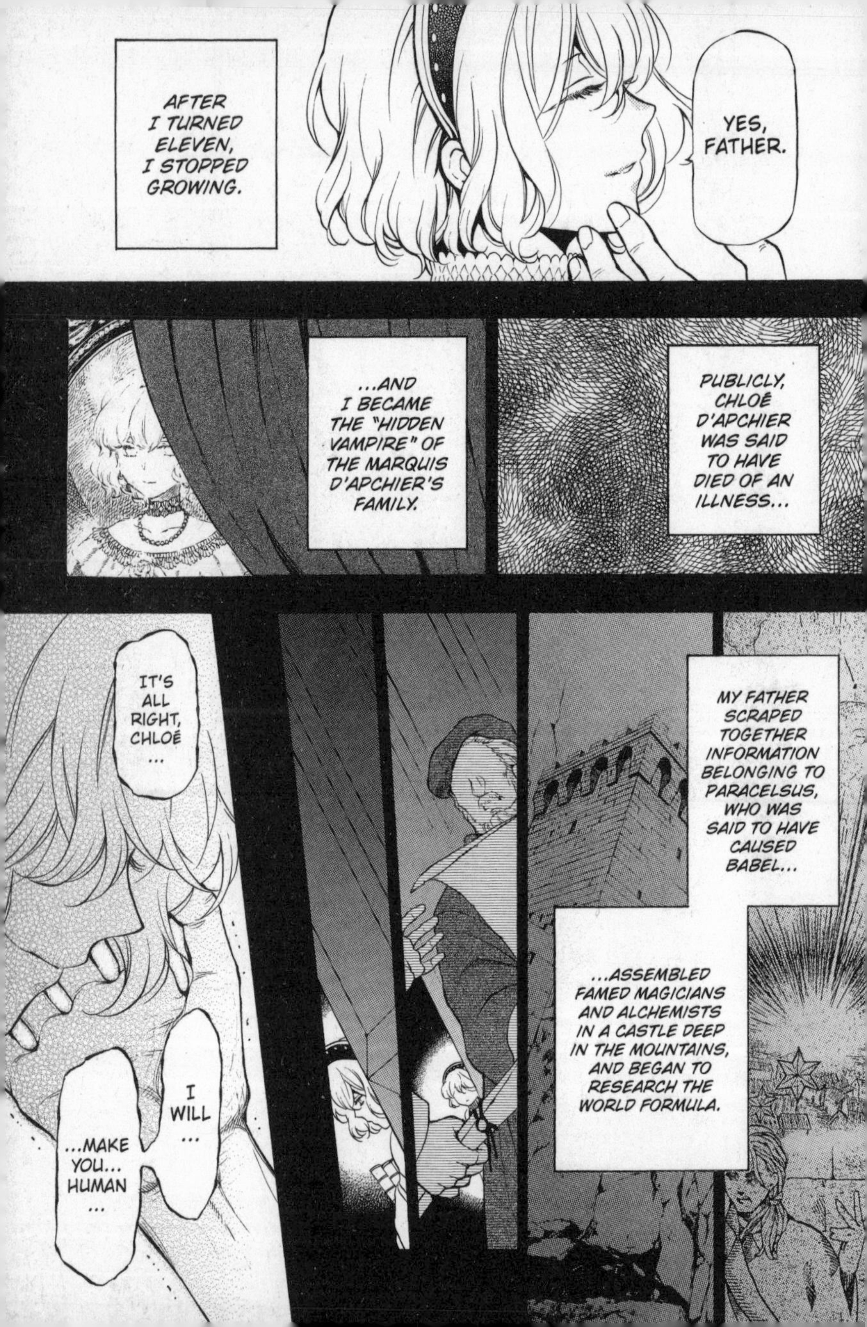
YES, FATHER.
AFTER I TURNED ELEVEN, I STOPPED GROWING.
PUBLICLY, CHLOÉ D'APCHIER WAS SAID TO HAVE DIED OF AN ILLNESS...
...AND I BECAME THE "HIDDEN VAMPIRE" OF THE MARQUIS D'APCHIER'S FAMILY.
MY FATHER SCRAPED TOGETHER INFORMATION BELONGING TO PARACELSUS, WHO WAS SAID TO HAVE CAUSED BABEL...
...ASSEMBLED FAMED MAGICIANS AND ALCHEMISTS IN A CASTLE DEEP IN THE MOUNTAINS, AND BEGAN TO RESEARCH THE WORLD FORMULA.
IT'S ALL RIGHT, CHLOÉ...
I WILL...
...MAKE YOU... HUMAN...

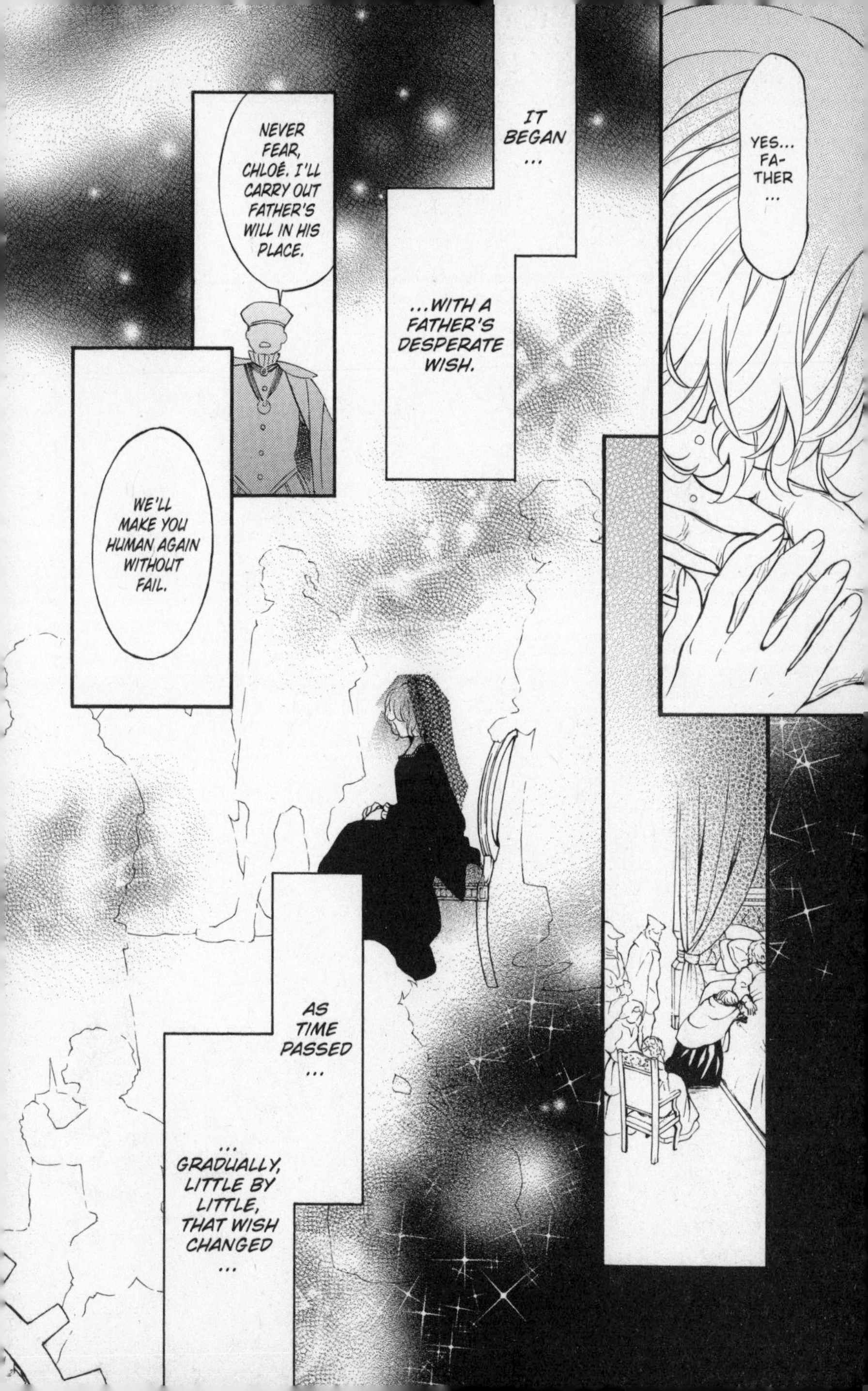
YES... FA-THER...
IT BEGAN...
...WITH A FATHER'S DESPERATE WISH.
NEVER FEAR, CHLOÉ. I'LL CARRY OUT FATHER'S WILL IN HIS PLACE.
WE'LL MAKE YOU HUMAN AGAIN WITHOUT FAIL.
AS TIME PASSED...
...GRADUALLY, LITTLE BY LITTLE, THAT WISH CHANGED...

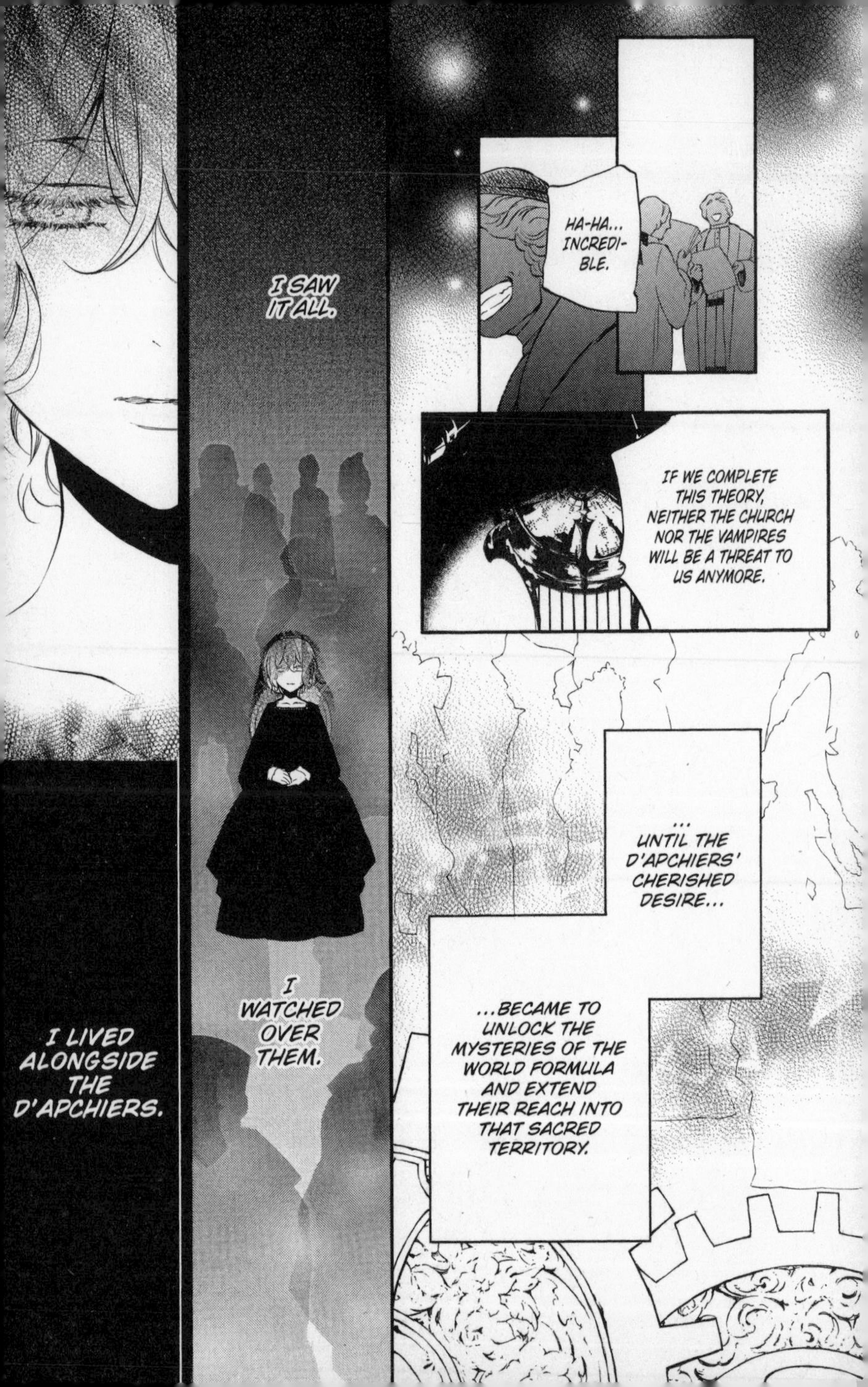
HA-HA... INCREDIBLE.
IF WE COMPLETE THIS THEORY, NEITHER THE CHURCH NOR THE VAMPIRES WILL BE A THREAT TO US ANYMORE.
...UNTIL THE D'APCHIERS' CHERISHED DESIRE...
...BECAME TO UNLOCK THE MYSTERIES OF THE WORLD FORMULA AND EXTEND THEIR REACH INTO THAT SACRED TERRITORY.
I SAW IT ALL.
I WATCHED OVER THEM.
I LIVED ALONGSIDE THE D'APCHIERS.

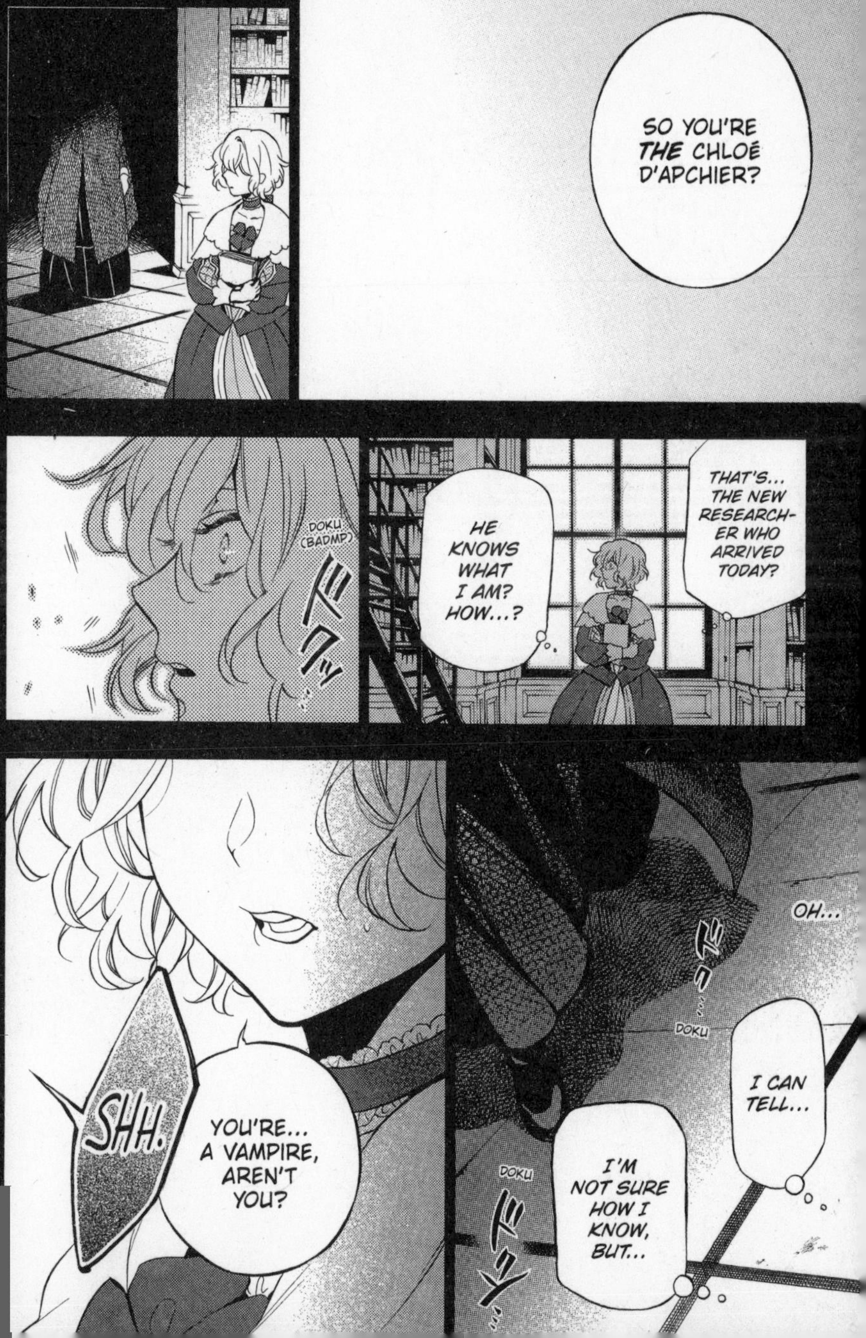

SO YOU'RE *THE* CHLOÉ D'APCHIER?
THAT'S... THE NEW RESEARCHER WHO ARRIVED TODAY?
HE KNOWS WHAT I AM? HOW...?
DOKU (BADMP)
OH...
DOKU
I CAN TELL...
I'M NOT SURE HOW I KNOW, BUT...
DOKU
SHH.
YOU'RE... A VAMPIRE, AREN'T YOU?

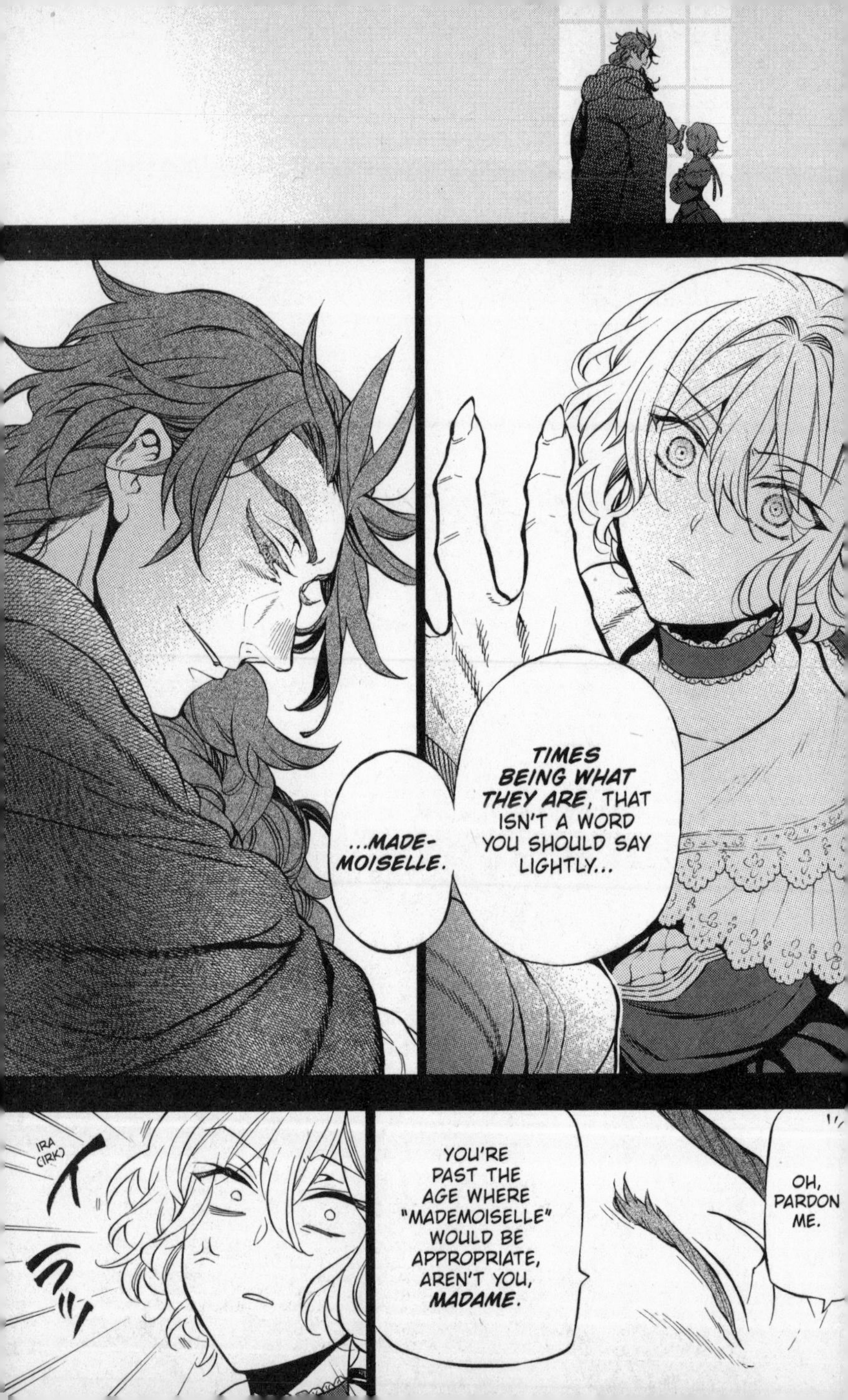
TIMES BEING WHAT THEY ARE, THAT ISN'T A WORD YOU SHOULD SAY LIGHTLY...
...MADE-MOISELLE.
OH, PARDON ME.
YOU'RE PAST THE AGE WHERE "MADEMOISELLE" WOULD BE APPROPRIATE, AREN'T YOU, MADAME.
IRA (IRK)

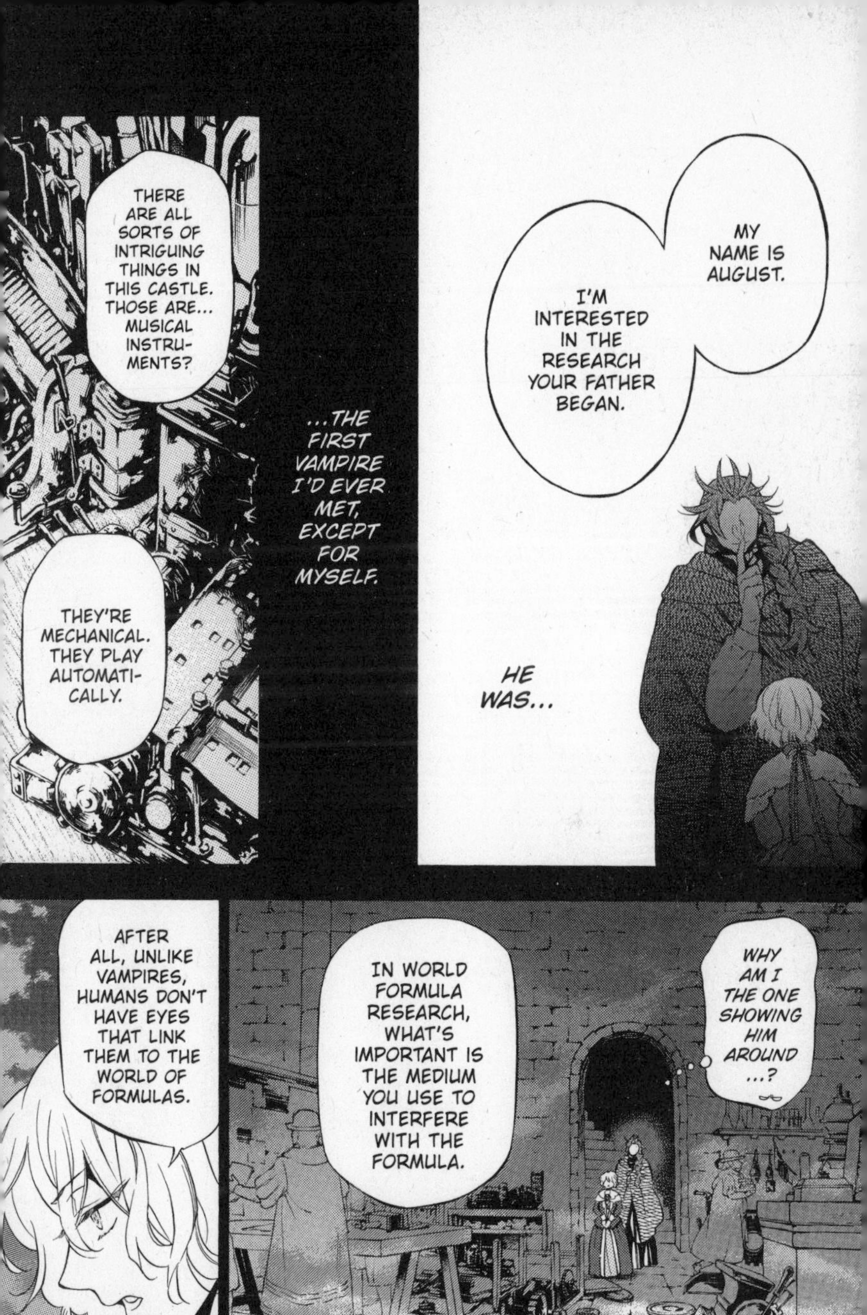
MY NAME IS AUGUST.
I'M INTERESTED IN THE RESEARCH YOUR FATHER BEGAN.
HE WAS...
...THE FIRST VAMPIRE I'D EVER MET, EXCEPT FOR MYSELF.
THERE ARE ALL SORTS OF INTRIGUING THINGS IN THIS CASTLE. THOSE ARE... MUSICAL INSTRU-MENTS?
THEY'RE MECHANICAL. THEY PLAY AUTOMATI-CALLY.
WHY AM I THE ONE SHOWING HIM AROUND ...?
IN WORLD FORMULA RESEARCH, WHAT'S IMPORTANT IS THE MEDIUM YOU USE TO INTERFERE WITH THE FORMULA.
AFTER ALL, UNLIKE VAMPIRES, HUMANS DON'T HAVE EYES THAT LINK THEM TO THE WORLD OF FORMULAS.

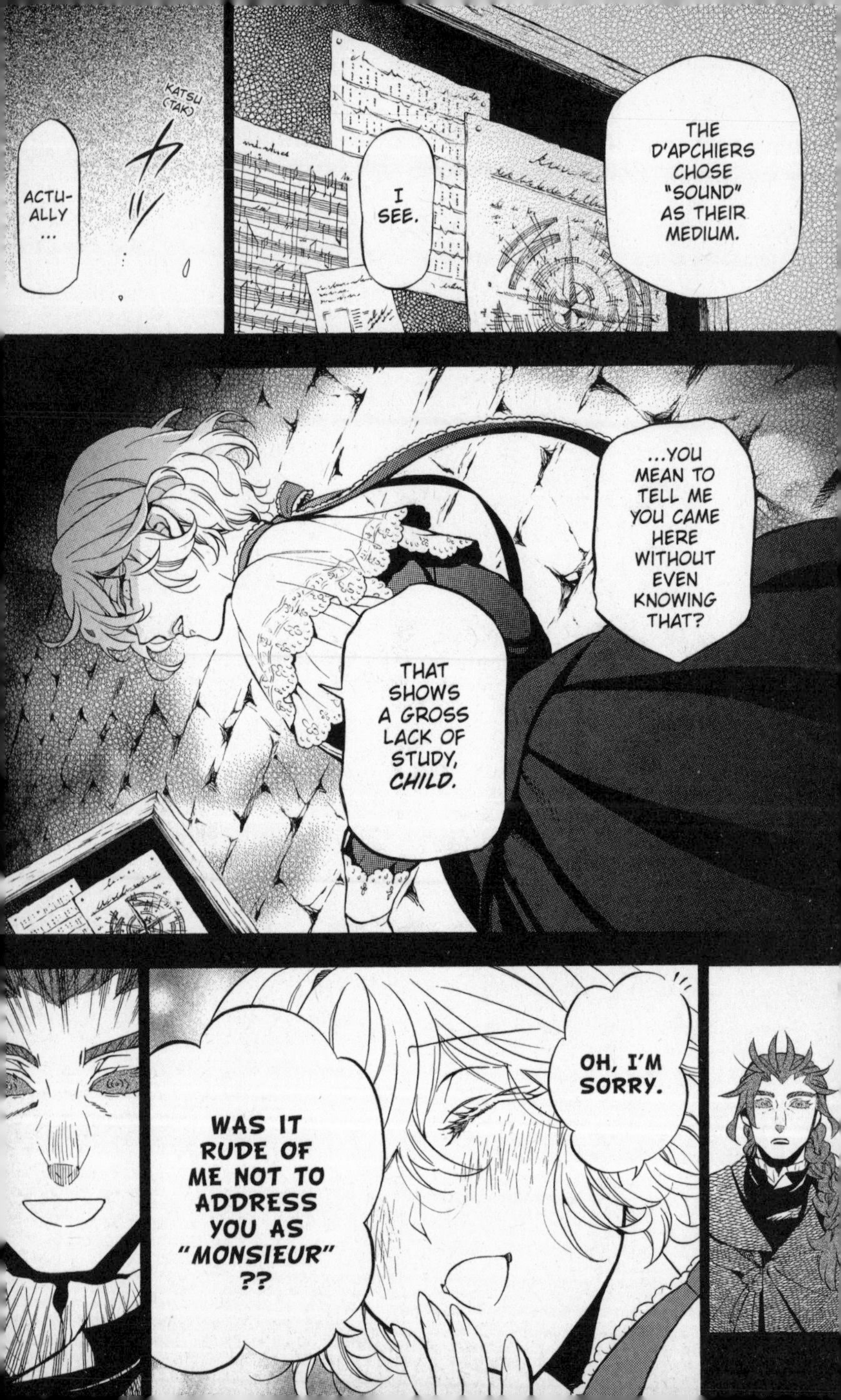
THE D'APCHIERS CHOSE "SOUND" AS THEIR MEDIUM.
I SEE.
KATSU (TAK)
ACTU-ALLY ...
...YOU MEAN TO TELL ME YOU CAME HERE WITHOUT EVEN KNOWING THAT?
THAT SHOWS A GROSS LACK OF STUDY, *CHILD.*
OH, I'M SORRY.
WAS IT RUDE OF ME NOT TO ADDRESS YOU AS "MONSIEUR"??

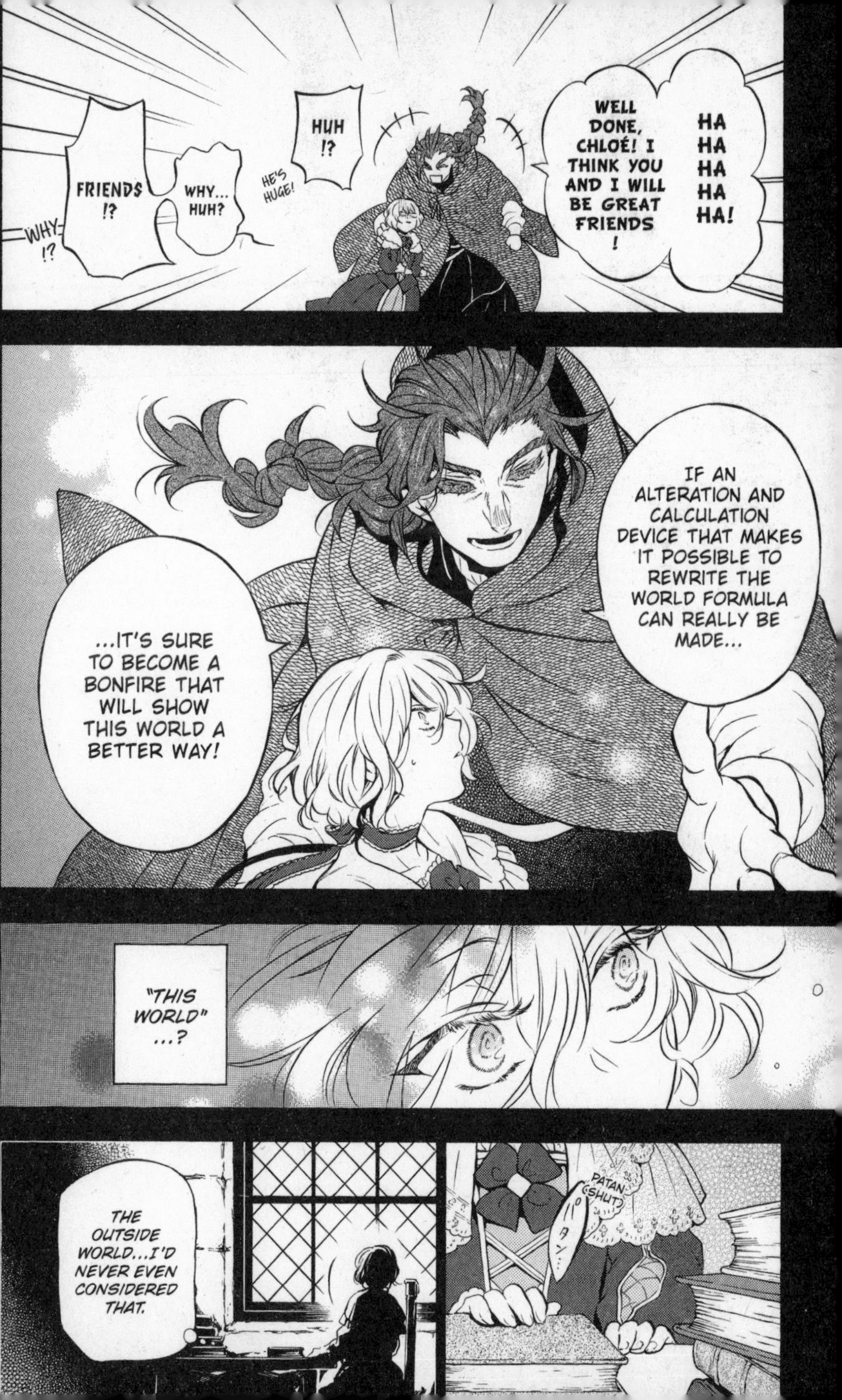
HA HA HA HA HA!
WELL DONE, CHLOÉ! I THINK YOU AND I WILL BE GREAT FRIENDS!
HUH!?
HE'S HUGE!
WHY... HUH?
FRIENDS!?
WHY!?
IF AN ALTERATION AND CALCULATION DEVICE THAT MAKES IT POSSIBLE TO REWRITE THE WORLD FORMULA CAN REALLY BE MADE...
...IT'S SURE TO BECOME A BONFIRE THAT WILL SHOW THIS WORLD A BETTER WAY!
"THIS WORLD" ...?
PATAN (SHUT)
パタン…
THE OUTSIDE WORLD...I'D NEVER EVEN CONSIDERED THAT.

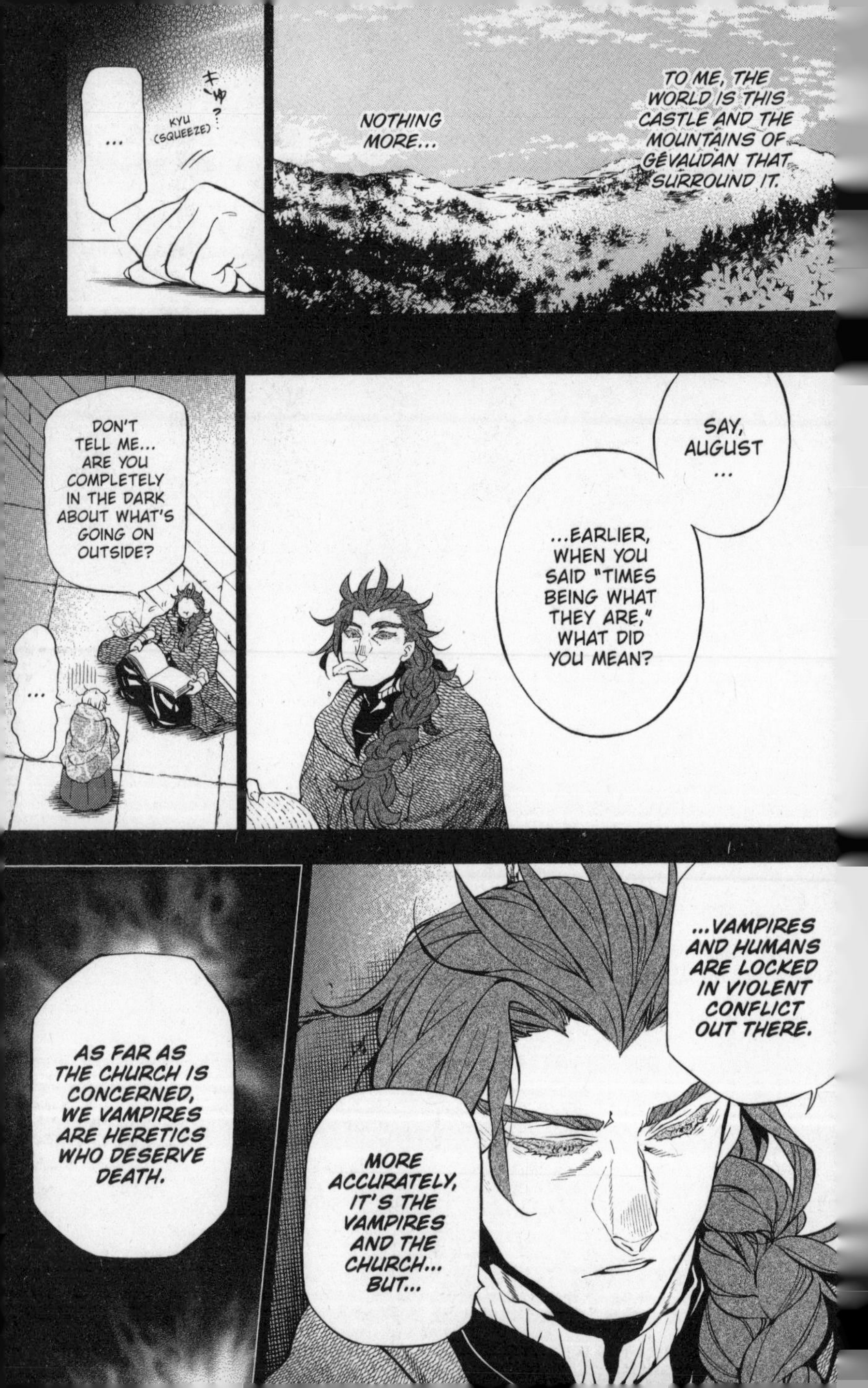
TO ME, THE WORLD IS THIS CASTLE AND THE MOUNTAINS OF GEVAUDAN THAT SURROUND IT.
NOTHING MORE...
...
KYU (SQUEEZE)
SAY, AUGUST...
...EARLIER, WHEN YOU SAID "TIMES BEING WHAT THEY ARE," WHAT DID YOU MEAN?
DON'T TELL ME... ARE YOU COMPLETELY IN THE DARK ABOUT WHAT'S GOING ON OUTSIDE?
...
...VAMPIRES AND HUMANS ARE LOCKED IN VIOLENT CONFLICT OUT THERE.
MORE ACCURATELY, IT'S THE VAMPIRES AND THE CHURCH... BUT...
AS FAR AS THE CHURCH IS CONCERNED, WE VAMPIRES ARE HERETICS WHO DESERVE DEATH.

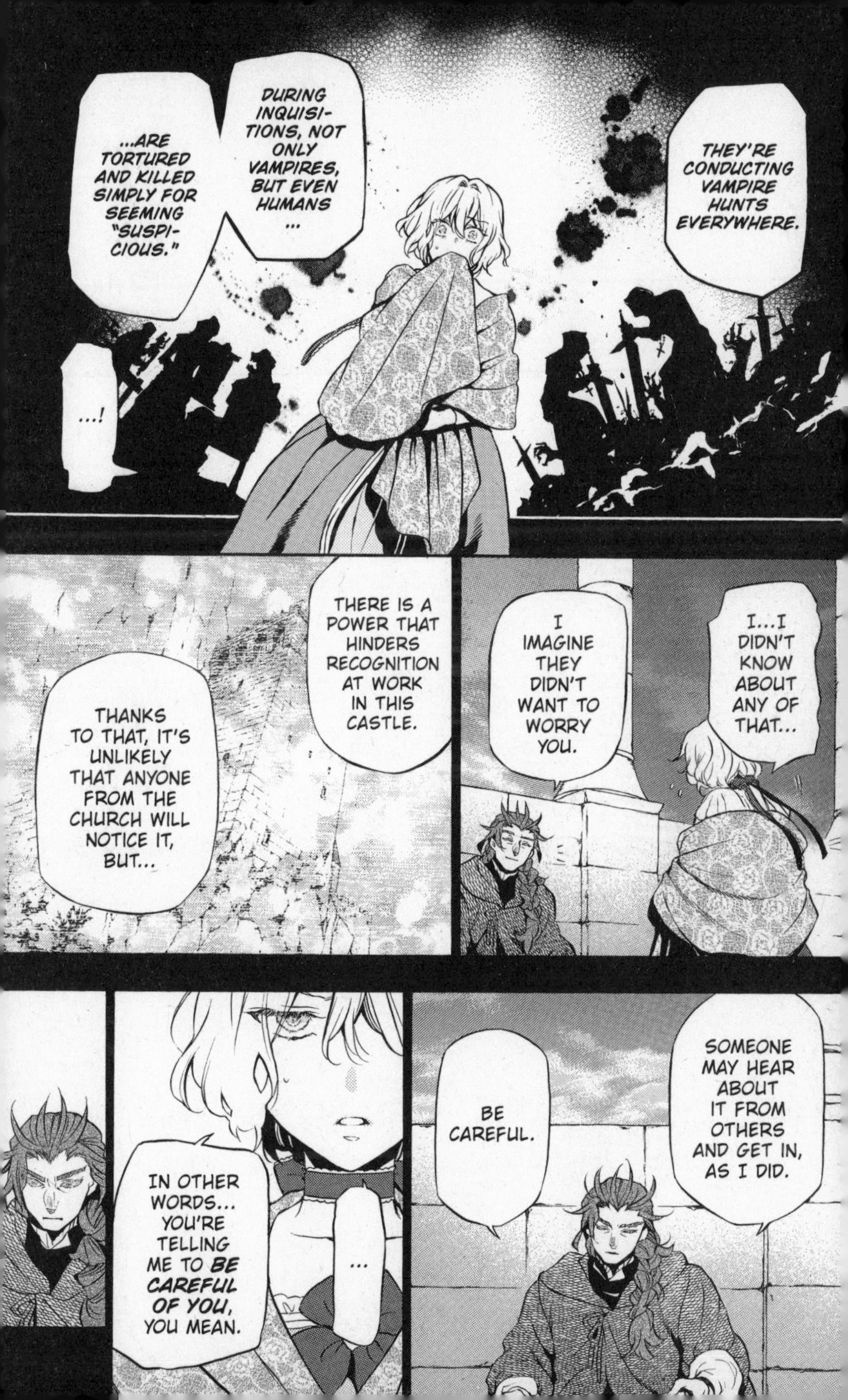
THEY'RE CONDUCTING VAMPIRE HUNTS EVERYWHERE.
DURING INQUISITIONS, NOT ONLY VAMPIRES, BUT EVEN HUMANS ...
...ARE TORTURED AND KILLED SIMPLY FOR SEEMING "SUSPICIOUS."
...!
I...I DIDN'T KNOW ABOUT ANY OF THAT...
I IMAGINE THEY DIDN'T WANT TO WORRY YOU.
THERE IS A POWER THAT HINDERS RECOGNITION AT WORK IN THIS CASTLE.
THANKS TO THAT, IT'S UNLIKELY THAT ANYONE FROM THE CHURCH WILL NOTICE IT, BUT...
SOMEONE MAY HEAR ABOUT IT FROM OTHERS AND GET IN, AS I DID.
BE CAREFUL.
...
IN OTHER WORDS... YOU'RE TELLING ME TO **BE CAREFUL OF YOU**, YOU MEAN.

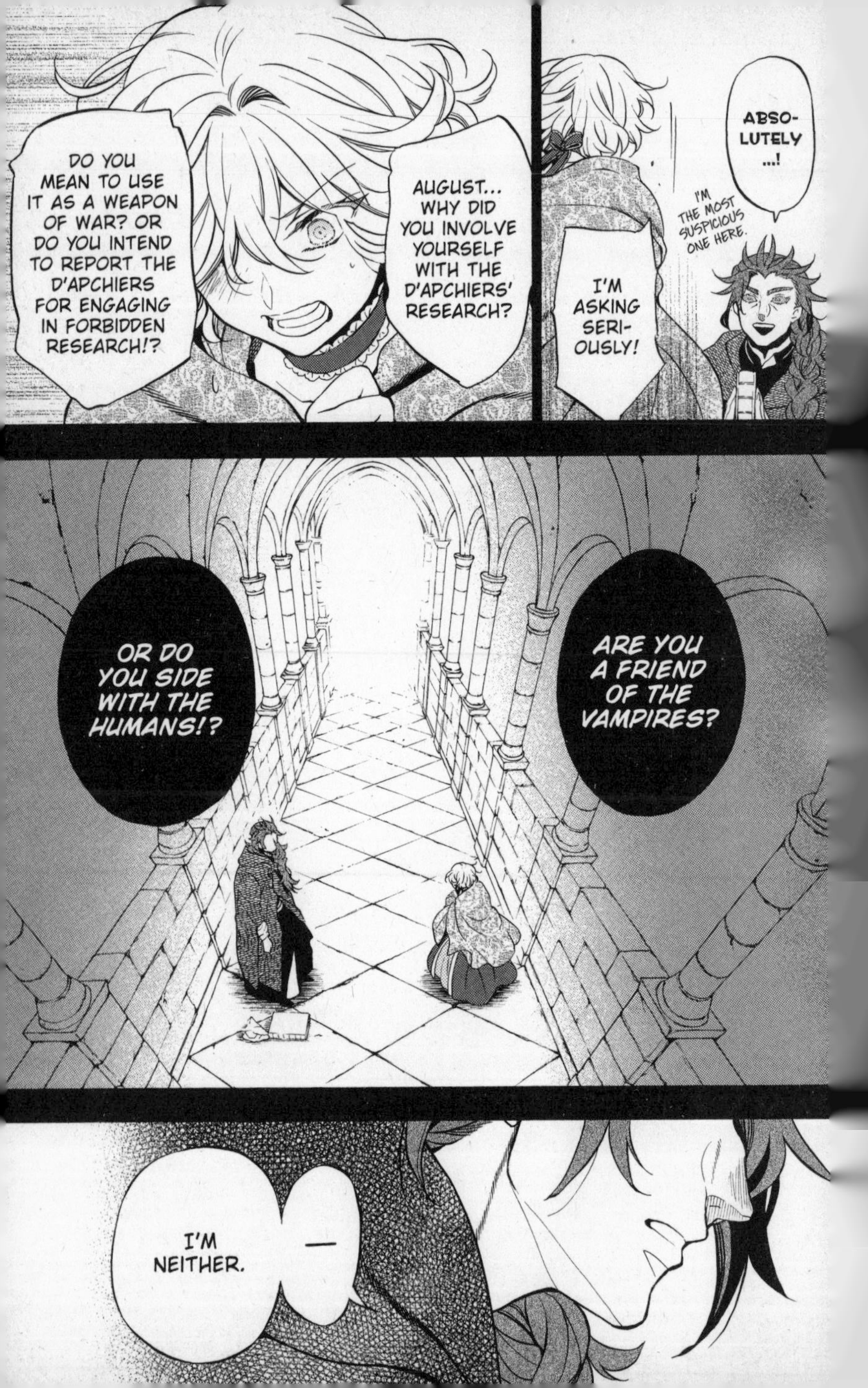
ABSO-LUTELY ...!
I'M THE MOST SUSPICIOUS ONE HERE.
I'M ASKING SERI-OUSLY!
AUGUST... WHY DID YOU INVOLVE YOURSELF WITH THE D'APCHIERS' RESEARCH?
DO YOU MEAN TO USE IT AS A WEAPON OF WAR? OR DO YOU INTEND TO REPORT THE D'APCHIERS FOR ENGAGING IN FORBIDDEN RESEARCH!?
ARE YOU A FRIEND OF THE VAMPIRES?
OR DO YOU SIDE WITH THE HUMANS!?
— I'M NEITHER.

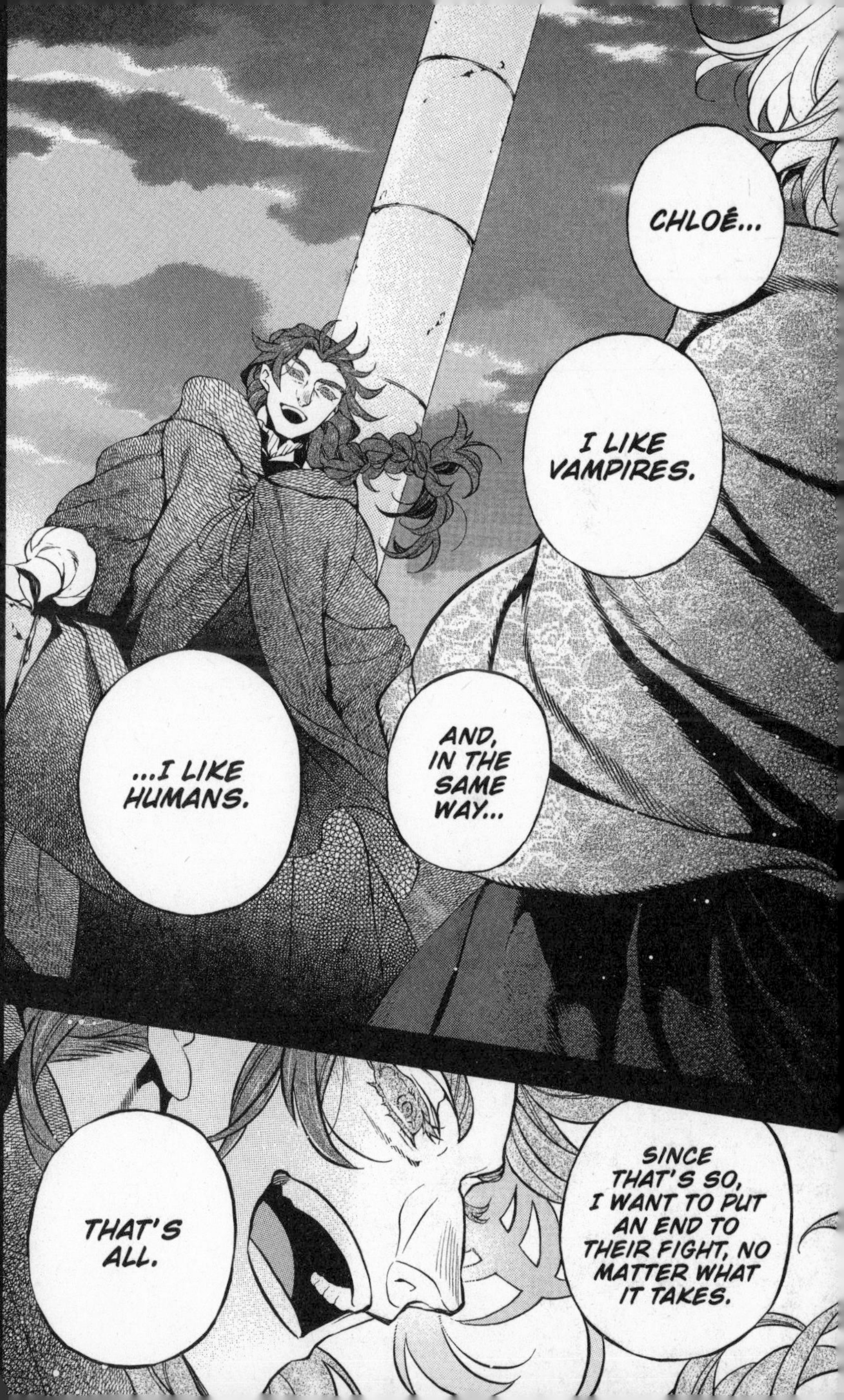
CHLOÉ...
I LIKE VAMPIRES.
AND, IN THE SAME WAY...
...I LIKE HUMANS.
SINCE THAT'S SO, I WANT TO PUT AN END TO THEIR FIGHT, NO MATTER WHAT IT TAKES.
THAT'S ALL.

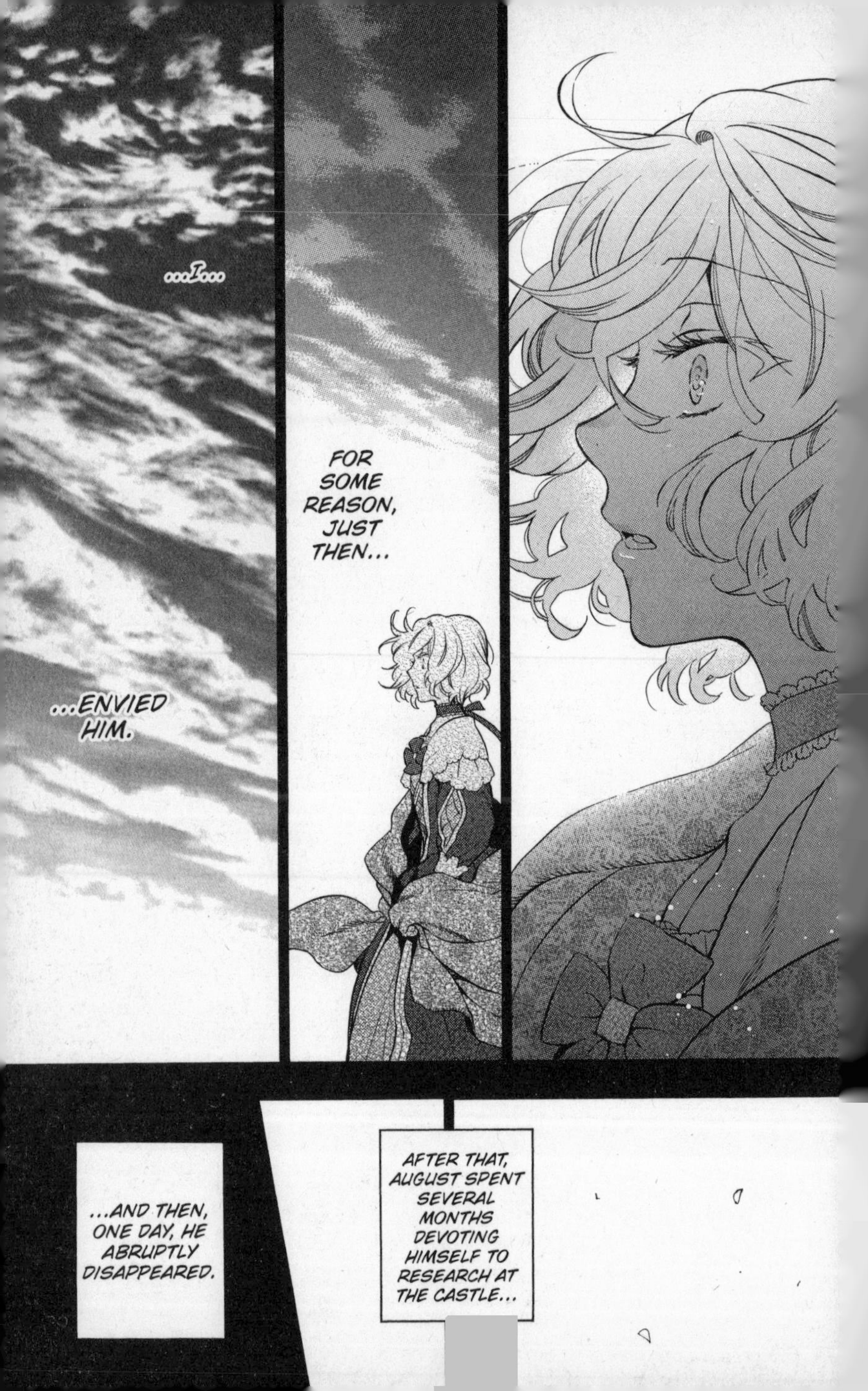
FOR SOME REASON, JUST THEN...
...I...
...ENVIED HIM.
AFTER THAT, AUGUST SPENT SEVERAL MONTHS DEVOTING HIMSELF TO RESEARCH AT THE CASTLE...
...AND THEN, ONE DAY, HE ABRUPTLY DISAPPEARED.

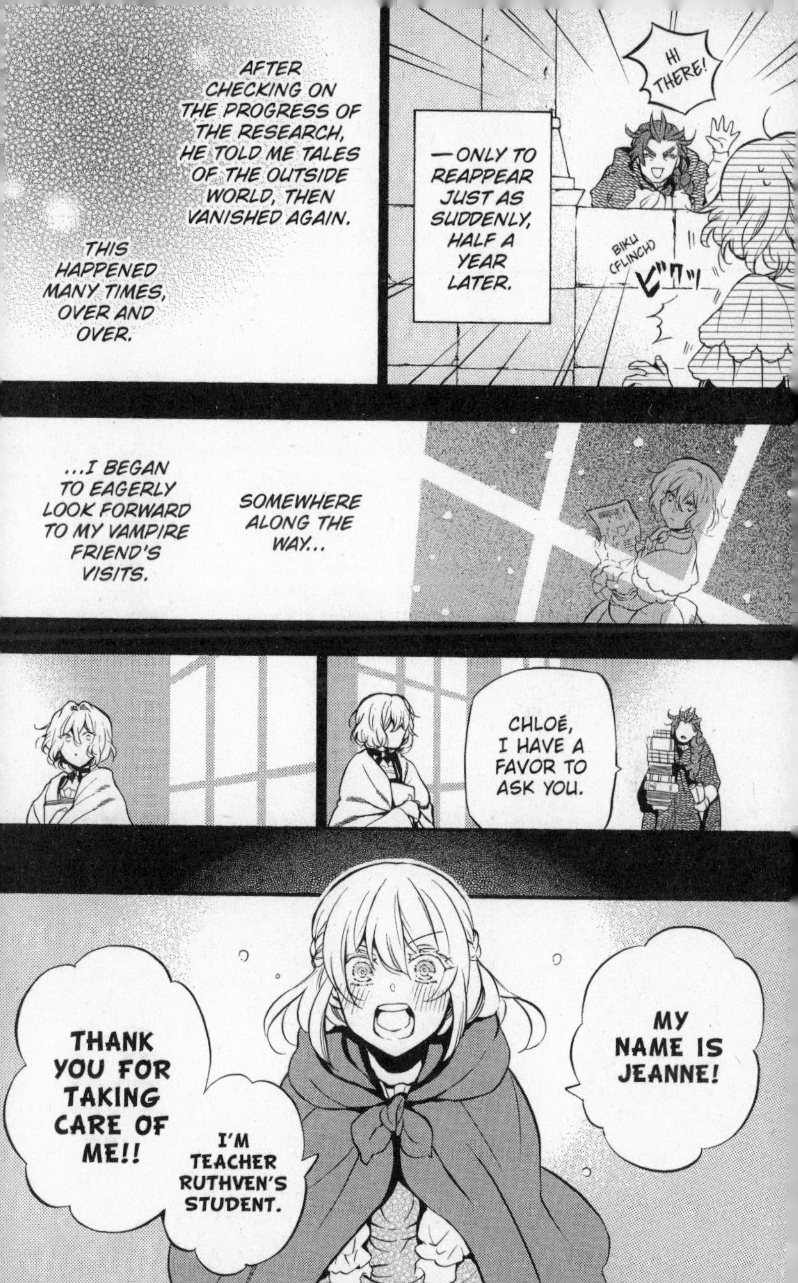
HI THERE!
—ONLY TO REAPPEAR JUST AS SUDDENLY, HALF A YEAR LATER.
BIKU (FLINCH)
ビクッ
AFTER CHECKING ON THE PROGRESS OF THE RESEARCH, HE TOLD ME TALES OF THE OUTSIDE WORLD, THEN VANISHED AGAIN.
THIS HAPPENED MANY TIMES, OVER AND OVER.
SOMEWHERE ALONG THE WAY...
...I BEGAN TO EAGERLY LOOK FORWARD TO MY VAMPIRE FRIEND'S VISITS.
CHLOÉ, I HAVE A FAVOR TO ASK YOU.
MY NAME IS JEANNE!
I'M TEACHER RUTHVEN'S STUDENT.
THANK YOU FOR TAKING CARE OF ME!!

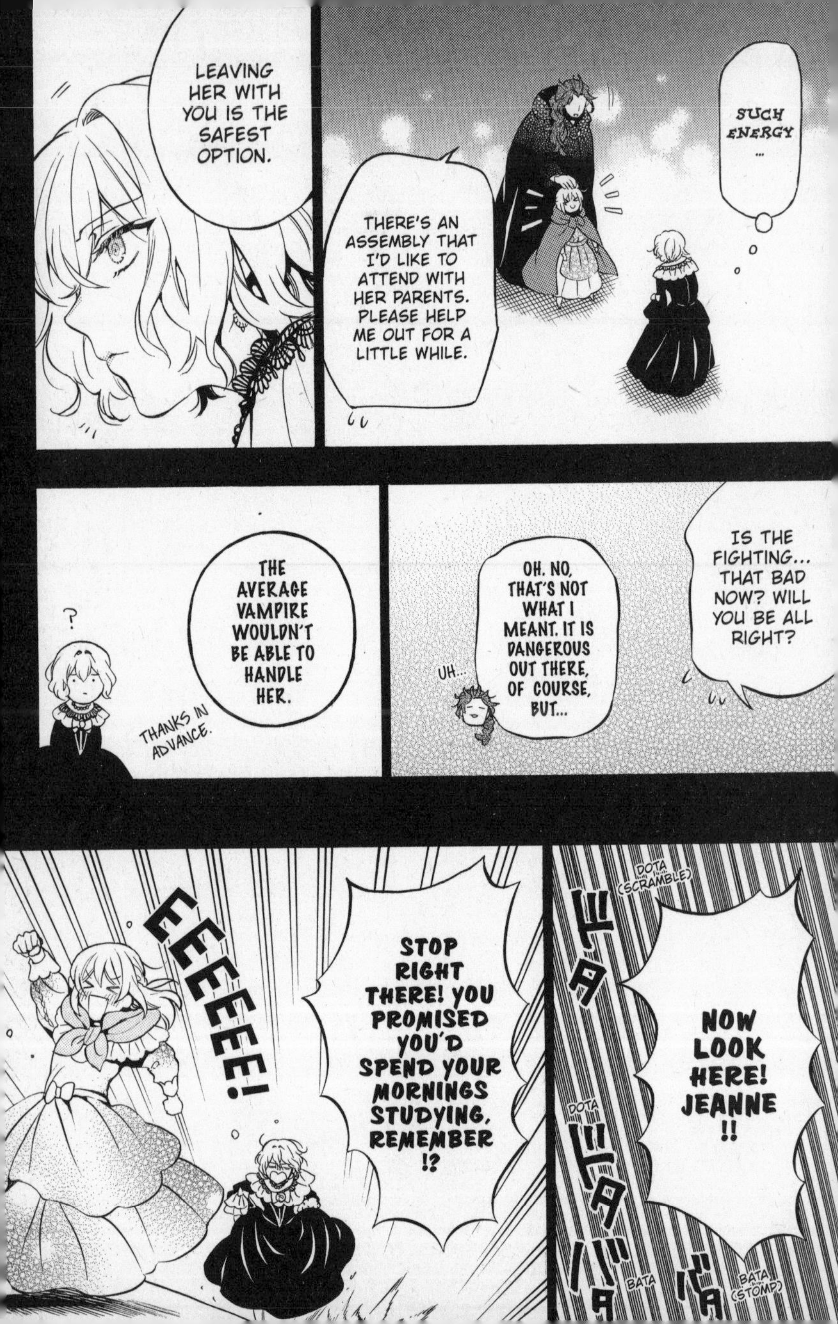
SUCH ENERGY...
THERE'S AN ASSEMBLY THAT I'D LIKE TO ATTEND WITH HER PARENTS. PLEASE HELP ME OUT FOR A LITTLE WHILE.
LEAVING HER WITH YOU IS THE SAFEST OPTION.
IS THE FIGHTING... THAT BAD NOW? WILL YOU BE ALL RIGHT?
OH. NO, THAT'S NOT WHAT I MEANT. IT IS DANGEROUS OUT THERE, OF COURSE, BUT...
UH...
THE AVERAGE VAMPIRE WOULDN'T BE ABLE TO HANDLE HER.
?
THANKS IN ADVANCE.
DOTA (SCRAMBLE)
NOW LOOK HERE! JEANNE!!
DOTA
BATA
BATA (STOMP)
STOP RIGHT THERE! YOU PROMISED YOU'D SPEND YOUR MORNINGS STUDYING, REMEMBER!?
EEEEEEE!

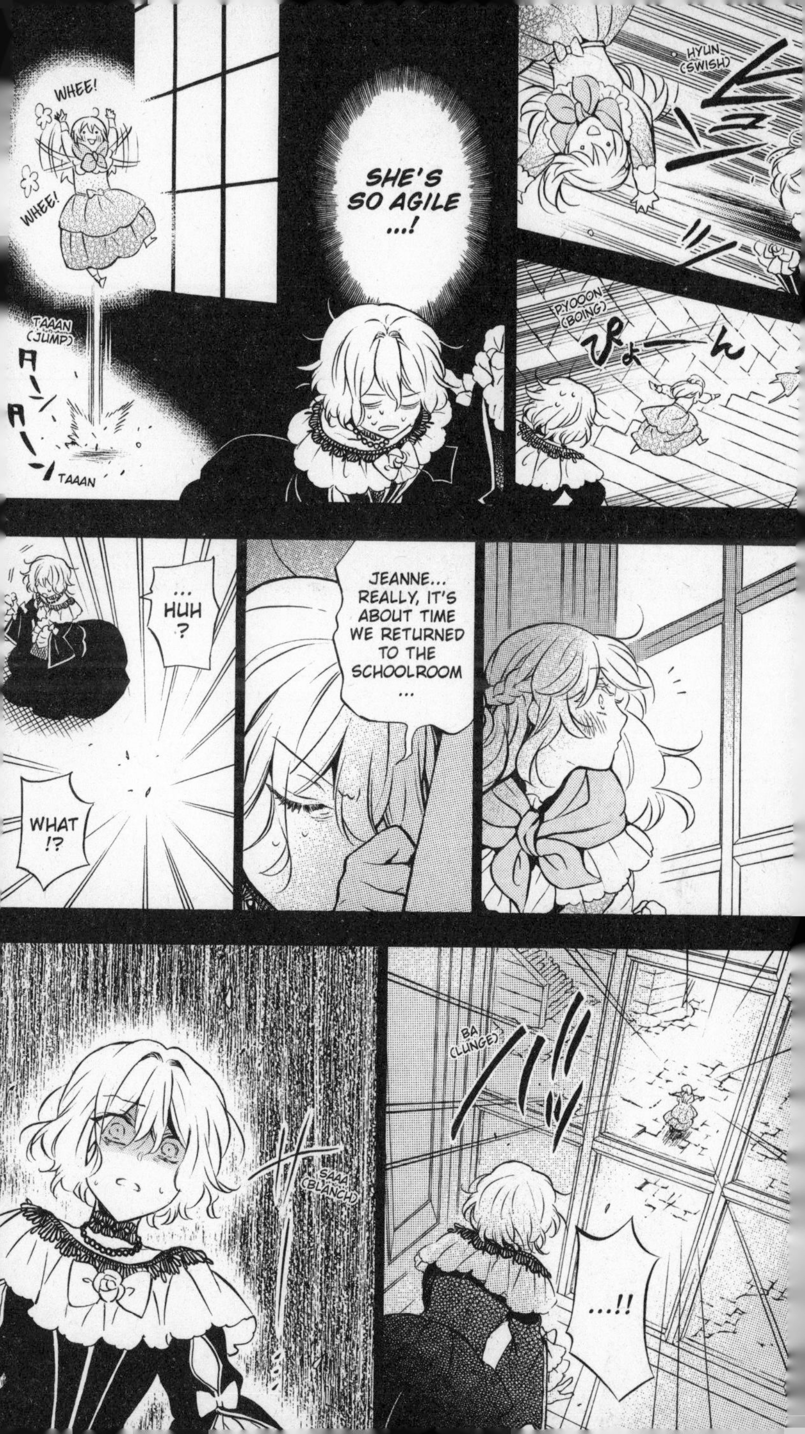
HYUN (SWISH)
PYOOON (BOING)
ぴょーん
SHE'S SO AGILE ...!
WHEE!
WHEE!
TAAAN (JUMP)
TAAAN
JEANNE... REALLY, IT'S ABOUT TIME WE RETURNED TO THE SCHOOLROOM ...
... HUH ?
WHAT !?
BA (LUNGE)
...!!
SAAA (BLANCH)

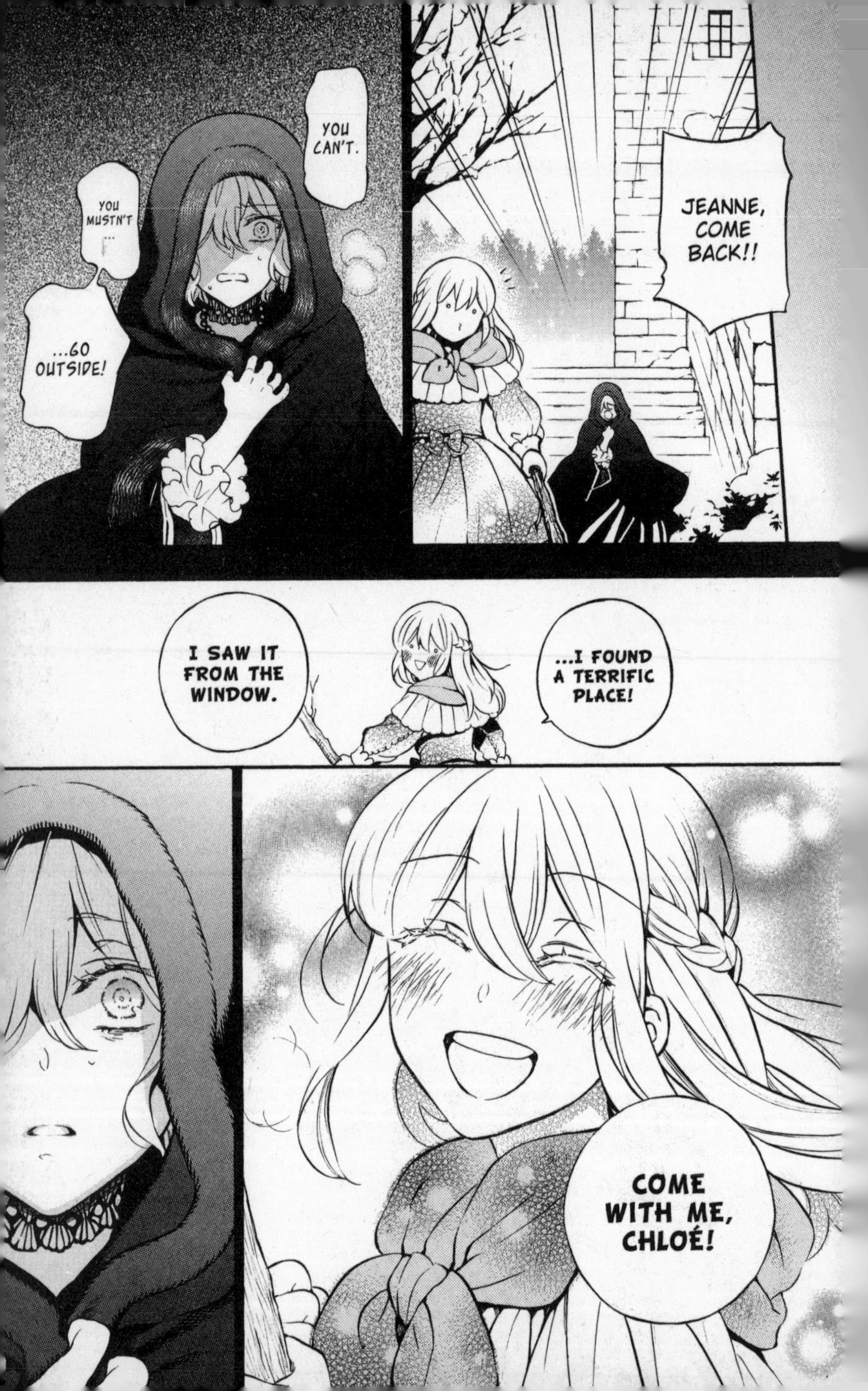
JEANNE, COME BACK!!
YOU CAN'T.
YOU MUSTN'T ...
...GO OUTSIDE!
...I FOUND A TERRIFIC PLACE!
I SAW IT FROM THE WINDOW.
COME WITH ME, CHLOÉ!

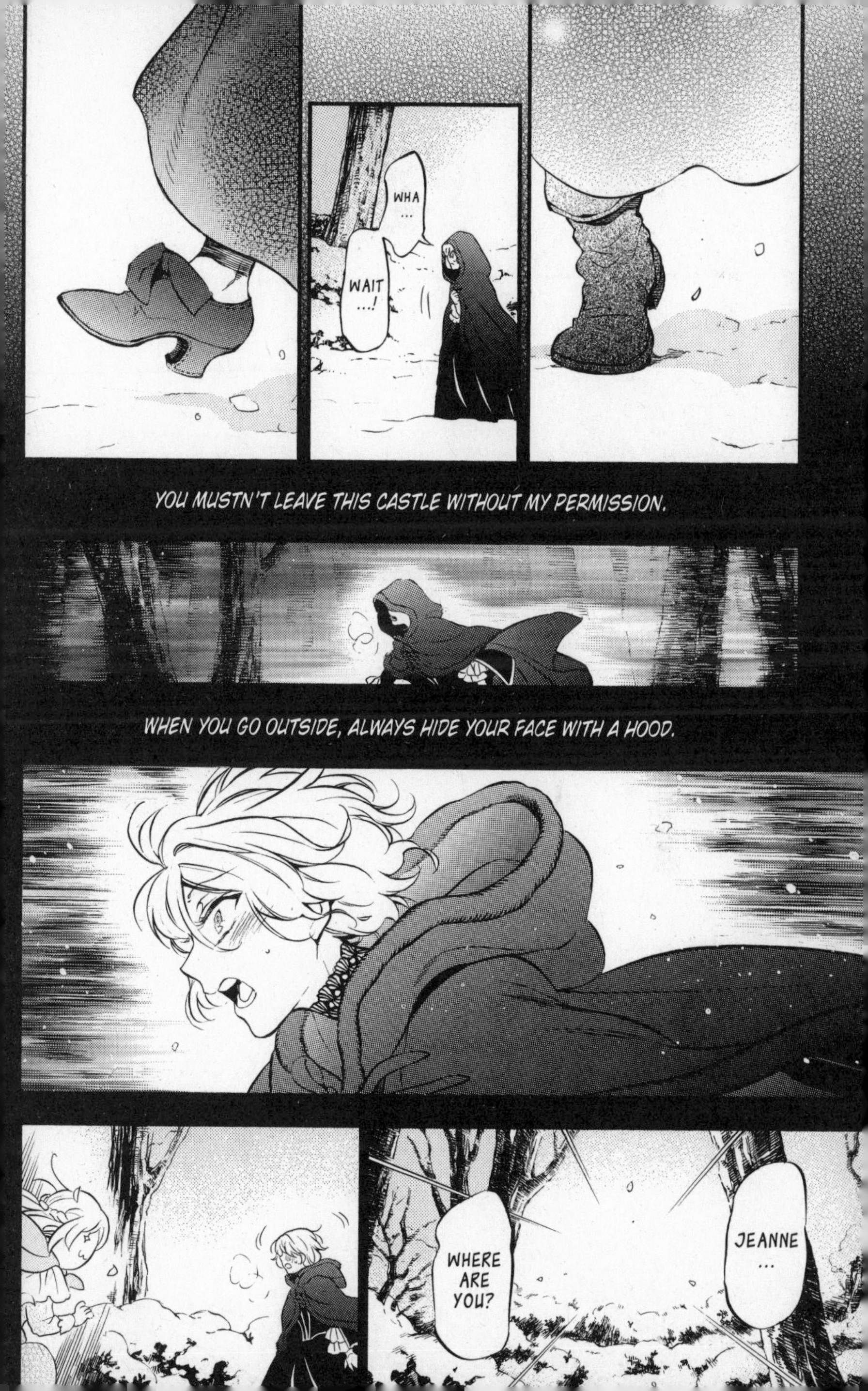
WHA ...
WAIT ...!
YOU MUSTN'T LEAVE THIS CASTLE WITHOUT MY PERMISSION.
WHEN YOU GO OUTSIDE, ALWAYS HIDE YOUR FACE WITH A HOOD.
JEANNE ...
WHERE ARE YOU?

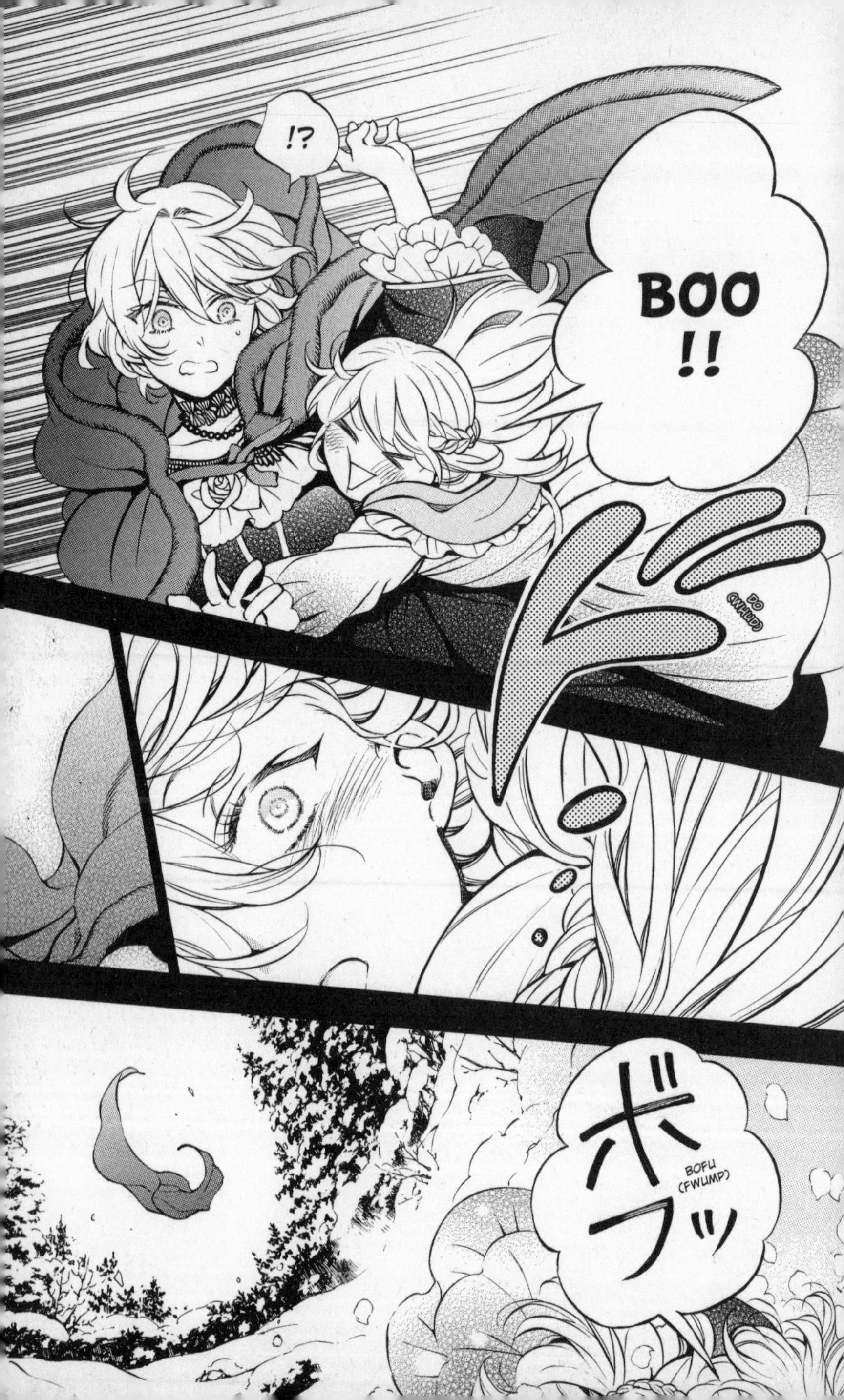
!?
BOO !!
DO (WHUD)
BOFU (FWUMP)

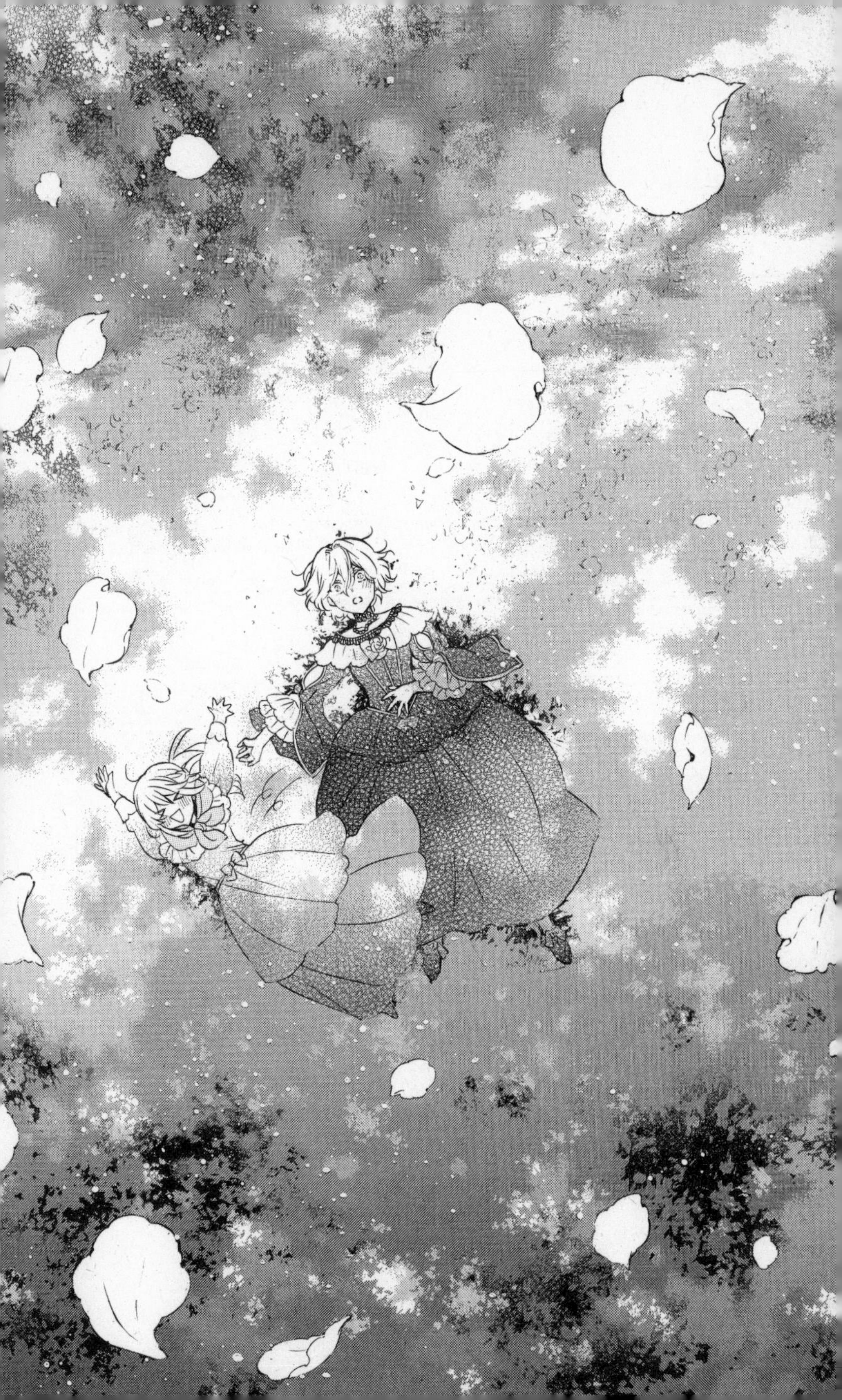

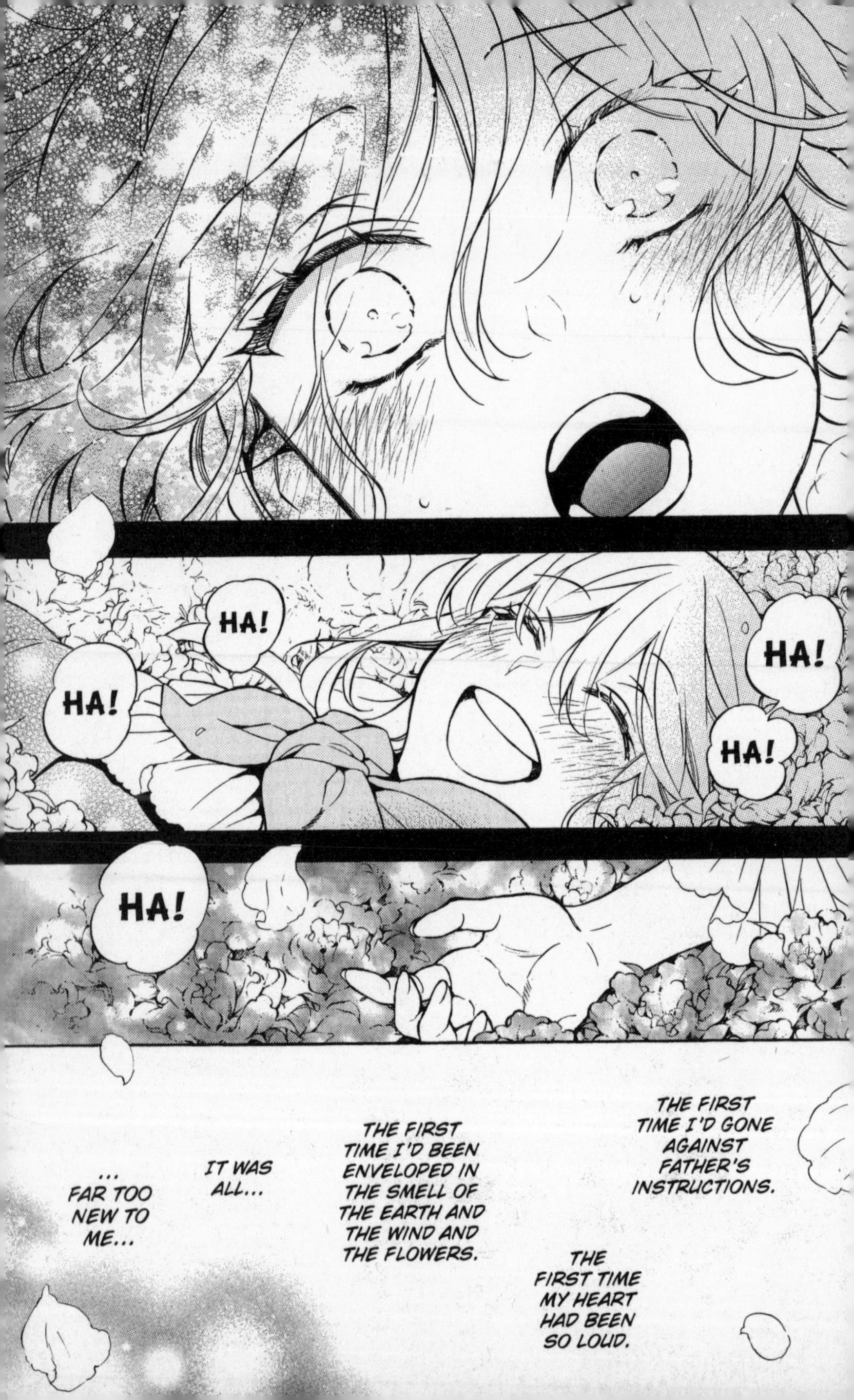
HA!
HA!
HA!
HA!
HA!
THE FIRST TIME I'D GONE AGAINST FATHER'S INSTRUCTIONS.
THE FIRST TIME MY HEART HAD BEEN SO LOUD.
THE FIRST TIME I'D BEEN ENVELOPED IN THE SMELL OF THE EARTH AND THE WIND AND THE FLOWERS.
IT WAS ALL...
... FAR TOO NEW TO ME...

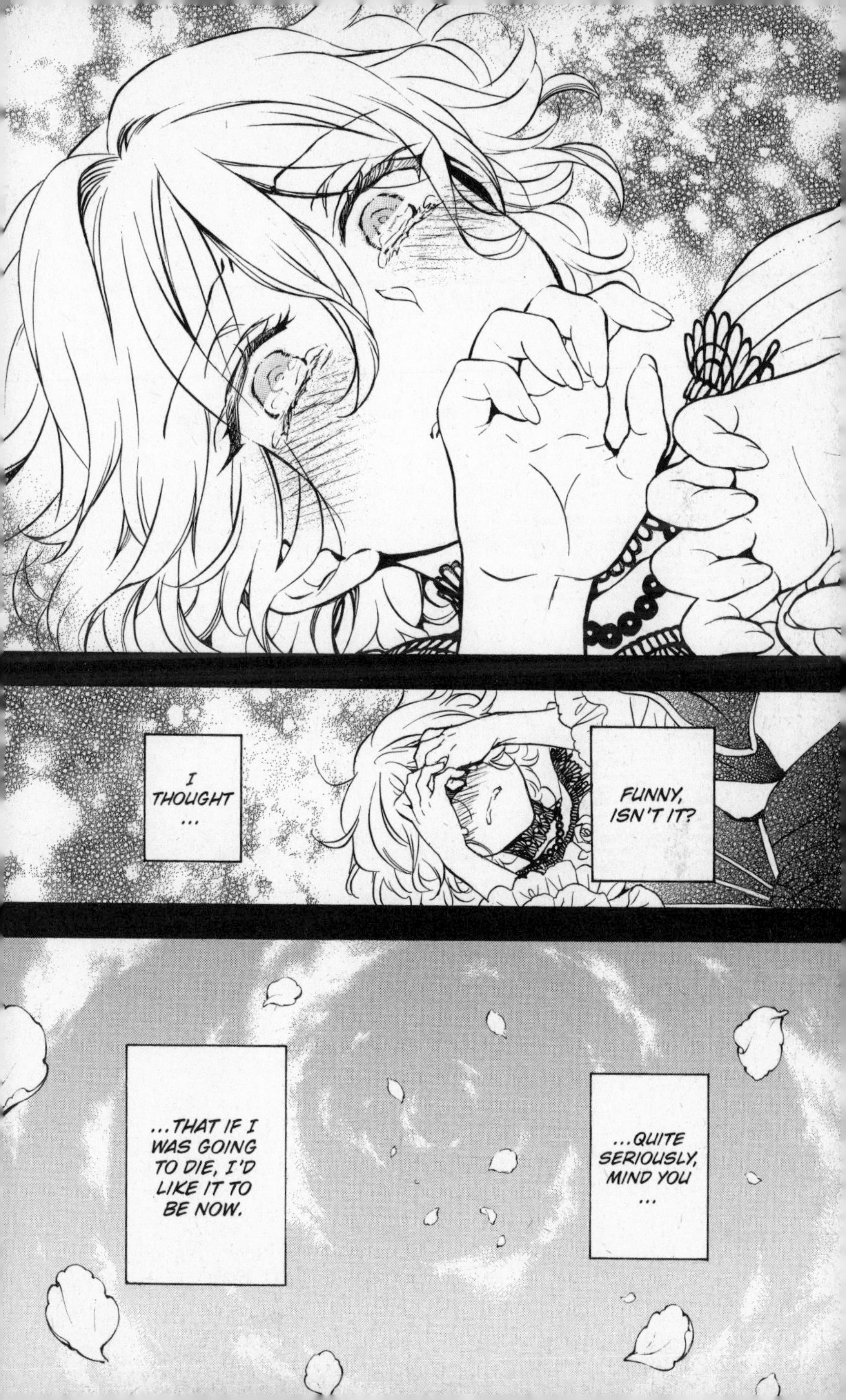
FUNNY, ISN'T IT?
I THOUGHT ...
...QUITE SERIOUSLY, MIND YOU ...
...THAT IF I WAS GOING TO DIE, I'D LIKE IT TO BE NOW.

Mémoire 31

Oiseau et Ciel THE VAMPIRE OF THE D'APCHIERS

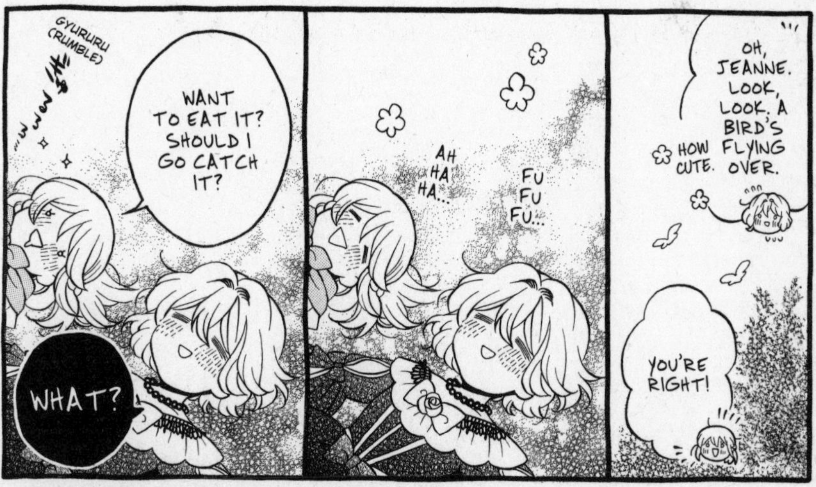
OH, JEANNE. LOOK, LOOK. A BIRD'S FLYING OVER.
HOW CUTE.
YOU'RE RIGHT!
FU FU FU...
AH HA HA...
WANT TO EAT IT? SHOULD I GO CATCH IT?
GYURURU (RUMBLE)
WHAT?

WILD CHILD

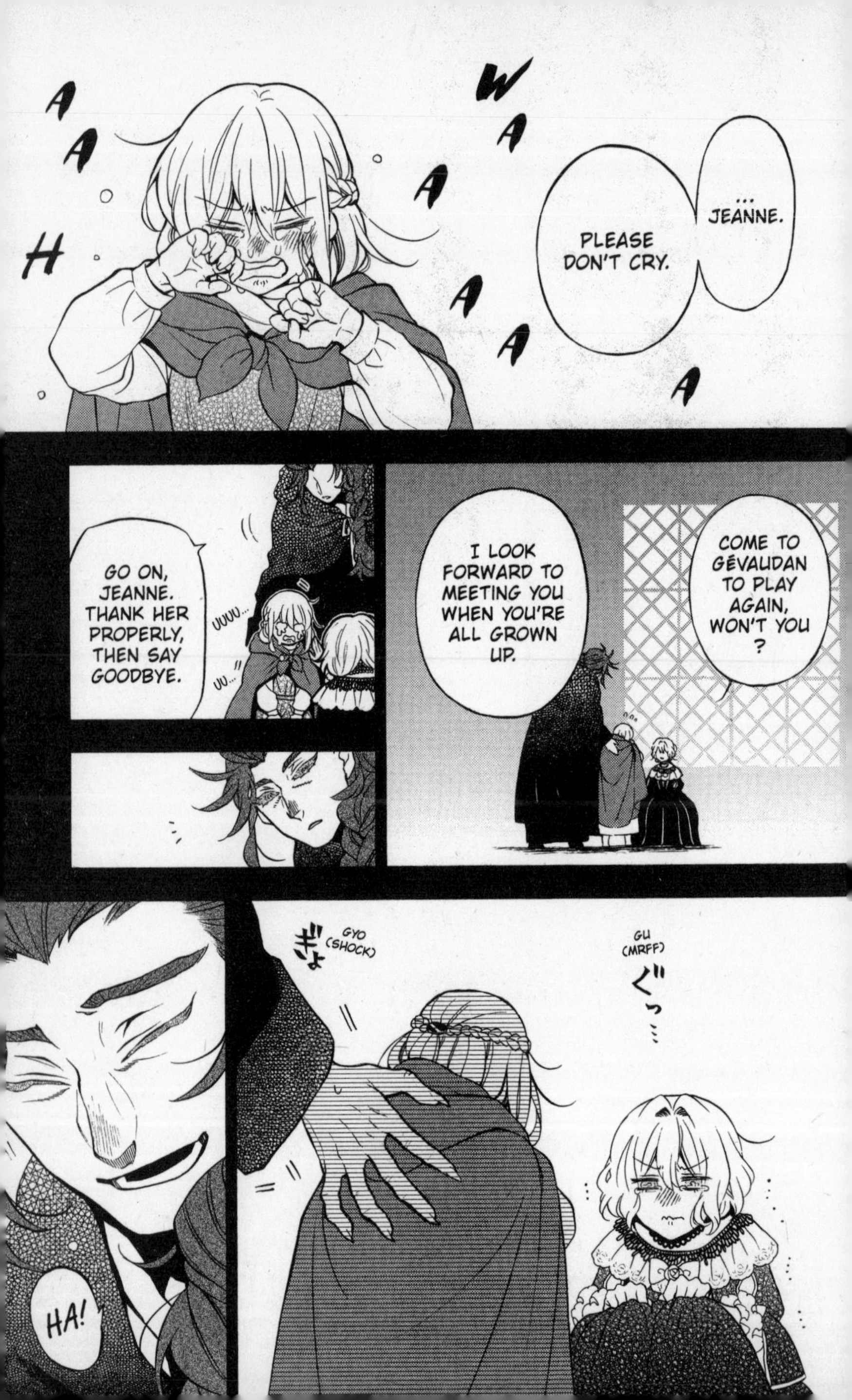
...JEANNE.
PLEASE DON'T CRY.
WAAAAAAA
AAAH
COME TO GÉVAUDAN TO PLAY AGAIN, WON'T YOU?
I LOOK FORWARD TO MEETING YOU WHEN YOU'RE ALL GROWN UP.
UUUU...
UU...!!
GO ON, JEANNE. THANK HER PROPERLY, THEN SAY GOODBYE.
ぐっ
GU (MRFF)
ぎょ
GYO (SHOCK)
HA!

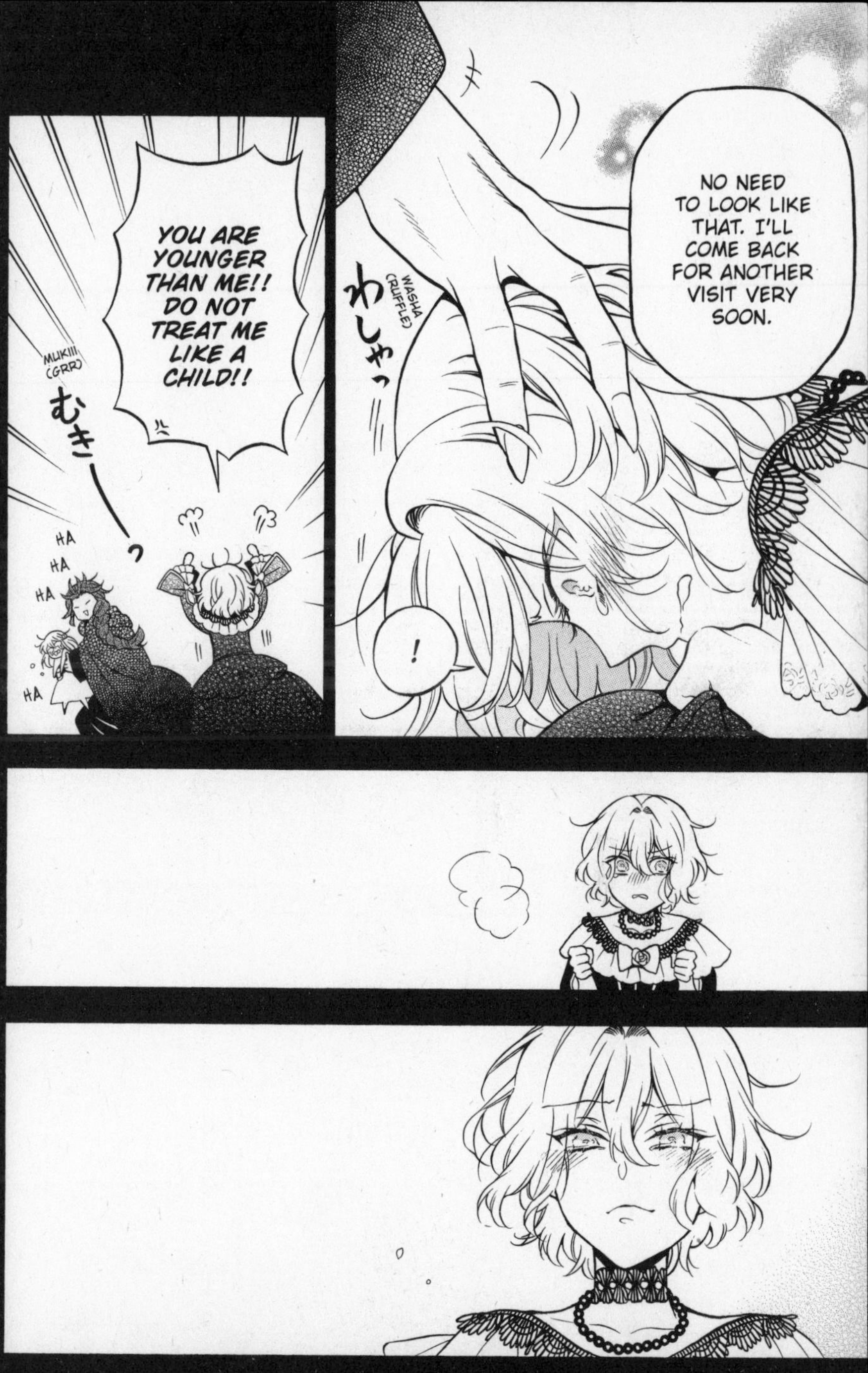
NO NEED TO LOOK LIKE THAT. I'LL COME BACK FOR ANOTHER VISIT VERY SOON.
わしゃっ
WASHA (RUFFLE)
!
YOU ARE YOUNGER THAN ME!! DO NOT TREAT ME LIKE A CHILD!!
むきーっ
MUKIII (GRR)
HA HA HA HA

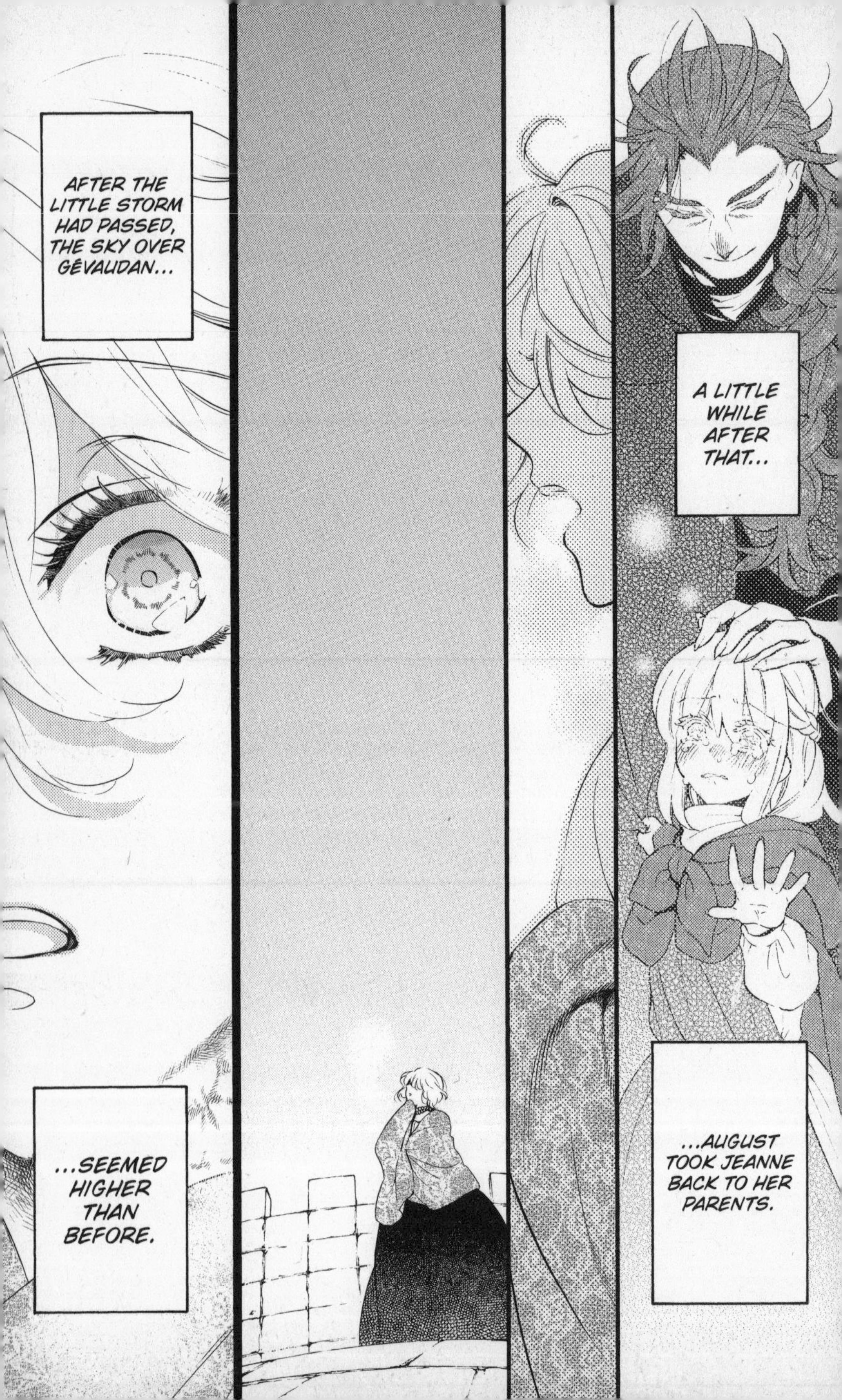
A LITTLE WHILE AFTER THAT...
...AUGUST TOOK JEANNE BACK TO HER PARENTS.
AFTER THE LITTLE STORM HAD PASSED, THE SKY OVER GÉVAUDAN...
...SEEMED HIGHER THAN BEFORE.

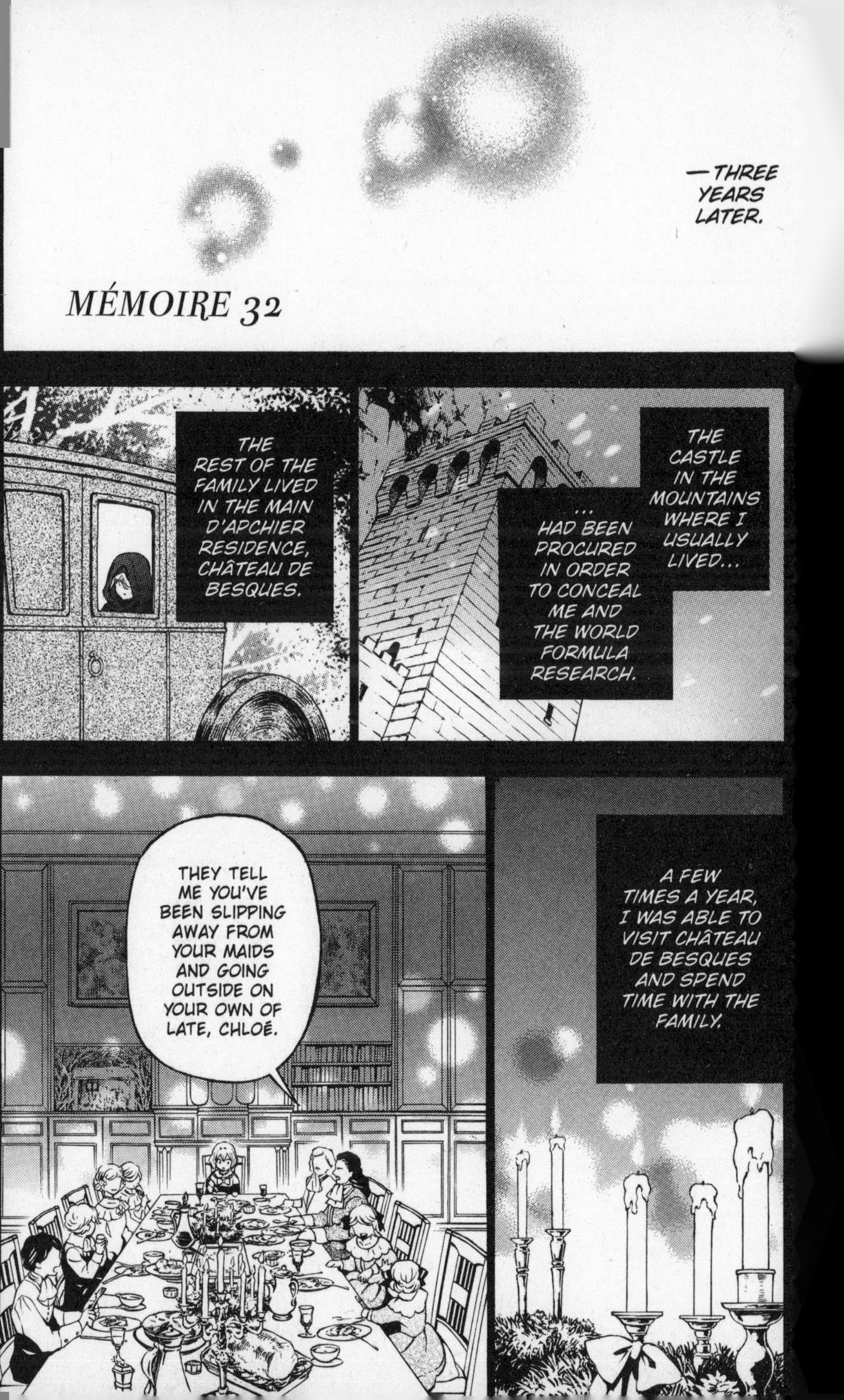
—THREE YEARS LATER.
MÉMOIRE 32
THE CASTLE IN THE MOUNTAINS WHERE I USUALLY LIVED...
...HAD BEEN PROCURED IN ORDER TO CONCEAL ME AND THE WORLD FORMULA RESEARCH.
THE REST OF THE FAMILY LIVED IN THE MAIN D'APCHIER RESIDENCE, CHÂTEAU DE BESQUES.
A FEW TIMES A YEAR, I WAS ABLE TO VISIT CHÂTEAU DE BESQUES AND SPEND TIME WITH THE FAMILY.
THEY TELL ME YOU'VE BEEN SLIPPING AWAY FROM YOUR MAIDS AND GOING OUTSIDE ON YOUR OWN OF LATE, CHLOÉ.

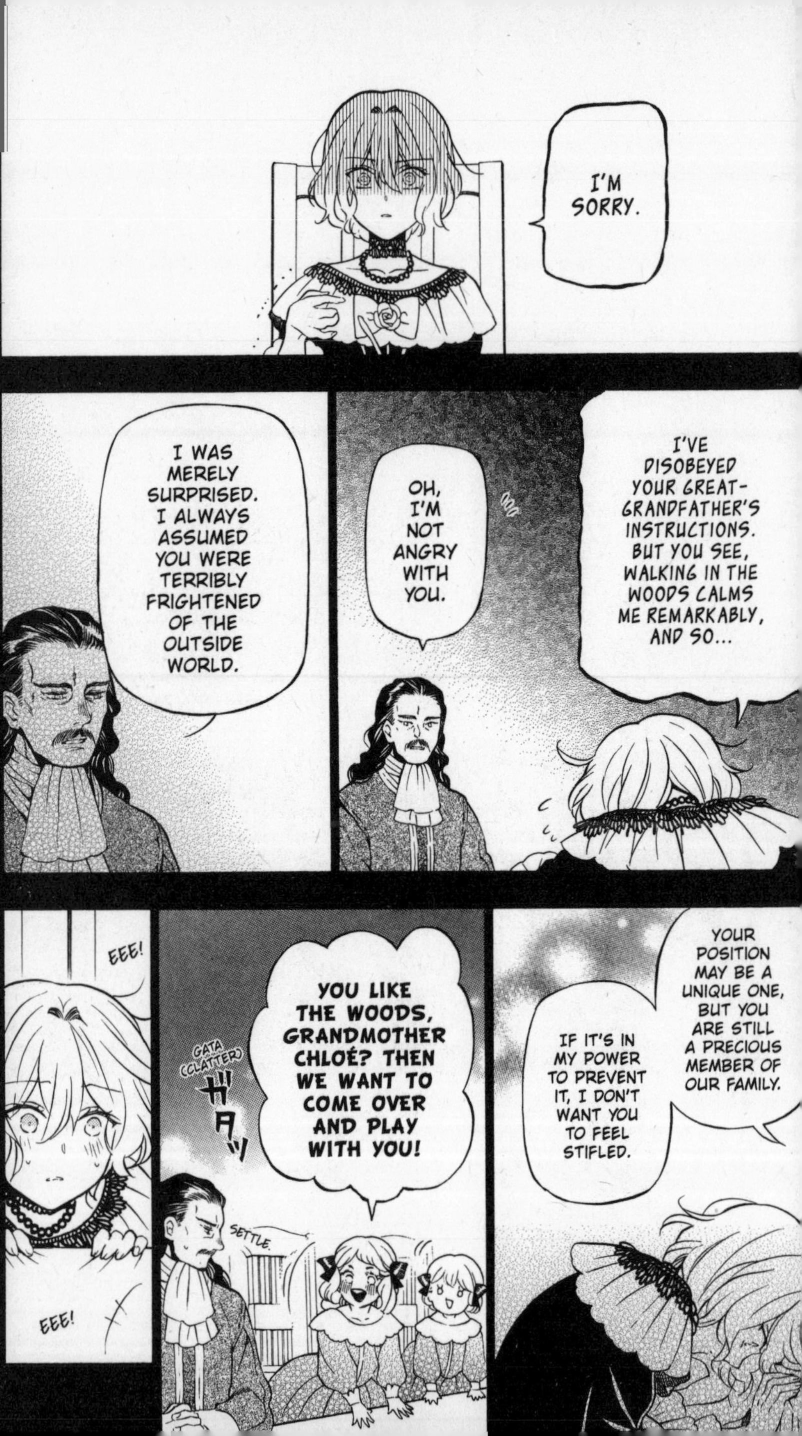
I'M SORRY.
I'VE DISOBEYED YOUR GREAT-GRANDFATHER'S INSTRUCTIONS. BUT YOU SEE, WALKING IN THE WOODS CALMS ME REMARKABLY, AND SO...
OH, I'M NOT ANGRY WITH YOU.
I WAS MERELY SURPRISED. I ALWAYS ASSUMED YOU WERE TERRIBLY FRIGHTENED OF THE OUTSIDE WORLD.
YOUR POSITION MAY BE A UNIQUE ONE, BUT YOU ARE STILL A PRECIOUS MEMBER OF OUR FAMILY.
IF IT'S IN MY POWER TO PREVENT IT, I DON'T WANT YOU TO FEEL STIFLED.
GATA (CLATTER)
ガタッ
YOU LIKE THE WOODS, GRANDMOTHER CHLOÉ? THEN WE WANT TO COME OVER AND PLAY WITH YOU!
SETTLE.
EEE!
EEE!

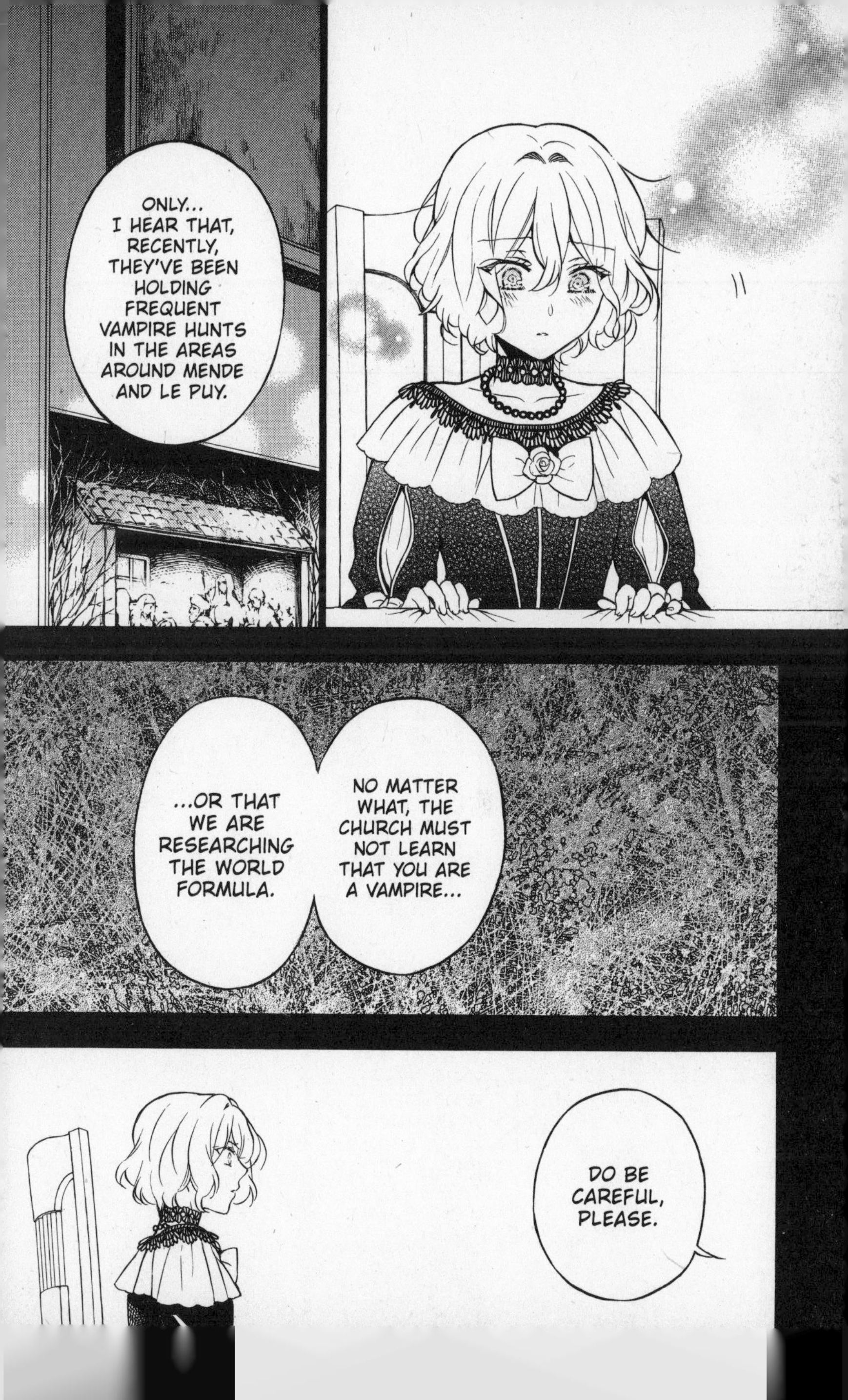
ONLY... I HEAR THAT, RECENTLY, THEY'VE BEEN HOLDING FREQUENT VAMPIRE HUNTS IN THE AREAS AROUND MENDE AND LE PUY.
NO MATTER WHAT, THE CHURCH MUST NOT LEARN THAT YOU ARE A VAMPIRE...
...OR THAT WE ARE RESEARCHING THE WORLD FORMULA.
DO BE CAREFUL, PLEASE.

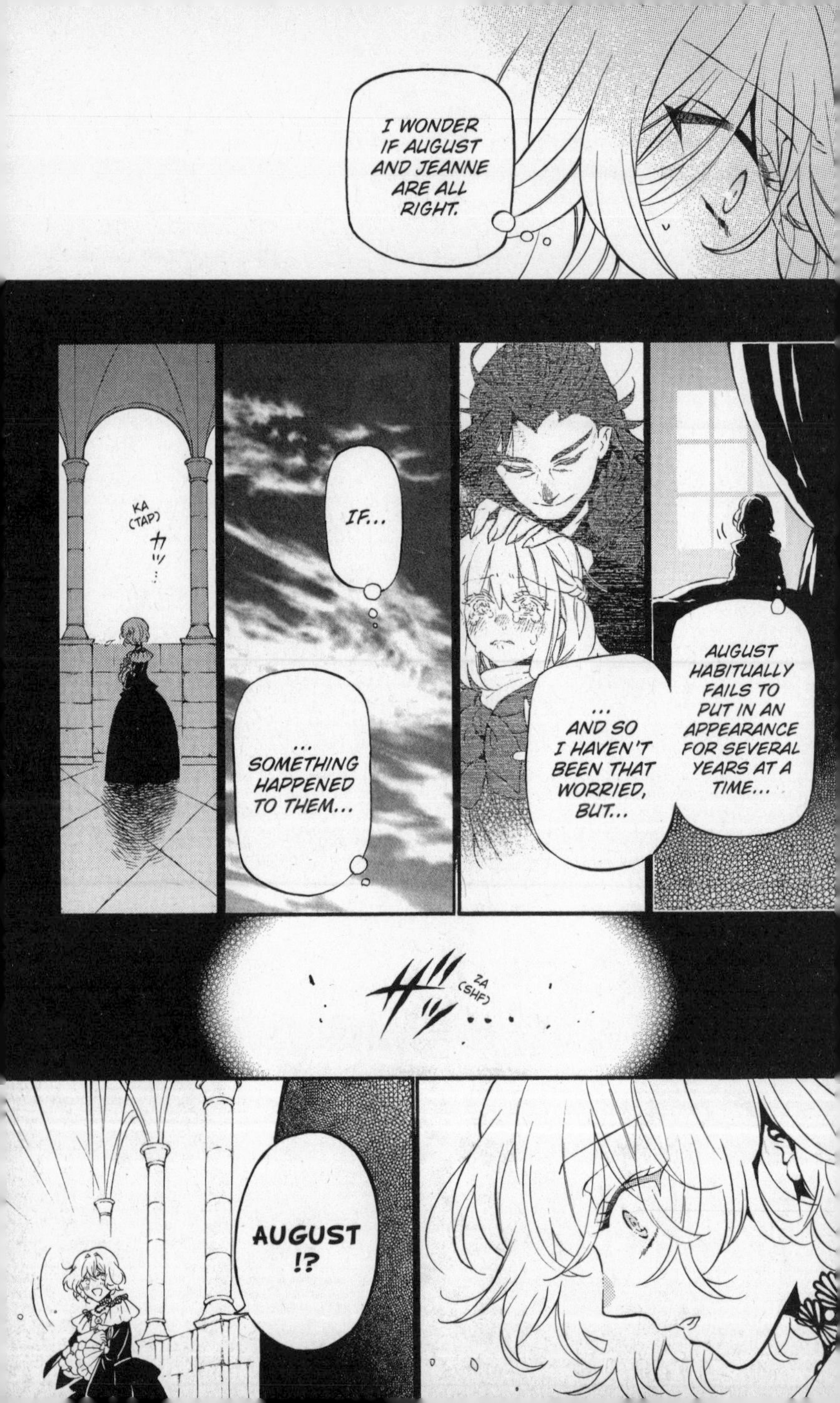
I WONDER IF AUGUST AND JEANNE ARE ALL RIGHT.
AUGUST HABITUALLY FAILS TO PUT IN AN APPEARANCE FOR SEVERAL YEARS AT A TIME...
...AND SO I HAVEN'T BEEN THAT WORRIED, BUT...
IF...
...SOMETHING HAPPENED TO THEM...
KA (TAP)
カッ…
ザッ
ZA (SHF)
AUGUST !?

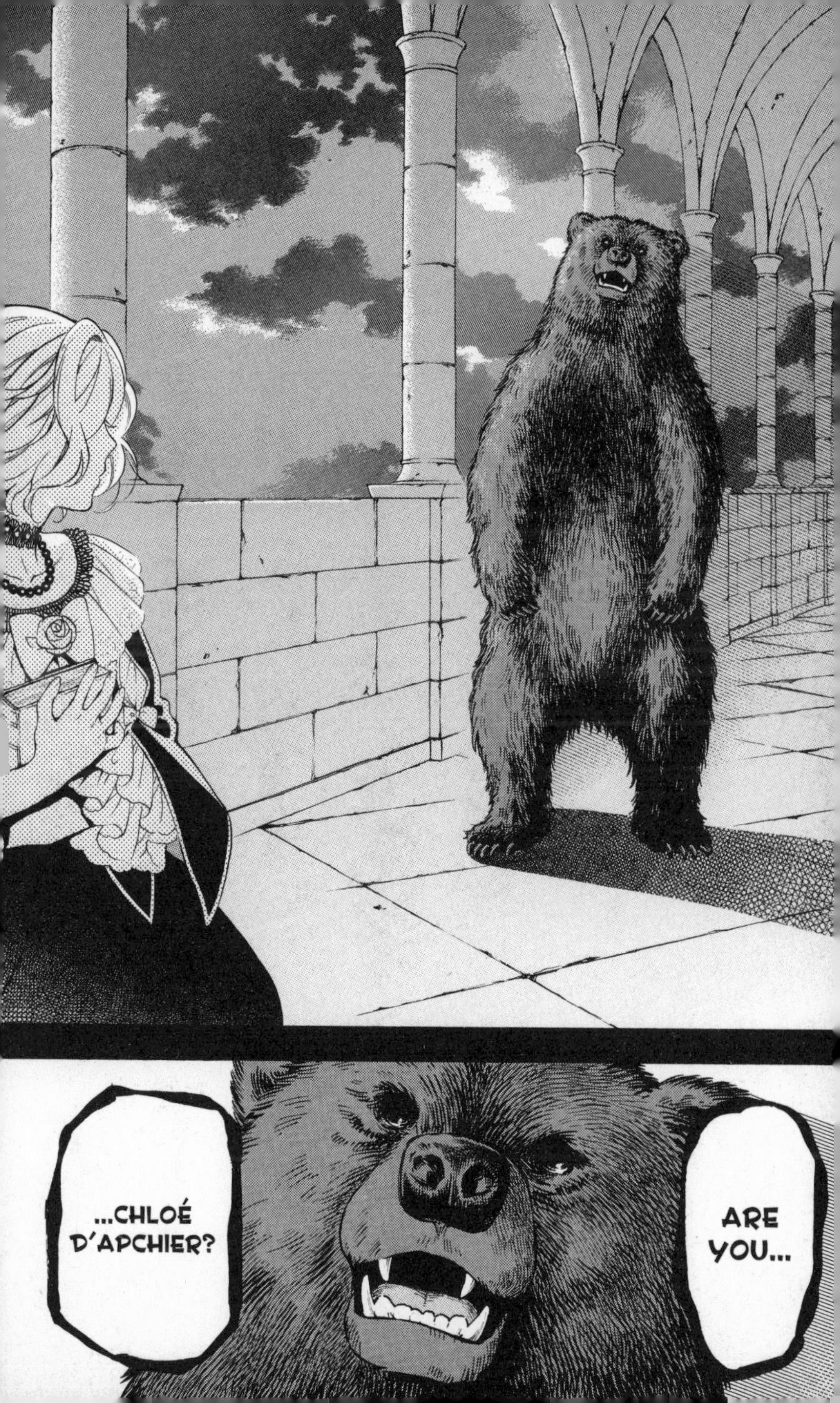
ARE YOU...
...CHLOÉ D'APCHIER?

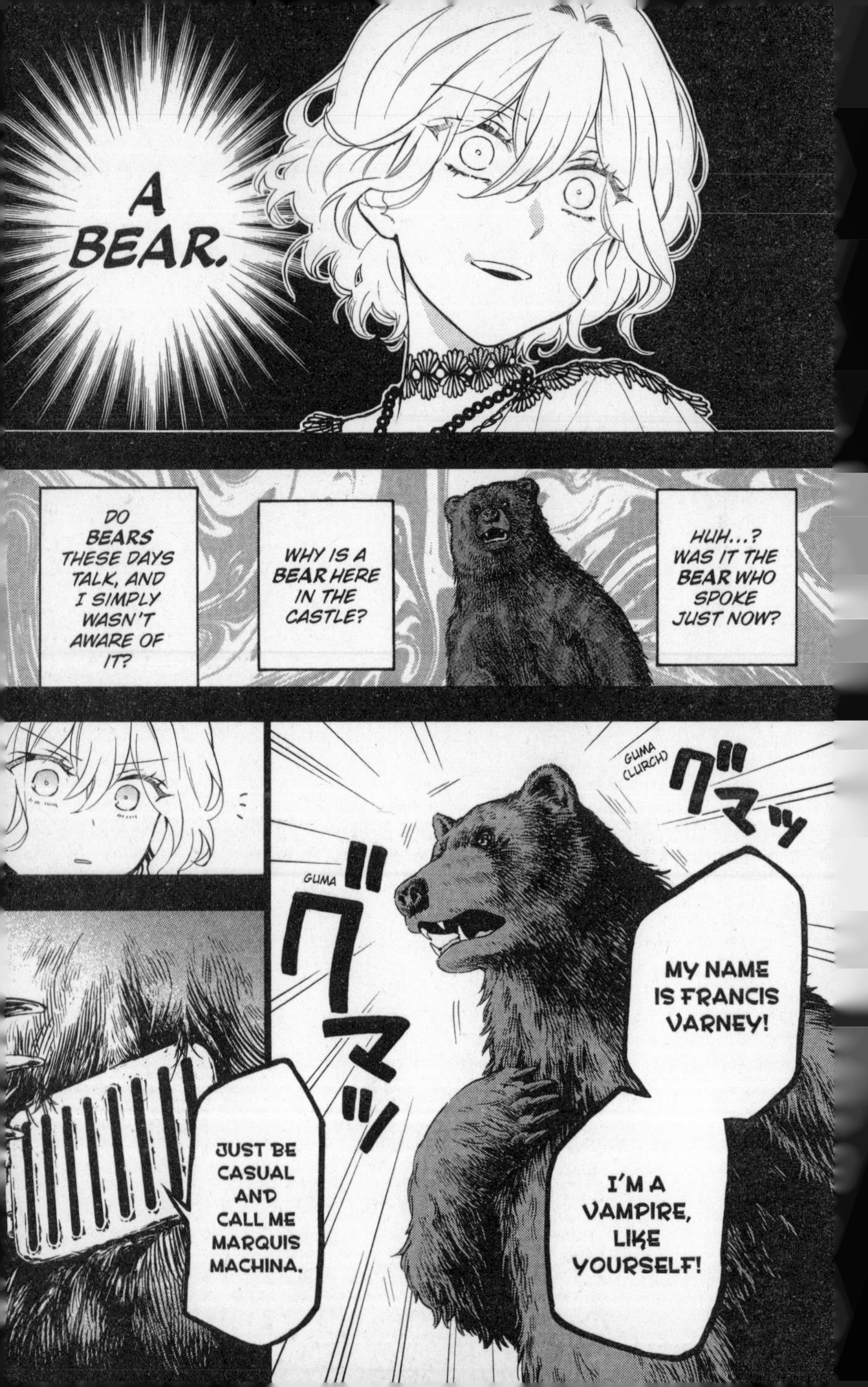
A BEAR.
HUH...? WAS IT THE BEAR WHO SPOKE JUST NOW?
WHY IS A BEAR HERE IN THE CASTLE?
DO BEARS THESE DAYS TALK, AND I SIMPLY WASN'T AWARE OF IT?
グマッ
GUMA (LURCH)
グマッ
GUMA
MY NAME IS FRANCIS VARNEY!
I'M A VAMPIRE, LIKE YOURSELF!
JUST BE CASUAL AND CALL ME MARQUIS MACHINA.

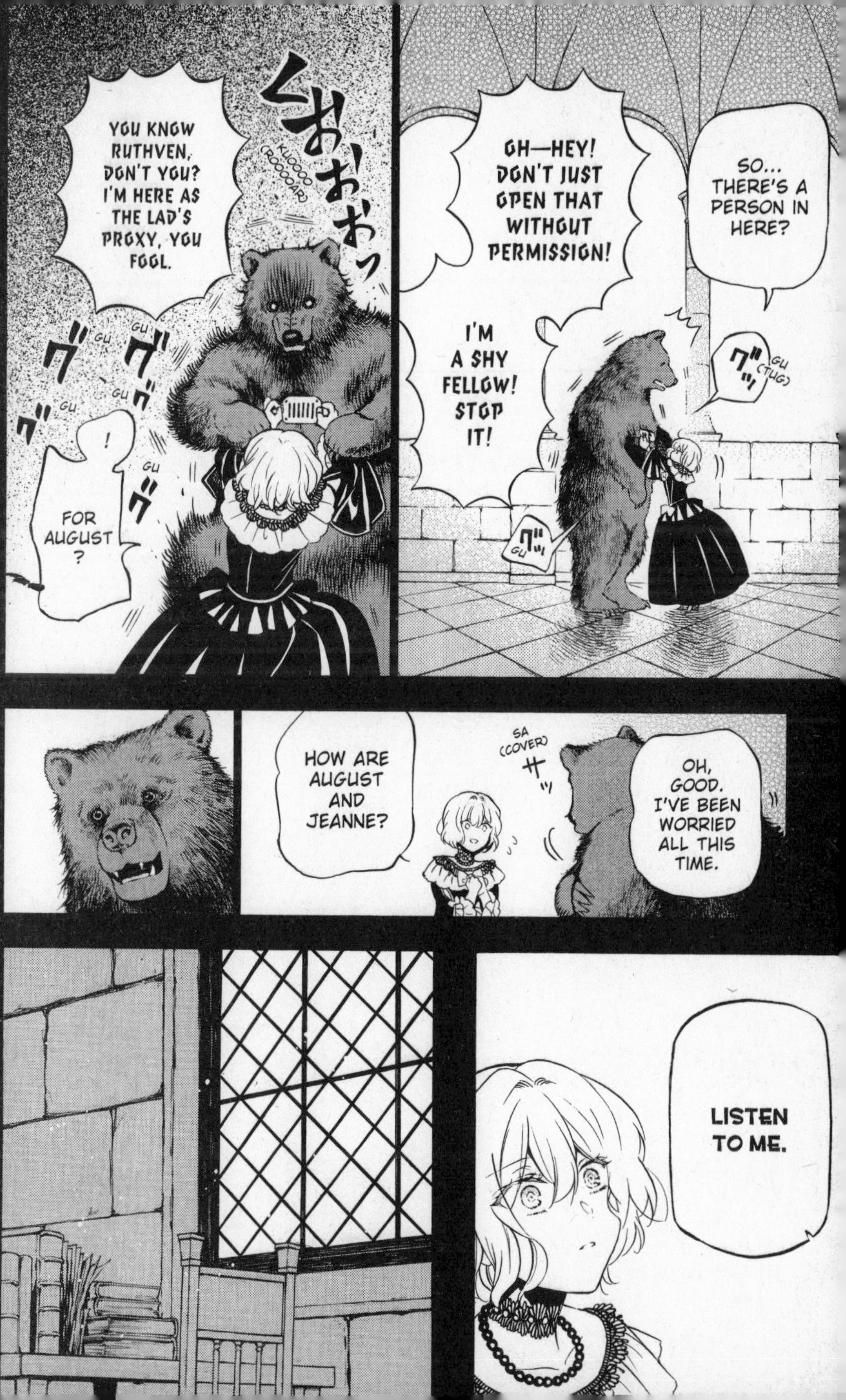
SO... THERE'S A PERSON IN HERE?
OH—HEY! DON'T JUST OPEN THAT WITHOUT PERMISSION!
GU (TUG)
I'M A SHY FELLOW! STOP IT!
GU
KUOOOO (ROOOOAR)
YOU KNOW RUTHVEN, DON'T YOU? I'M HERE AS THE LAD'S PROXY, YOU FOOL.
GU
GU
GU
GU
! FOR AUGUST ?
SA (COVER)
OH, GOOD. I'VE BEEN WORRIED ALL THIS TIME.
HOW ARE AUGUST AND JEANNE?
LISTEN TO ME.

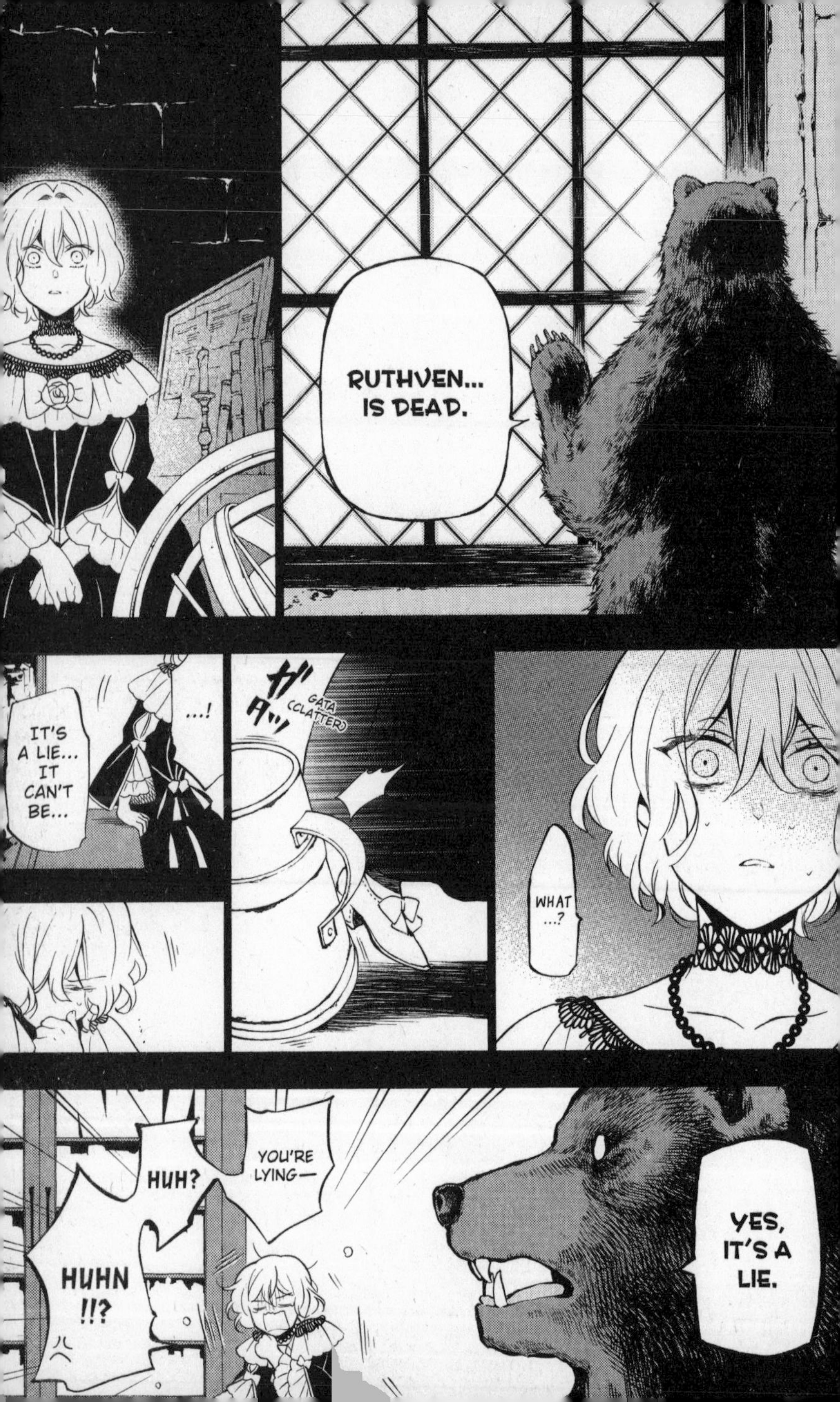
RUTHVEN... IS DEAD.
WHAT ...?
ガタッ
GATA (CLATTER)
...!
IT'S A LIE... IT CAN'T BE...
YES, IT'S A LIE.
YOU'RE LYING—
HUH?
HUHN !!?

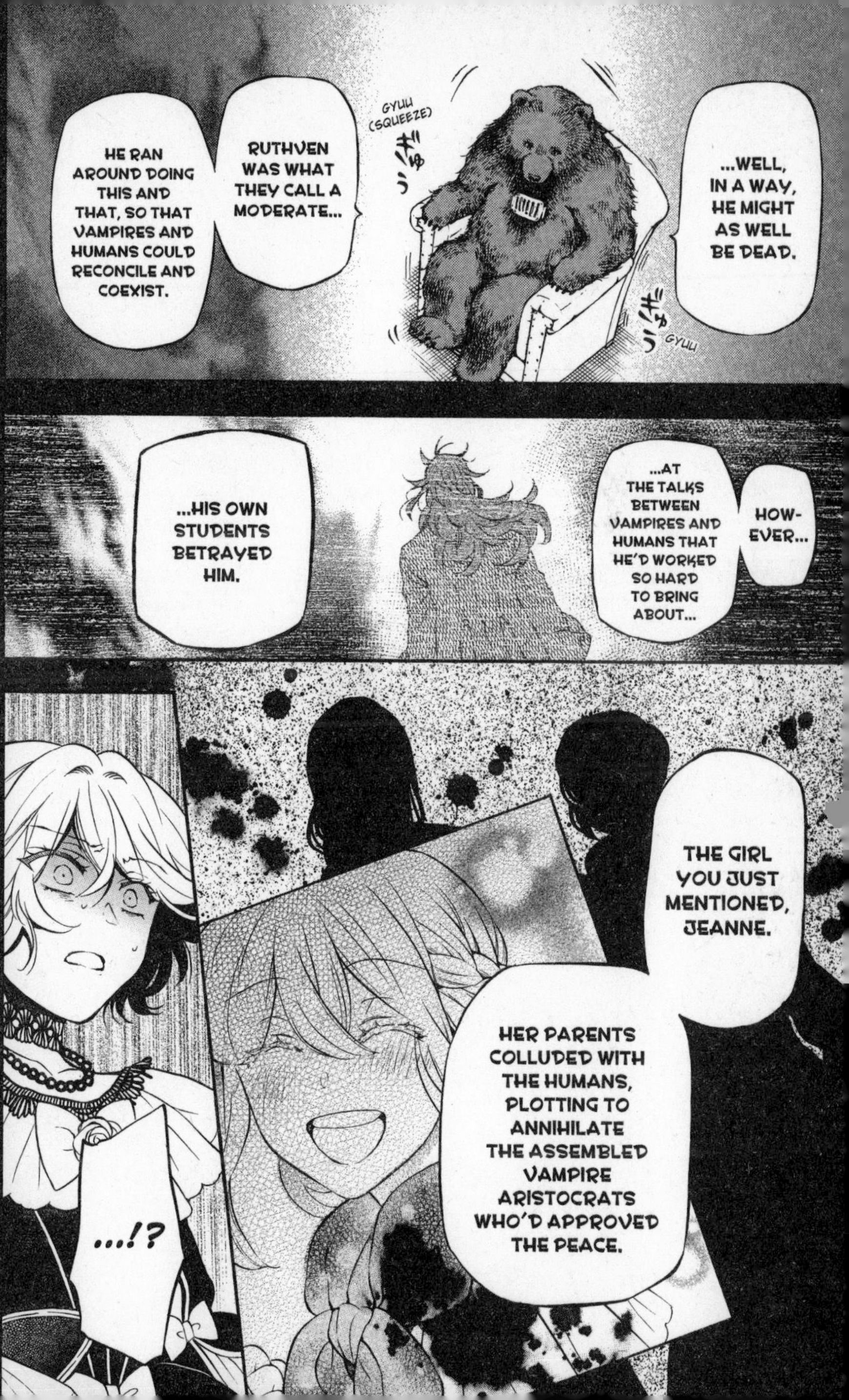
...WELL, IN A WAY, HE MIGHT AS WELL BE DEAD.
GYUU (SQUEEZE)
GYUU
RUTHVEN WAS WHAT THEY CALL A MODERATE...
HE RAN AROUND DOING THIS AND THAT, SO THAT VAMPIRES AND HUMANS COULD RECONCILE AND COEXIST.
HOW-EVER...
...AT THE TALKS BETWEEN VAMPIRES AND HUMANS THAT HE'D WORKED SO HARD TO BRING ABOUT...
...HIS OWN STUDENTS BETRAYED HIM.
THE GIRL YOU JUST MENTIONED, JEANNE.
HER PARENTS COLLUDED WITH THE HUMANS, PLOTTING TO ANNIHILATE THE ASSEMBLED VAMPIRE ARISTOCRATS WHO'D APPROVED THE PEACE.
...!?

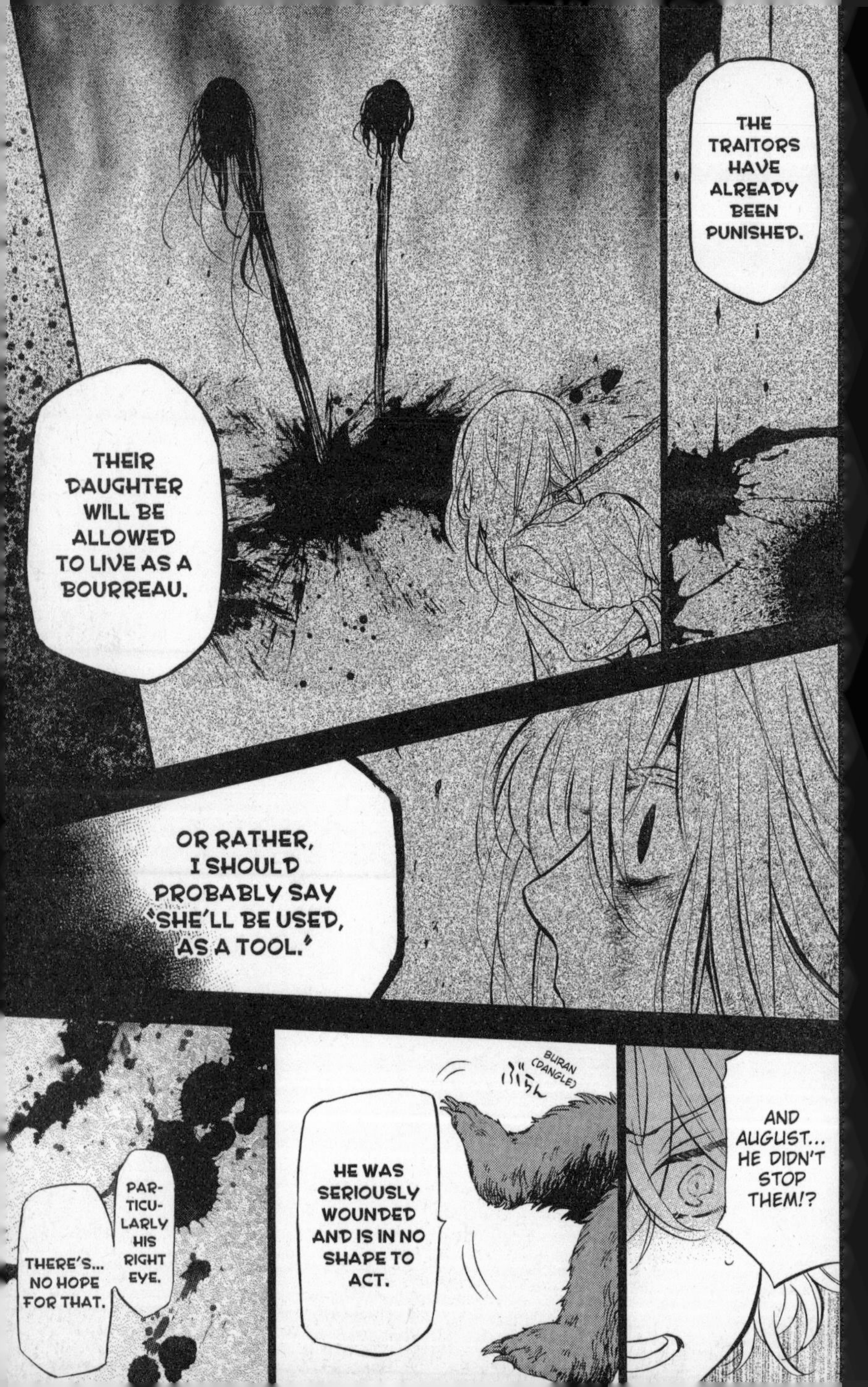
THE TRAITORS HAVE ALREADY BEEN PUNISHED.
THEIR DAUGHTER WILL BE ALLOWED TO LIVE AS A BOURREAU.
OR RATHER, I SHOULD PROBABLY SAY "SHE'LL BE USED, AS A TOOL."
AND AUGUST... HE DIDN'T STOP THEM!?
ぶらん BURAN (DANGLE)
HE WAS SERIOUSLY WOUNDED AND IS IN NO SHAPE TO ACT.
PAR-TICU-LARLY HIS RIGHT EYE.
THERE'S... NO HOPE FOR THAT.

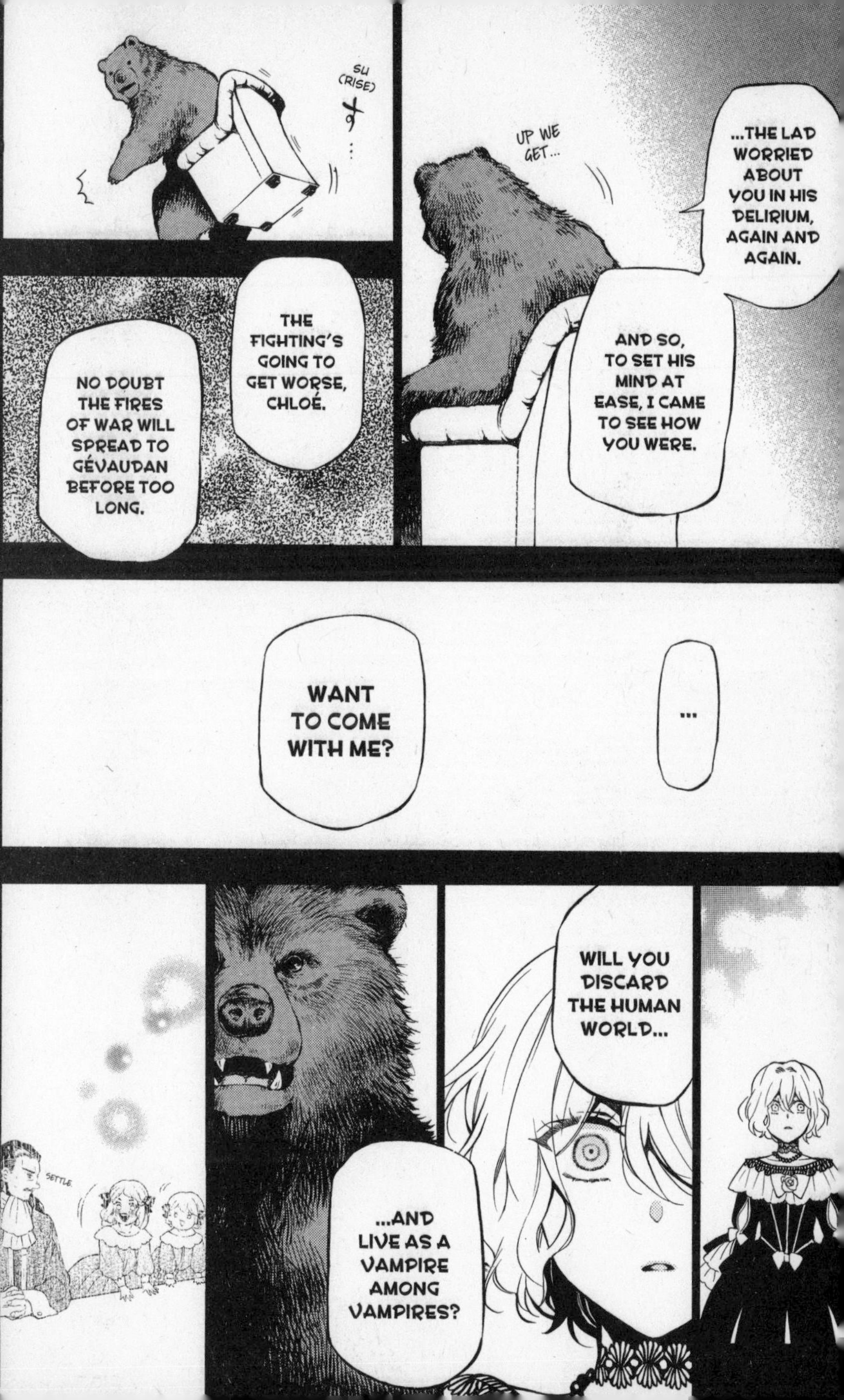
...THE LAD WORRIED ABOUT YOU IN HIS DELIRIUM, AGAIN AND AGAIN.
UP WE GET...
AND SO, TO SET HIS MIND AT EASE, I CAME TO SEE HOW YOU WERE.
SU (RISE)
す...
THE FIGHTING'S GOING TO GET WORSE, CHLOÉ.
NO DOUBT THE FIRES OF WAR WILL SPREAD TO GÉVAUDAN BEFORE TOO LONG.
...
WANT TO COME WITH ME?
WILL YOU DISCARD THE HUMAN WORLD...
...AND LIVE AS A VAMPIRE AMONG VAMPIRES?
SETTLE.

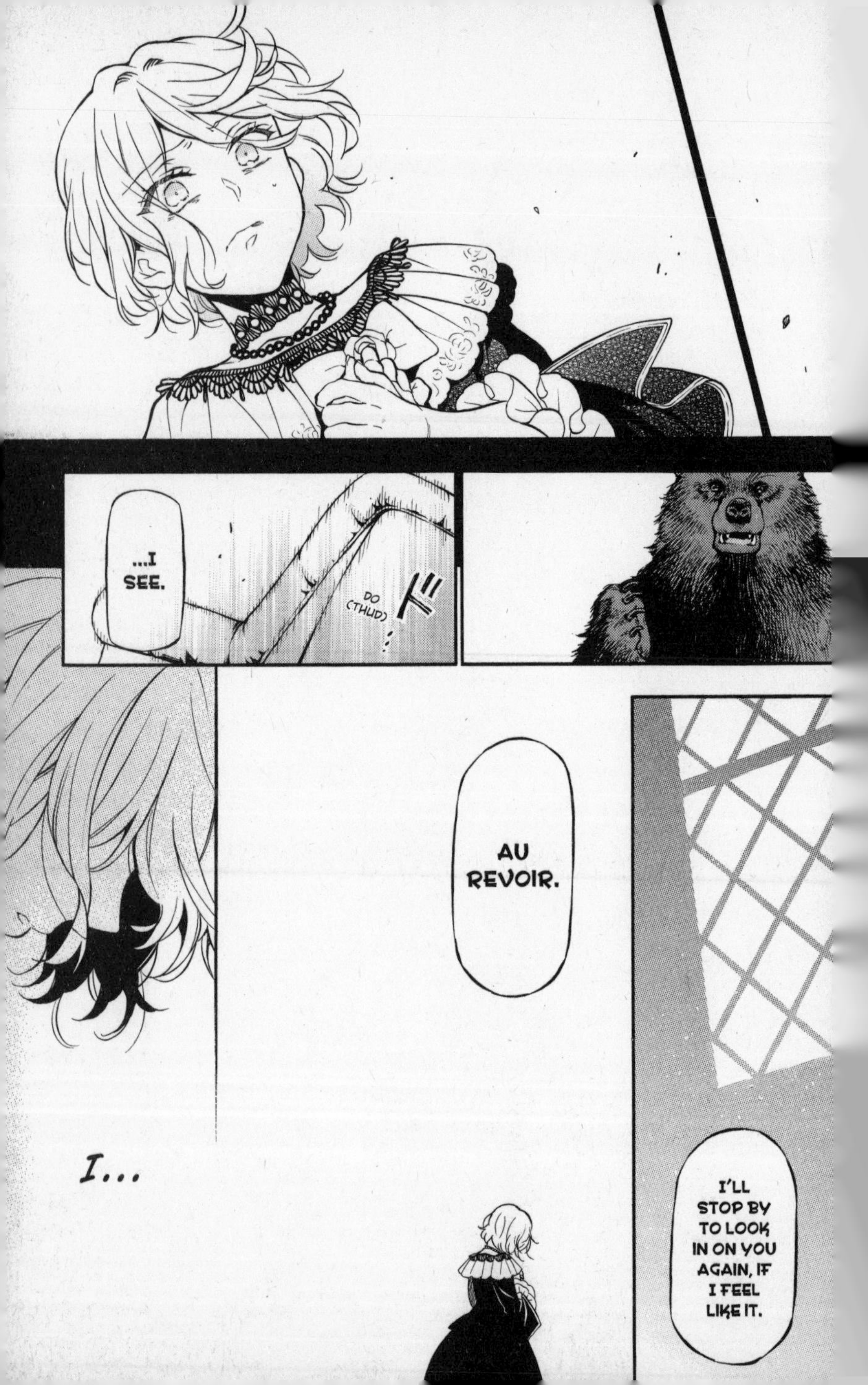
...I SEE.
DO (THUD)
AU REVOIR.
I'LL STOP BY TO LOOK IN ON YOU AGAIN, IF I FEEL LIKE IT.
I...

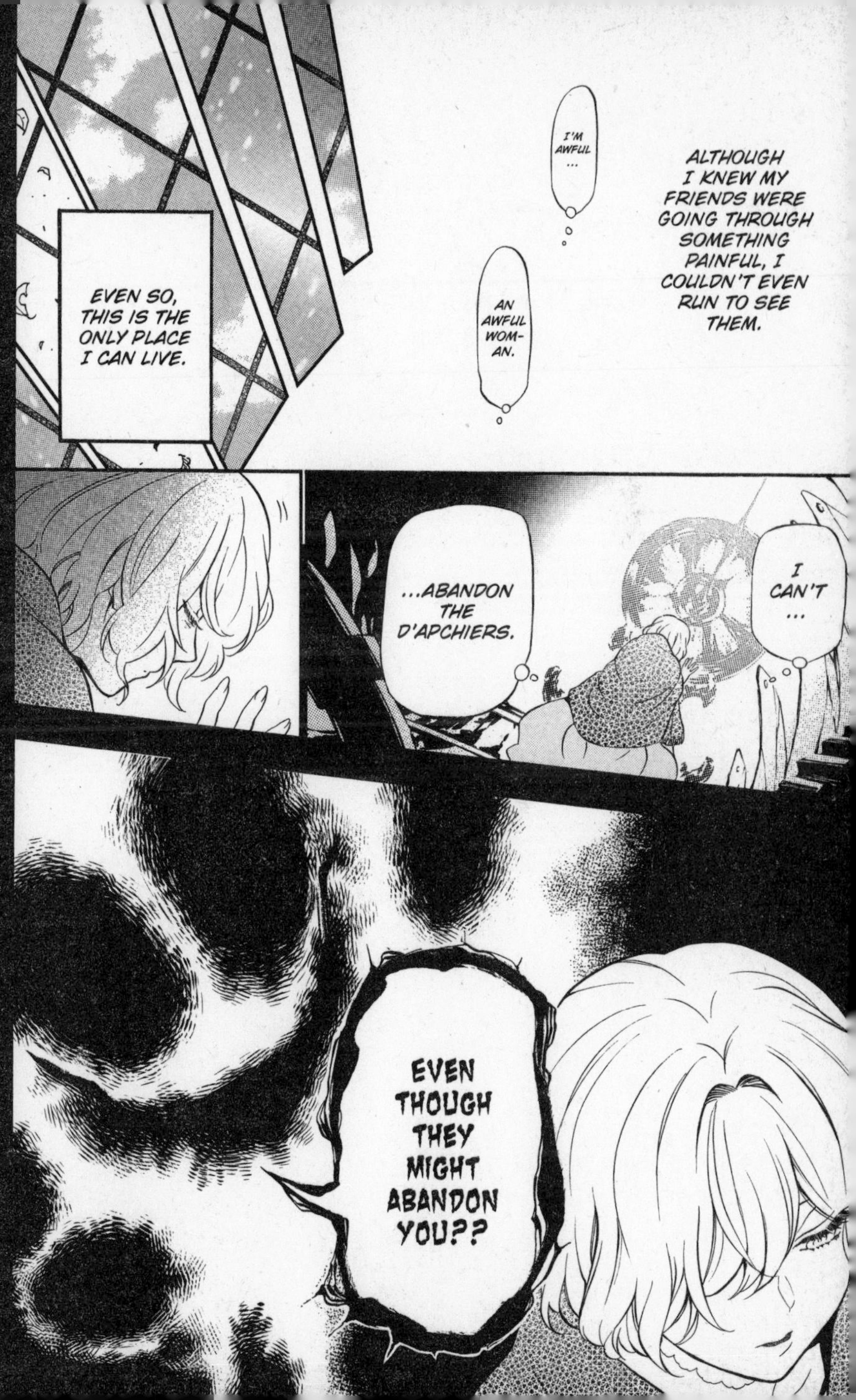
ALTHOUGH I KNEW MY FRIENDS WERE GOING THROUGH SOMETHING PAINFUL, I COULDN'T EVEN RUN TO SEE THEM.
I'M AWFUL ...
AN AWFUL WOM-AN.
EVEN SO, THIS IS THE ONLY PLACE I CAN LIVE.
I CAN'T ...
...ABANDON THE D'APCHIERS.
EVEN THOUGH THEY MIGHT ABANDON YOU??

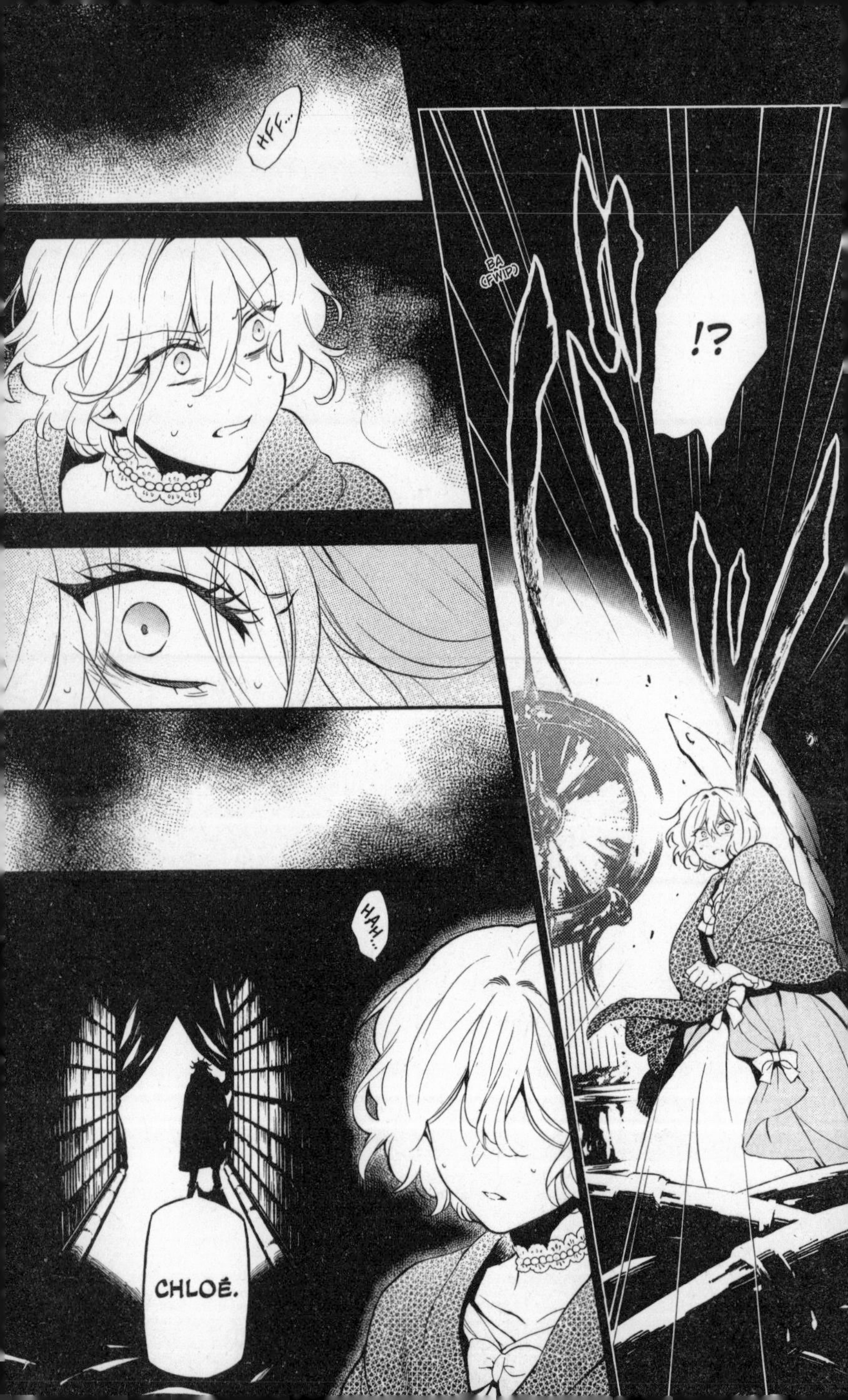
BA (FWIP)
!?
HFF...
HAH...
CHLOÉ.

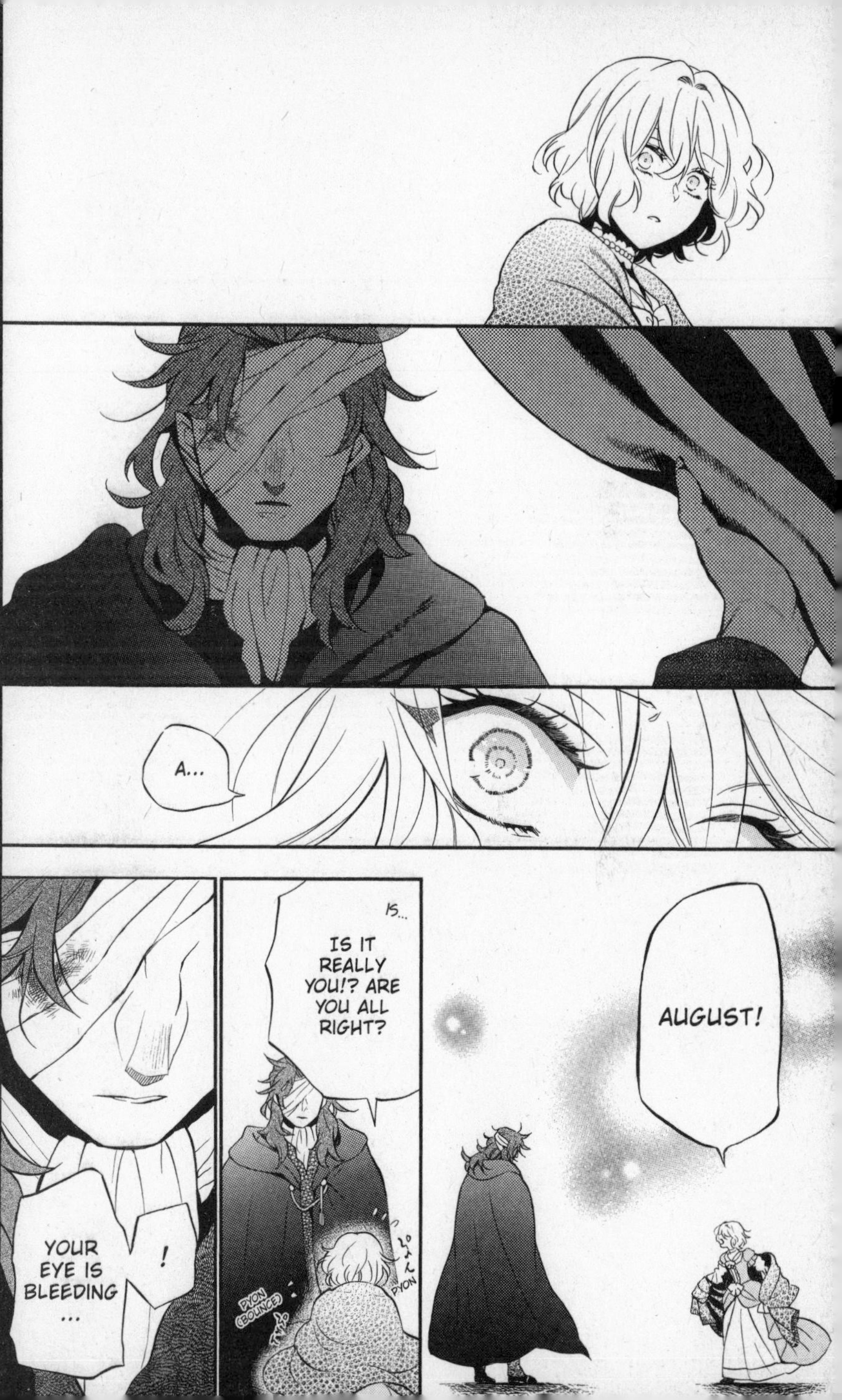
A...
AUGUST!
IS...
IS IT REALLY YOU!? ARE YOU ALL RIGHT?
DYON
DYON (BOUNCE)
!
YOUR EYE IS BLEEDING ...

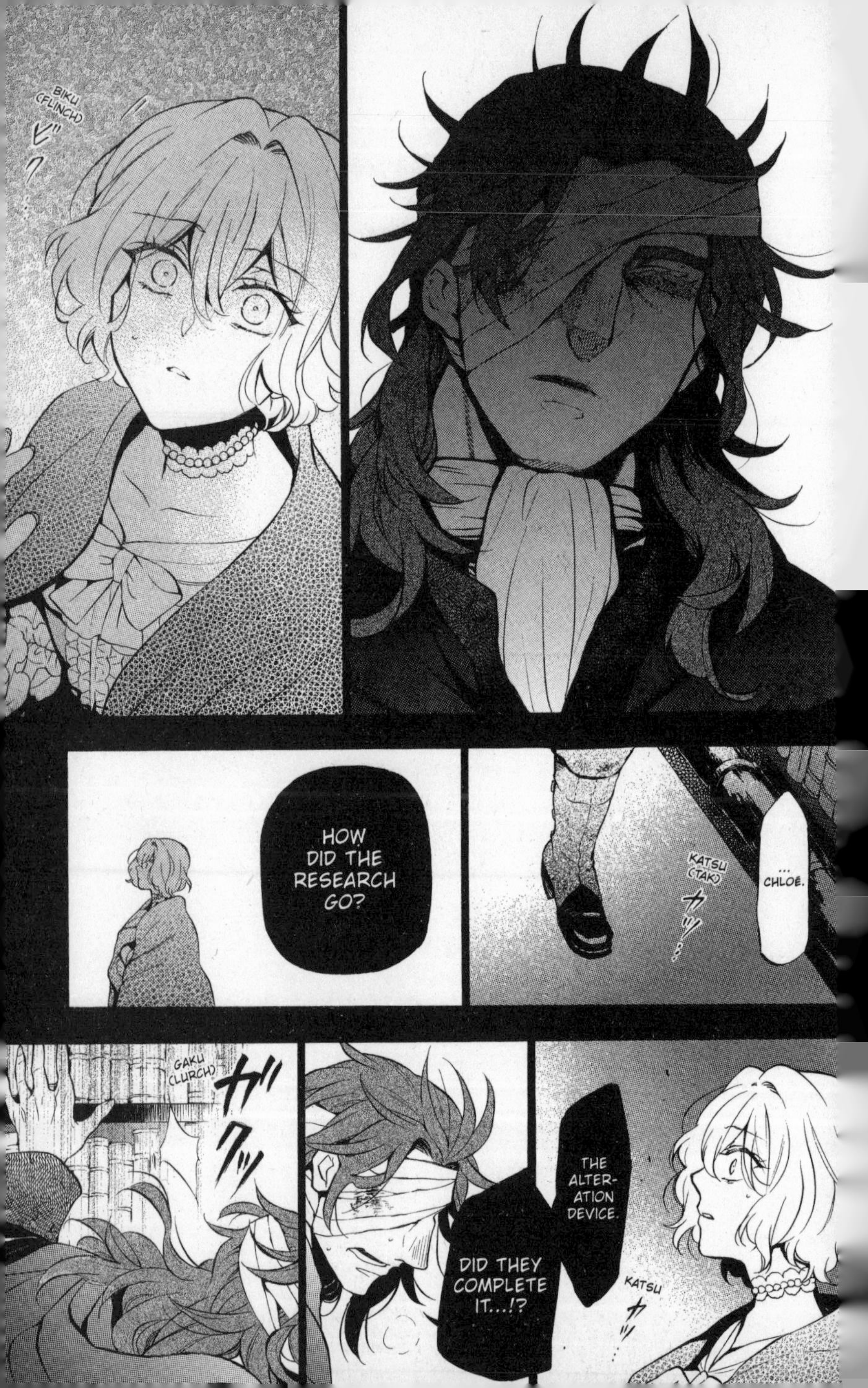
BIKU (FLINCH)
ビク…
...CHLOE.
KATSU (TAK)
HOW DID THE RESEARCH GO?
THE ALTER-ATION DEVICE.
KATSU
DID THEY COMPLETE IT...!?
GAKU (LURCH)

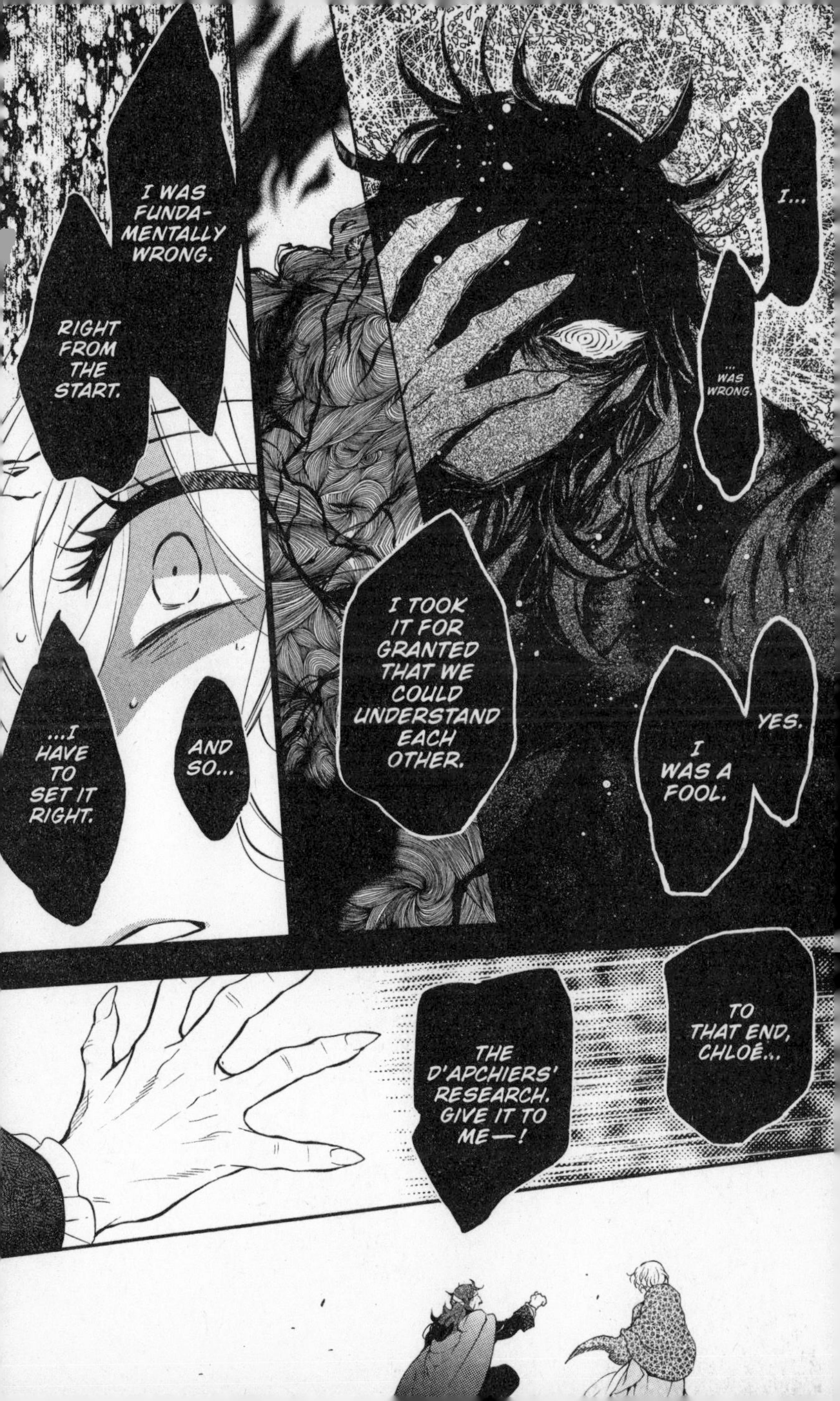
I...
...WAS WRONG.
YES. I WAS A FOOL.
I TOOK IT FOR GRANTED THAT WE COULD UNDERSTAND EACH OTHER.
I WAS FUNDAMENTALLY WRONG.
RIGHT FROM THE START.
AND SO...
...I HAVE TO SET IT RIGHT.
TO THAT END, CHLOÉ...
THE D'APCHIERS' RESEARCH. GIVE IT TO ME—!

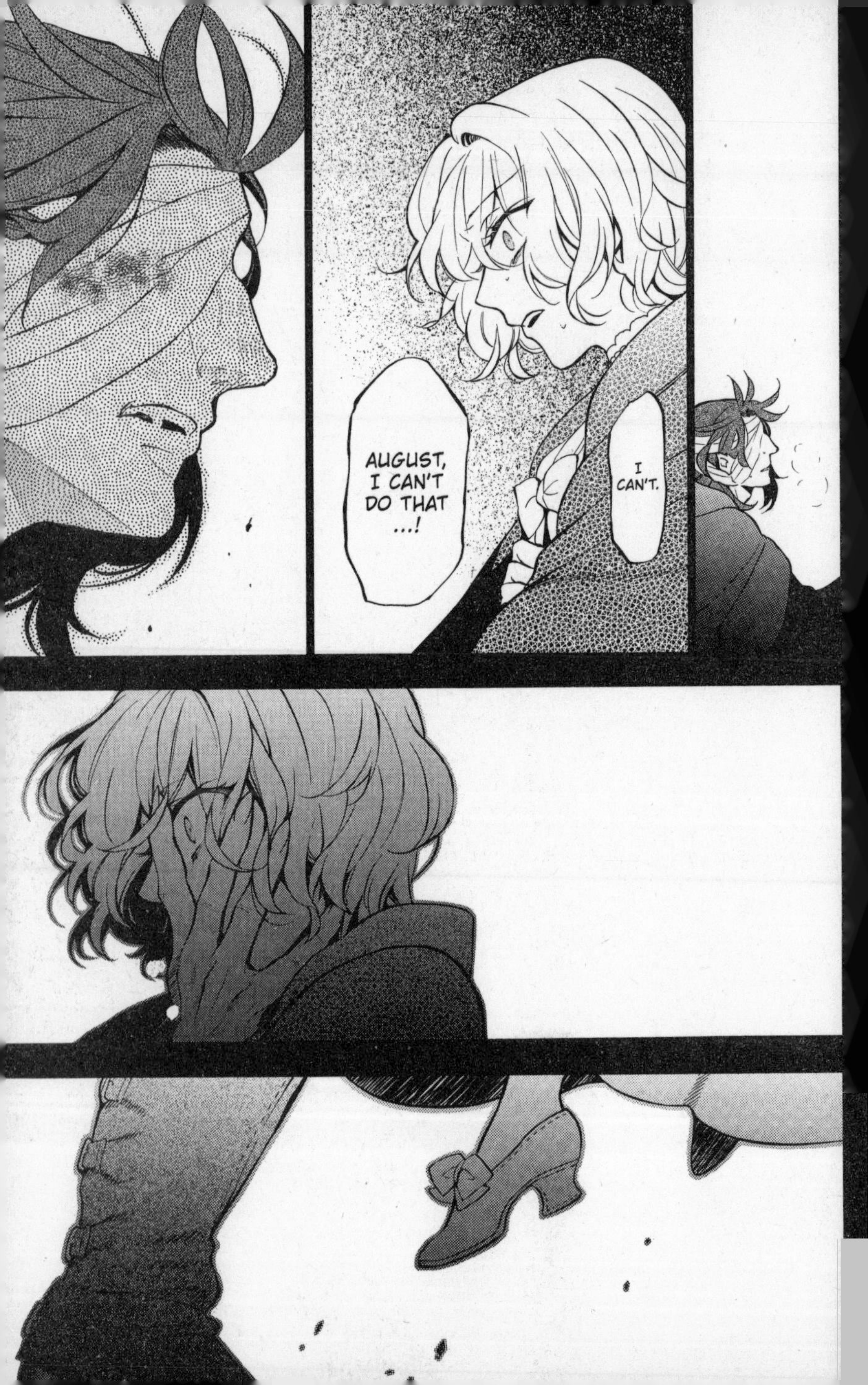
I CAN'T.
AUGUST, I CAN'T DO THAT ...!

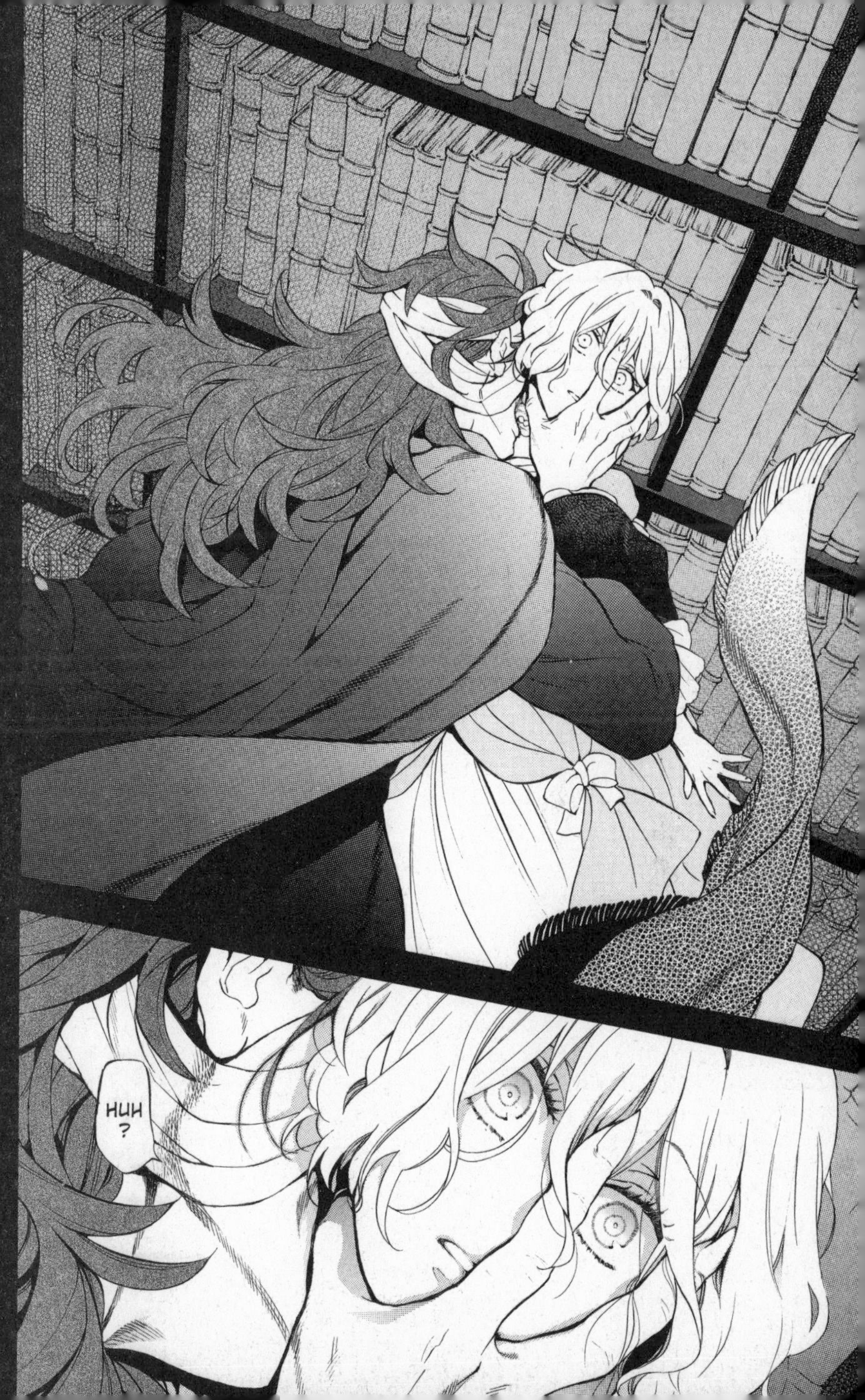
HUH
?

Mémoire 32 Visiteur FOOTFALLS OF THE BEAST

Les Mémoires de Vanitas

THE CASE STUDY OF
VANITAS

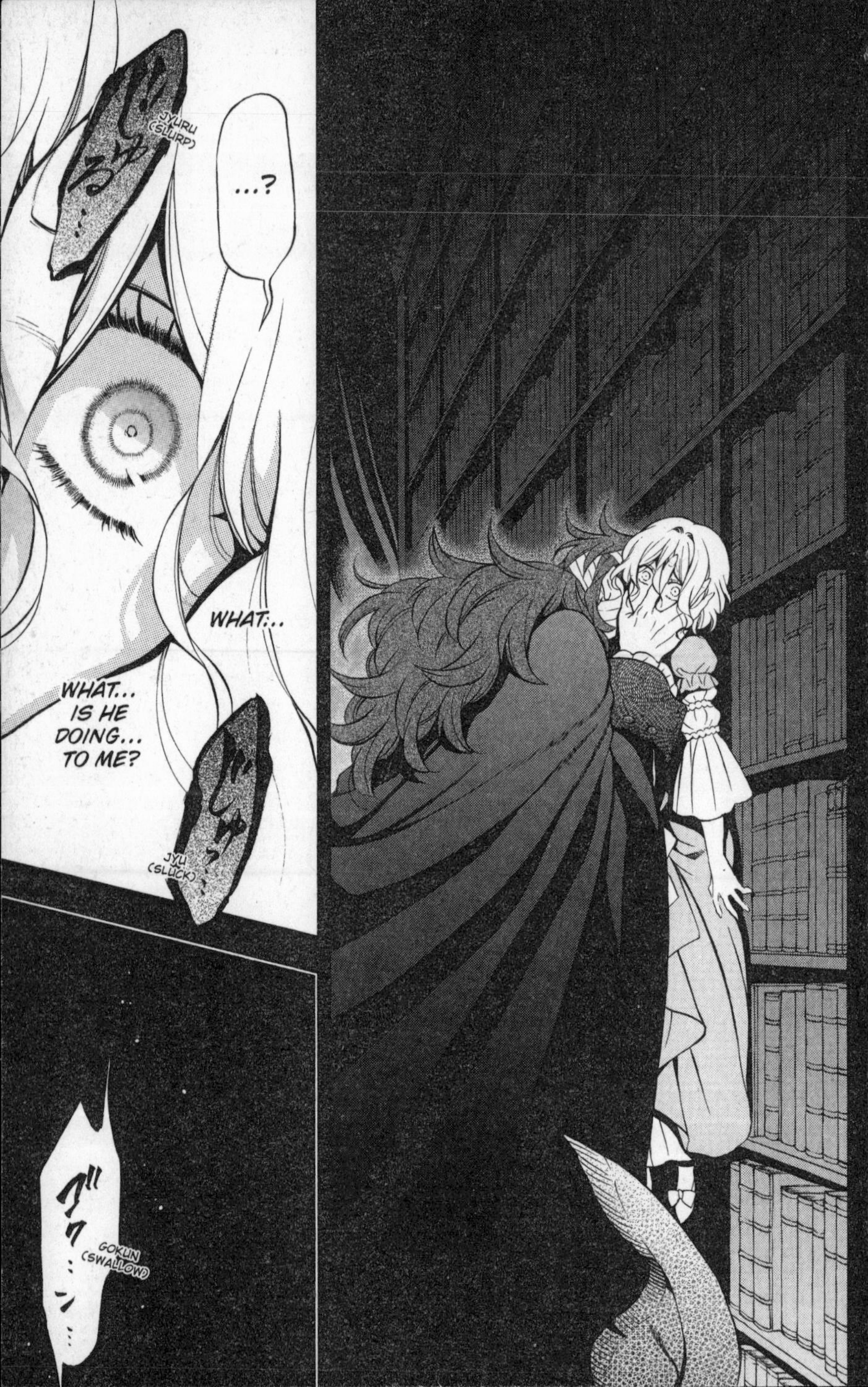
...?
JYURU (SLURP)
WHAT...
WHAT... IS HE DOING... TO ME?
JYU (SLUCK)
GOKUN (SWALLOW)

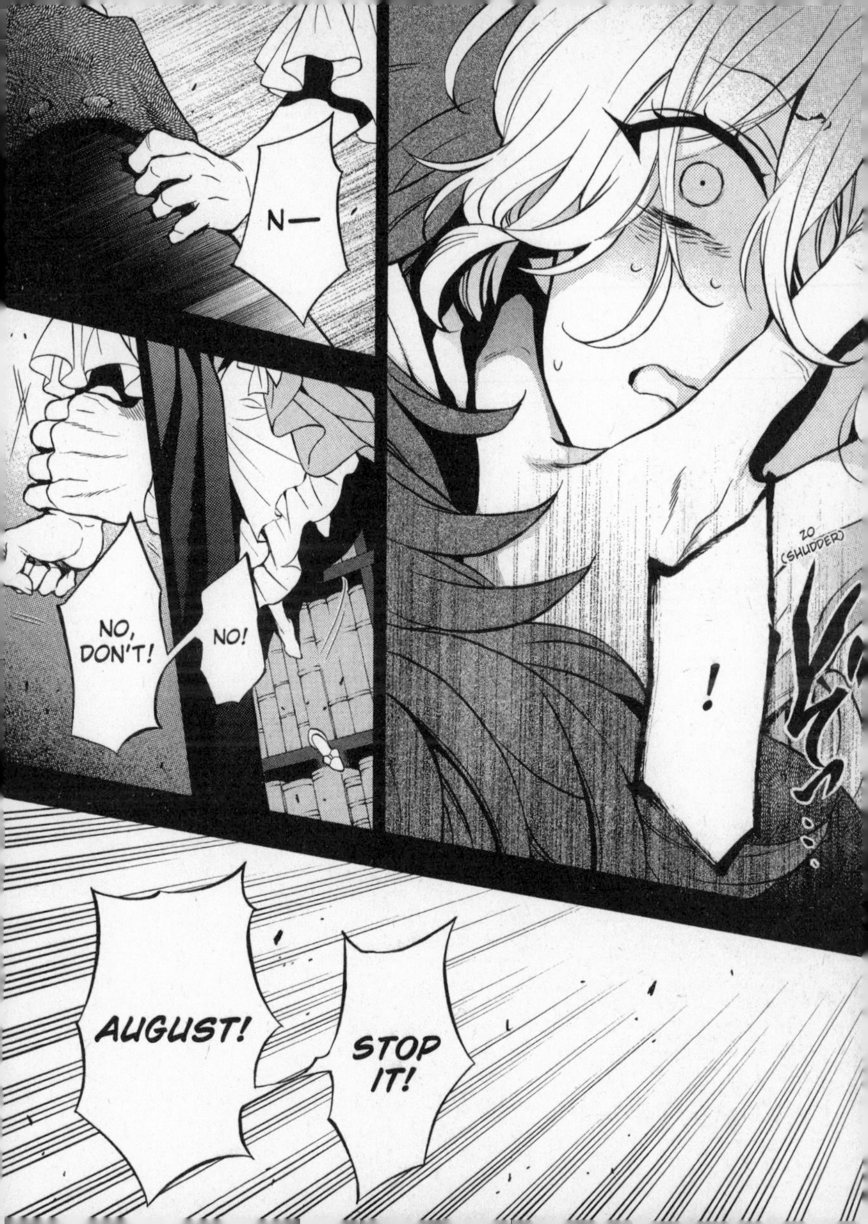
ZO (SHUDDER)
!
N—
NO!
NO, DON'T!
AUGUST!
STOP IT!

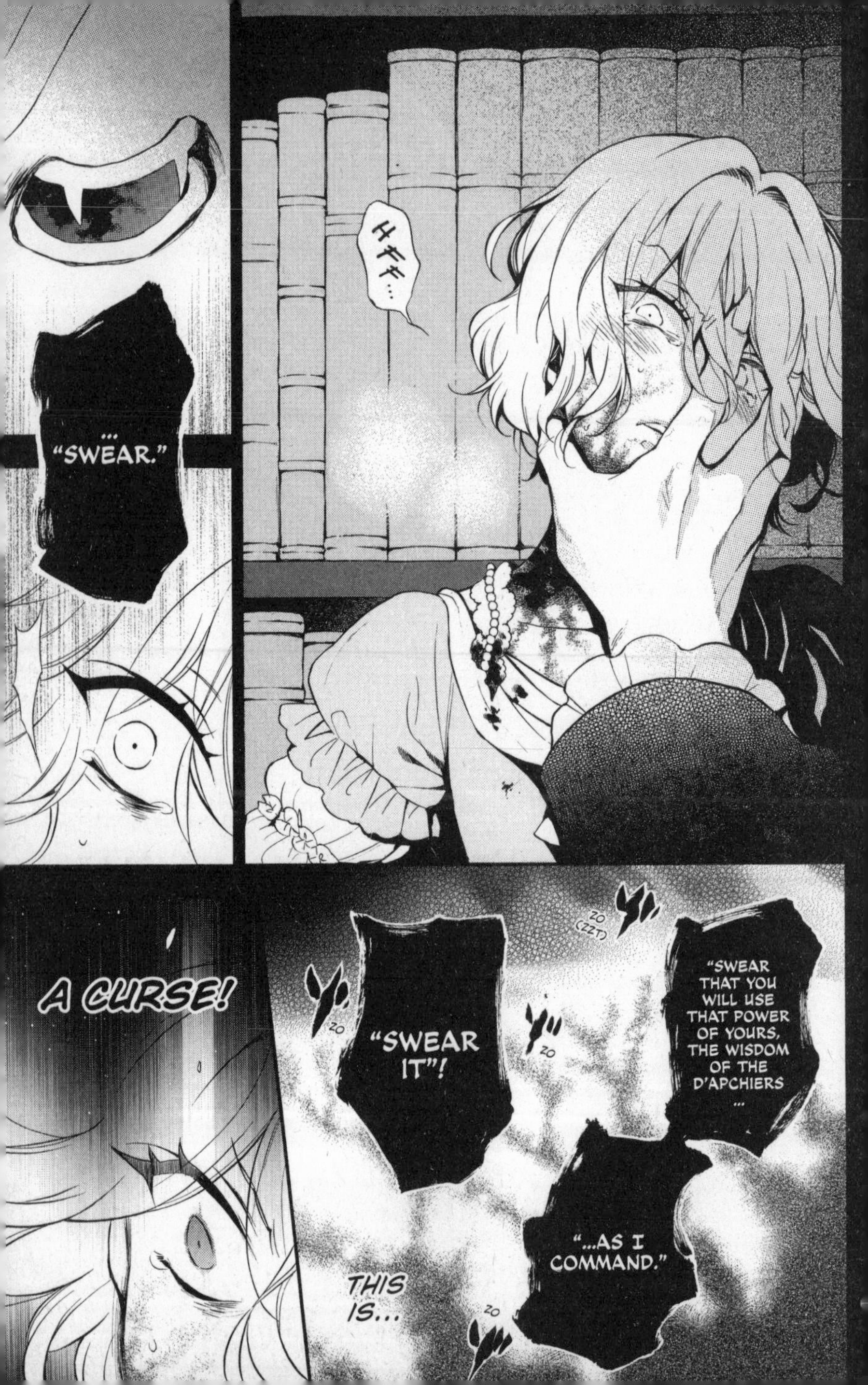
HFF...
... "SWEAR."
ZO (ZZT)
"SWEAR THAT YOU WILL USE THAT POWER OF YOURS, THE WISDOM OF THE D'APCHIERS ...
"SWEAR IT"!
ZO
ZO
"...AS I COMMAND."
ZO
THIS IS...
A CURSE!

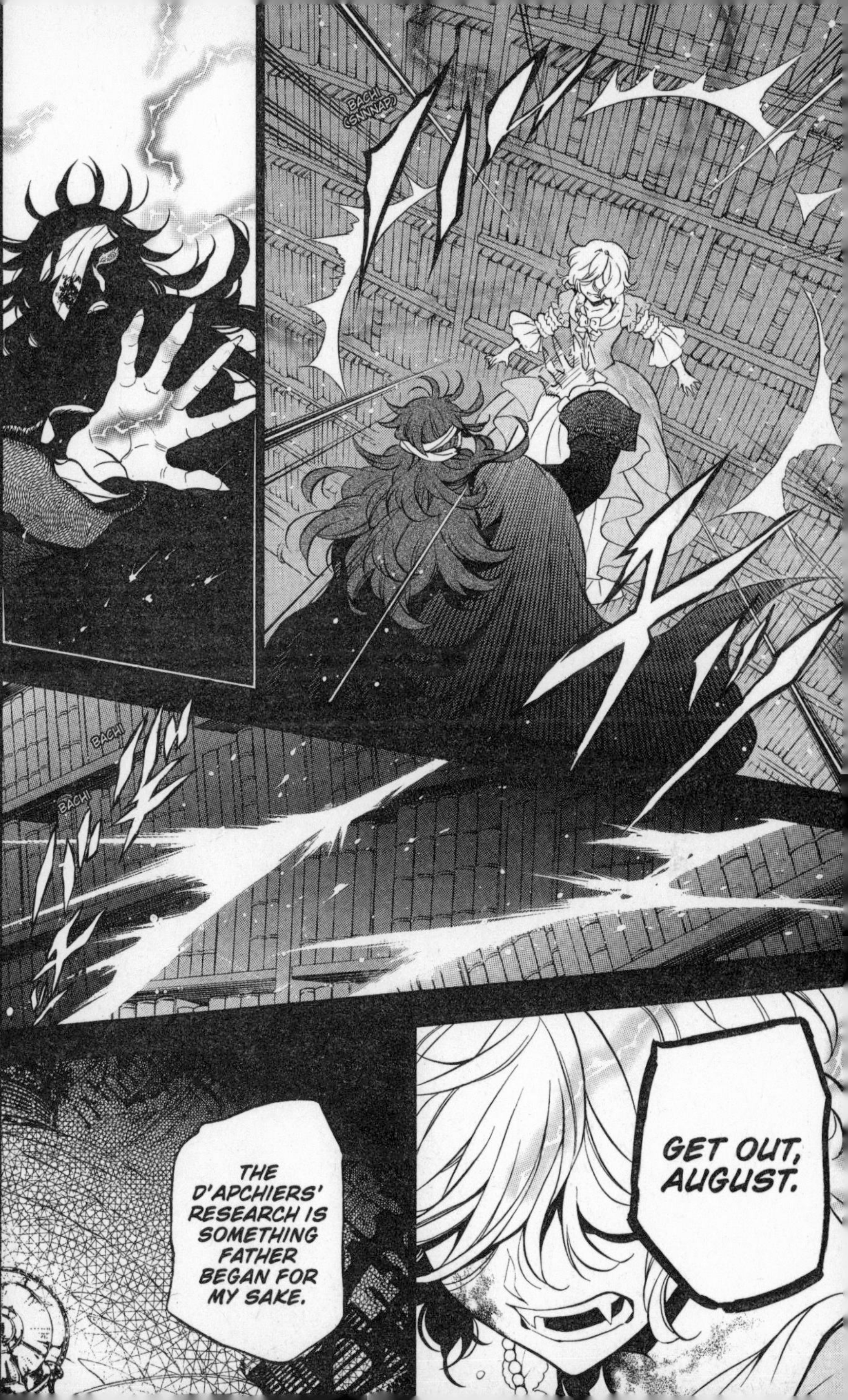
BACHI (SNNNAP)
BACHI
BACHI
GET OUT, AUGUST.
THE D'APCHIERS' RESEARCH IS SOMETHING FATHER BEGAN FOR MY SAKE.

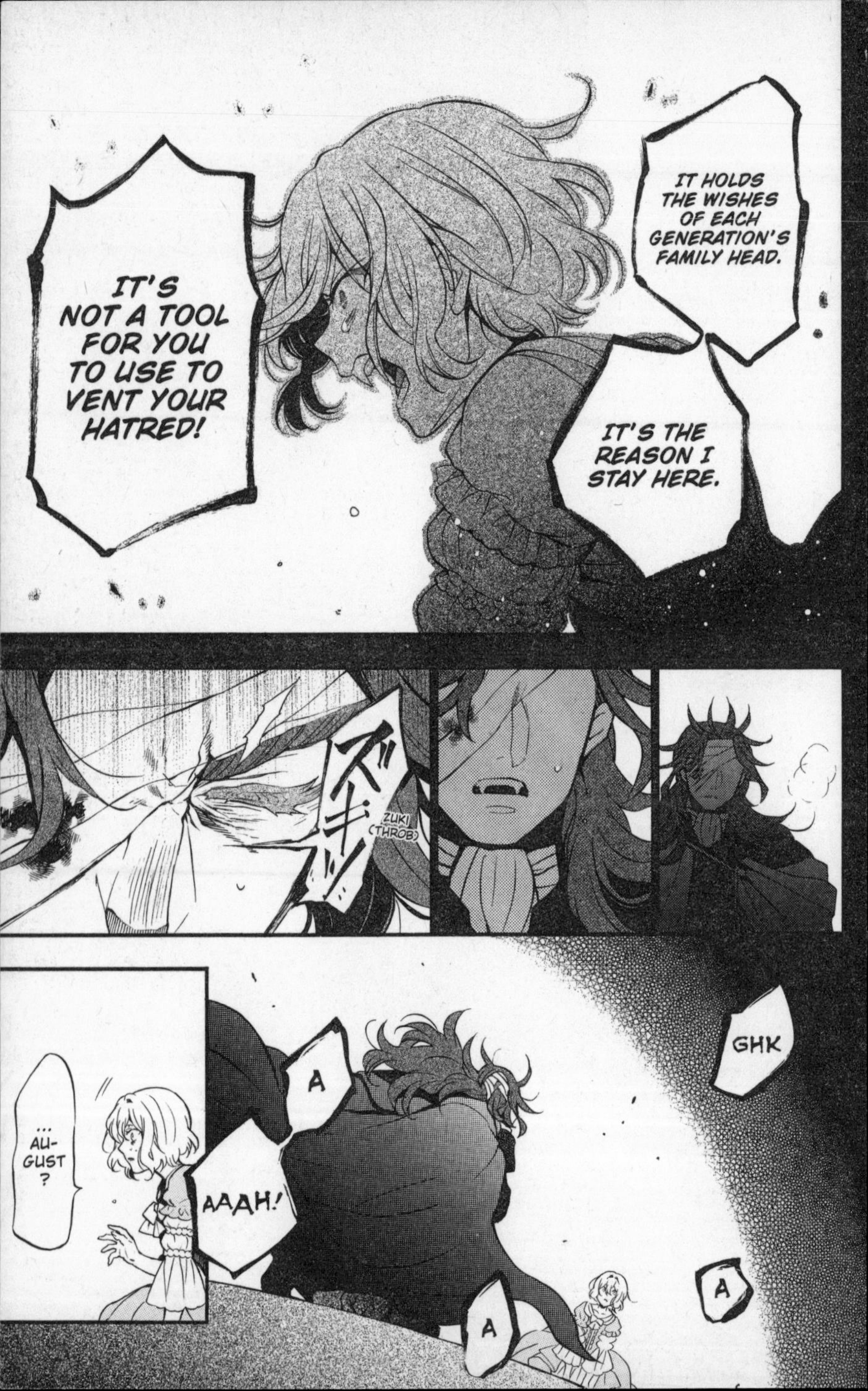
IT HOLDS THE WISHES OF EACH GENERATION'S FAMILY HEAD.
IT'S THE REASON I STAY HERE.
IT'S NOT A TOOL FOR YOU TO USE TO VENT YOUR HATRED!
ZUKI (THROB)
GHK
A
A
AAAH!
A
...AUGUST?

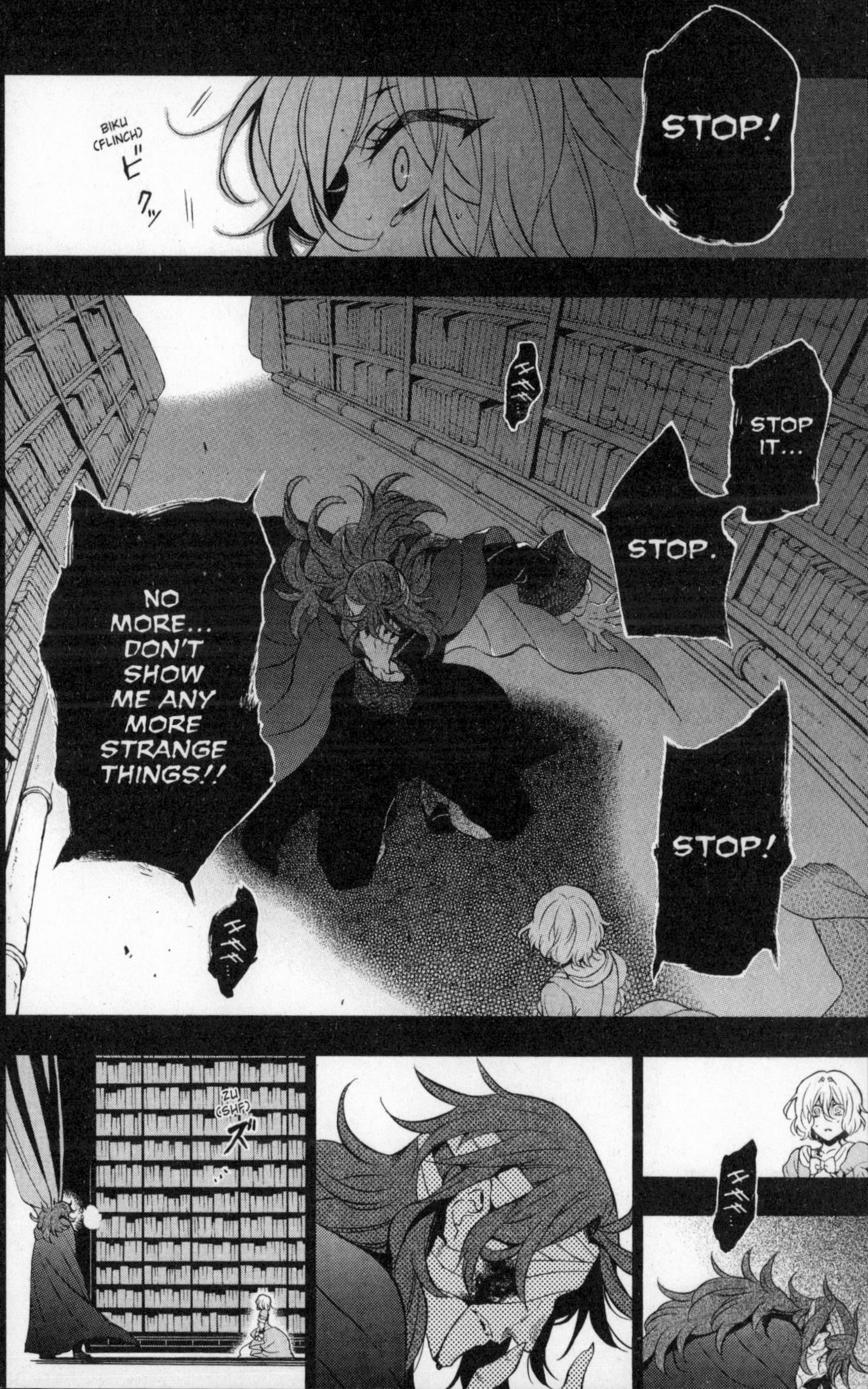
STOP!
BIKU (FLINCH) ビクッ
STOP IT...
HFF...
STOP.
NO MORE... DON'T SHOW ME ANY MORE STRANGE THINGS!!
STOP!
HFF...
HFF...
ZU (SHF) ズ

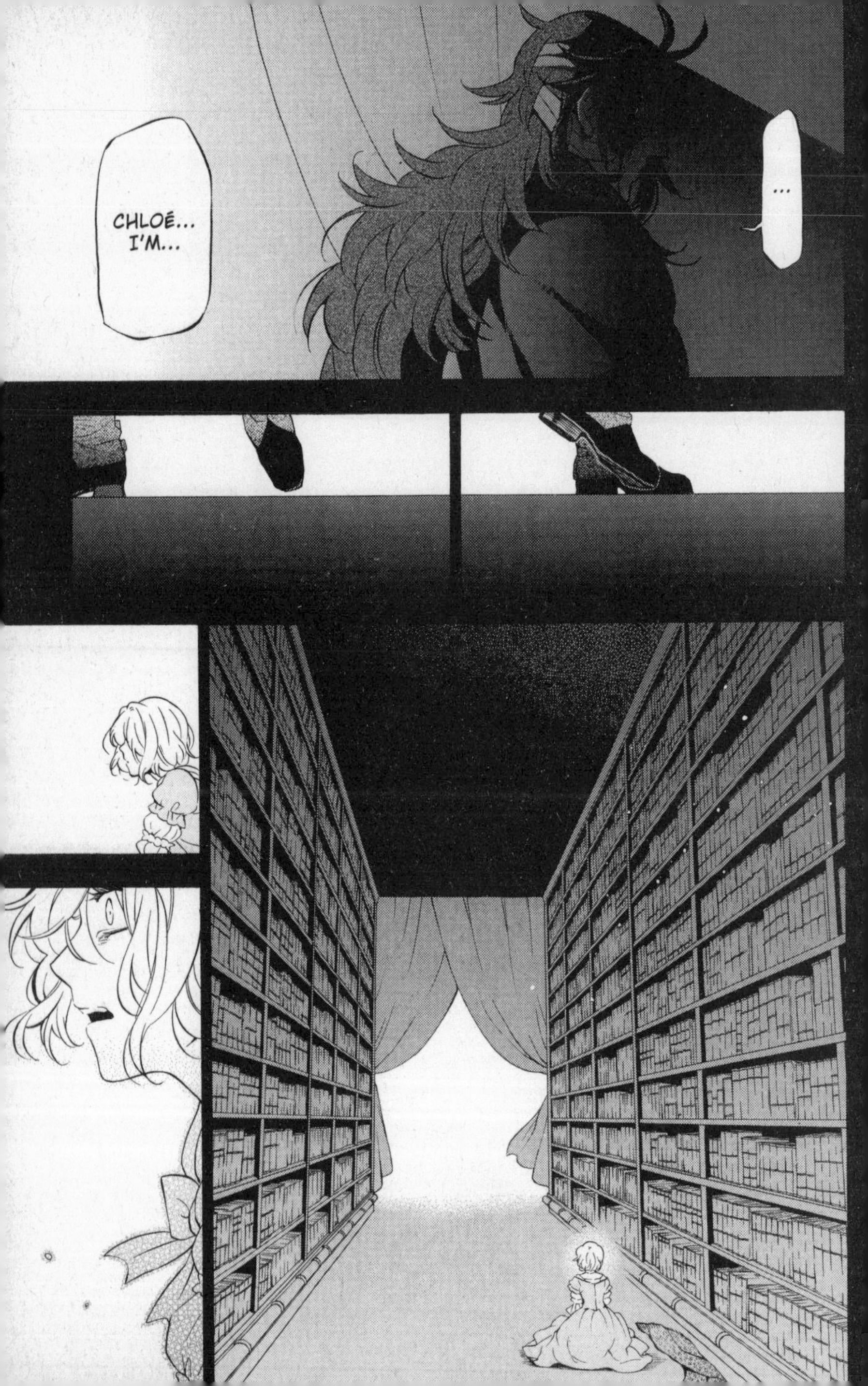
...
CHLOÉ... I'M...

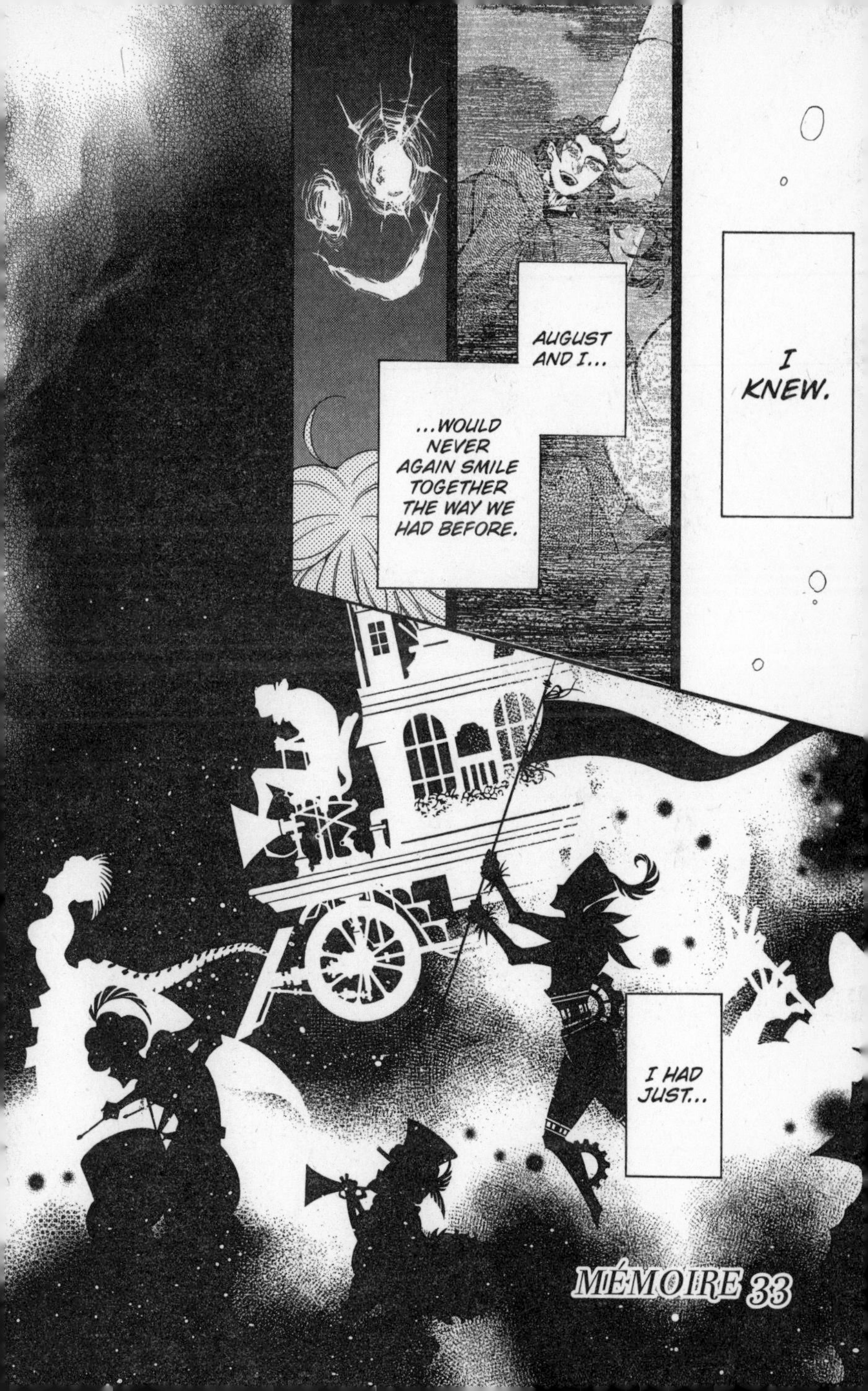
I KNEW.
AUGUST AND I...
...WOULD NEVER AGAIN SMILE TOGETHER THE WAY WE HAD BEFORE.
I HAD JUST...
MÉMOIRE 33

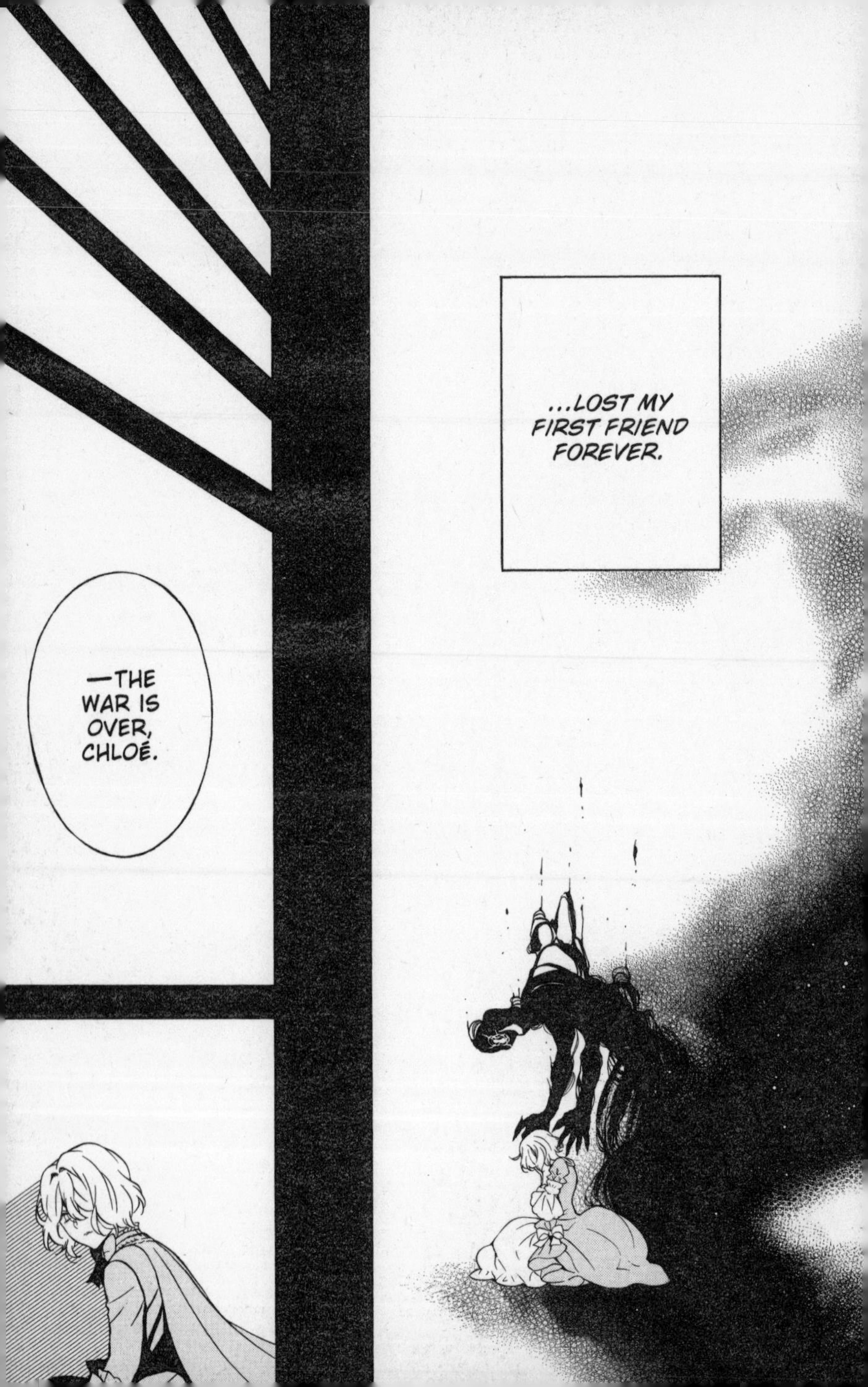
...LOST MY FIRST FRIEND FOREVER.
—THE WAR IS OVER, CHLOÉ.

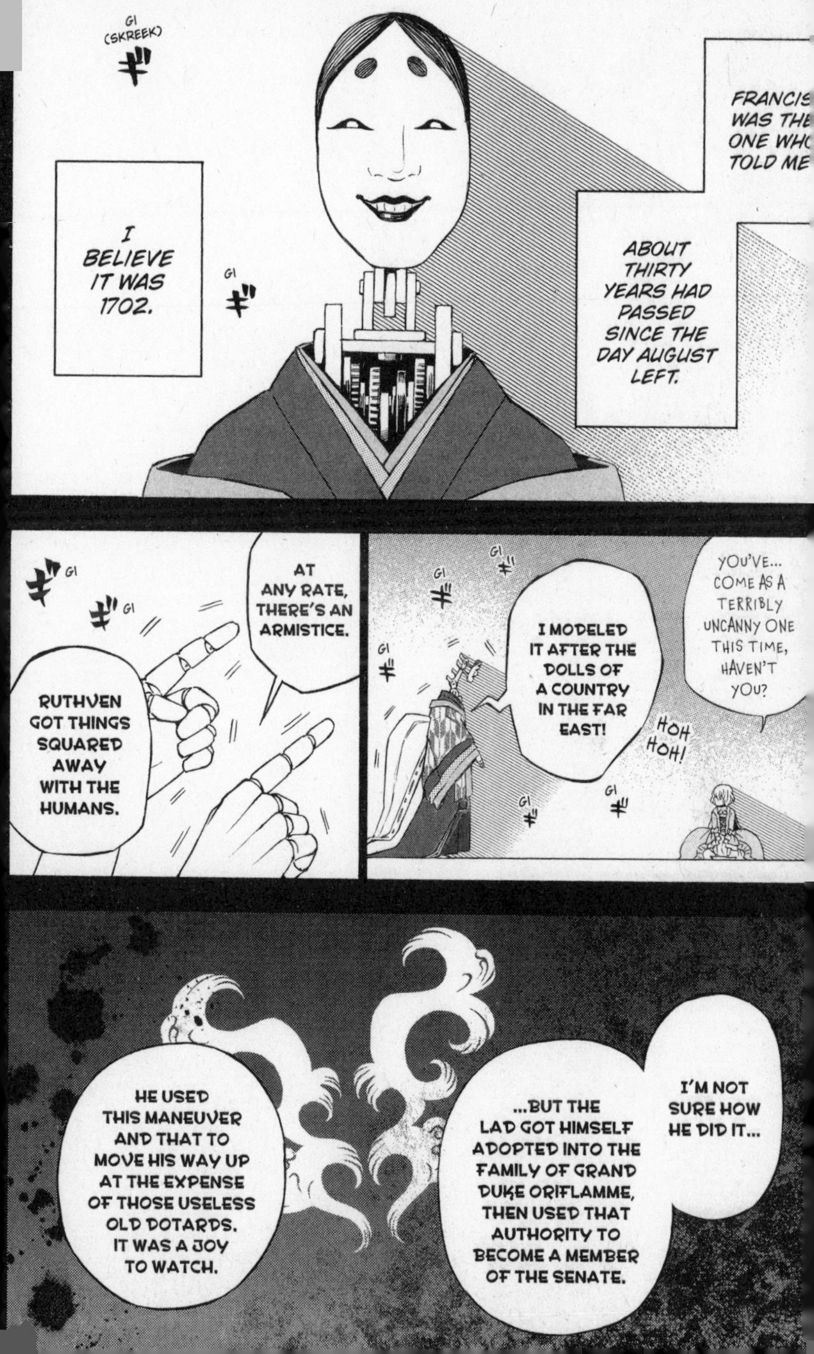
FRANCIS WAS THE ONE WHO TOLD ME
ABOUT THIRTY YEARS HAD PASSED SINCE THE DAY AUGUST LEFT.
GI (SKREEK)
GI
I BELIEVE IT WAS 1702.
YOU'VE... COME AS A TERRIBLY UNCANNY ONE THIS TIME, HAVEN'T YOU?
HOH HOH!
I MODELED IT AFTER THE DOLLS OF A COUNTRY IN THE FAR EAST!
GI
GI
GI
GI
GI
AT ANY RATE, THERE'S AN ARMISTICE.
GI
GI
RUTHVEN GOT THINGS SQUARED AWAY WITH THE HUMANS.
I'M NOT SURE HOW HE DID IT...
...BUT THE LAD GOT HIMSELF ADOPTED INTO THE FAMILY OF GRAND DUKE ORIFLAMME, THEN USED THAT AUTHORITY TO BECOME A MEMBER OF THE SENATE.
HE USED THIS MANEUVER AND THAT TO MOVE HIS WAY UP AT THE EXPENSE OF THOSE USELESS OLD DOTARDS. IT WAS A JOY TO WATCH.

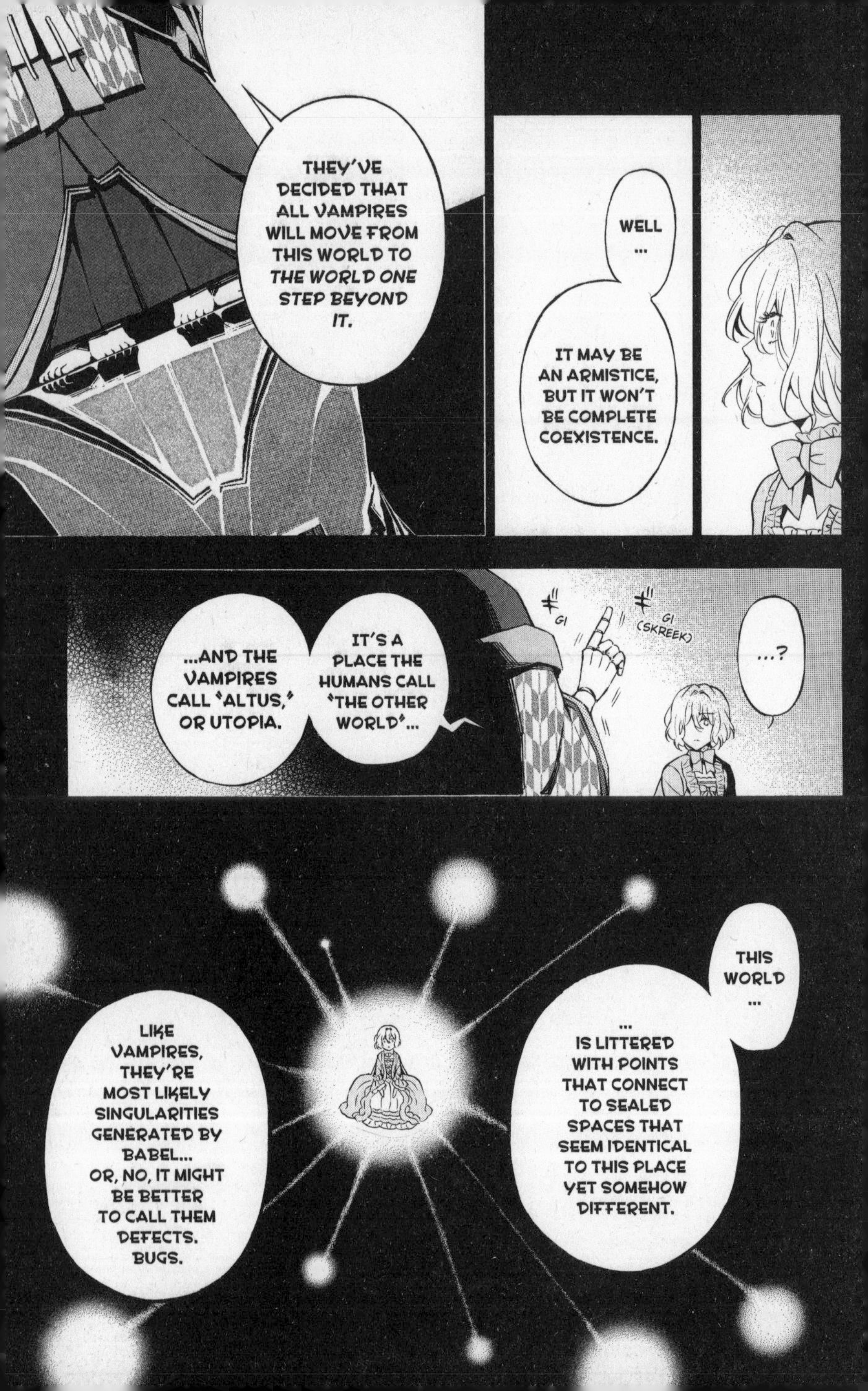
WELL ...
IT MAY BE AN ARMISTICE, BUT IT WON'T BE COMPLETE COEXISTENCE.
THEY'VE DECIDED THAT ALL VAMPIRES WILL MOVE FROM THIS WORLD TO *THE WORLD ONE STEP BEYOND* IT.
...?
GI (SKREEK)
GI
IT'S A PLACE THE HUMANS CALL "THE OTHER WORLD"...
...AND THE VAMPIRES CALL "ALTUS," OR UTOPIA.
THIS WORLD ...
... IS LITTERED WITH POINTS THAT CONNECT TO SEALED SPACES THAT SEEM IDENTICAL TO THIS PLACE YET SOMEHOW DIFFERENT.
LIKE VAMPIRES, THEY'RE MOST LIKELY SINGULARITIES GENERATED BY BABEL... OR, NO, IT MIGHT BE BETTER TO CALL THEM DEFECTS. BUGS.

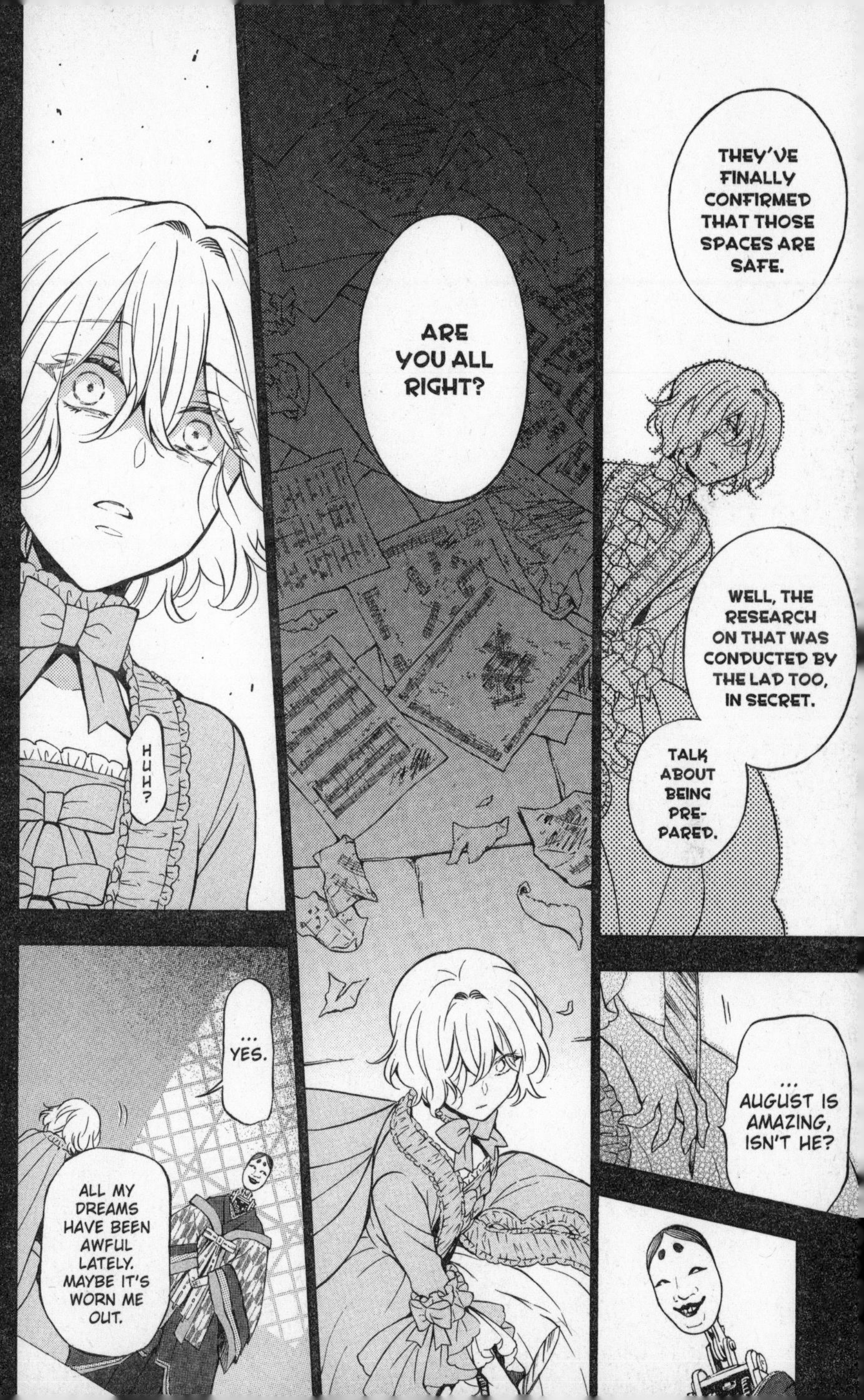
THEY'VE FINALLY CONFIRMED THAT THOSE SPACES ARE SAFE.
WELL, THE RESEARCH ON THAT WAS CONDUCTED BY THE LAD TOO, IN SECRET.
TALK ABOUT BEING PRE-PARED.
ARE YOU ALL RIGHT?
HUH?
... AUGUST IS AMAZING, ISN'T HE?
... YES.
ALL MY DREAMS HAVE BEEN AWFUL LATELY. MAYBE IT'S WORN ME OUT.

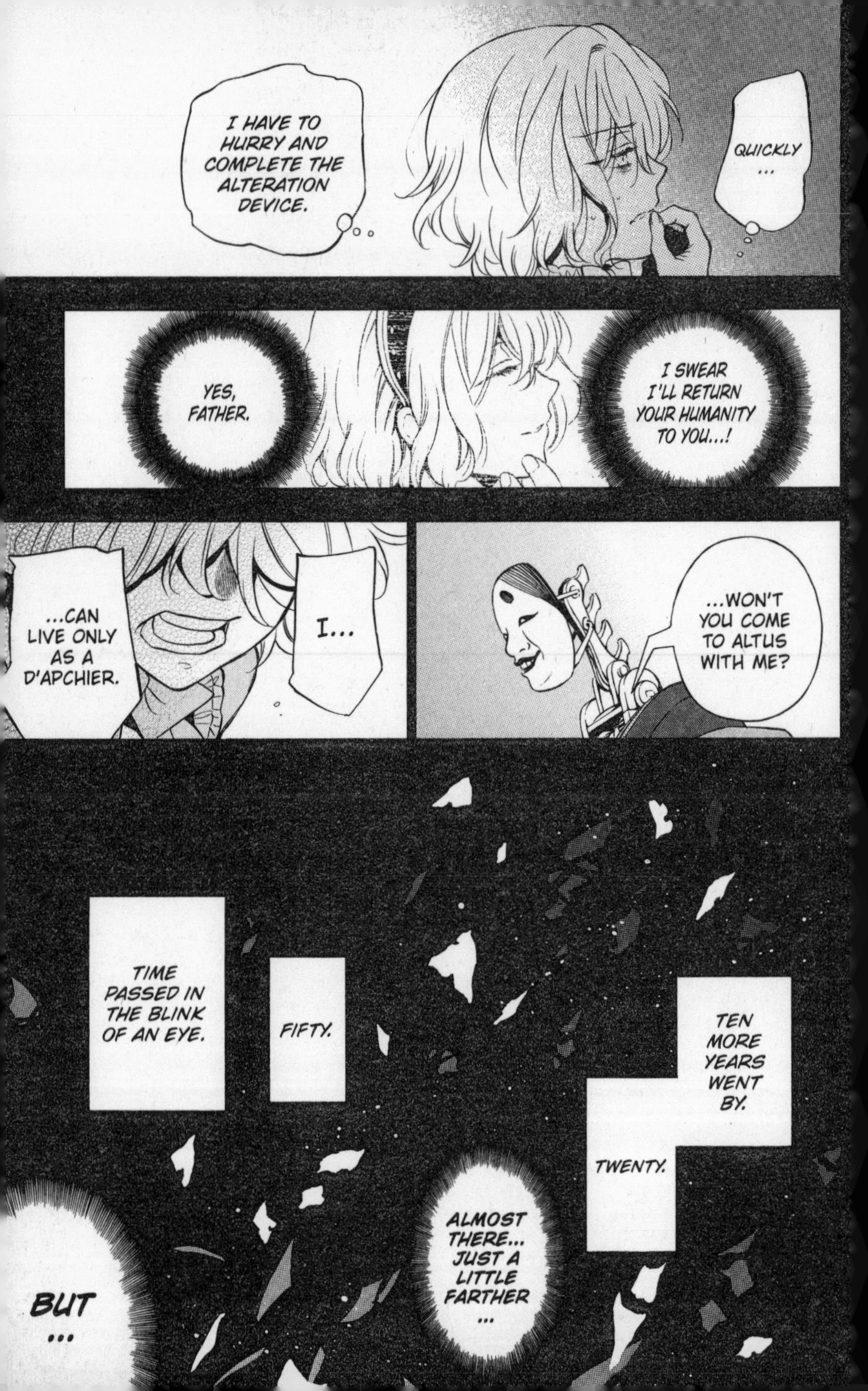
QUICKLY ...
I HAVE TO HURRY AND COMPLETE THE ALTERATION DEVICE.
I SWEAR I'LL RETURN YOUR HUMANITY TO YOU...!
YES, FATHER.
...WON'T YOU COME TO ALTUS WITH ME?
I...
...CAN LIVE ONLY AS A D'APCHIER.
TEN MORE YEARS WENT BY.
TWENTY.
FIFTY.
TIME PASSED IN THE BLINK OF AN EYE.
ALMOST THERE... JUST A LITTLE FARTHER ...
BUT ...

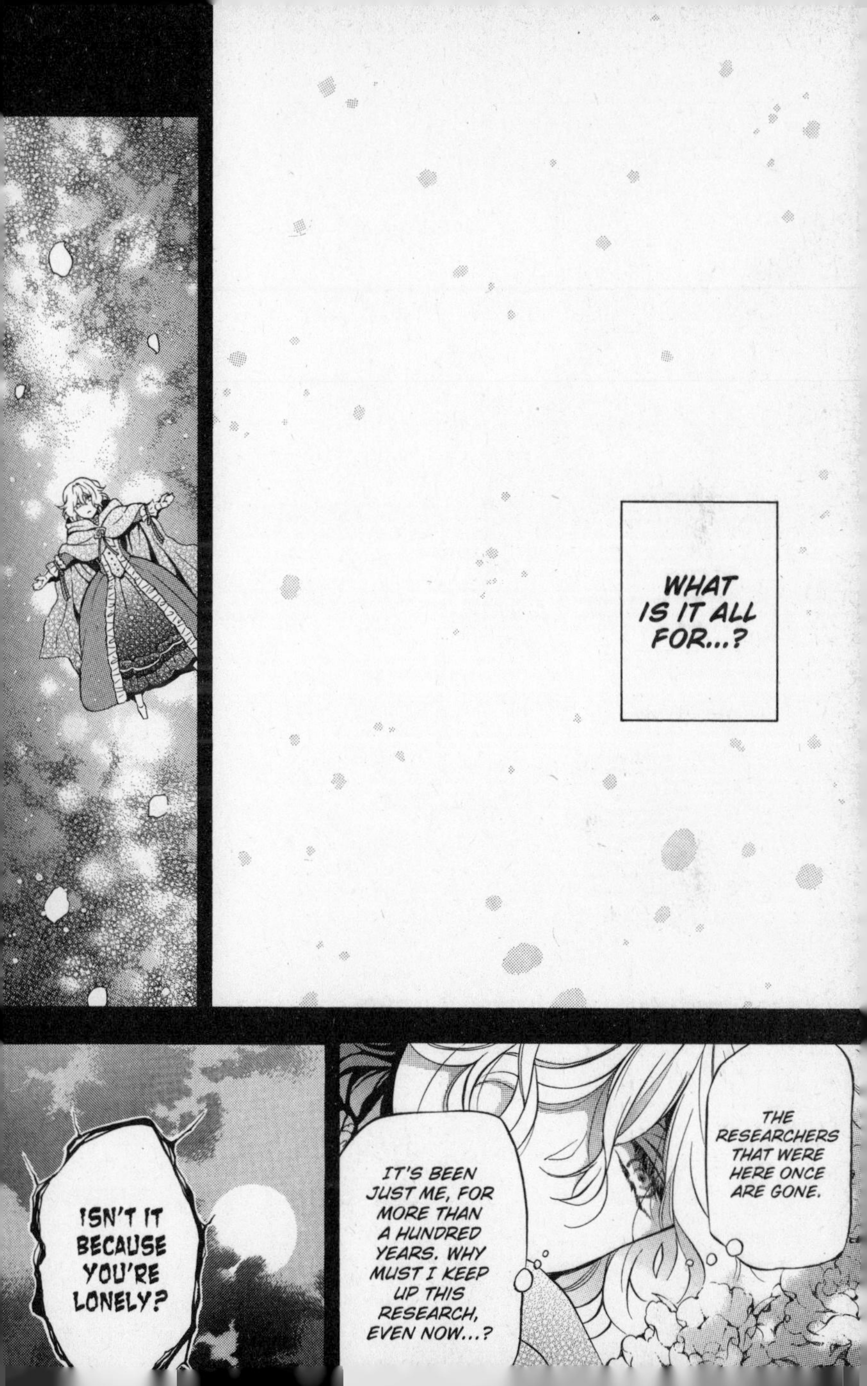
WHAT IS IT ALL FOR...?
THE RESEARCHERS THAT WERE HERE ONCE ARE GONE.
IT'S BEEN JUST ME, FOR MORE THAN A HUNDRED YEARS. WHY MUST I KEEP UP THIS RESEARCH, EVEN NOW...?
ISN'T IT BECAUSE YOU'RE LONELY?

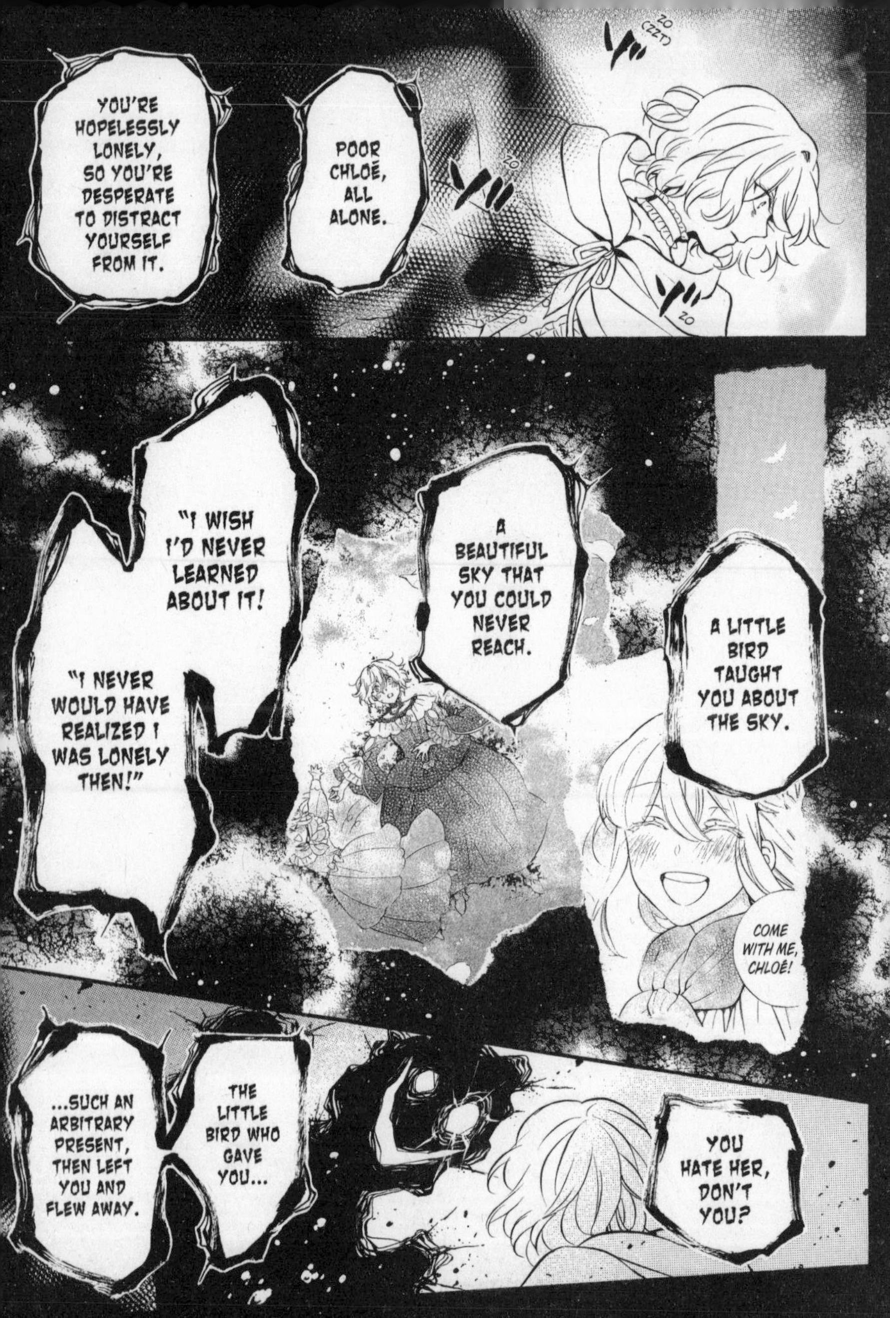
ZO (ZZZT)
ZO
ZO
POOR CHLOÉ, ALL ALONE.
YOU'RE HOPELESSLY LONELY, SO YOU'RE DESPERATE TO DISTRACT YOURSELF FROM IT.
A LITTLE BIRD TAUGHT YOU ABOUT THE SKY.
COME WITH ME, CHLOÉ!
A BEAUTIFUL SKY THAT YOU COULD NEVER REACH.
"I WISH I'D NEVER LEARNED ABOUT IT!
"I NEVER WOULD HAVE REALIZED I WAS LONELY THEN!"
YOU HATE HER, DON'T YOU?
THE LITTLE BIRD WHO GAVE YOU...
...SUCH AN ARBITRARY PRESENT, THEN LEFT YOU AND FLEW AWAY.

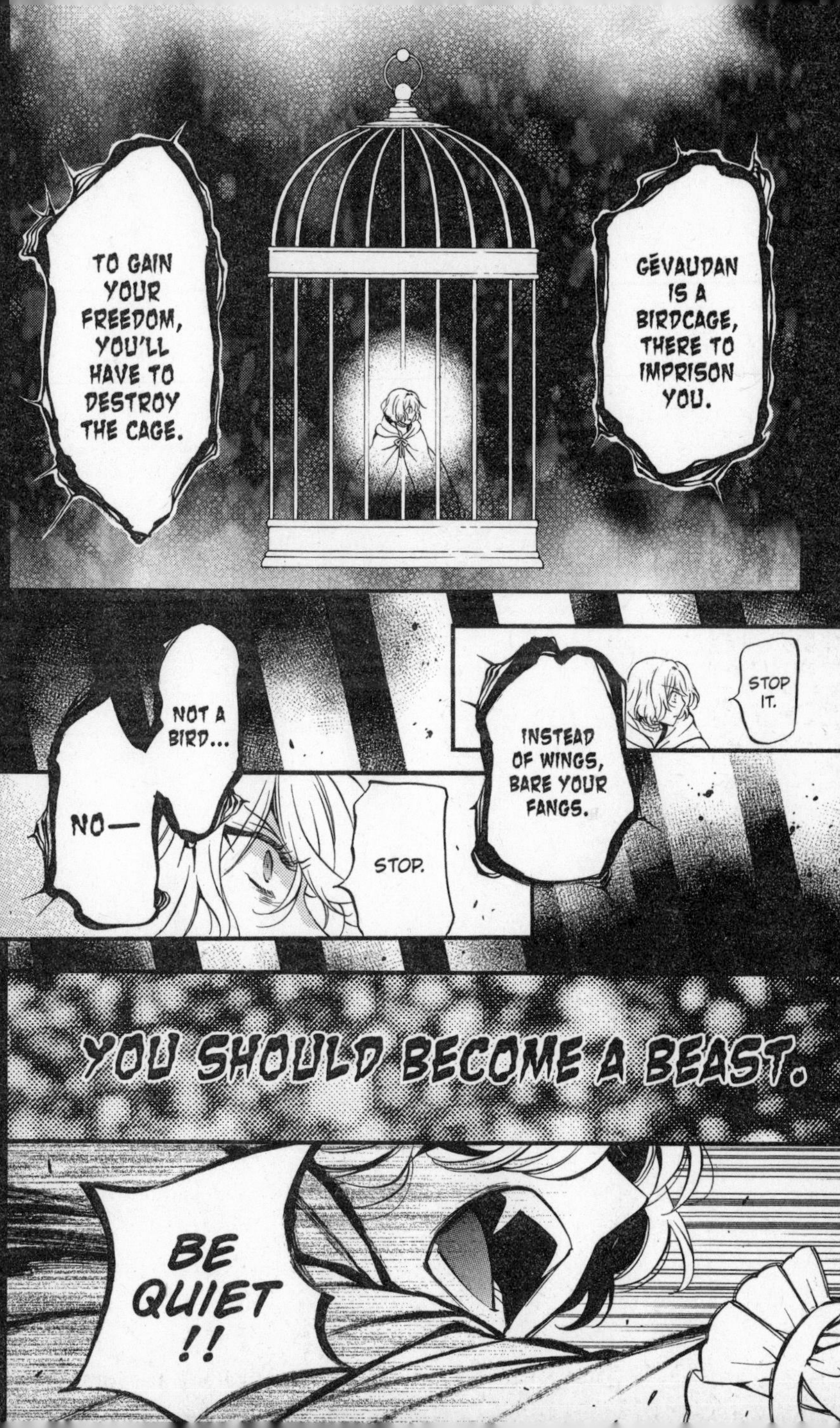
GĒVAUDAN IS A BIRDCAGE, THERE TO IMPRISON YOU.
TO GAIN YOUR FREEDOM, YOU'LL HAVE TO DESTROY THE CAGE.
STOP IT.
INSTEAD OF WINGS, BARE YOUR FANGS.
STOP.
NOT A BIRD...
NO—
YOU SHOULD BECOME A BEAST.
BE QUIET!!

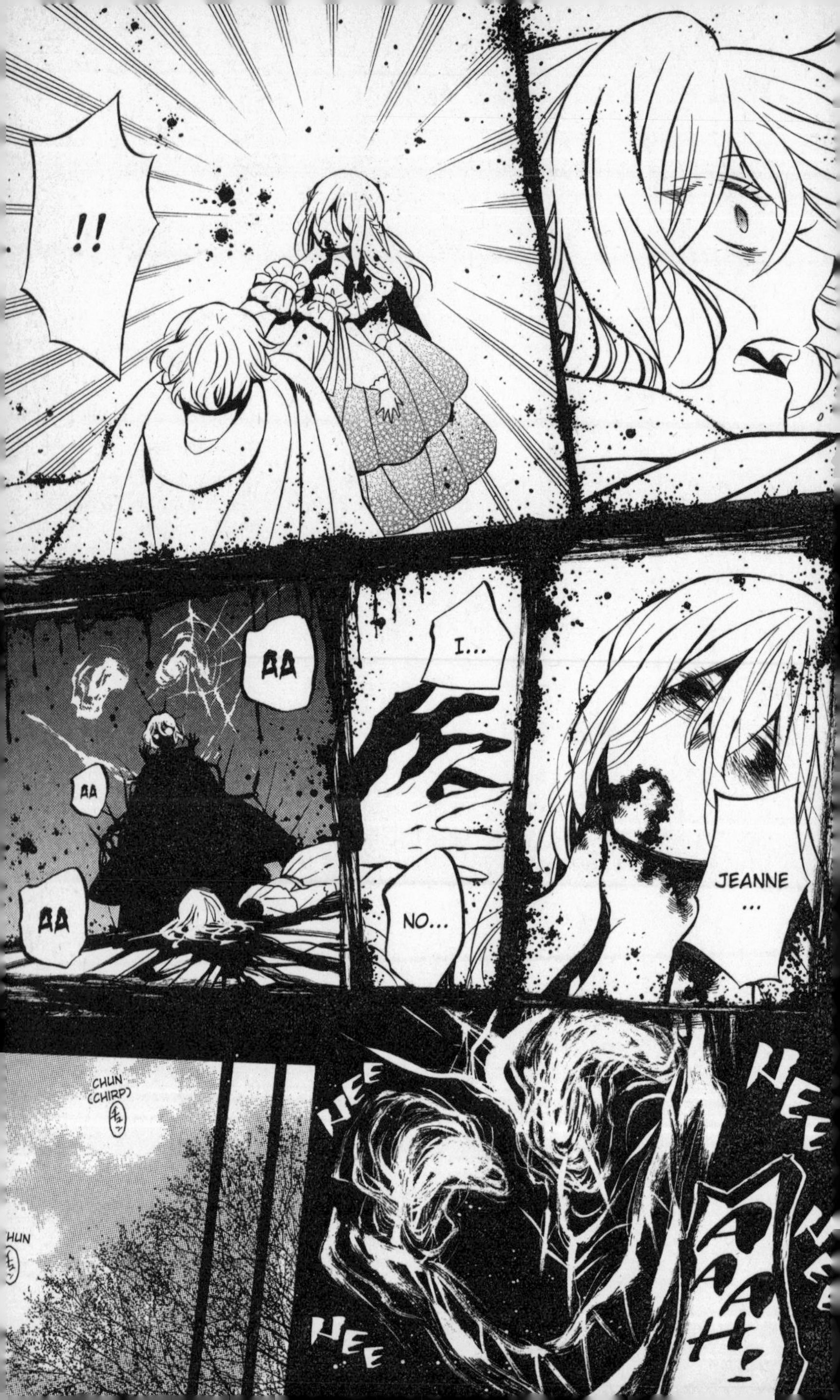
!!
JEANNE ...
I...
NO...
AA
AA
AA
HEE
AAAH!
HEE
HEE
HEE
CHUN (CHIRP)

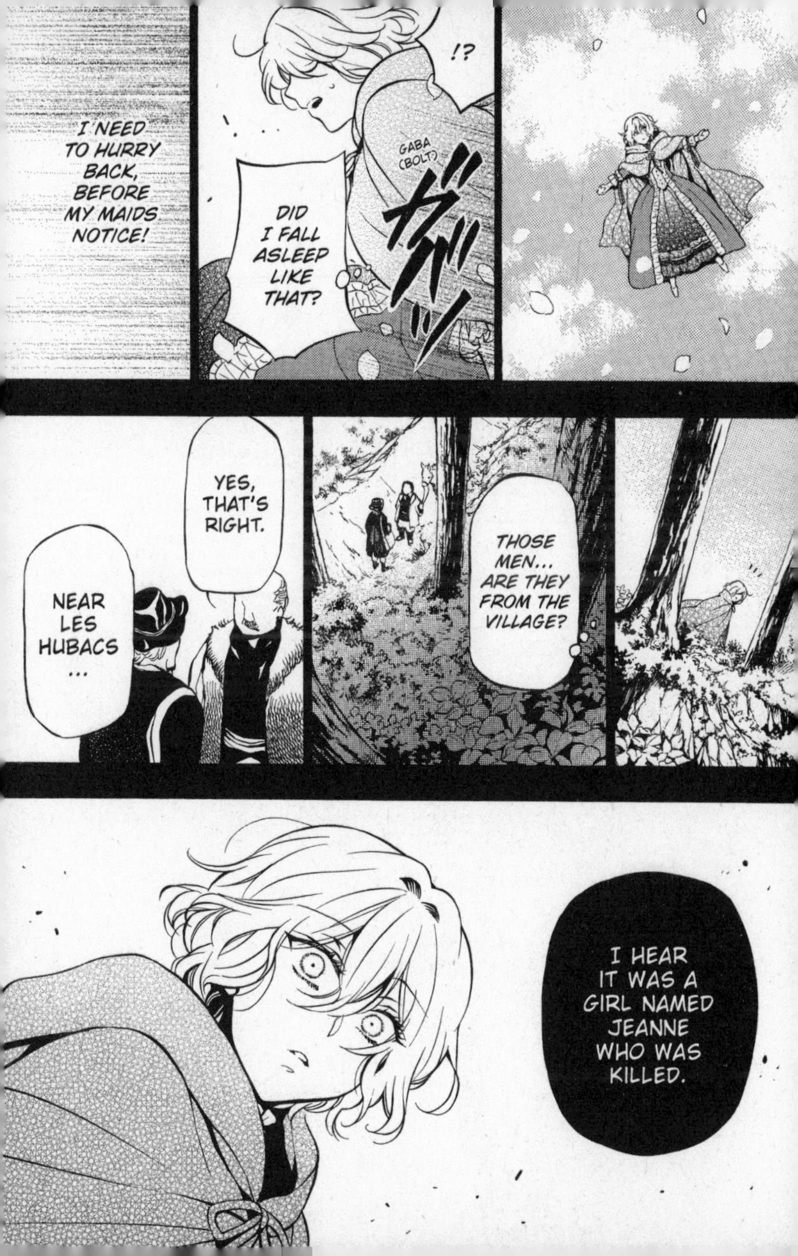
!?
GABA (BOLT)
ガバッ
DID I FALL ASLEEP LIKE THAT?
I NEED TO HURRY BACK, BEFORE MY MAIDS NOTICE!
THOSE MEN... ARE THEY FROM THE VILLAGE?
YES, THAT'S RIGHT.
NEAR LES HUBACS ...
I HEAR IT WAS A GIRL NAMED JEANNE WHO WAS KILLED.

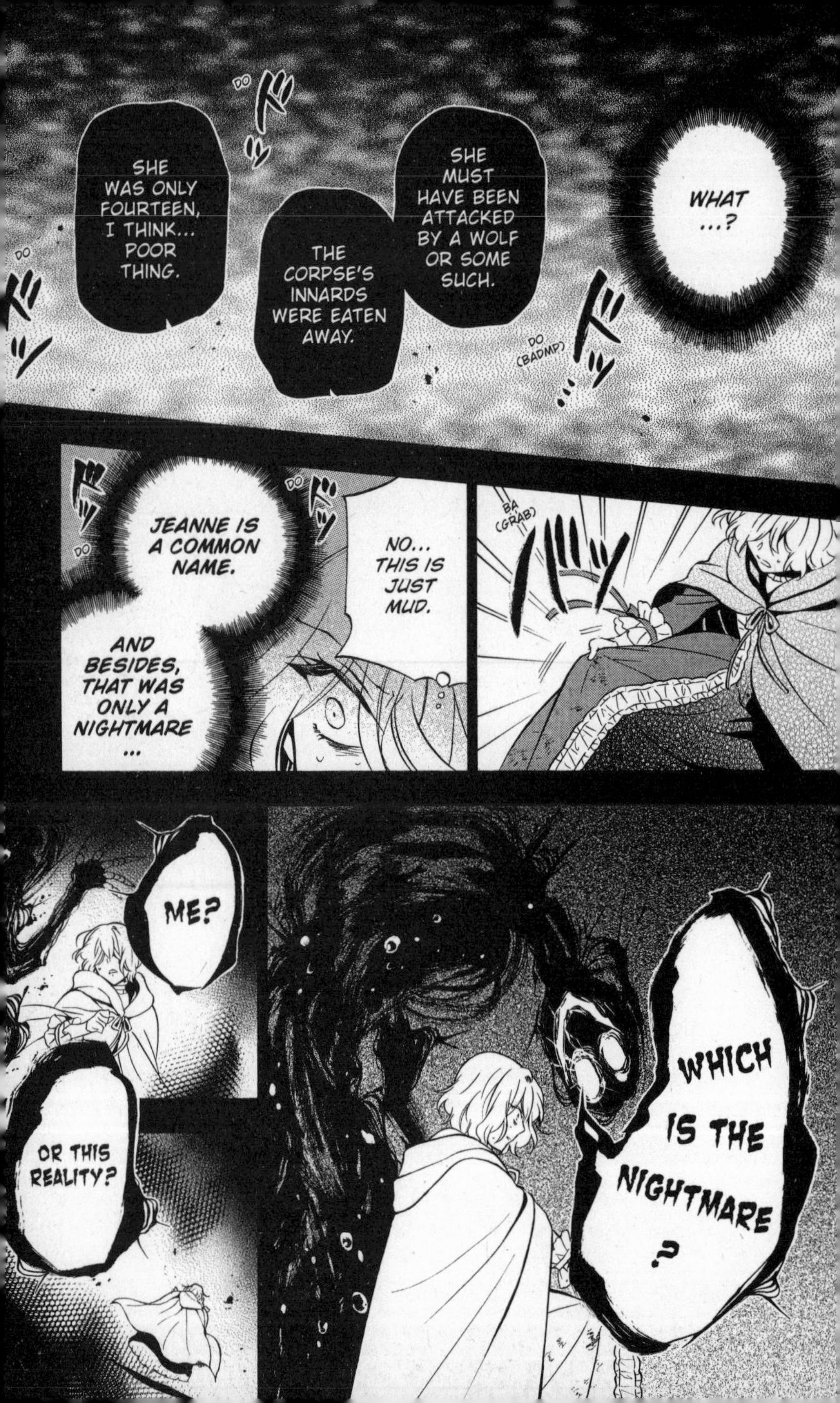
WHAT...?
DO (BADMP)
SHE MUST HAVE BEEN ATTACKED BY A WOLF OR SOME SUCH.
THE CORPSE'S INNARDS WERE EATEN AWAY.
DO
SHE WAS ONLY FOURTEEN, I THINK... POOR THING.
DO
BA (GRAB)
NO... THIS IS JUST MUD.
DO
JEANNE IS A COMMON NAME.
DO
AND BESIDES, THAT WAS ONLY A NIGHTMARE...
WHICH IS THE NIGHTMARE?
ME?
OR THIS REALITY?

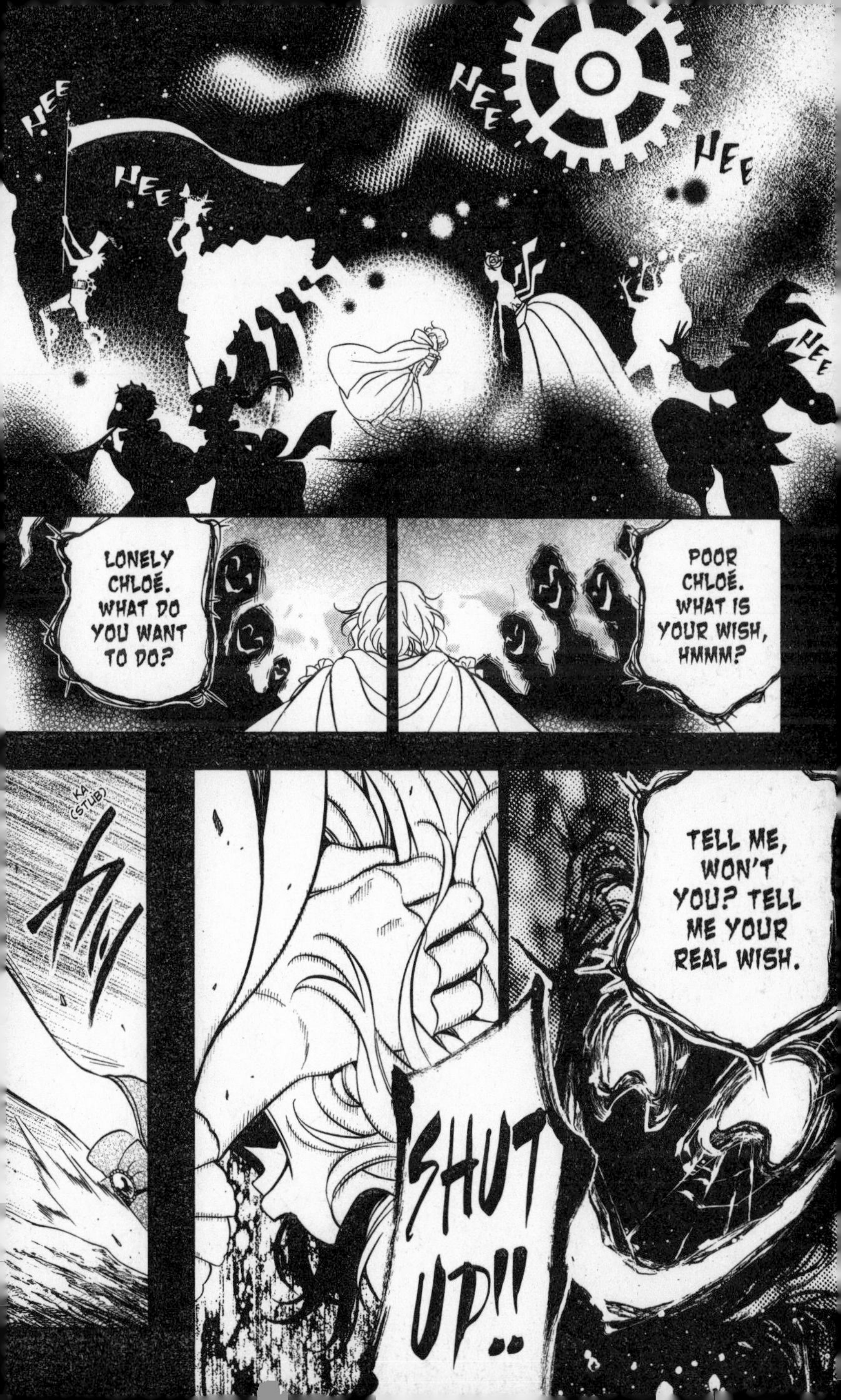
HEE
HEE
HEE
HEE
HEE
POOR CHLOÉ. WHAT IS YOUR WISH, HMMM?
LONELY CHLOÉ. WHAT DO YOU WANT TO DO?
TELL ME, WON'T YOU? TELL ME YOUR REAL WISH.
SHUT UP!!
KA (STUB)

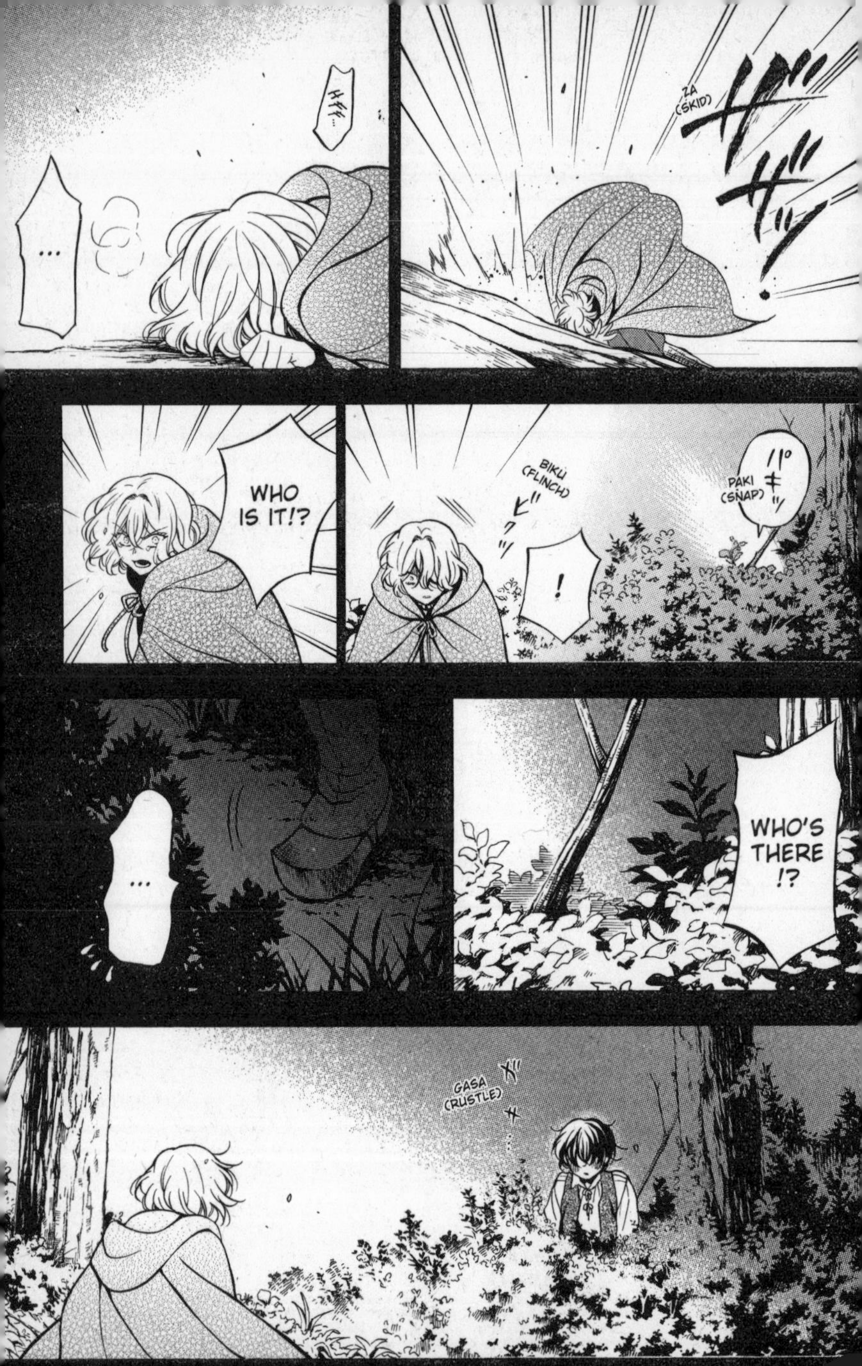

ZA (SKID)
ザザッ
ザザ…
...
PAKI (SNAP)
パキッ
BIKU (FLINCH)
ビクッ
!
WHO IS IT!?
WHO'S THERE !?
...
GASA (RUSTLE)
ガサ

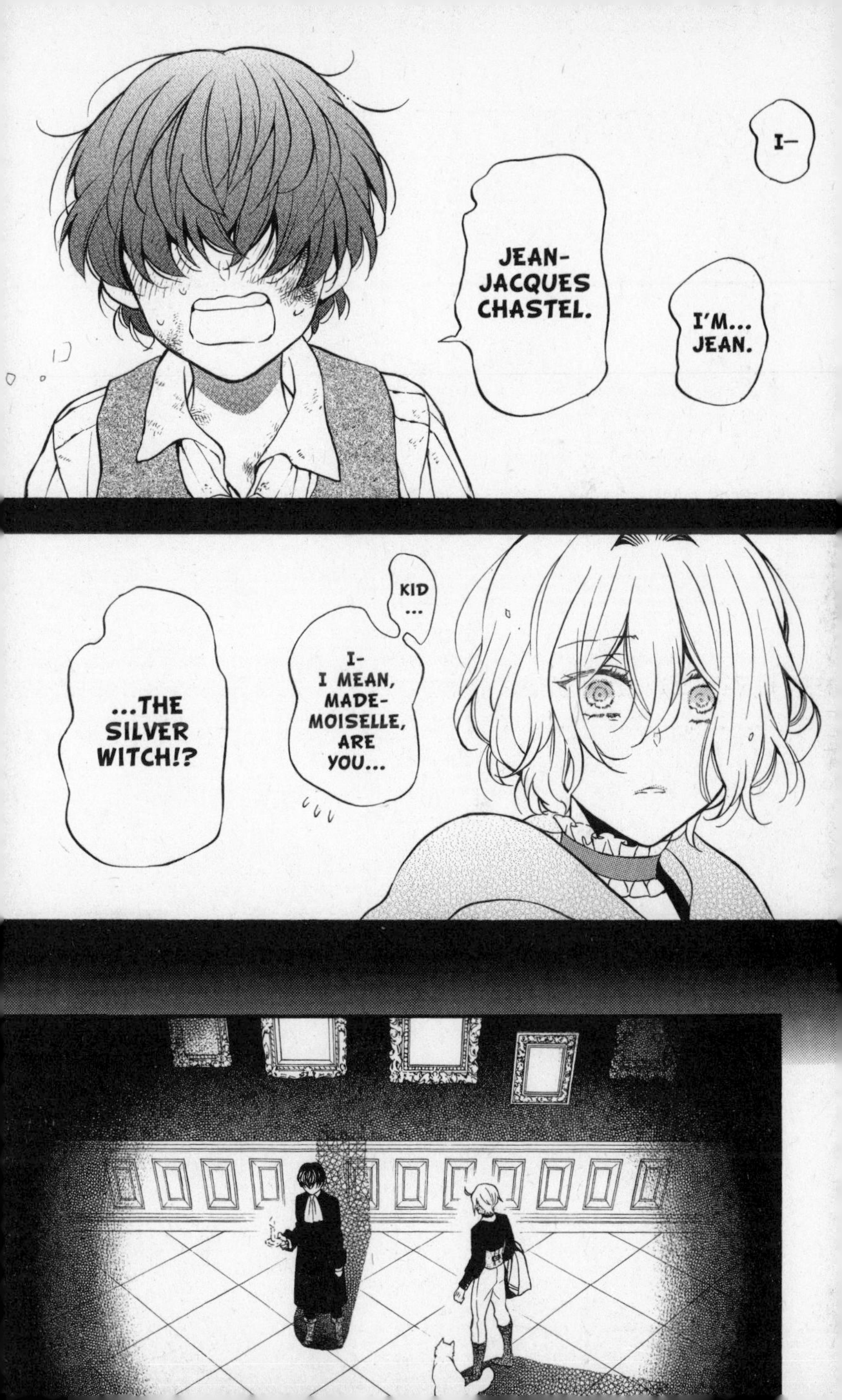
I—
I'M... JEAN.
JEAN-JACQUES CHASTEL.
KID ...
I- I MEAN, MADE-MOISELLE, ARE YOU...
...THE SILVER WITCH!?

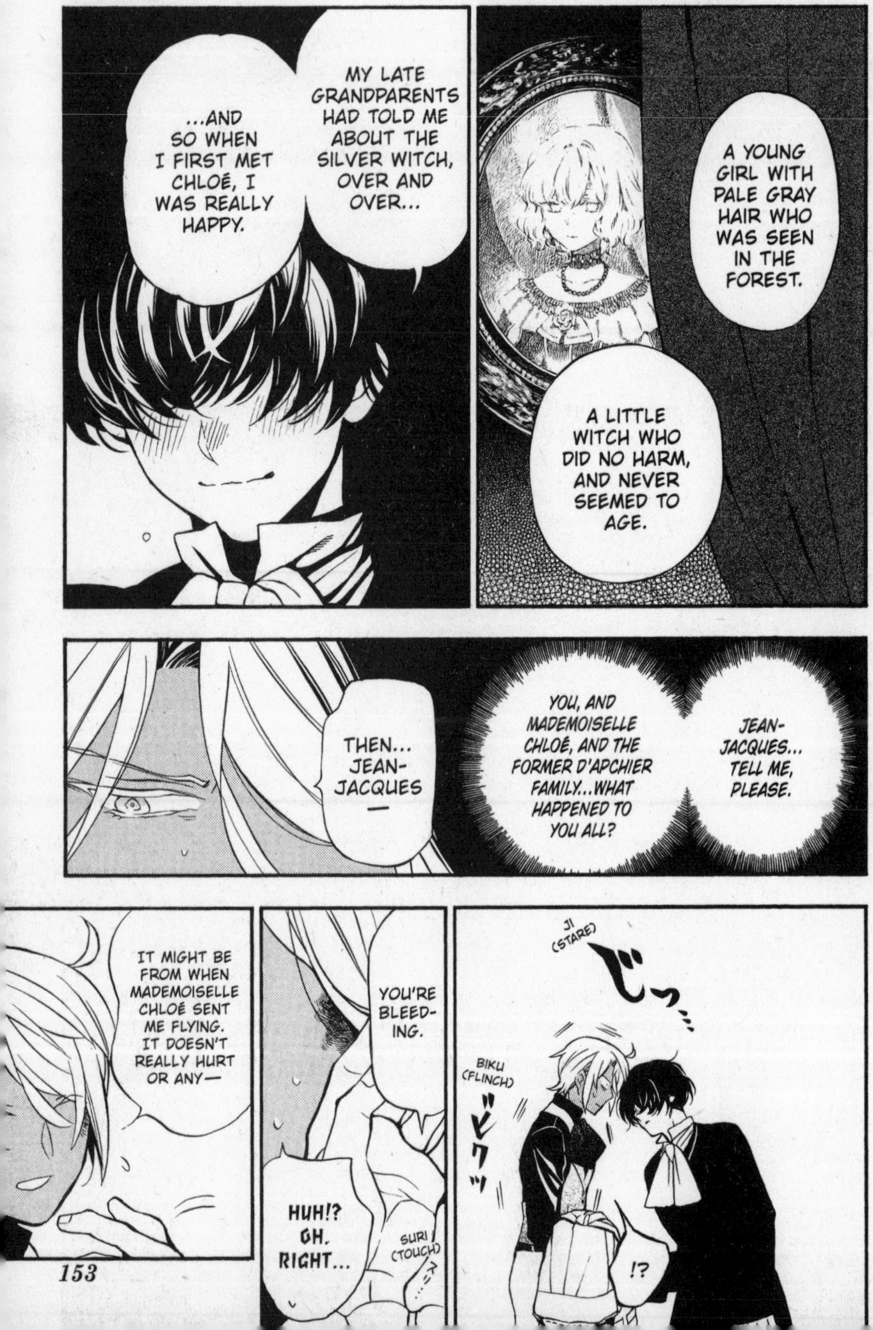
A YOUNG GIRL WITH PALE GRAY HAIR WHO WAS SEEN IN THE FOREST.
A LITTLE WITCH WHO DID NO HARM, AND NEVER SEEMED TO AGE.
MY LATE GRANDPARENTS HAD TOLD ME ABOUT THE SILVER WITCH, OVER AND OVER...
...AND SO WHEN I FIRST MET CHLOÉ, I WAS REALLY HAPPY.
JEAN-JACQUES... TELL ME, PLEASE.
YOU, AND MADEMOISELLE CHLOÉ, AND THE FORMER D'APCHIER FAMILY...WHAT HAPPENED TO YOU ALL?
THEN... JEAN-JACQUES—
JI (STARE)
BIKU (FLINCH)
!?
YOU'RE BLEED-ING.
HUH!? GH. RIGHT...
SURI (TOUCH)
IT MIGHT BE FROM WHEN MADEMOISELLE CHLOÉ SENT ME FLYING. IT DOESN'T REALLY HURT OR ANY—

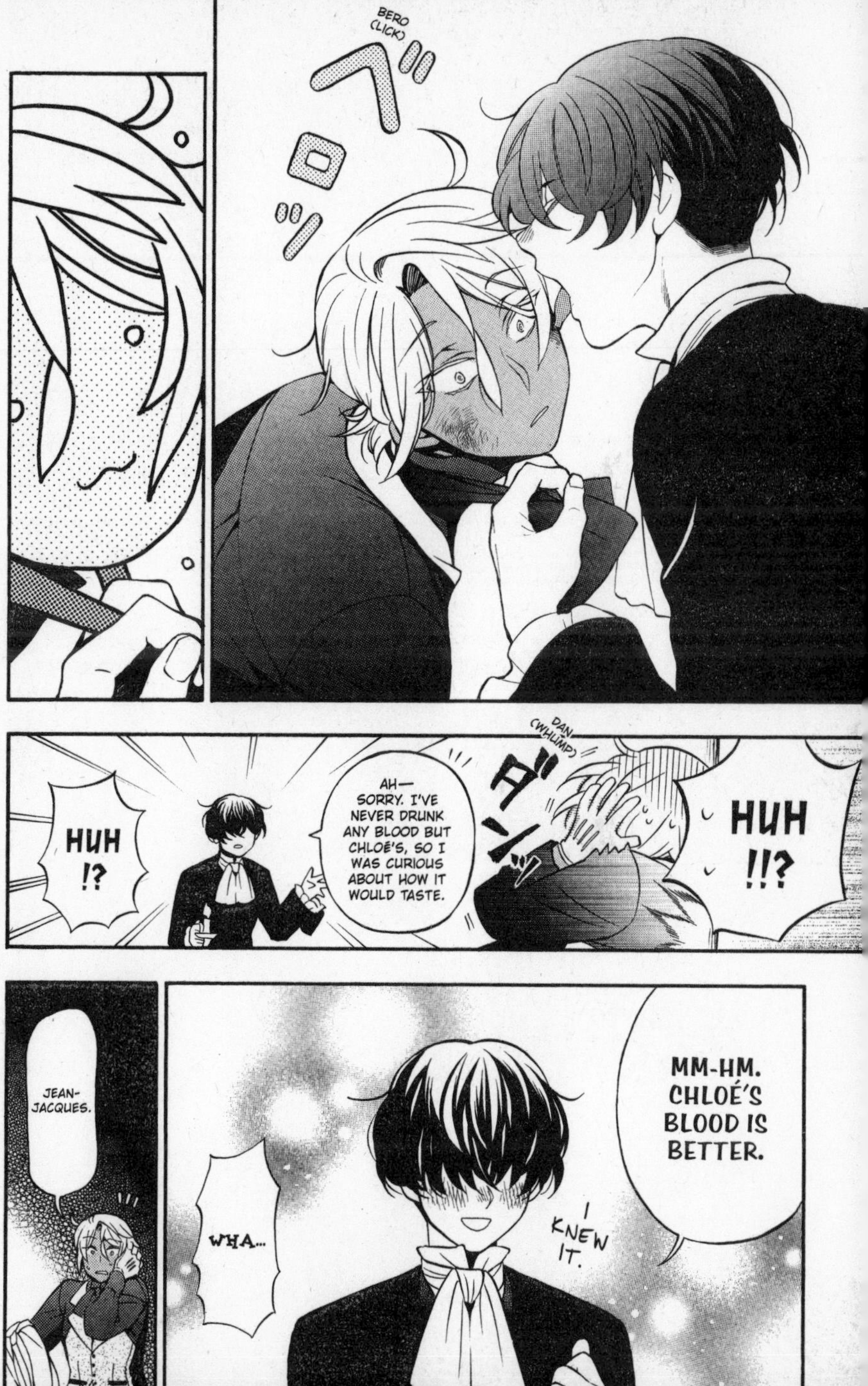

BERO (LICK)
ベロッ
HUH !!?
DAN (WHUMP)
ダン
AH— SORRY. I'VE NEVER DRUNK ANY BLOOD BUT CHLOÉ'S, SO I WAS CURIOUS ABOUT HOW IT WOULD TASTE.
HUH !?
MM-HM. CHLOÉ'S BLOOD IS BETTER.
I KNEW IT.
WHA...
JEAN-JACQUES.

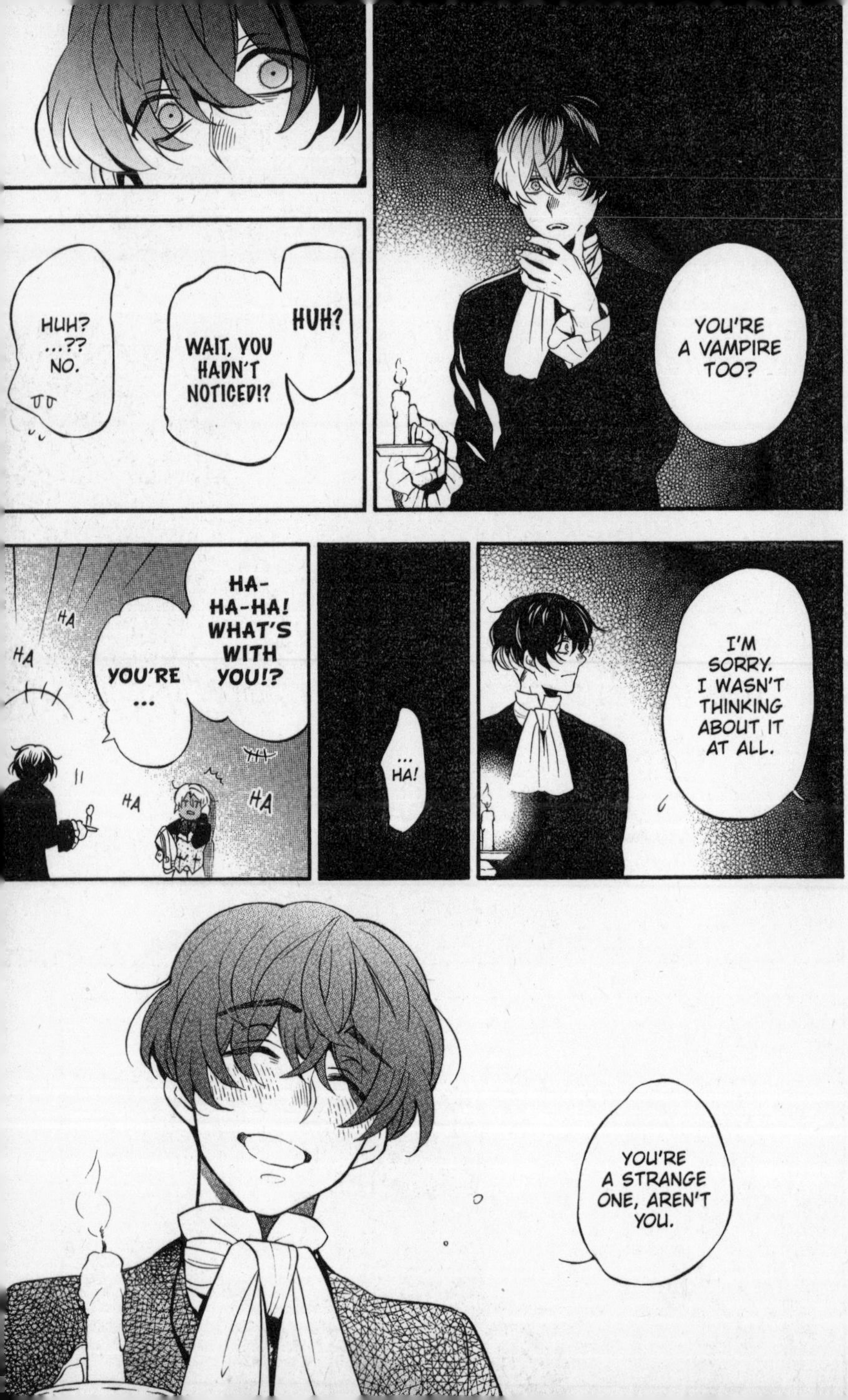
YOU'RE A VAMPIRE TOO?
HUH? WAIT, YOU HADN'T NOTICED!?
HUH? ...?? NO.
I'M SORRY. I WASN'T THINKING ABOUT IT AT ALL.
...HA!
HA-HA-HA! WHAT'S WITH YOU!?
YOU'RE ...
HA
HA
HA
HA
YOU'RE A STRANGE ONE, AREN'T YOU.

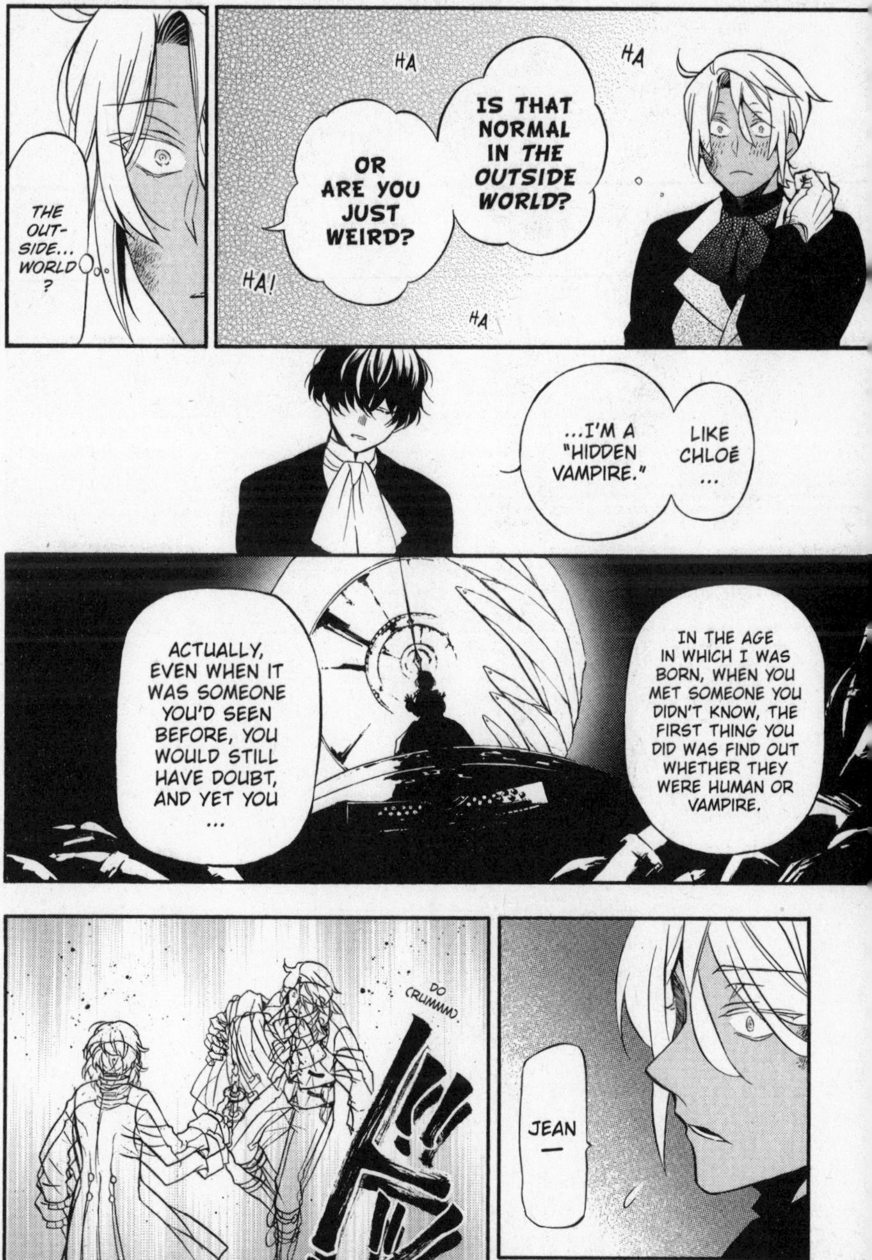
HA
IS THAT NORMAL IN THE OUTSIDE WORLD?
HA
OR ARE YOU JUST WEIRD?
HA!
HA
THE OUT-SIDE... WORLD?
...I'M A "HIDDEN VAMPIRE."
LIKE CHLOÉ ...
IN THE AGE IN WHICH I WAS BORN, WHEN YOU MET SOMEONE YOU DIDN'T KNOW, THE FIRST THING YOU DID WAS FIND OUT WHETHER THEY WERE HUMAN OR VAMPIRE.
ACTUALLY, EVEN WHEN IT WAS SOMEONE YOU'D SEEN BEFORE, YOU WOULD STILL HAVE DOUBT, AND YET YOU ...
JEAN —
DO CRUMMM

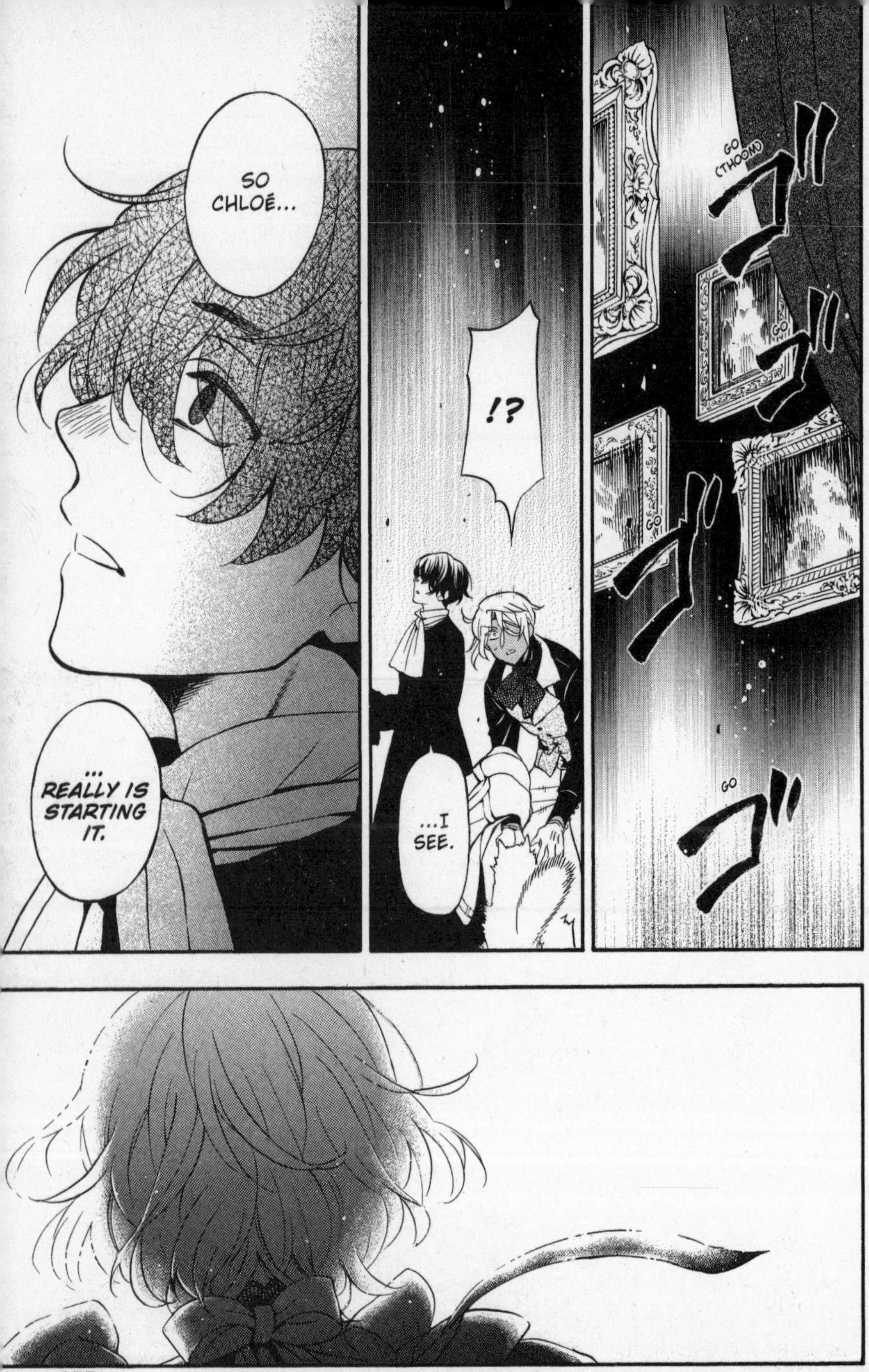
GO (THOOM)
GO
GO
GO
!?
...I SEE.
SO CHLOÉ...
...REALLY IS STARTING IT.

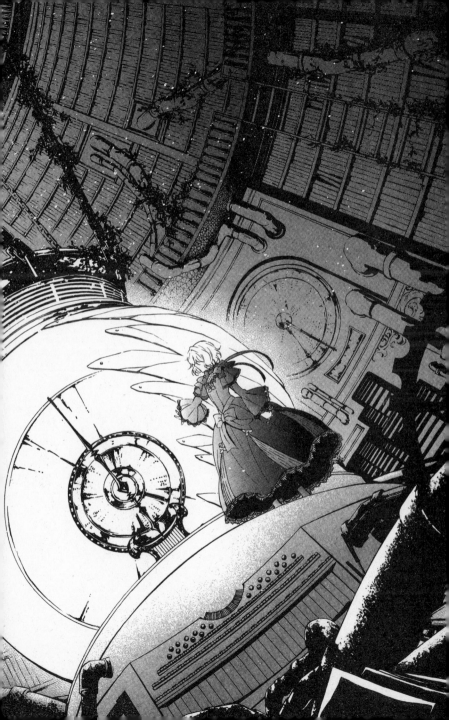

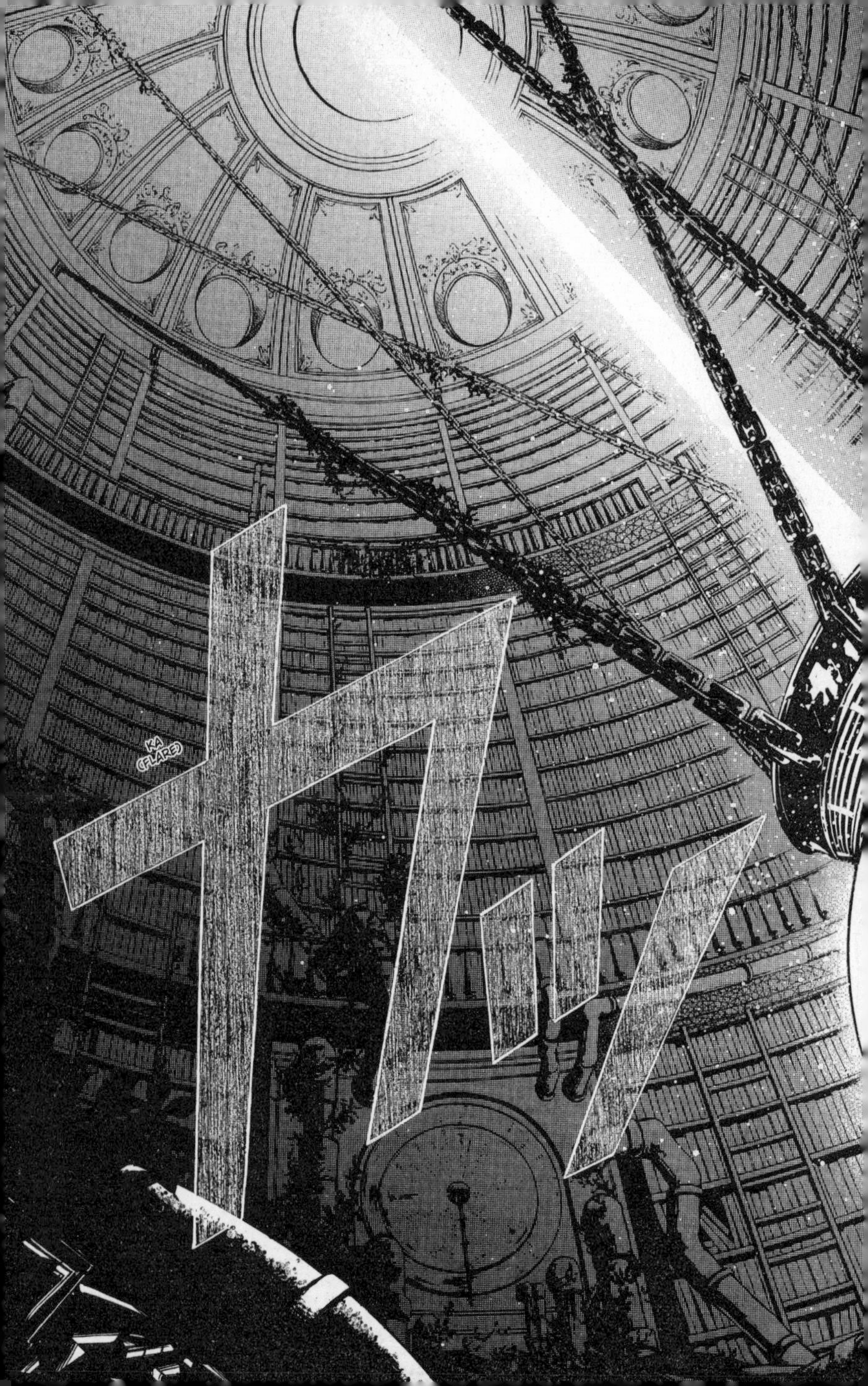
カッ
KA (FLARE)

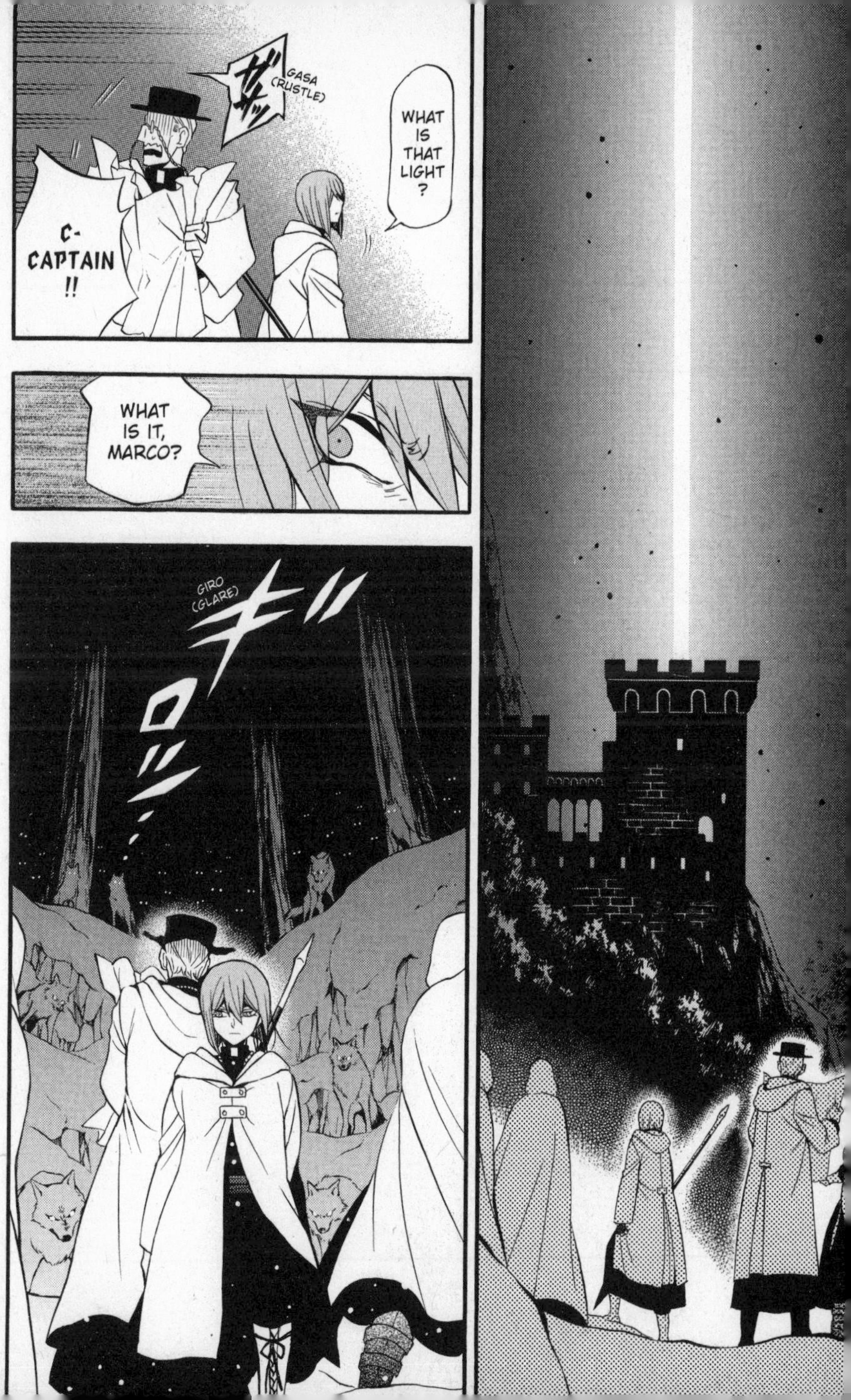
WHAT IS THAT LIGHT?
GASA (RUSTLE)
C-CAPTAIN!!
WHAT IS IT, MARCO?
GIRO (GLARE)

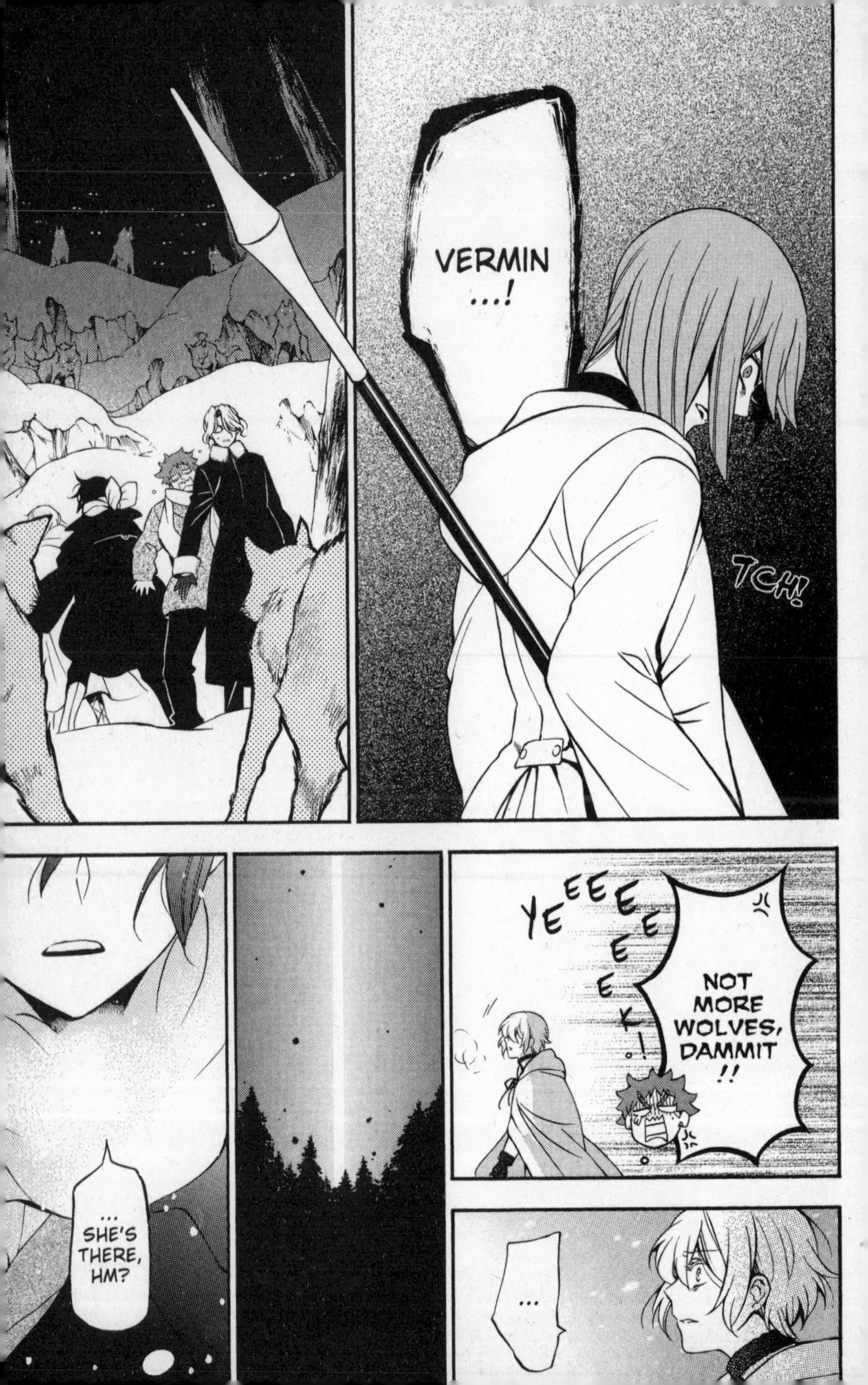
VERMIN ...!
TCH!
YEEEEEEEK!
NOT MORE WOLVES, DAMMIT!!
...
... SHE'S THERE, HM?

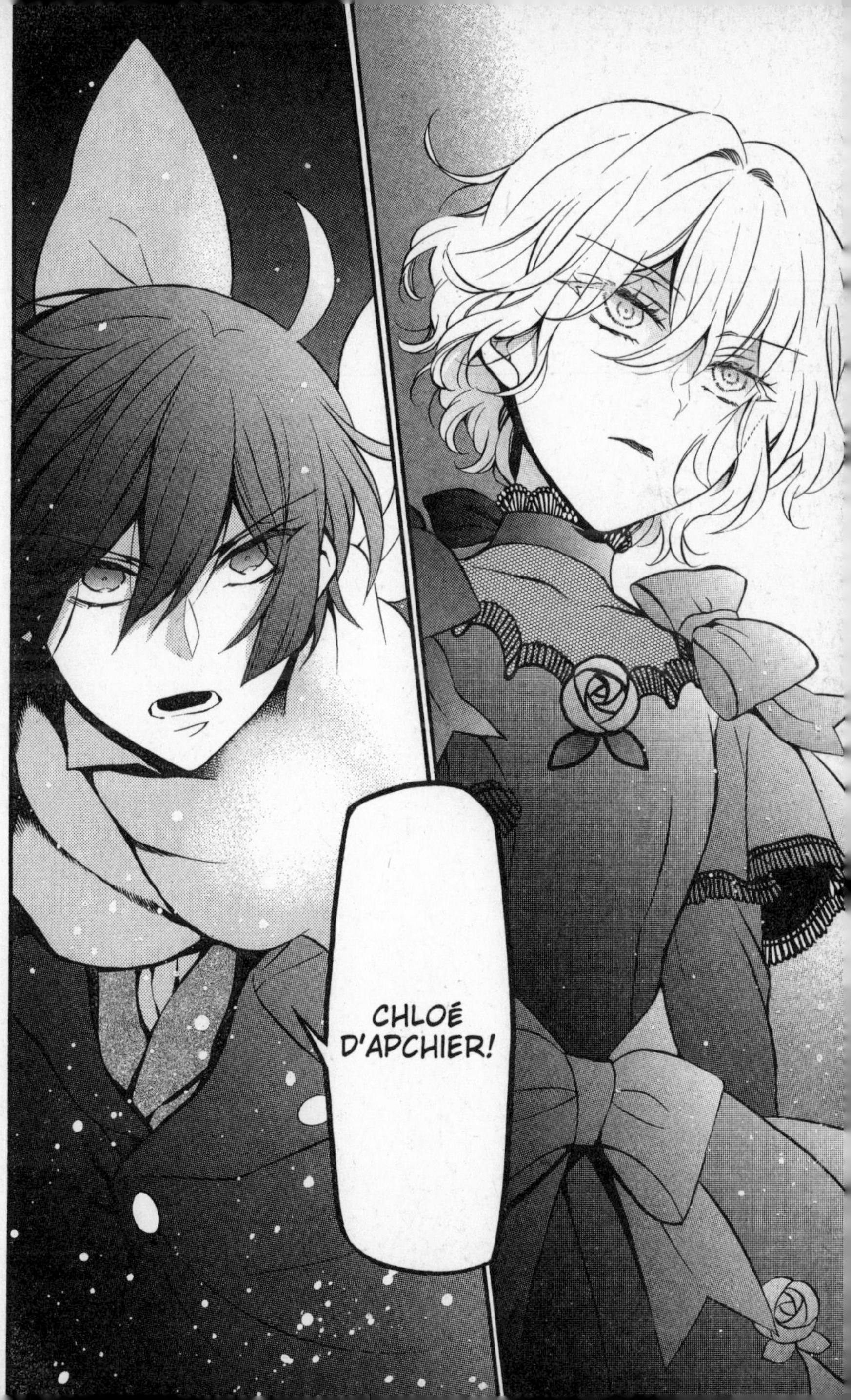
CHLOÉ D'APCHIER!

Mémoire 55 *Cauchemar* RUMBLE

Les Mémoires de Vanitas

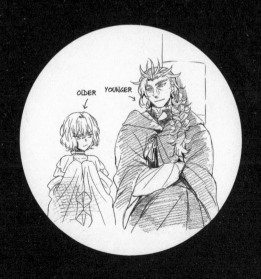

OLDER   YOUNGER

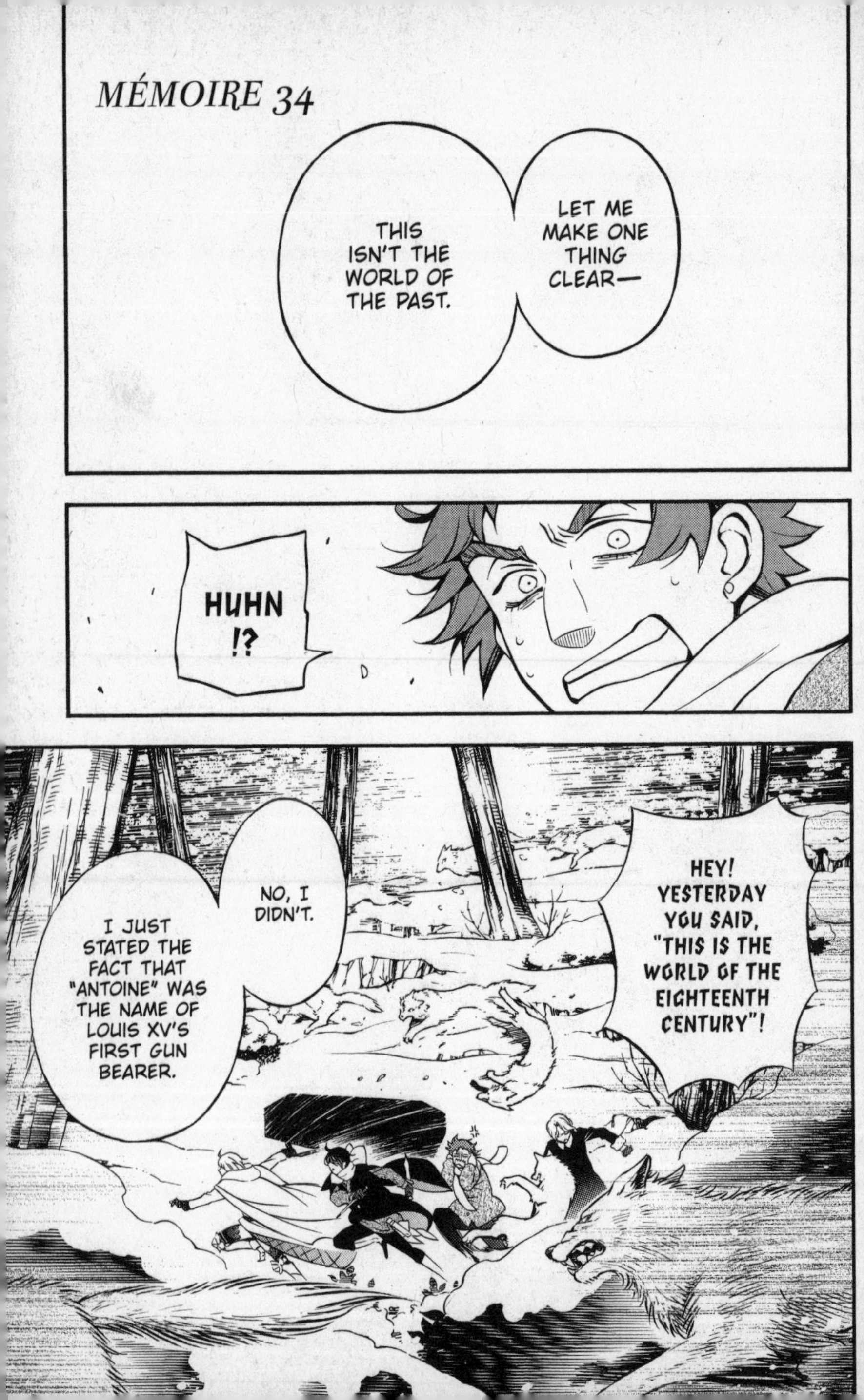
MÉMOIRE 34
LET ME MAKE ONE THING CLEAR—
THIS ISN'T THE WORLD OF THE PAST.
HUHN !?
HEY! YESTERDAY YOU SAID, "THIS IS THE WORLD OF THE EIGHTEENTH CENTURY"!
NO, I DIDN'T.
I JUST STATED THE FACT THAT "ANTOINE" WAS THE NAME OF LOUIS XV'S FIRST GUN BEARER.

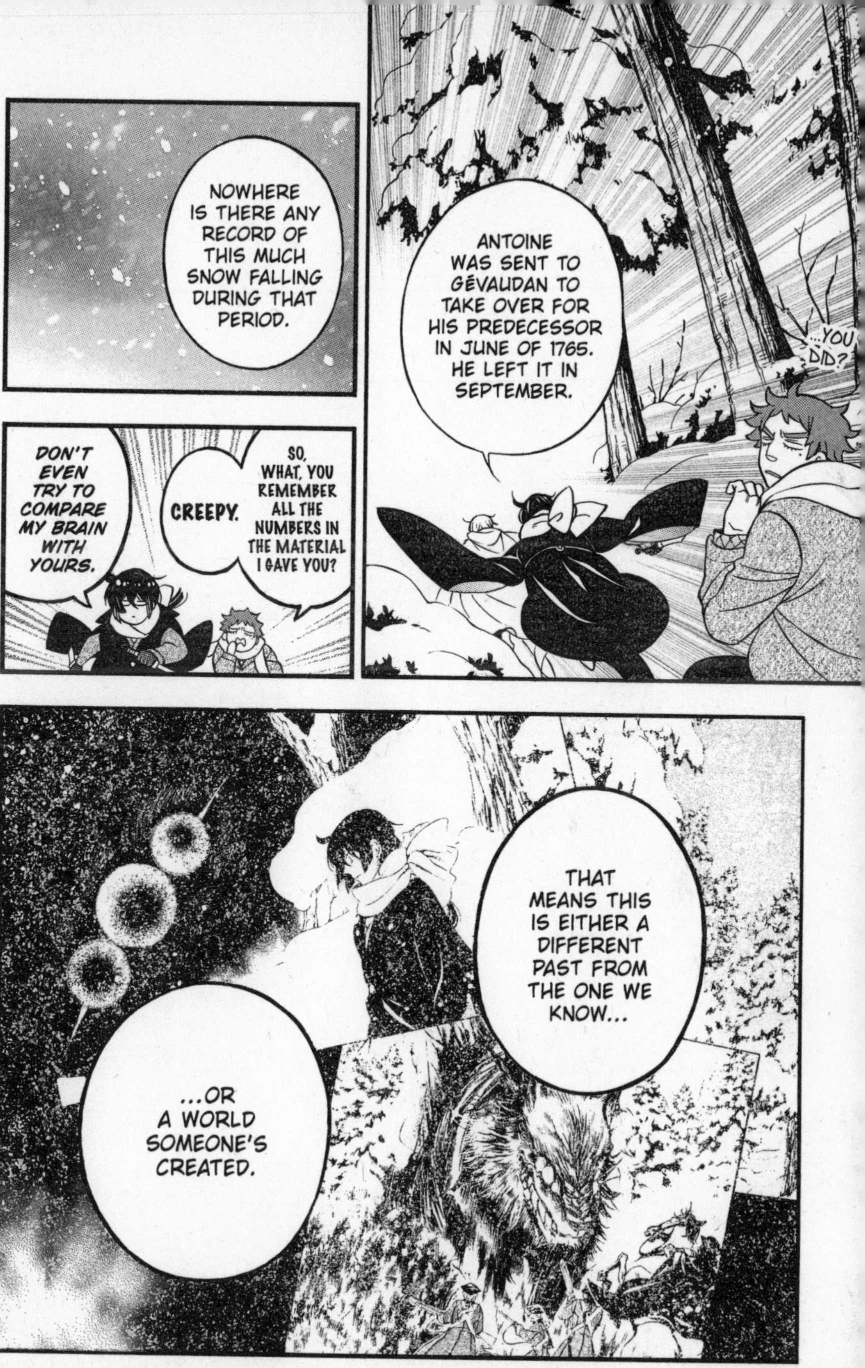
ANTOINE WAS SENT TO GÉVAUDAN TO TAKE OVER FOR HIS PREDECESSOR IN JUNE OF 1765. HE LEFT IT IN SEPTEMBER.
...YOU DID?
NOWHERE IS THERE ANY RECORD OF THIS MUCH SNOW FALLING DURING THAT PERIOD.
SO, WHAT, YOU REMEMBER ALL THE NUMBERS IN THE MATERIAL I GAVE YOU?
CREEPY.
DON'T EVEN TRY TO COMPARE MY BRAIN WITH YOURS.
THAT MEANS THIS IS EITHER A DIFFERENT PAST FROM THE ONE WE KNOW...
...OR A WORLD SOMEONE'S CREATED.

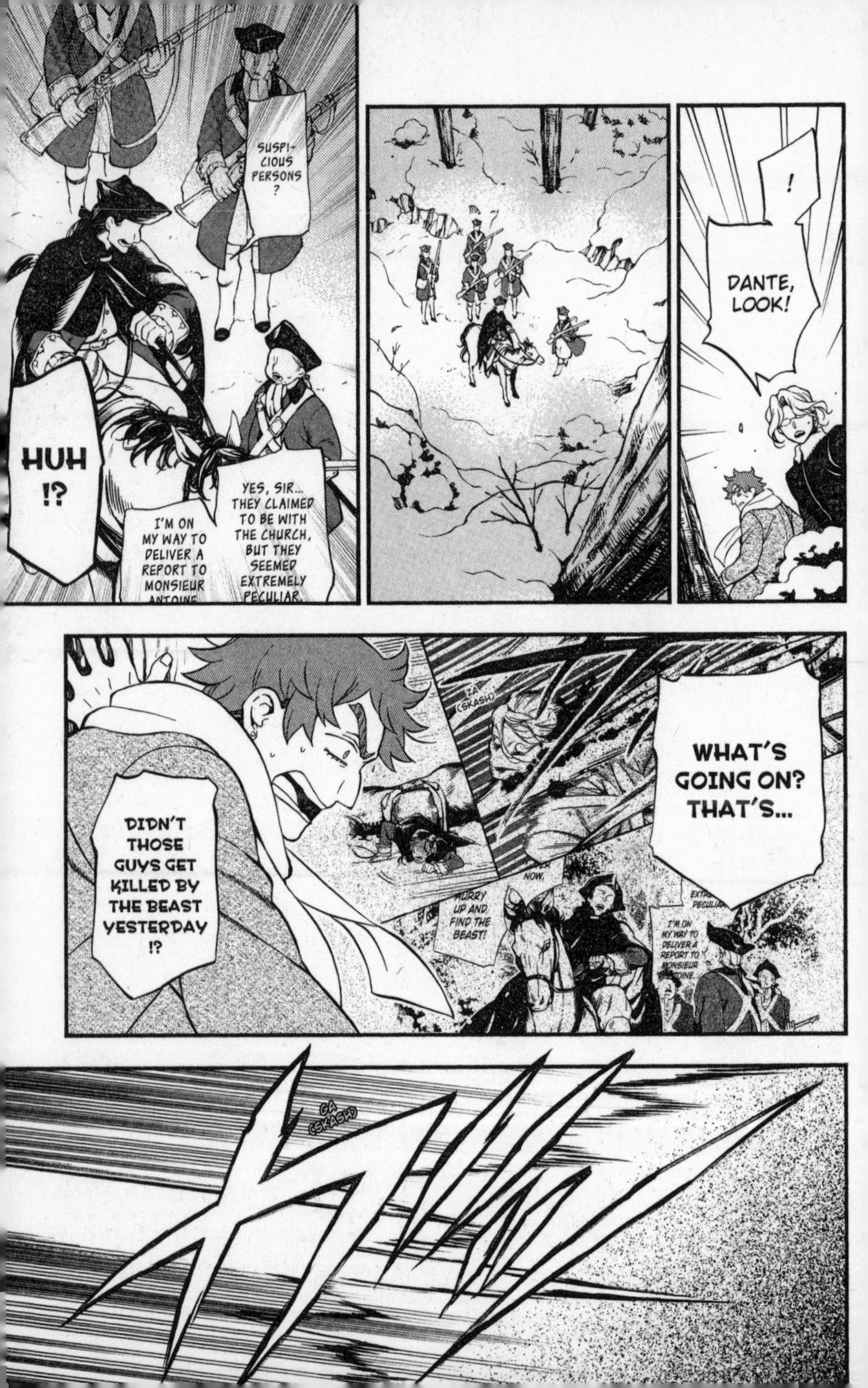
!
DANTE, LOOK!
SUSPICIOUS PERSONS?
YES, SIR... THEY CLAIMED TO BE WITH THE CHURCH, BUT THEY SEEMED EXTREMELY PECULIAR
I'M ON MY WAY TO DELIVER A REPORT TO MONSIEUR ANTOINE
HUH!?
WHAT'S GOING ON? THAT'S...
ZA (SKASH)
NOW.
HURRY UP AND FIND THE BEAST!
DIDN'T THOSE GUYS GET KILLED BY THE BEAST YESTERDAY!?
GA (SKASH)

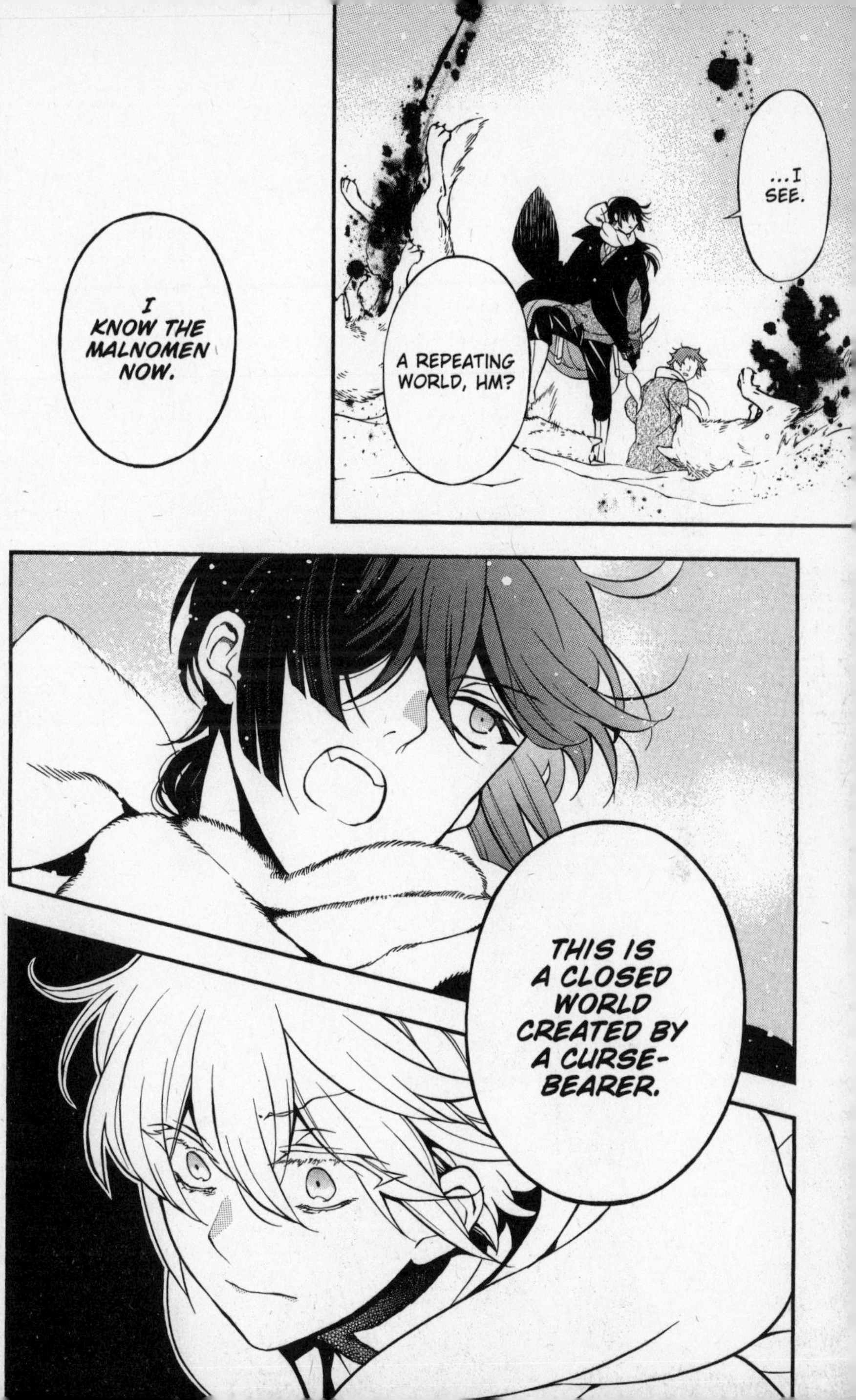
...I SEE.
A REPEATING WORLD, HM?
I KNOW THE MALNOMEN NOW.
THIS IS A CLOSED WORLD CREATED BY A CURSE-BEARER.

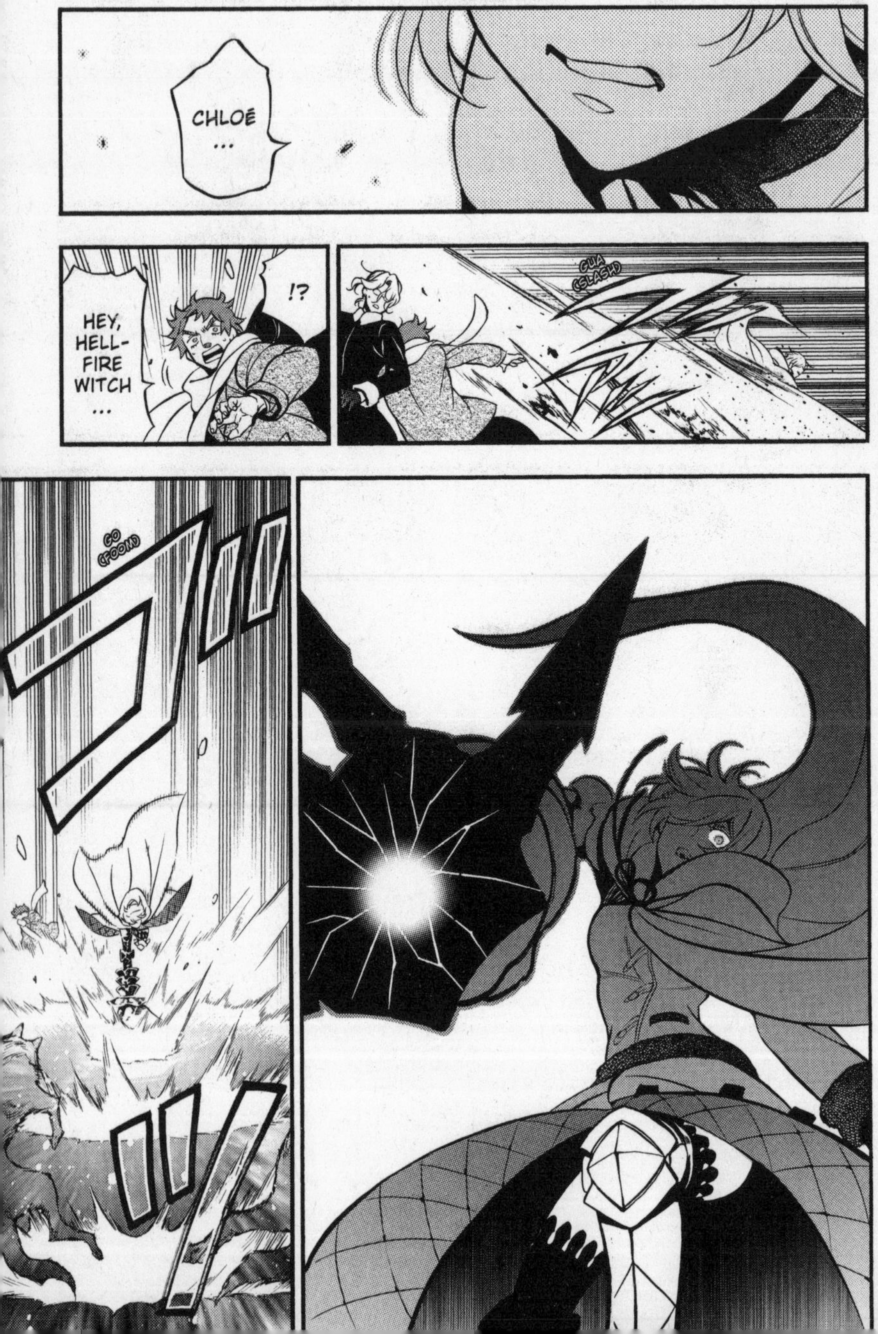
CHLOÉ ...
GUA (SLASH)
!?
HEY, HELL-FIRE WITCH ...
GO (FOOM)

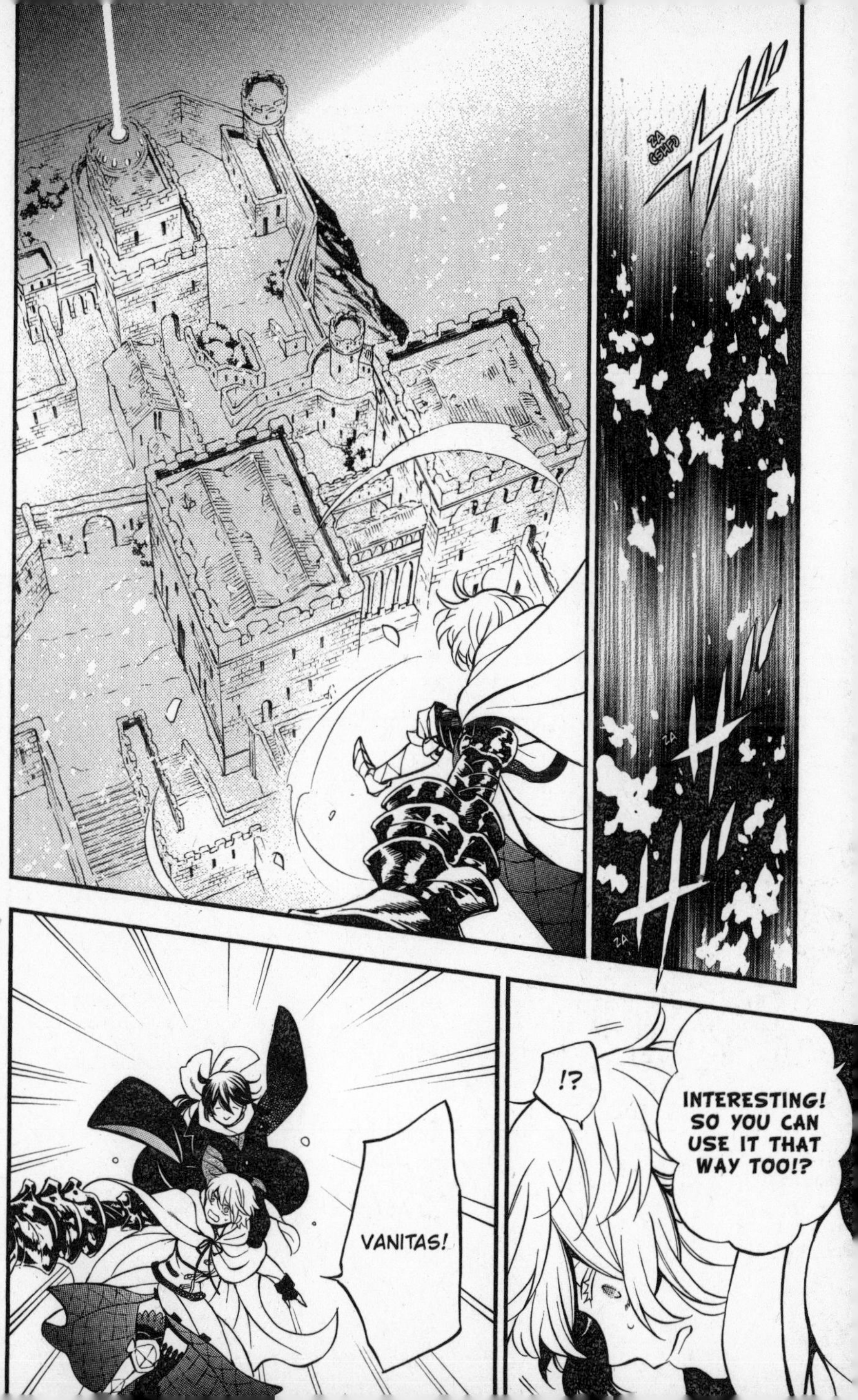
ZA (SHF)
ZA
ZA
!?
INTERESTING! SO YOU CAN USE IT THAT WAY TOO!?
VANITAS!

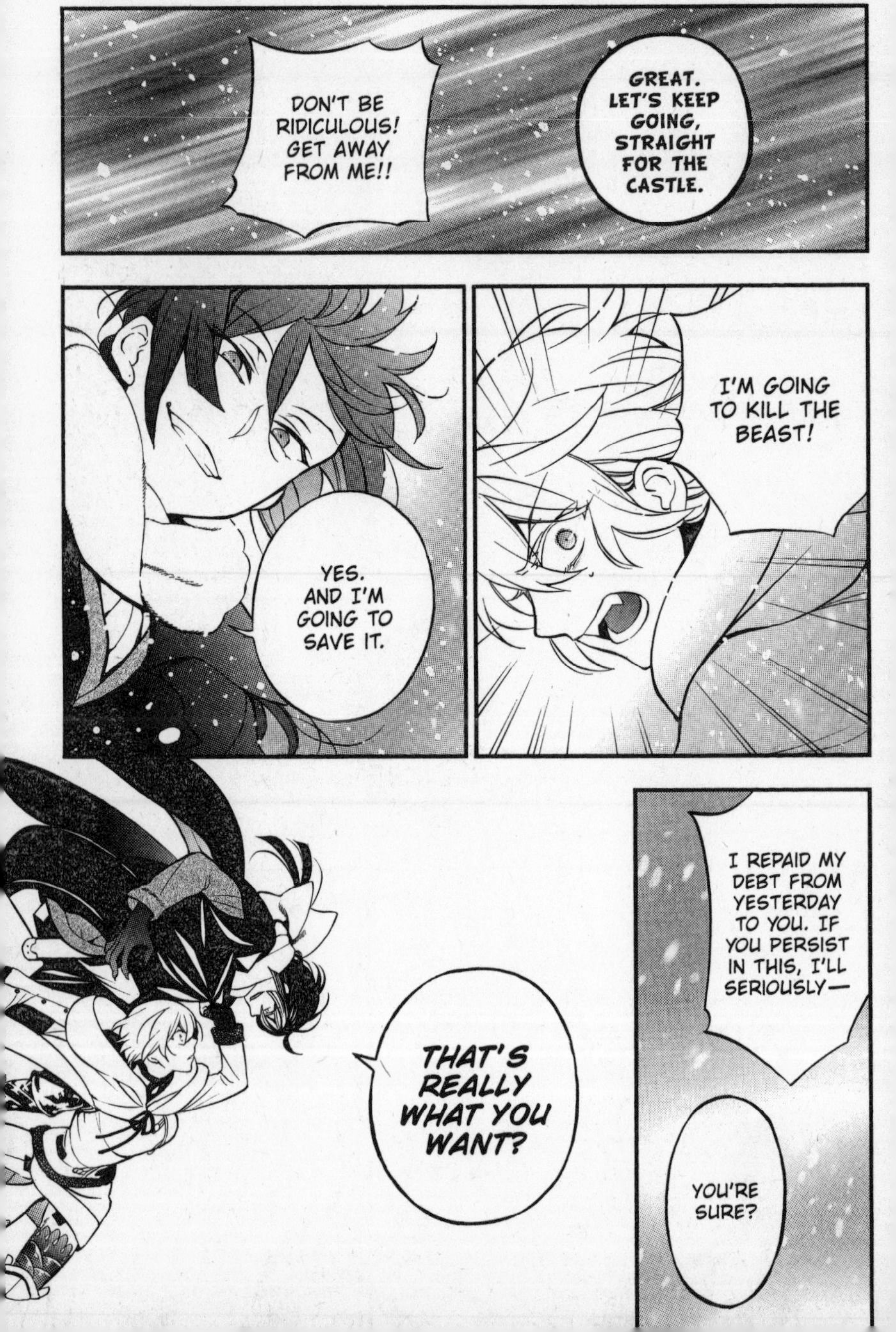
GREAT. LET'S KEEP GOING, STRAIGHT FOR THE CASTLE.
DON'T BE RIDICULOUS! GET AWAY FROM ME!!
I'M GOING TO KILL THE BEAST!
YES. AND I'M GOING TO SAVE IT.
I REPAID MY DEBT FROM YESTERDAY TO YOU. IF YOU PERSIST IN THIS, I'LL SERIOUSLY—
YOU'RE SURE?
THAT'S REALLY WHAT YOU WANT?

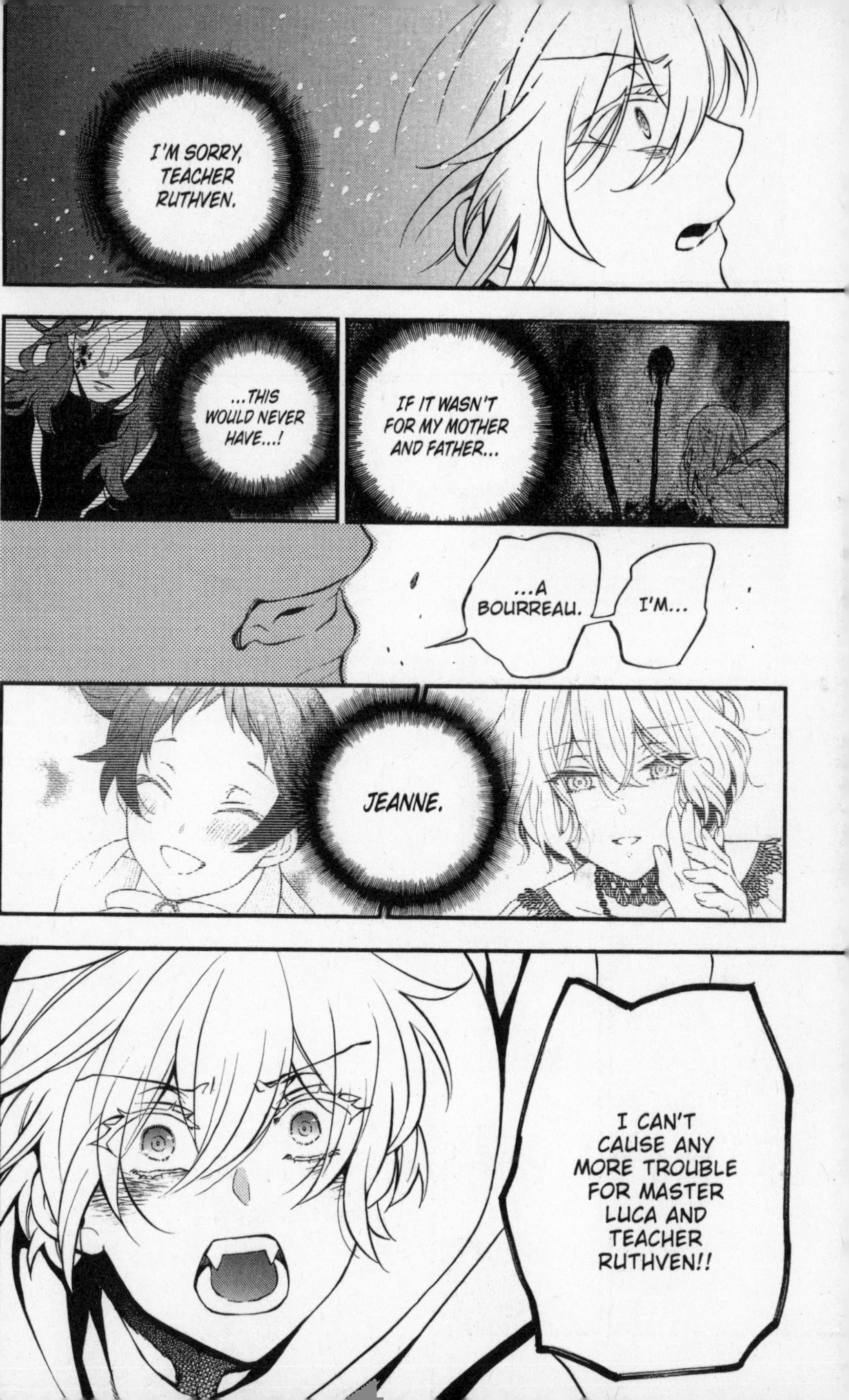
I'M SORRY, TEACHER RUTHVEN.
IF IT WASN'T FOR MY MOTHER AND FATHER...
...THIS WOULD NEVER HAVE...!
I'M...
...A BOURREAU.
JEANNE.
I CAN'T CAUSE ANY MORE TROUBLE FOR MASTER LUCA AND TEACHER RUTHVEN!!

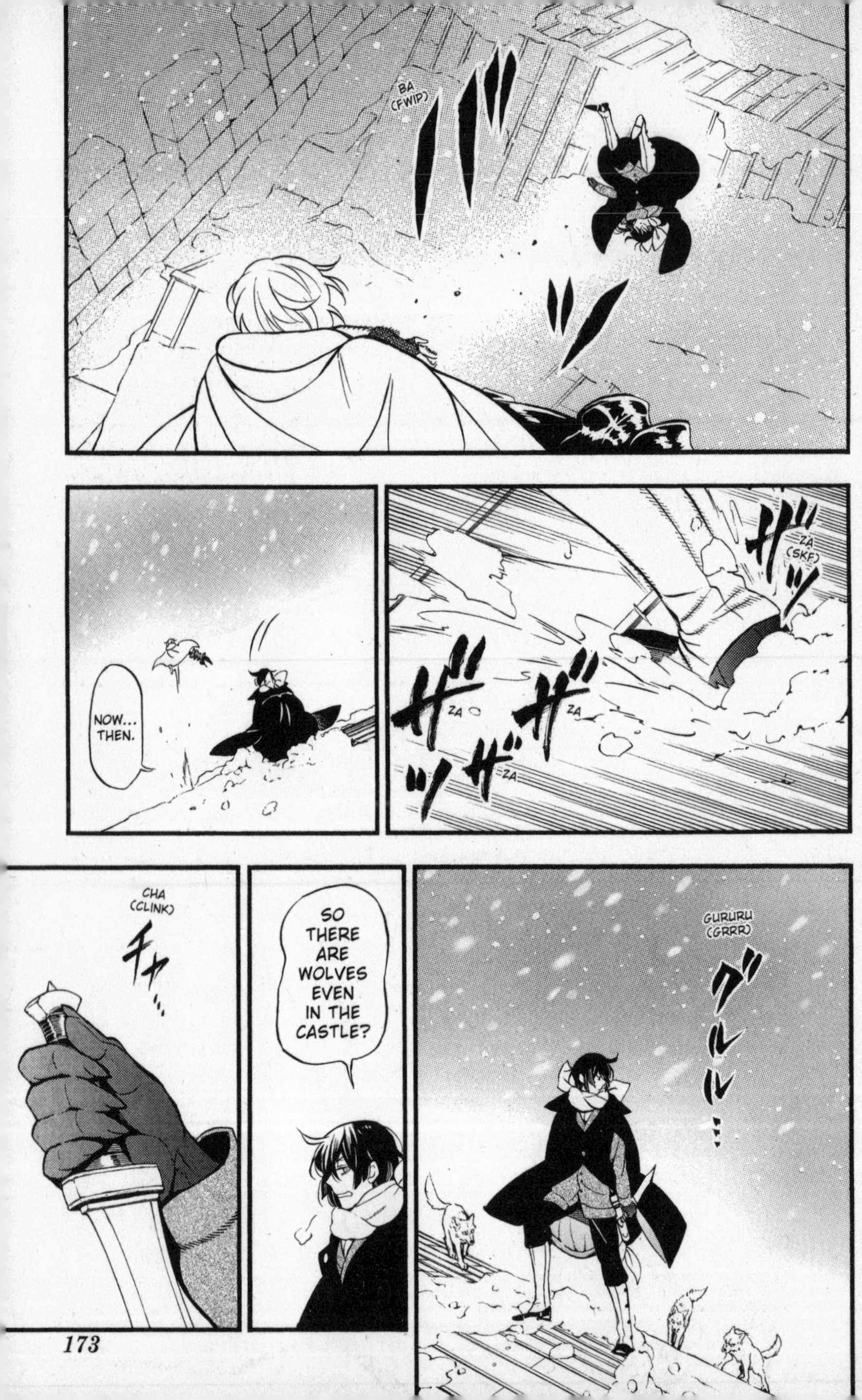

BA (FWIP)
ZA (SKF)
ZA
ZA
ZA
NOW... THEN.
GURURU (GRRR)
SO THERE ARE WOLVES EVEN IN THE CASTLE?
CHA (CLINK)

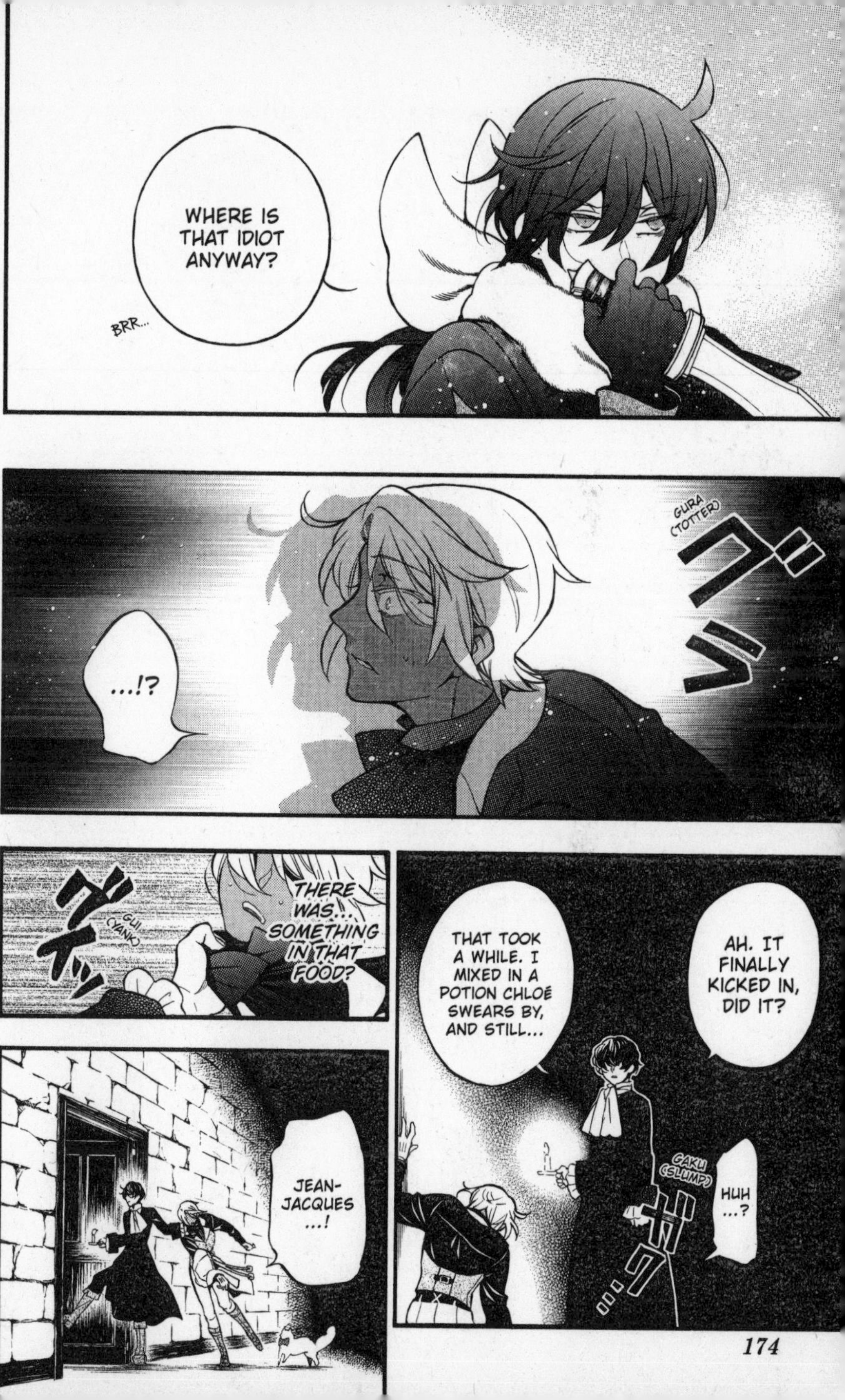
WHERE IS THAT IDIOT ANYWAY?
BRR...
GURA (TOTTER)
...!?
AH. IT FINALLY KICKED IN, DID IT?
THAT TOOK A WHILE. I MIXED IN A POTION CHLOÉ SWEARS BY, AND STILL...
GAKU (SLUMP)
HUH ...?
THERE WAS... SOMETHING IN THAT FOOD?
GUI (YANK)
JEAN-JACQUES ...!

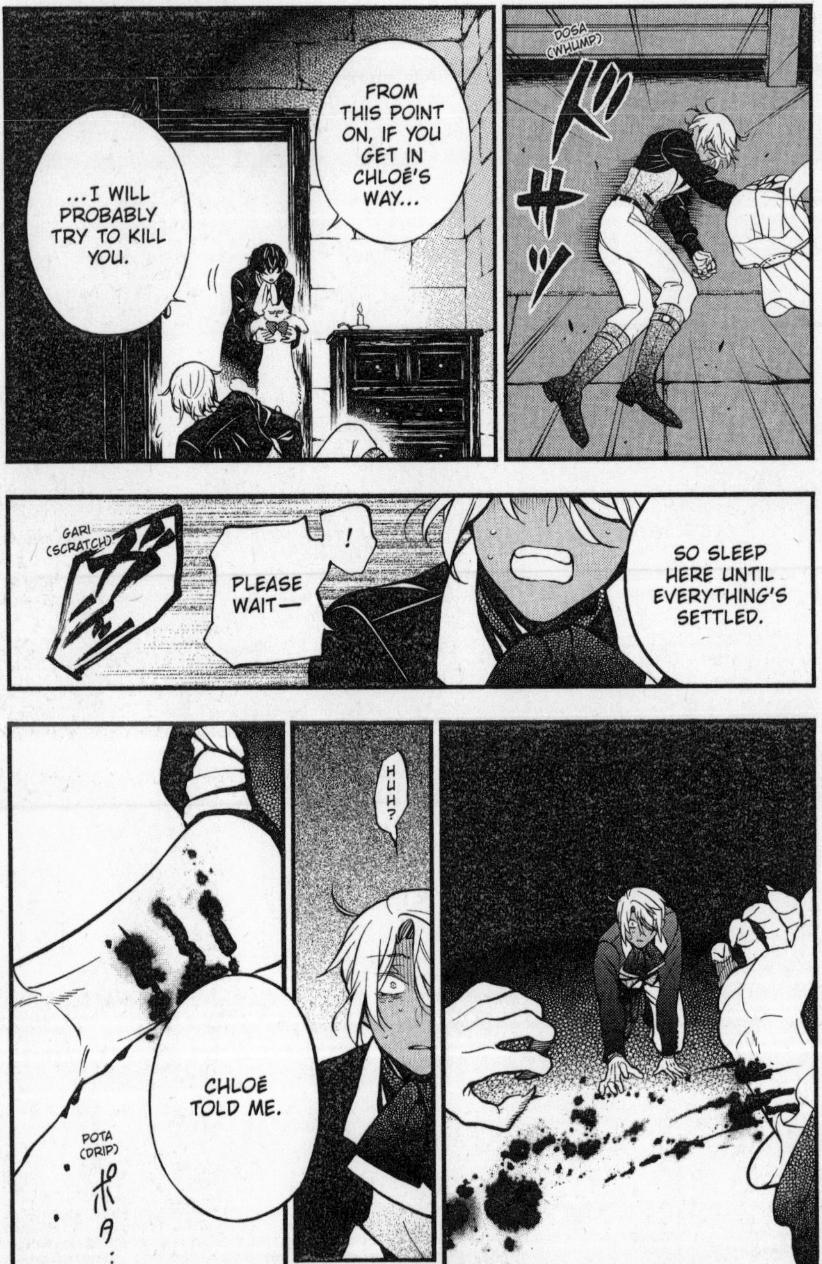
DOSA (WHUMP)
FROM THIS POINT ON, IF YOU GET IN CHLOÉ'S WAY...
...I WILL PROBABLY TRY TO KILL YOU.
SO SLEEP HERE UNTIL EVERYTHING'S SETTLED.
!
PLEASE WAIT—
GARI (SCRATCH)
HUH?
CHLOÉ TOLD ME.
POTA (DRIP)

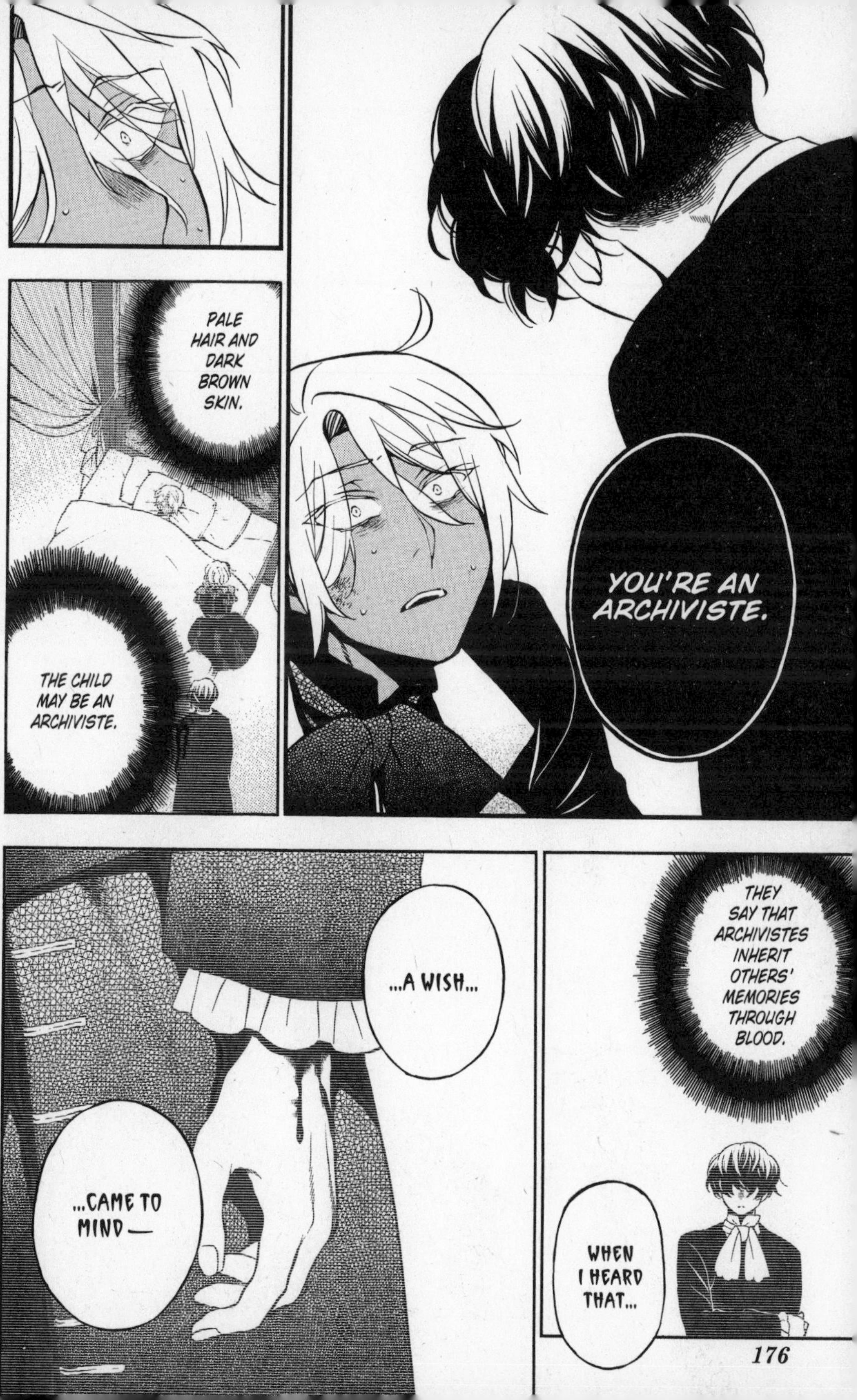
YOU'RE AN ARCHIVISTE.
PALE HAIR AND DARK BROWN SKIN.
THE CHILD MAY BE AN ARCHIVISTE.
THEY SAY THAT ARCHIVISTES INHERIT OTHERS' MEMORIES THROUGH BLOOD.
WHEN I HEARD THAT...
...A WISH...
...CAME TO MIND—

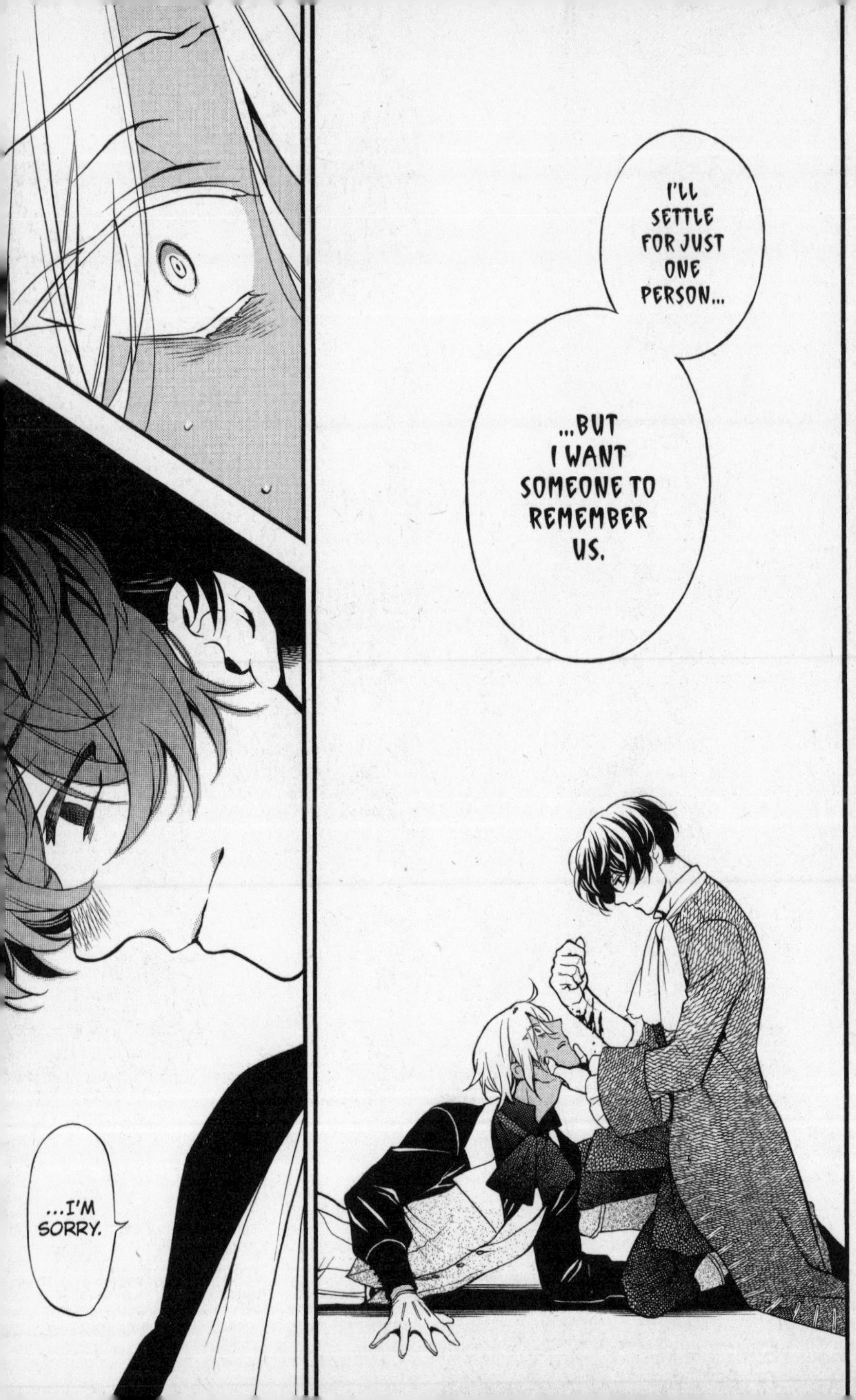
I'LL SETTLE FOR JUST ONE PERSON...
...BUT I WANT SOMEONE TO REMEMBER US.
...I'M SORRY.

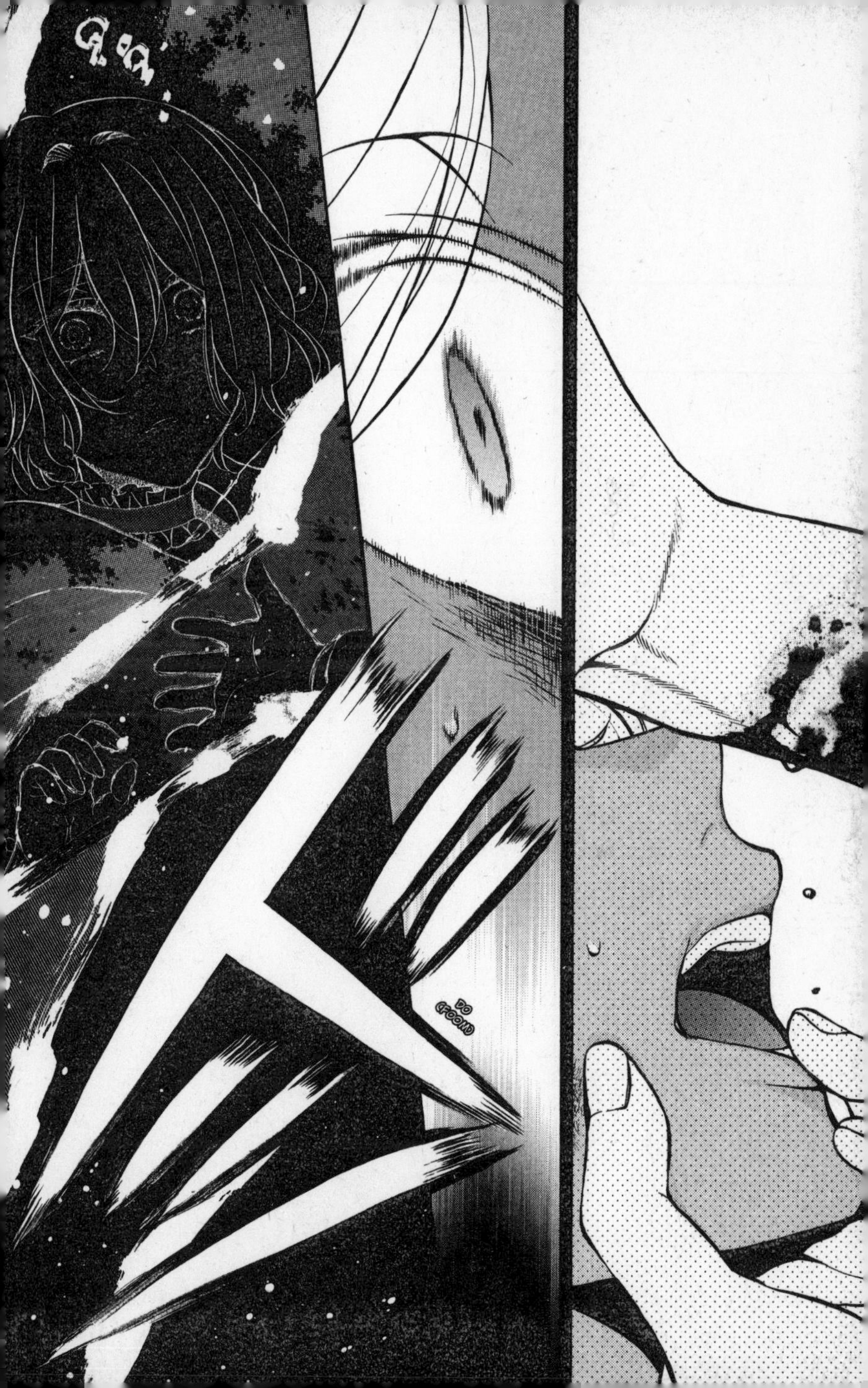
DO
(FOOM)

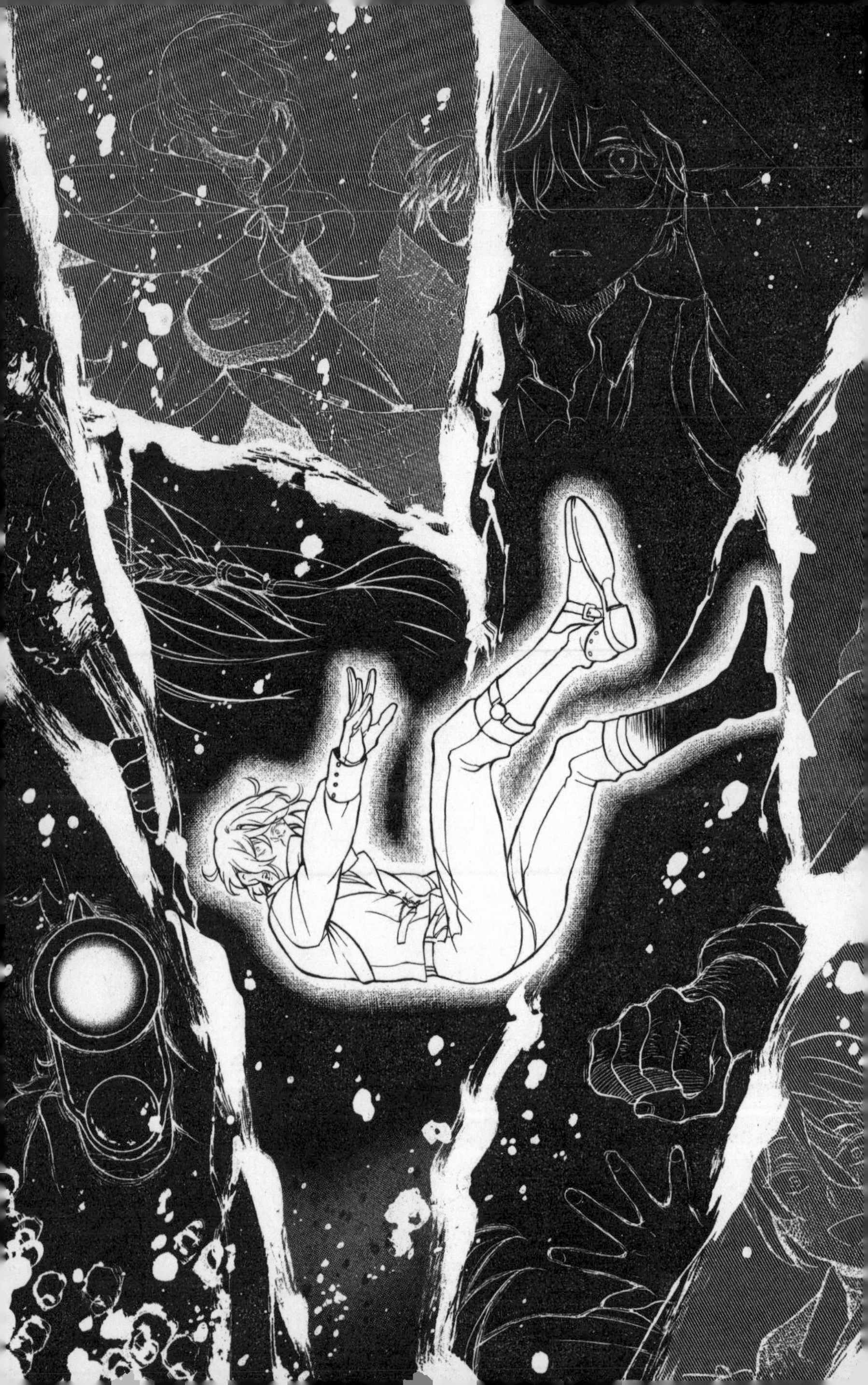

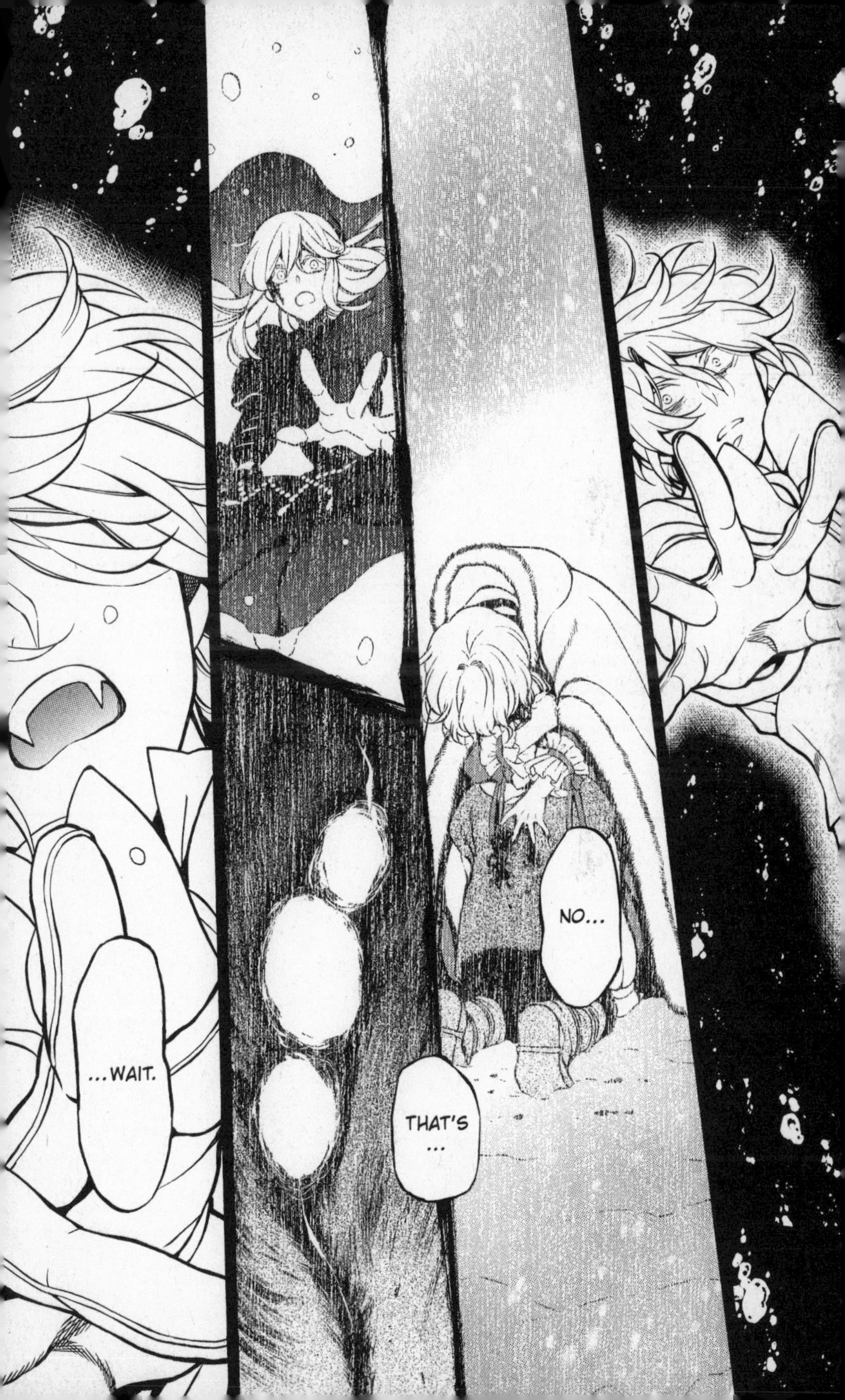
NO...
THAT'S ...
...WAIT.

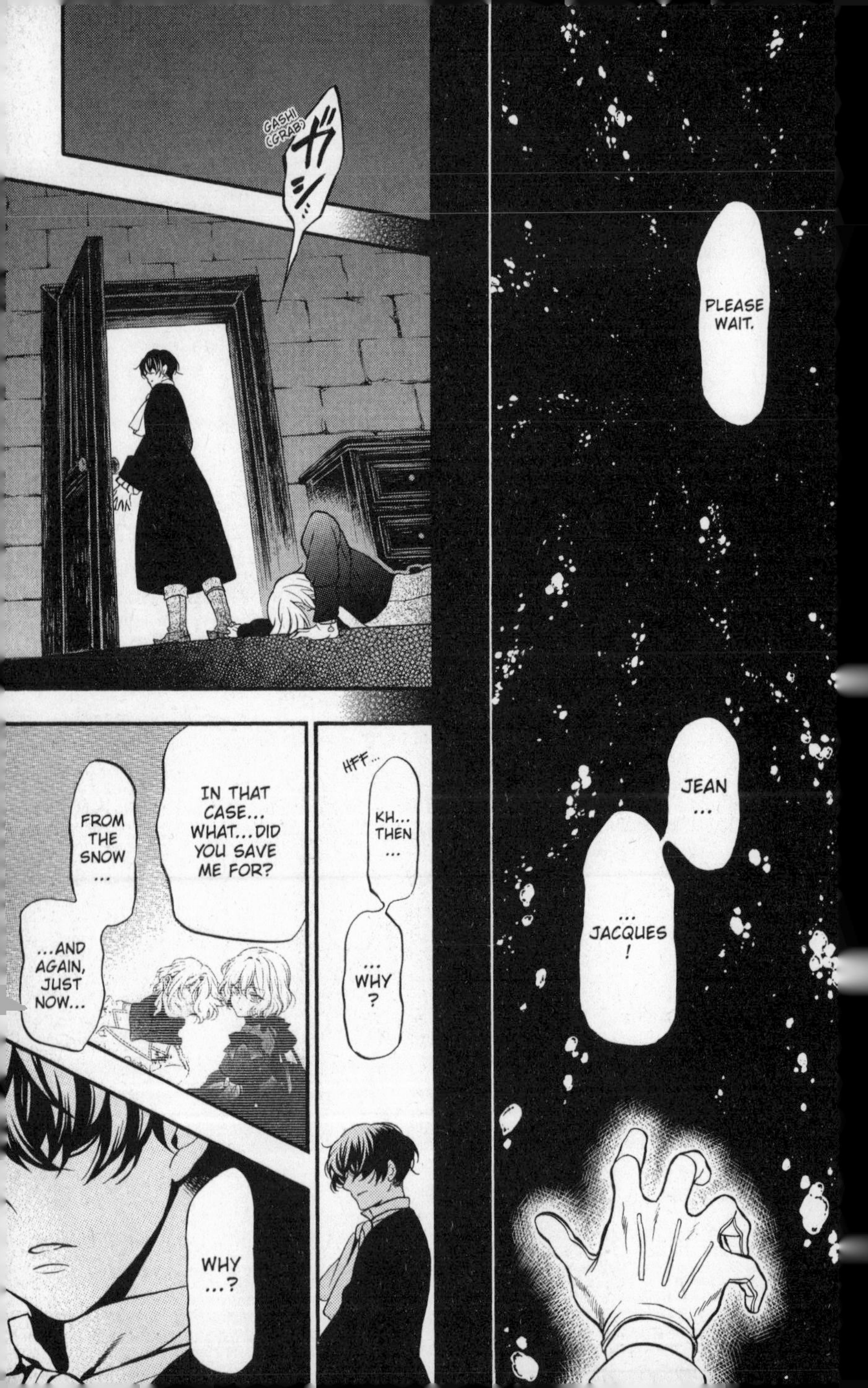
PLEASE WAIT.
JEAN...
...JACQUES!
GASHI (GRAB)
HFF...
KH... THEN...
...WHY?
IN THAT CASE... WHAT...DID YOU SAVE ME FOR?
FROM THE SNOW...
...AND AGAIN, JUST NOW...
WHY...?

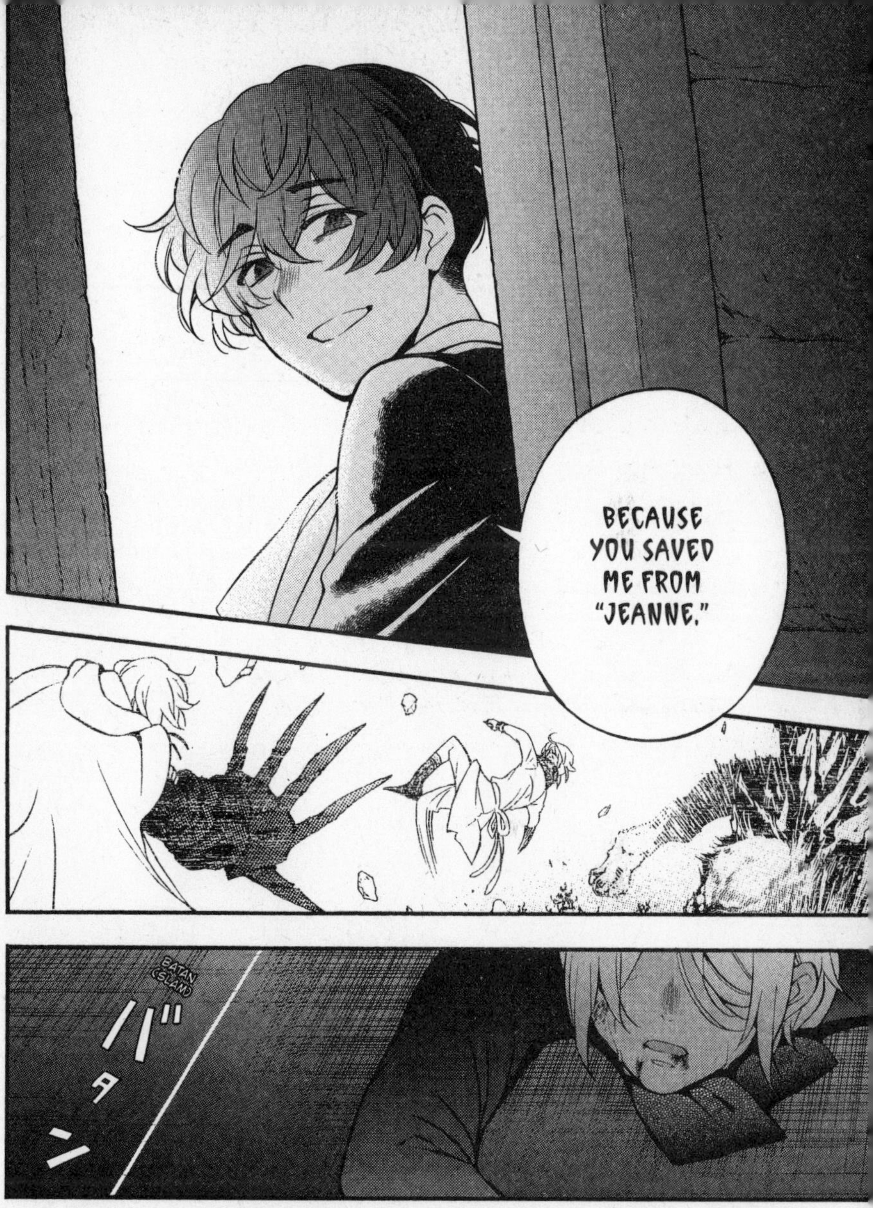
BECAUSE YOU SAVED ME FROM "JEANNE."
BATAN (SLAM)
バタン

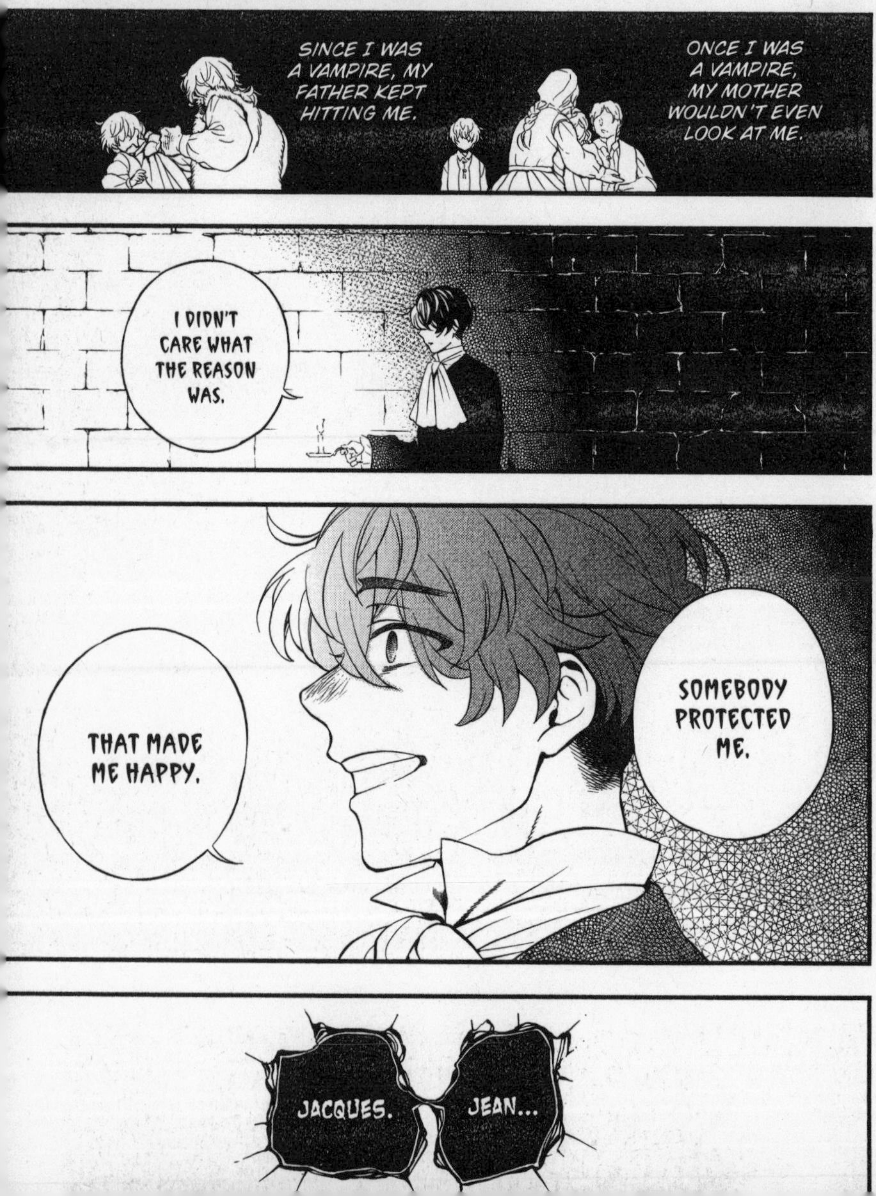
ONCE I WAS A VAMPIRE, MY MOTHER WOULDN'T EVEN LOOK AT ME.
SINCE I WAS A VAMPIRE, MY FATHER KEPT HITTING ME.
I DIDN'T CARE WHAT THE REASON WAS.
SOMEBODY PROTECTED ME.
THAT MADE ME HAPPY.
JEAN...
JACQUES.

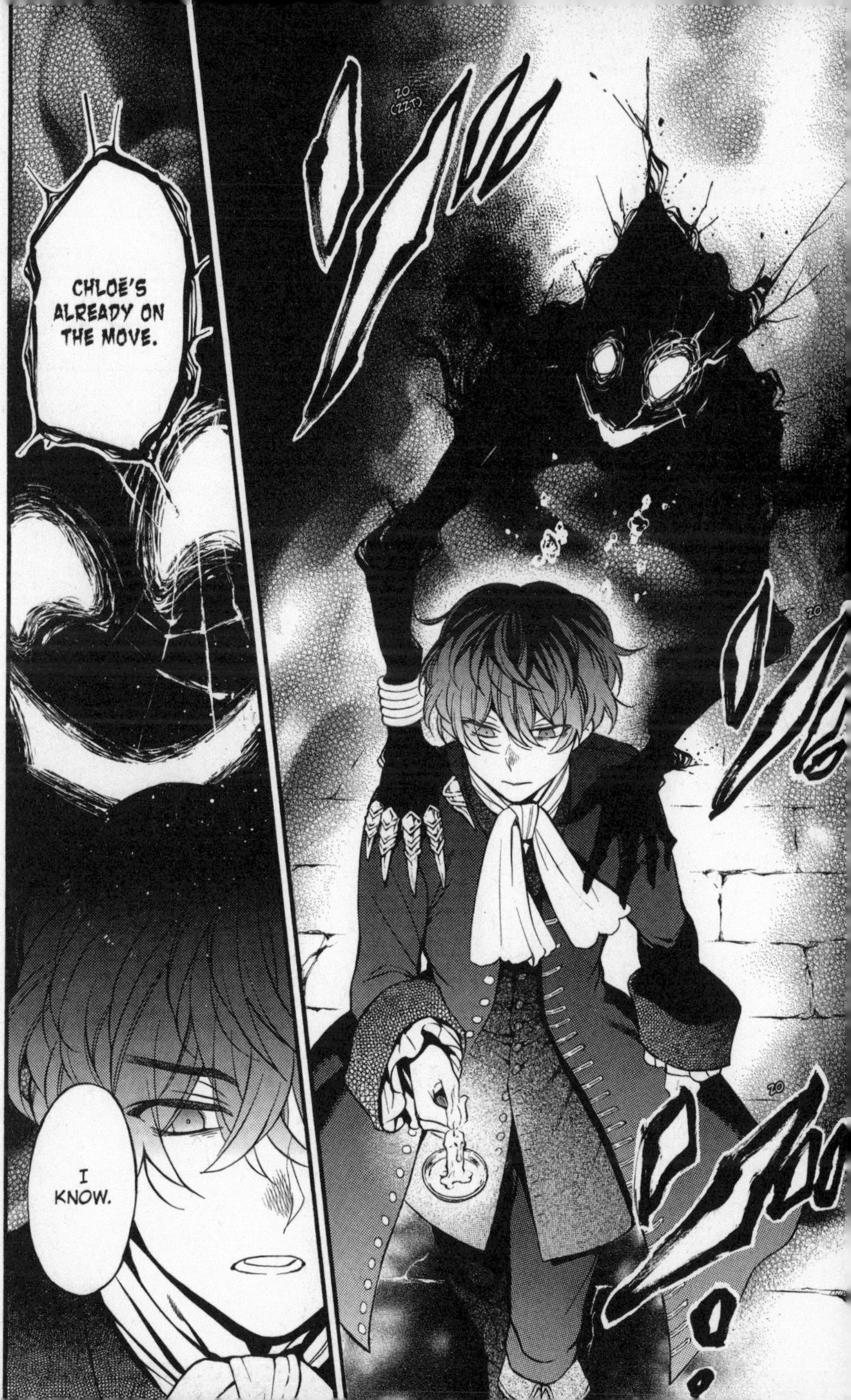
ZO
(ZZZT)
ZO
ZO
CHLOÉ'S ALREADY ON THE MOVE.
I KNOW.

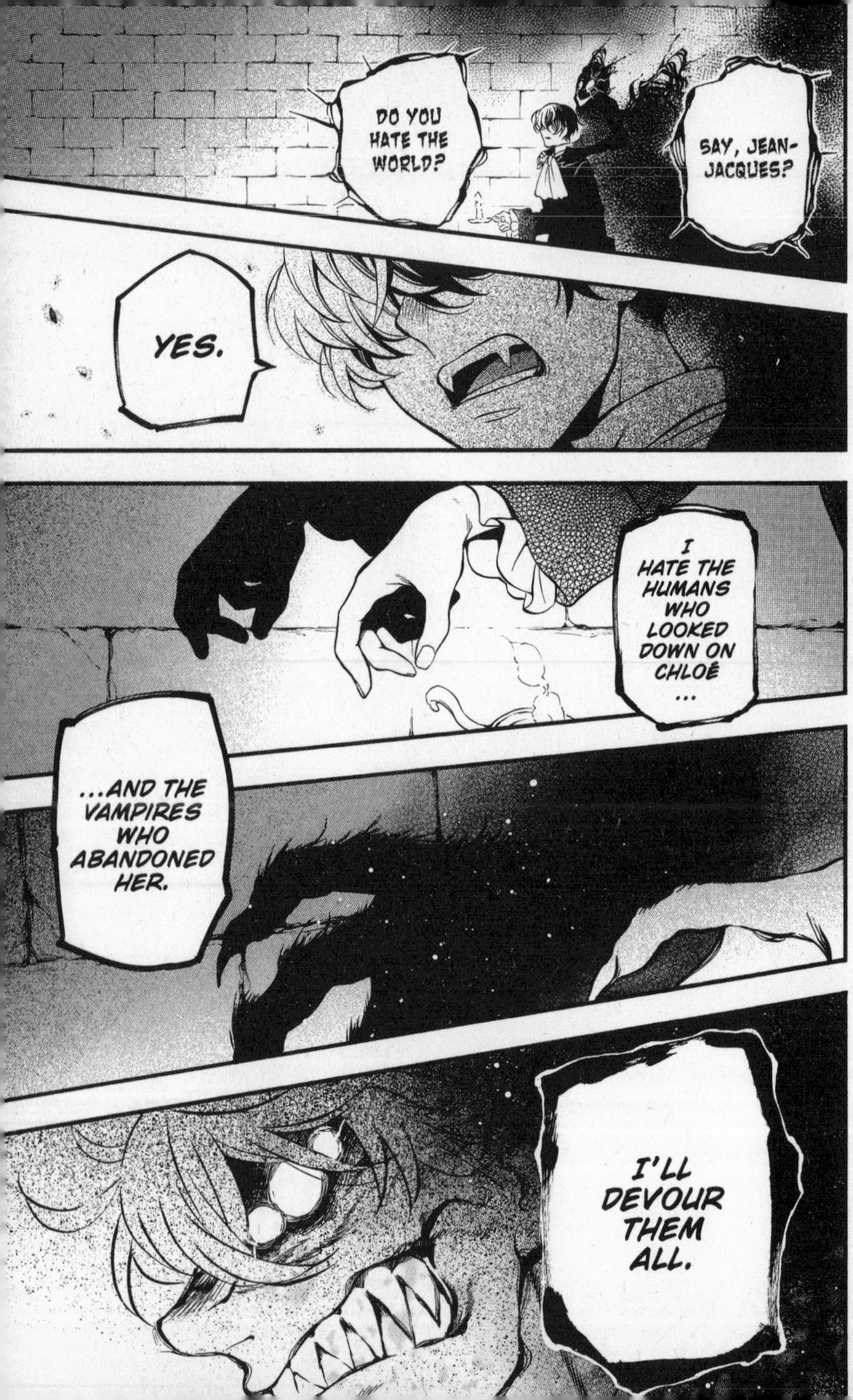
SAY, JEAN-JACQUES?
DO YOU HATE THE WORLD?
YES.
I HATE THE HUMANS WHO LOOKED DOWN ON CHLOÉ...
...AND THE VAMPIRES WHO ABANDONED HER.
I'LL DEVOUR THEM ALL.

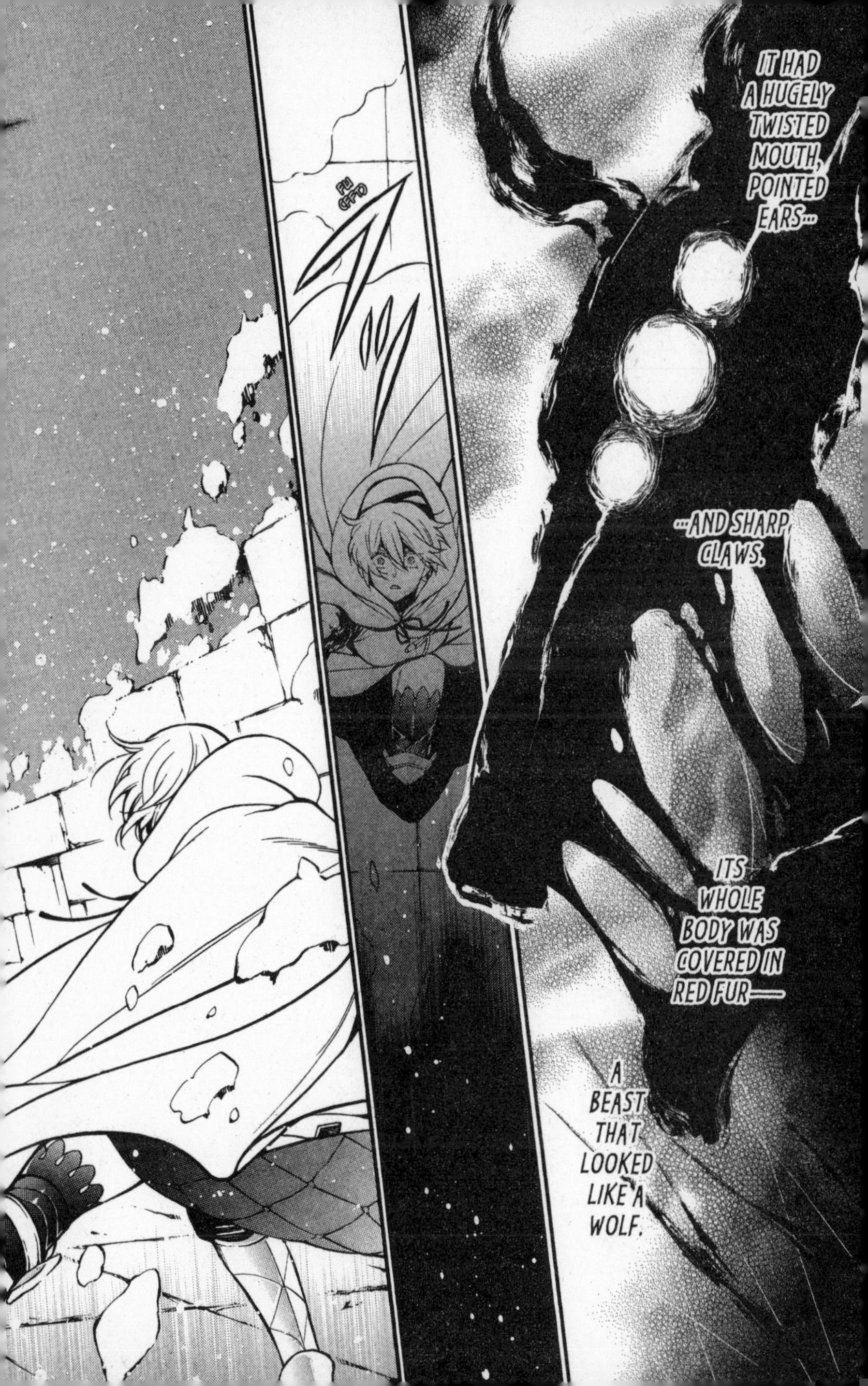
IT HAD A HUGELY TWISTED MOUTH, POINTED EARS...
...AND SHARP CLAWS.
ITS WHOLE BODY WAS COVERED IN RED FUR—
A BEAST THAT LOOKED LIKE A WOLF.
FU (FFT)

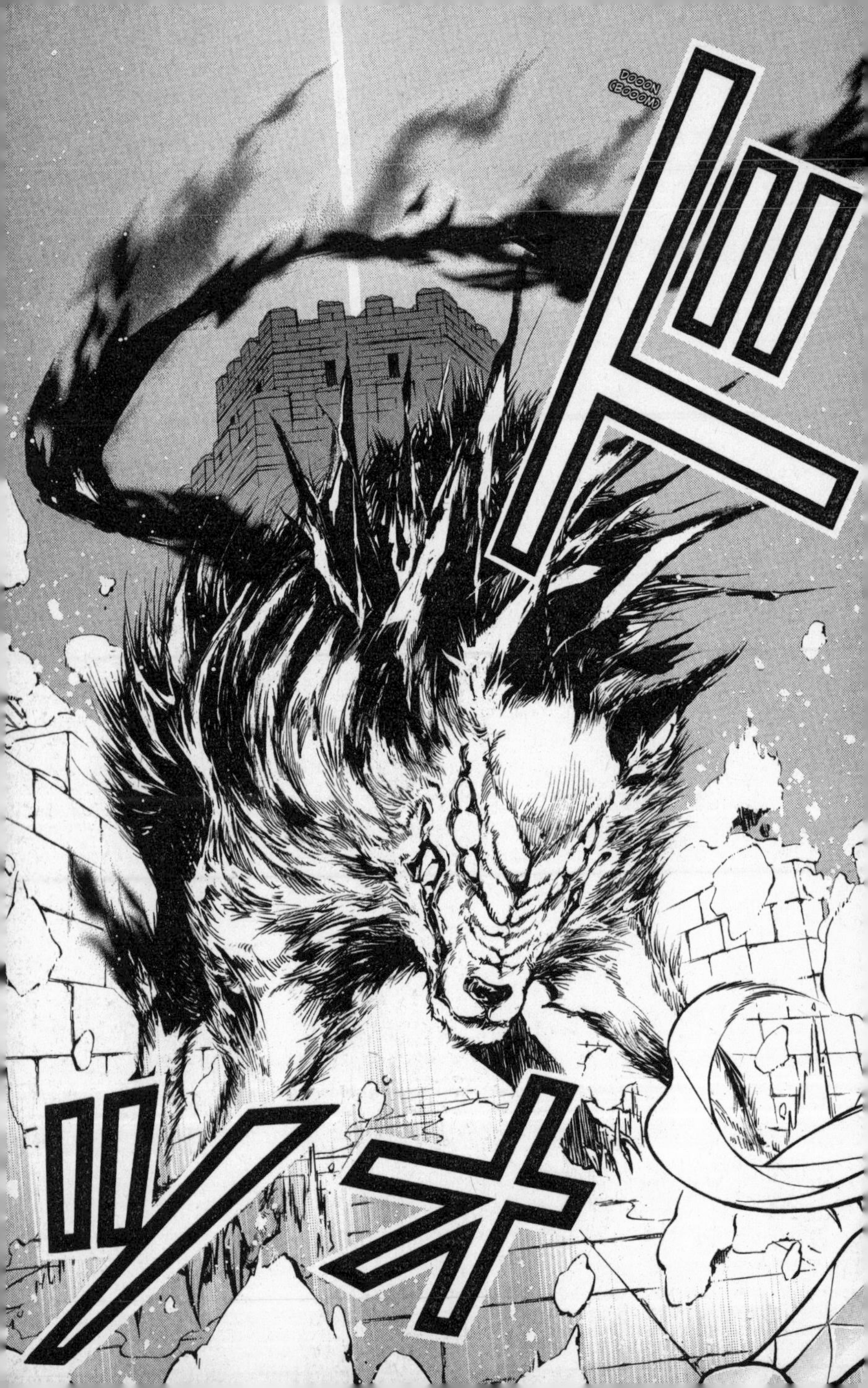
DOOON
(BOOOM)
ドドン

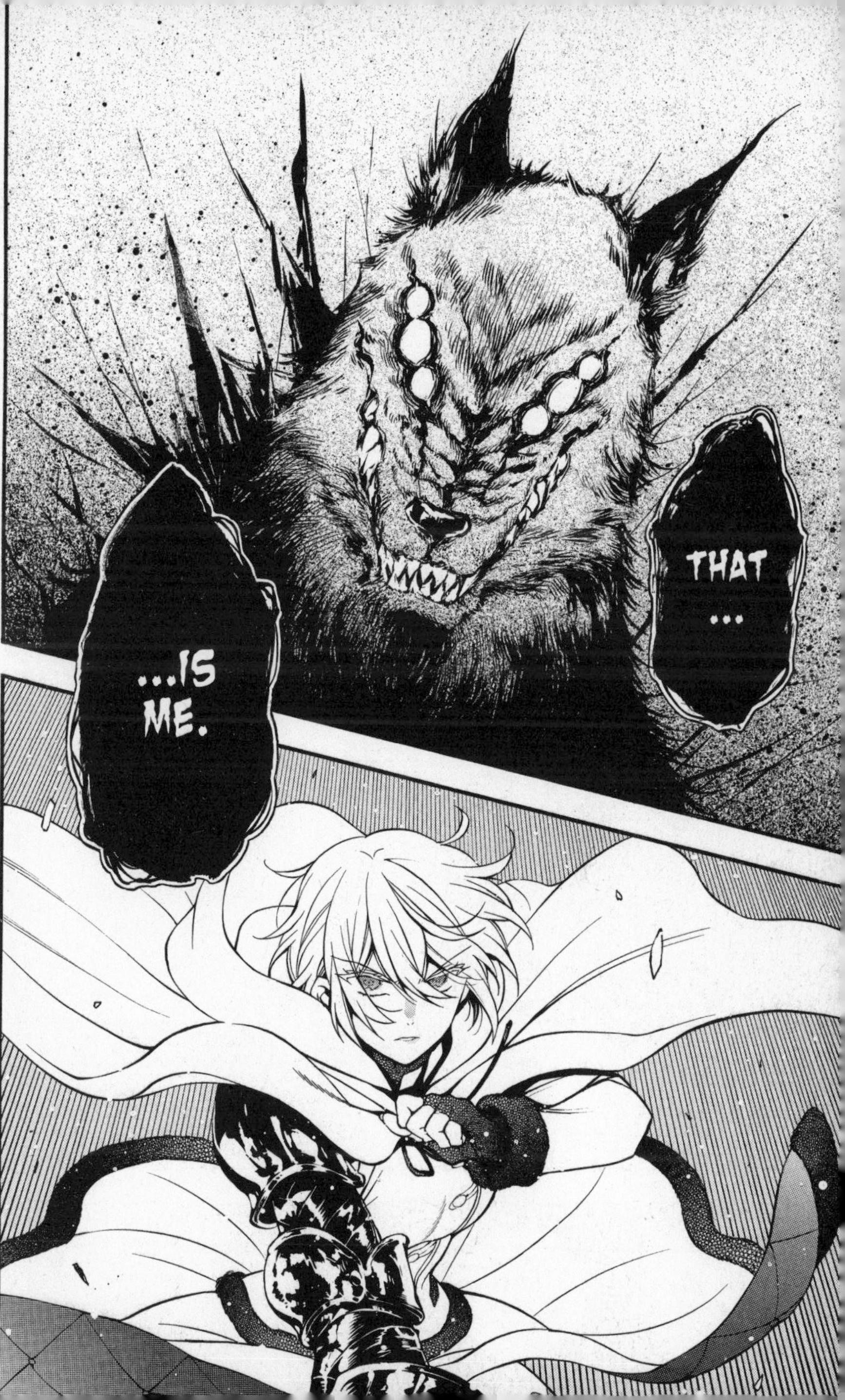
THAT ...
...IS ME.

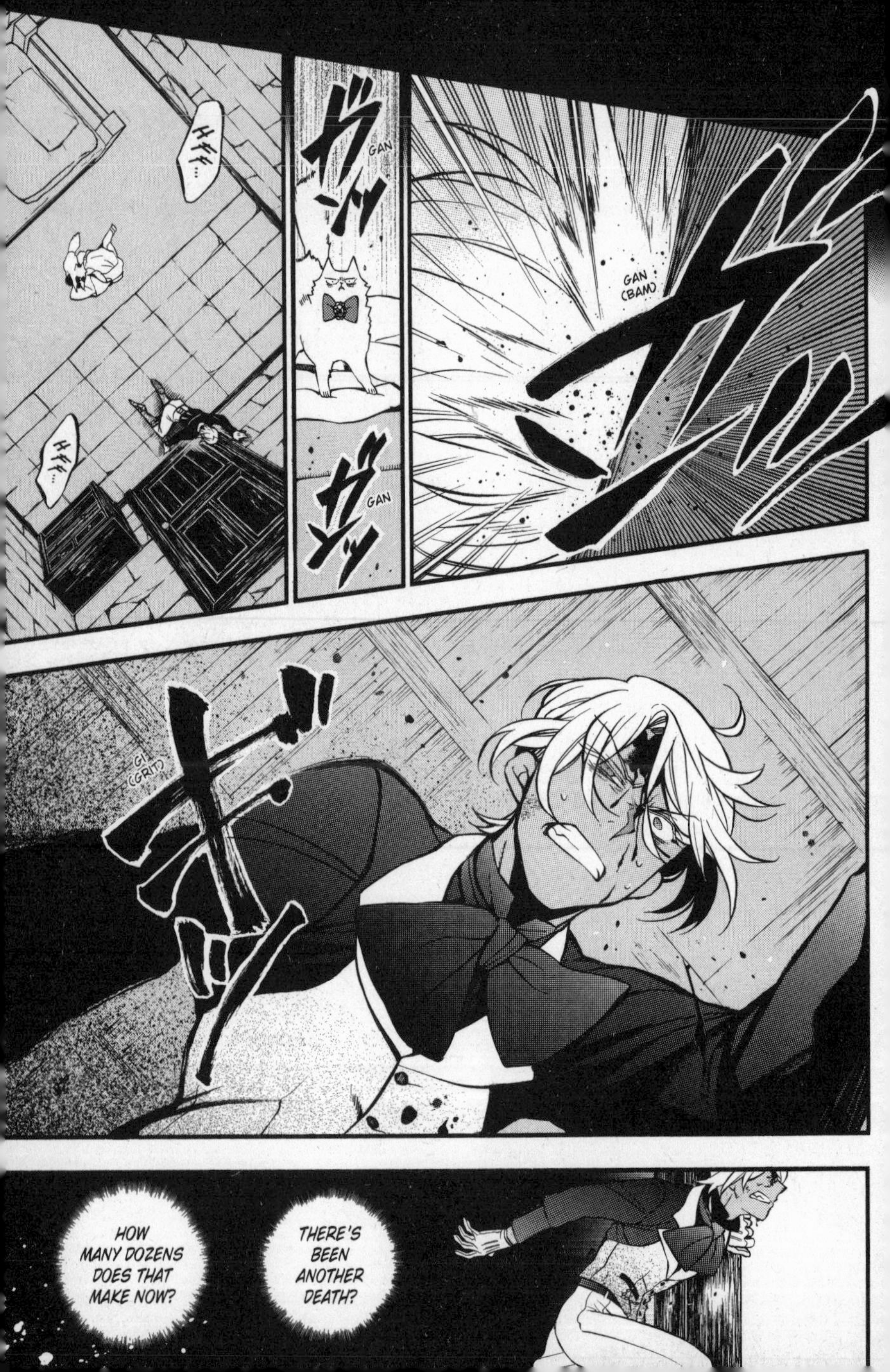
GAN (BAM)
GAN
GAN
GI (GRIT)
THERE'S BEEN ANOTHER DEATH?
HOW MANY DOZENS DOES THAT MAKE NOW?

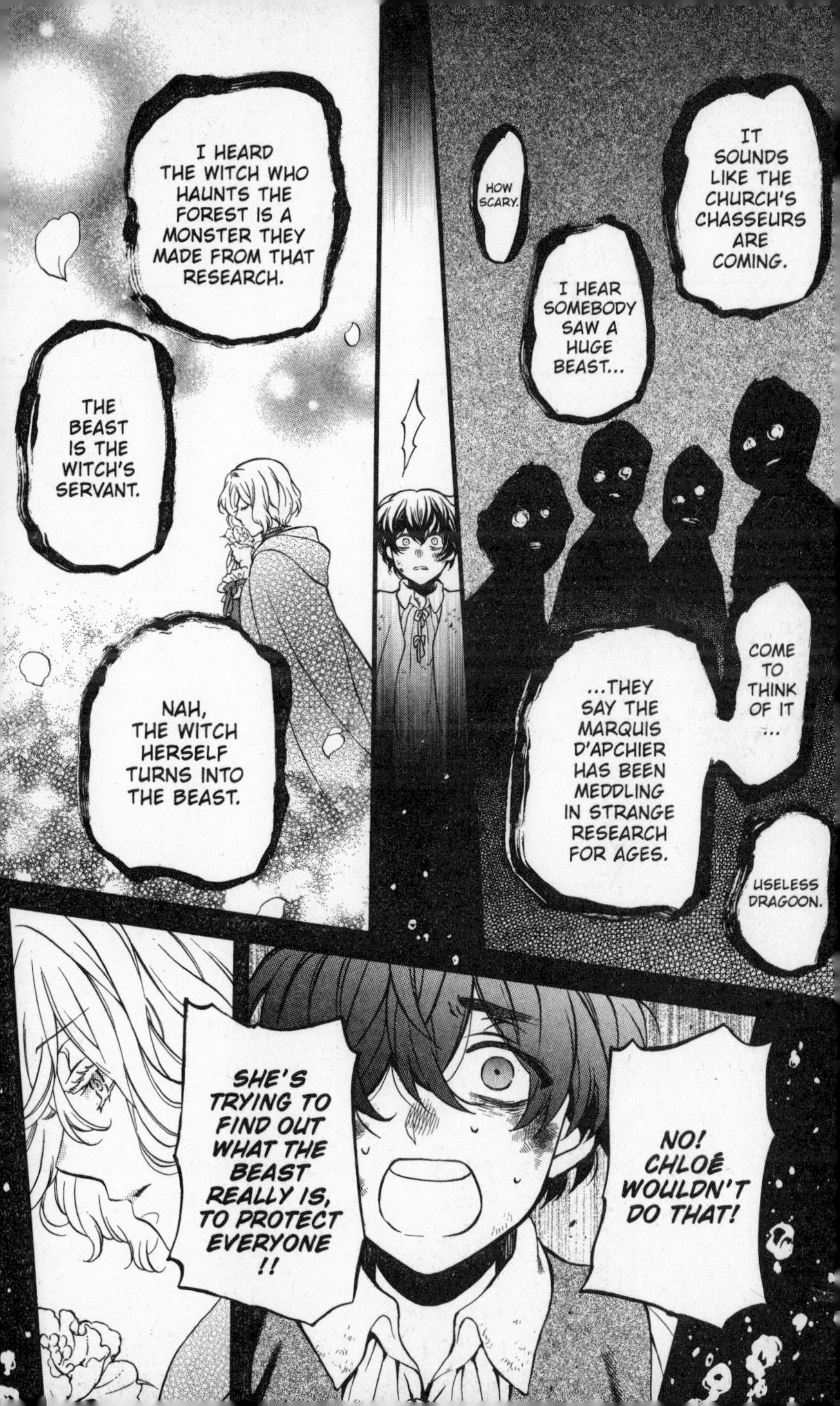
IT SOUNDS LIKE THE CHURCH'S CHASSEURS ARE COMING.
HOW SCARY.
I HEAR SOMEBODY SAW A HUGE BEAST...
COME TO THINK OF IT...
...THEY SAY THE MARQUIS D'APCHIER HAS BEEN MEDDLING IN STRANGE RESEARCH FOR AGES.
USELESS DRAGOON.
I HEARD THE WITCH WHO HAUNTS THE FOREST IS A MONSTER THEY MADE FROM THAT RESEARCH.
THE BEAST IS THE WITCH'S SERVANT.
NAH, THE WITCH HERSELF TURNS INTO THE BEAST.
NO! CHLOÉ WOULDN'T DO THAT!
SHE'S TRYING TO FIND OUT WHAT THE BEAST REALLY IS, TO PROTECT EVERYONE!!

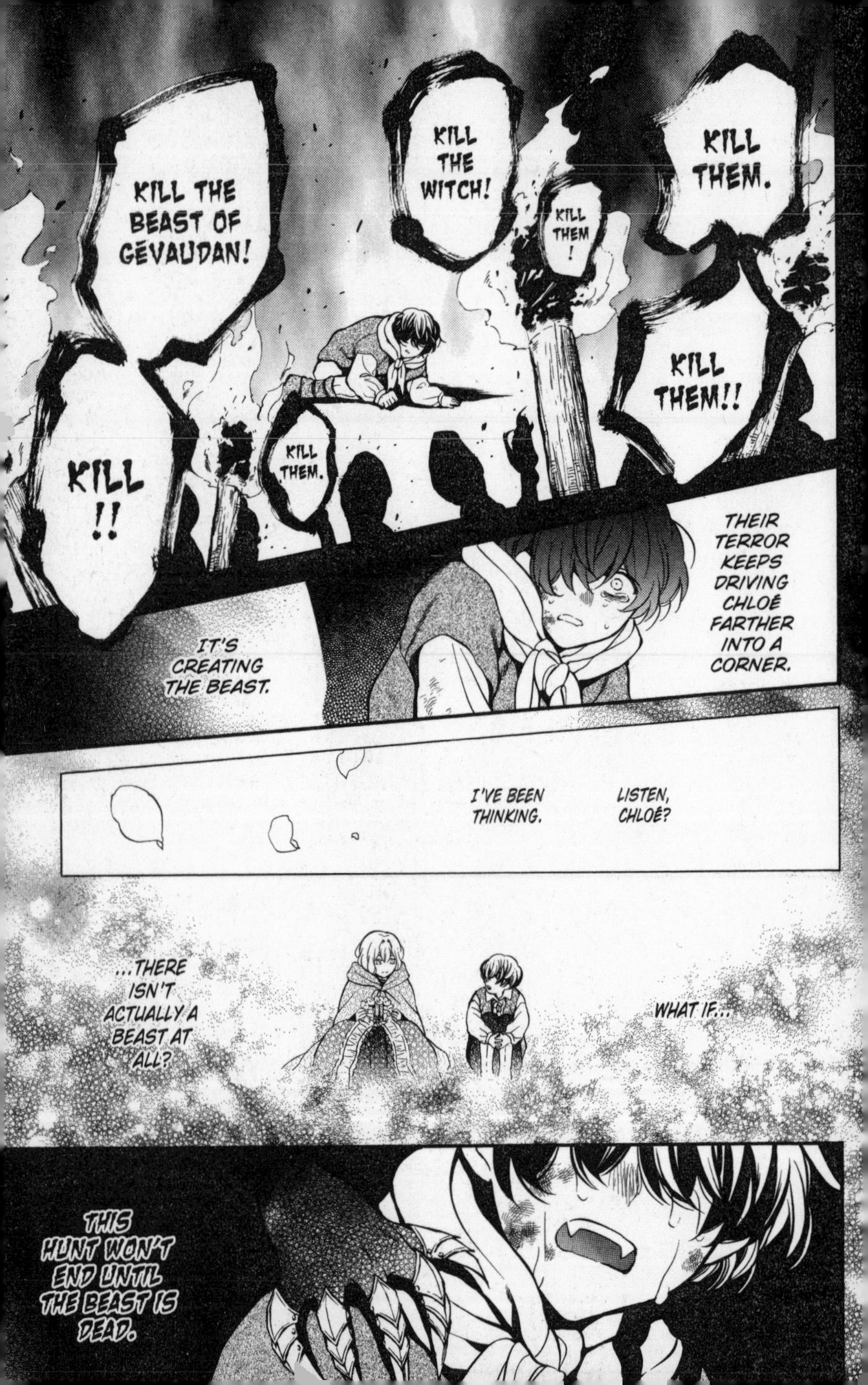
KILL THEM.
KILL THEM!!
KILL THEM !
KILL THE WITCH!
KILL THE BEAST OF GEVAUDAN!
KILL THEM.
KILL !!
THEIR TERROR KEEPS DRIVING CHLOÉ FARTHER INTO A CORNER.
IT'S CREATING THE BEAST.
LISTEN, CHLOÉ?
I'VE BEEN THINKING.
WHAT IF...
...THERE ISN'T ACTUALLY A BEAST AT ALL?
THIS HUNT WON'T END UNTIL THE BEAST IS DEAD.

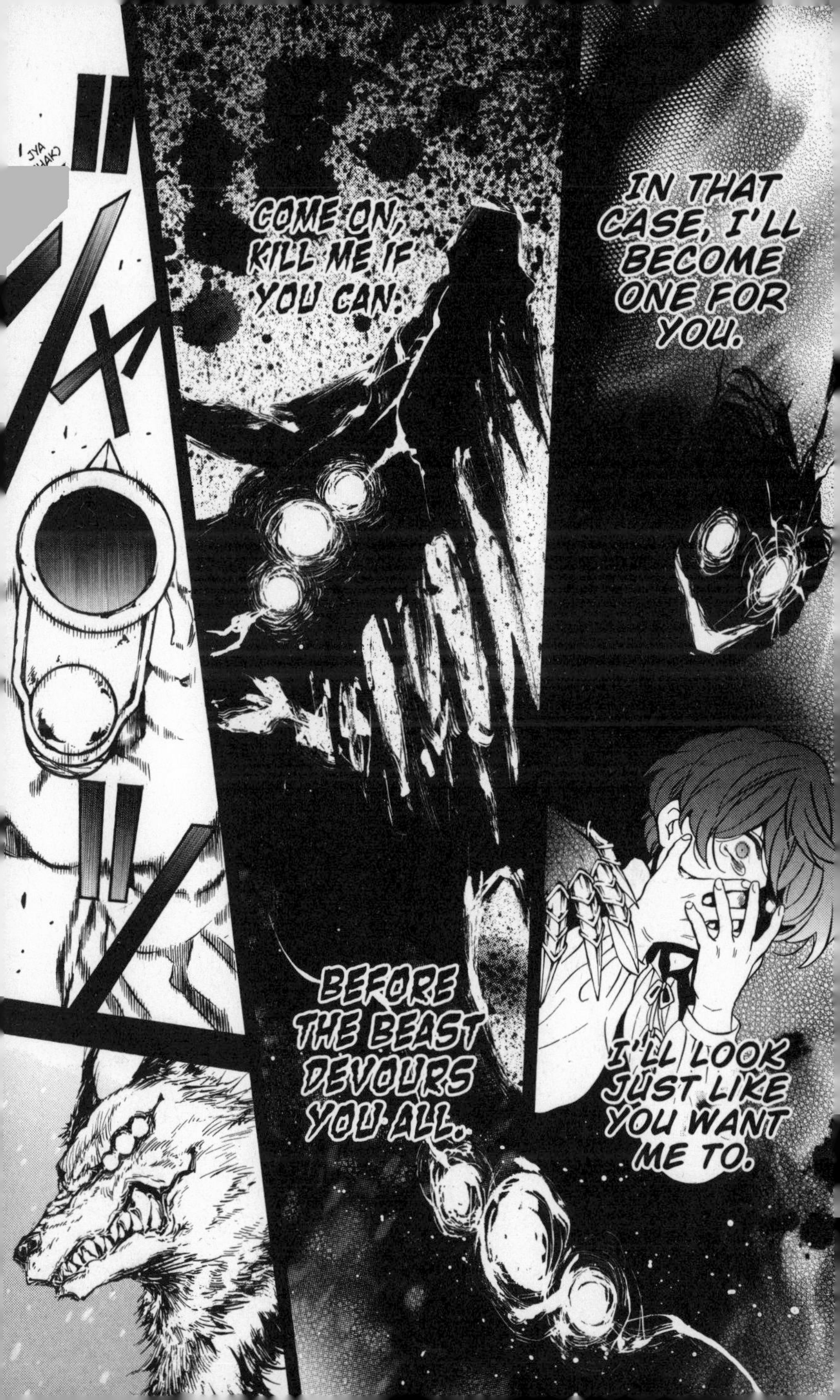
IN THAT CASE, I'LL BECOME ONE FOR YOU.
I'LL LOOK JUST LIKE YOU WANT ME TO.
COME ON, KILL ME IF YOU CAN.
BEFORE THE BEAST DEVOURS YOU ALL.
JYA

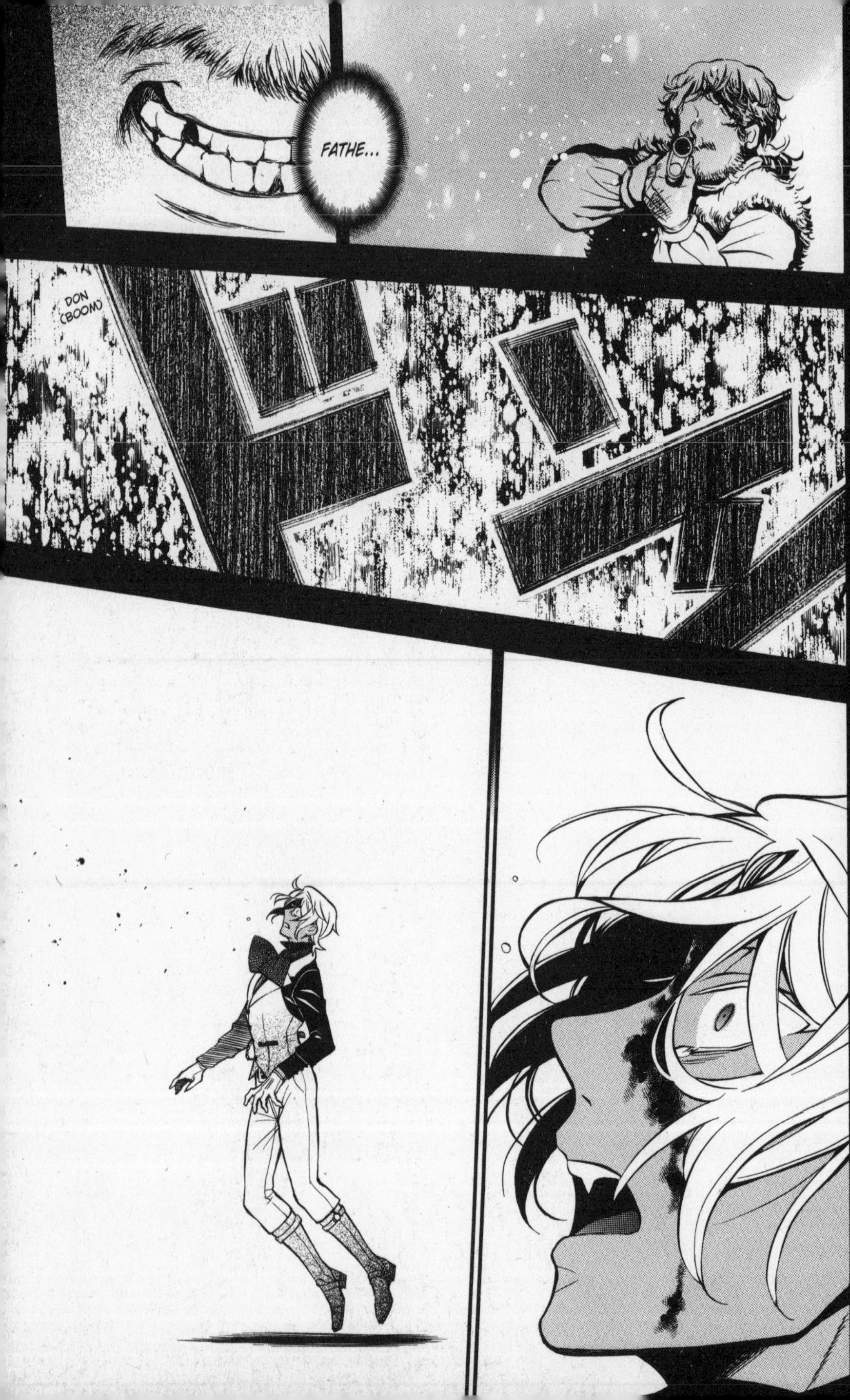
FATHE...
DON
(BOOM)

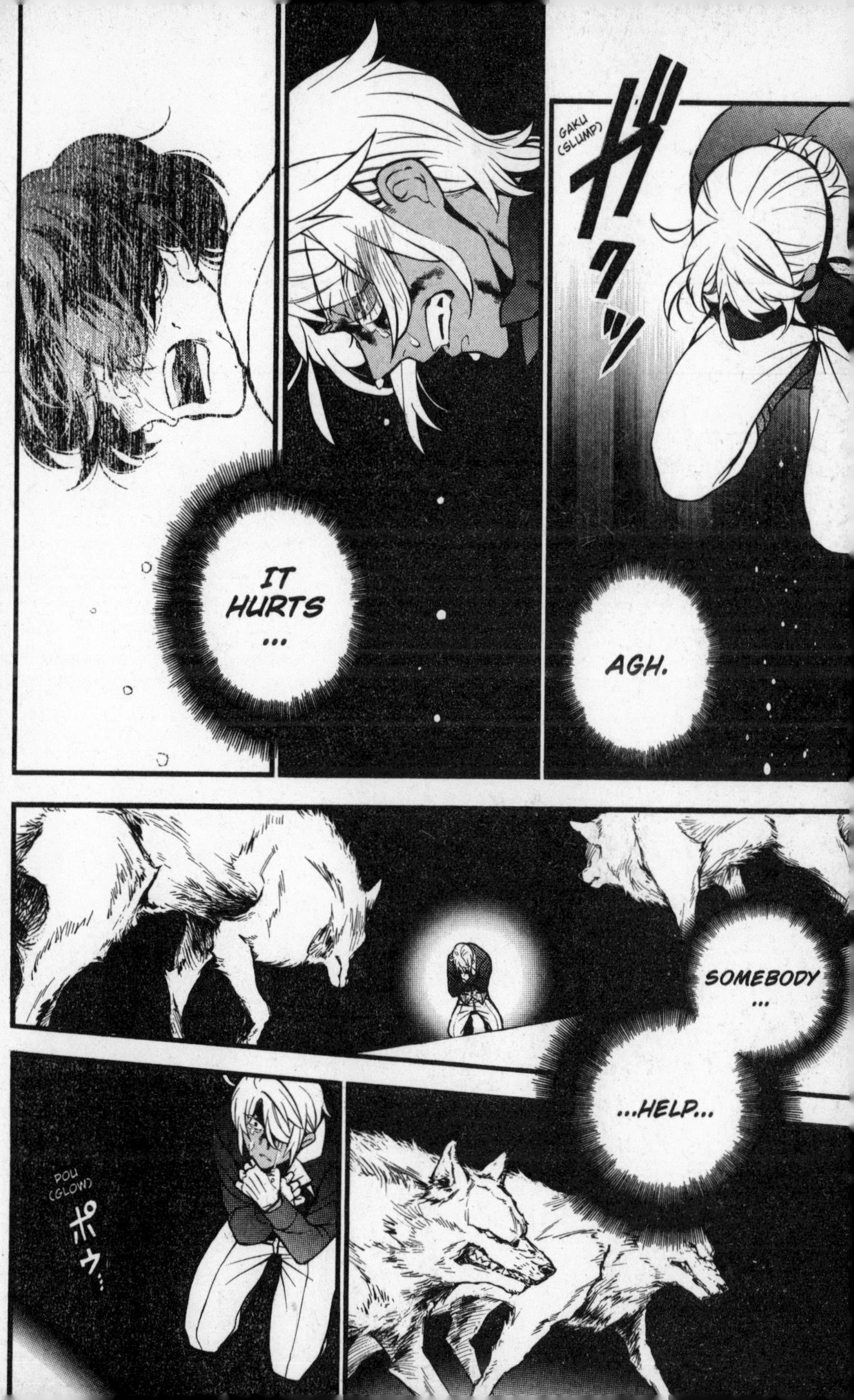
GAKU (SLUMP)
ガクッ
AGH.
IT HURTS ...
SOMEBODY ...
...HELP...
POU (GLOW)
ポウ…

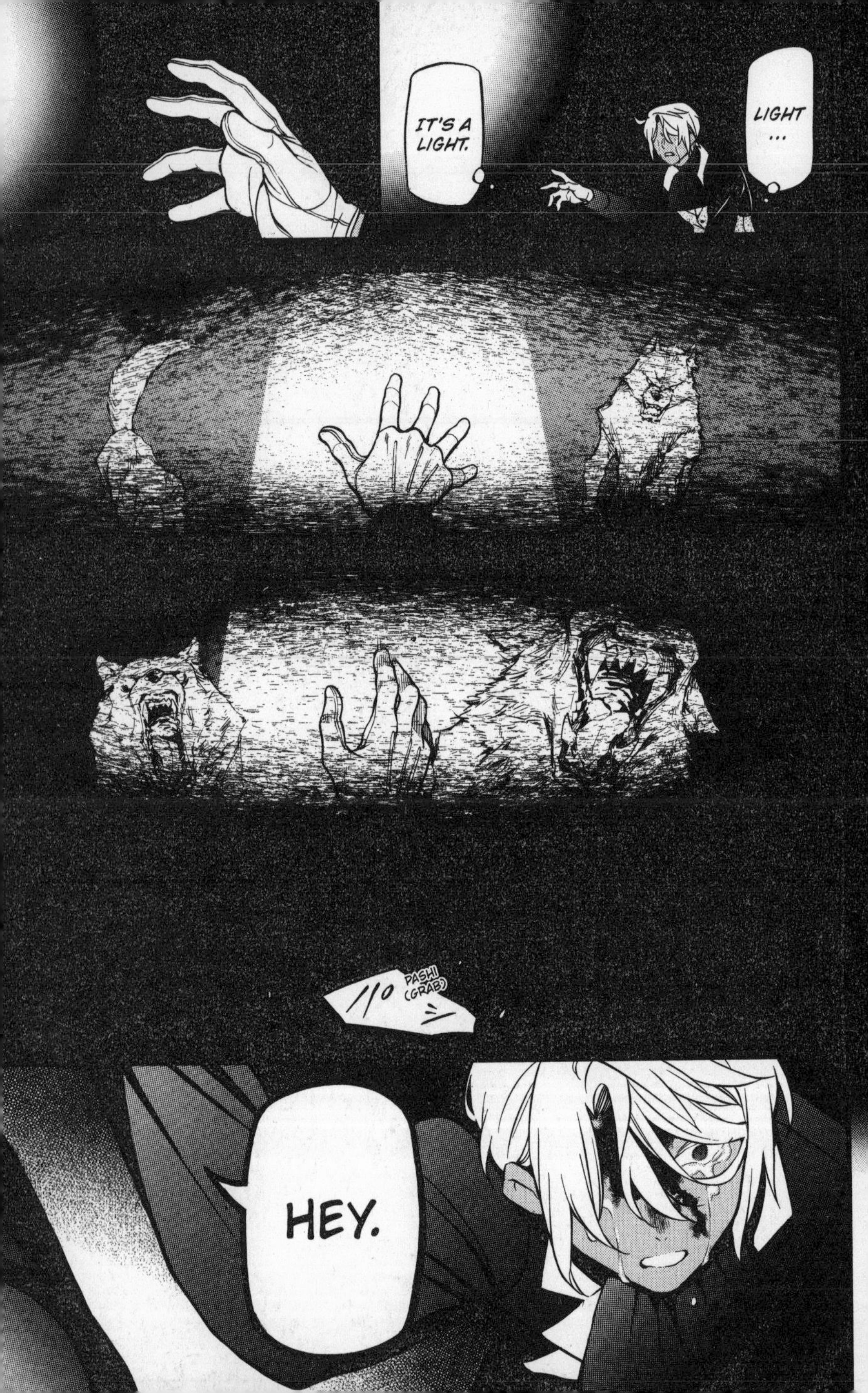
LIGHT ...
IT'S A LIGHT.
PASHI (GRAB)
HEY.

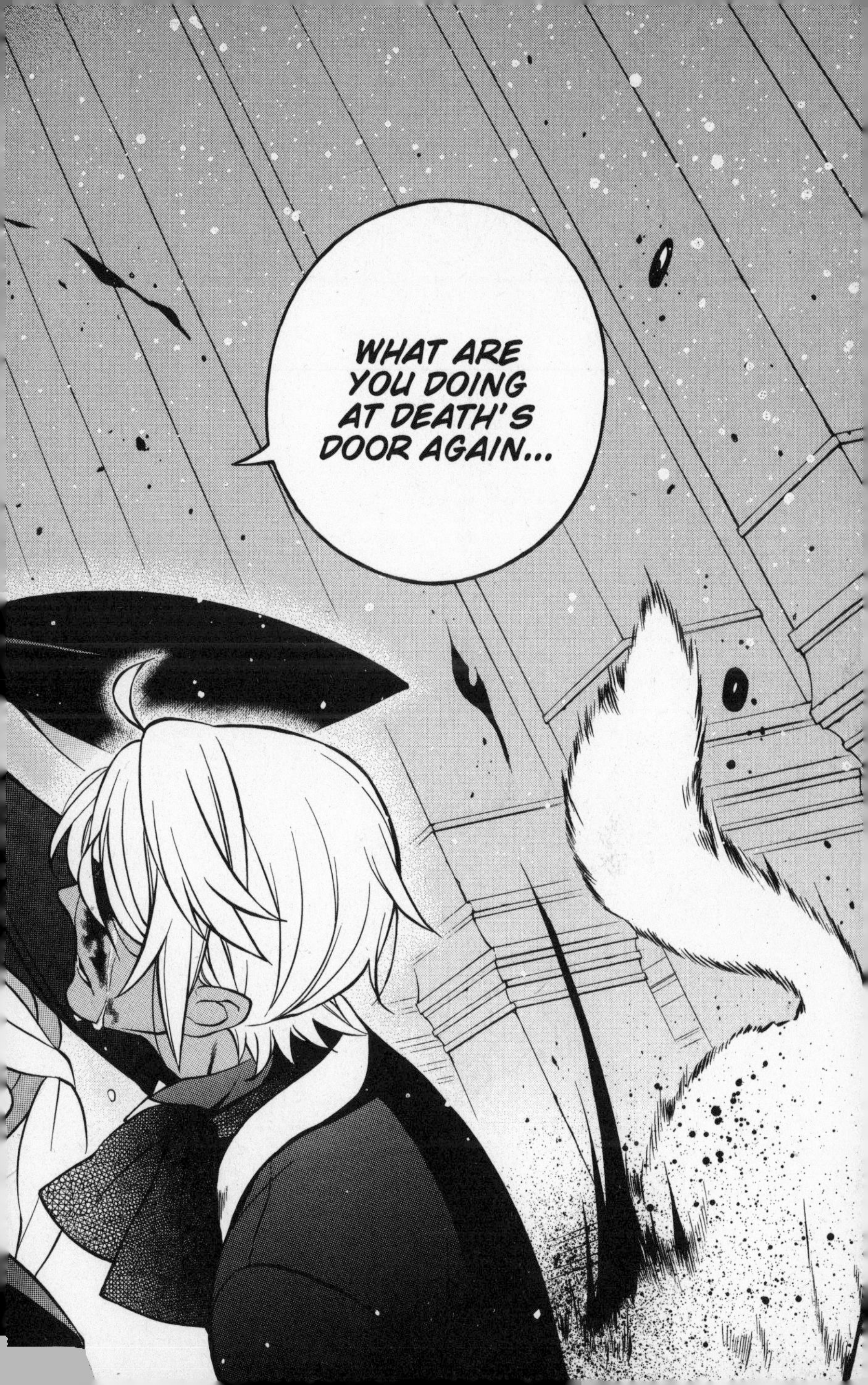
WHAT ARE YOU DOING AT DEATH'S DOOR AGAIN...

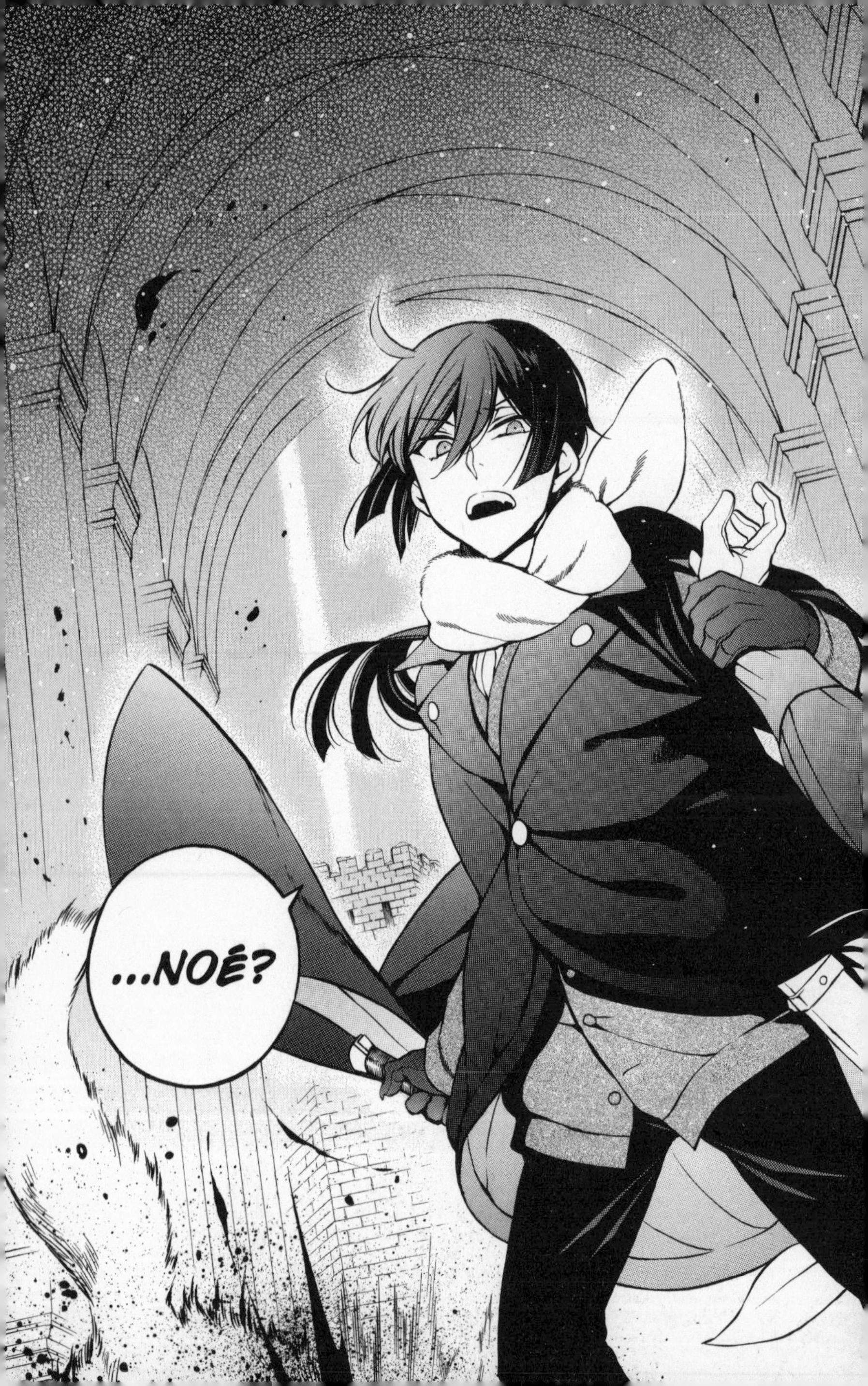
...NOÉ?

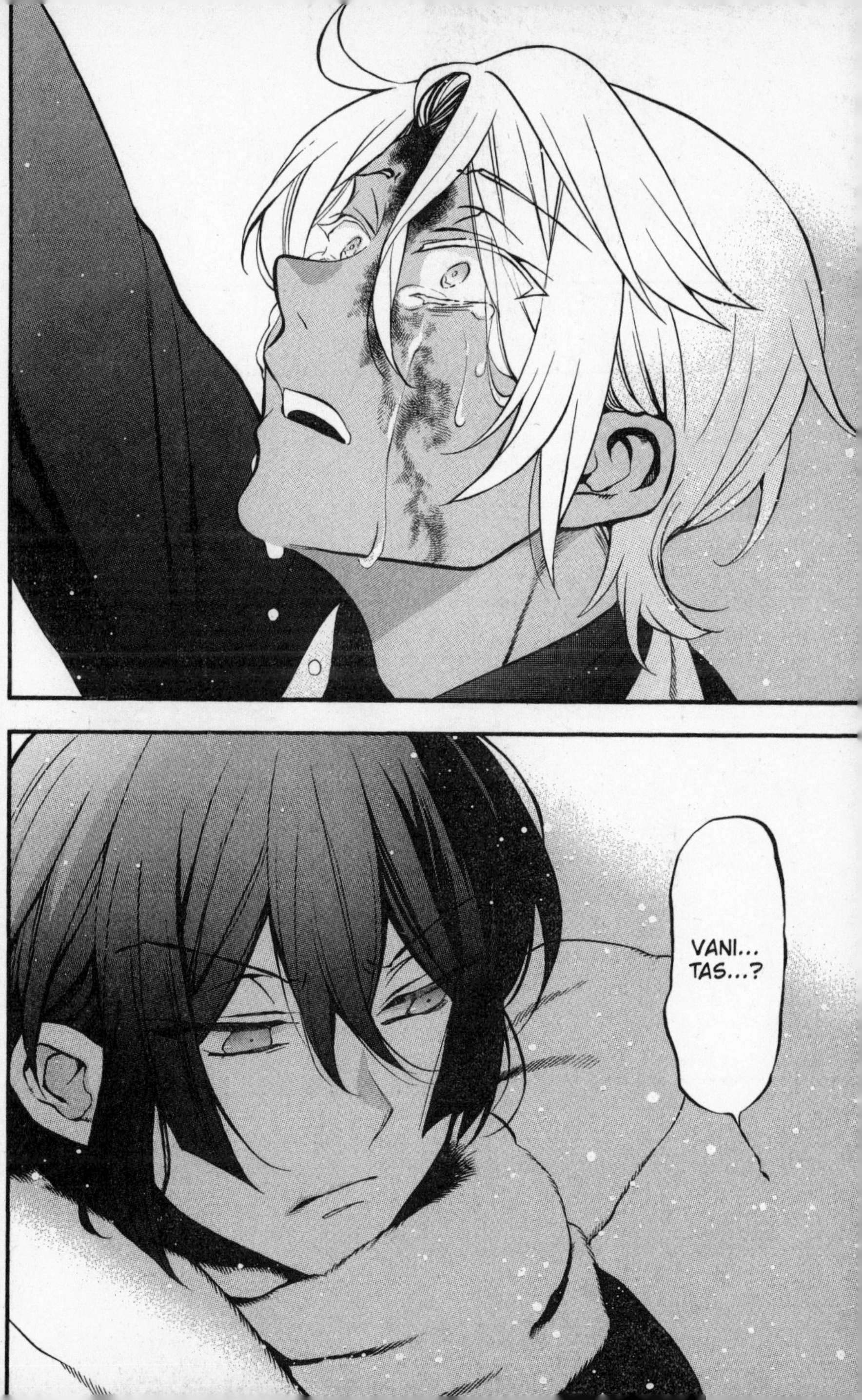
VANI... TAS...?

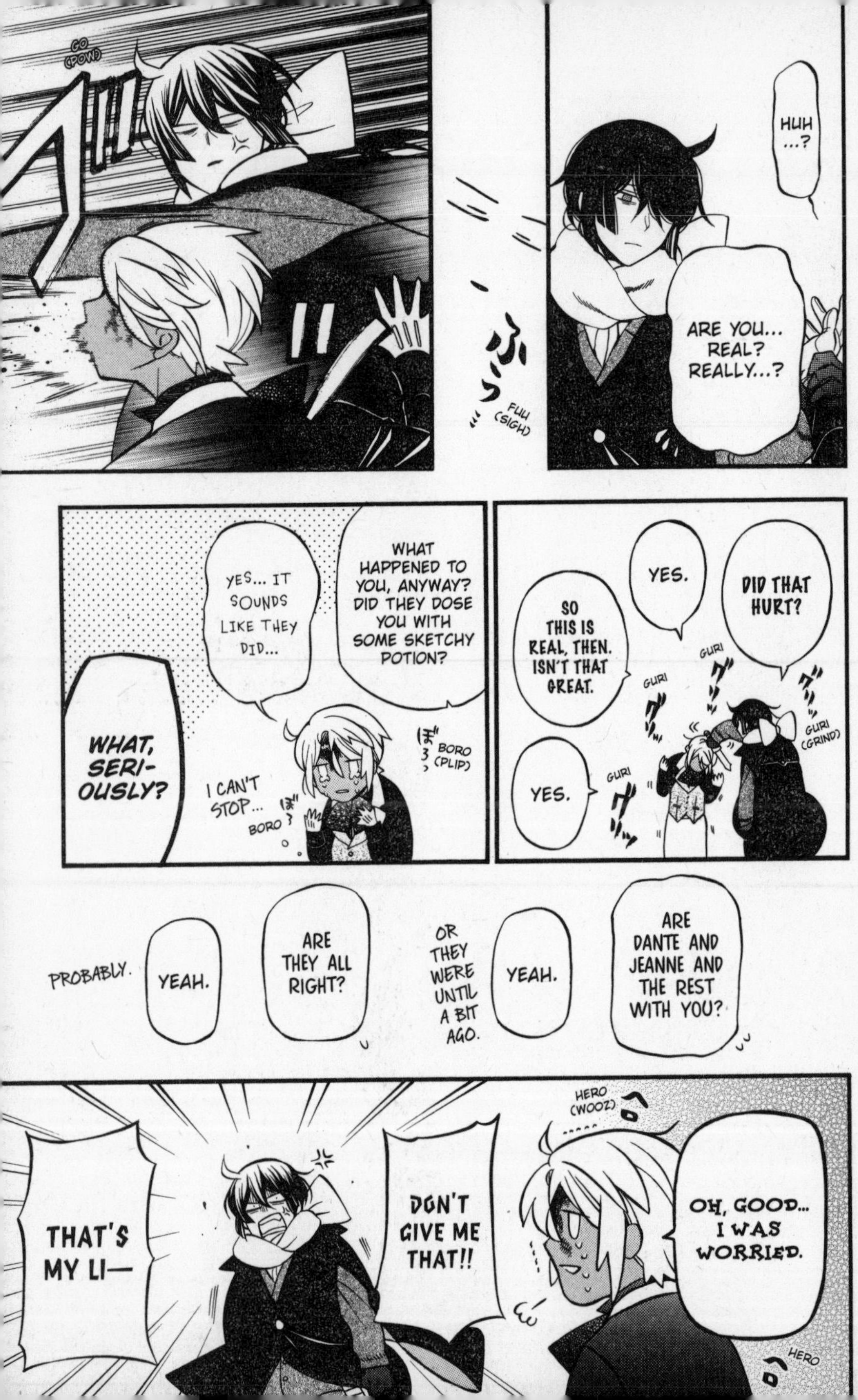
HUH ...?
ARE YOU... REAL? REALLY...?
FUU (SIGH)
GO (POW)
DID THAT HURT?
YES.
GURI (GRIND)
GURI
SO THIS IS REAL, THEN. ISN'T THAT GREAT.
GURI
YES.
GURI
WHAT HAPPENED TO YOU, ANYWAY? DID THEY DOSE YOU WITH SOME SKETCHY POTION?
YES... IT SOUNDS LIKE THEY DID...
BORO (PLIP)
WHAT, SERIOUSLY?
I CAN'T STOP...
BORO
ARE DANTE AND JEANNE AND THE REST WITH YOU?
YEAH.
OR THEY WERE UNTIL A BIT AGO.
ARE THEY ALL RIGHT?
YEAH.
PROBABLY.
HERO (WOOZ)
OH, GOOD... I WAS WORRIED.
HERO
DON'T GIVE ME THAT!!
THAT'S MY LI—

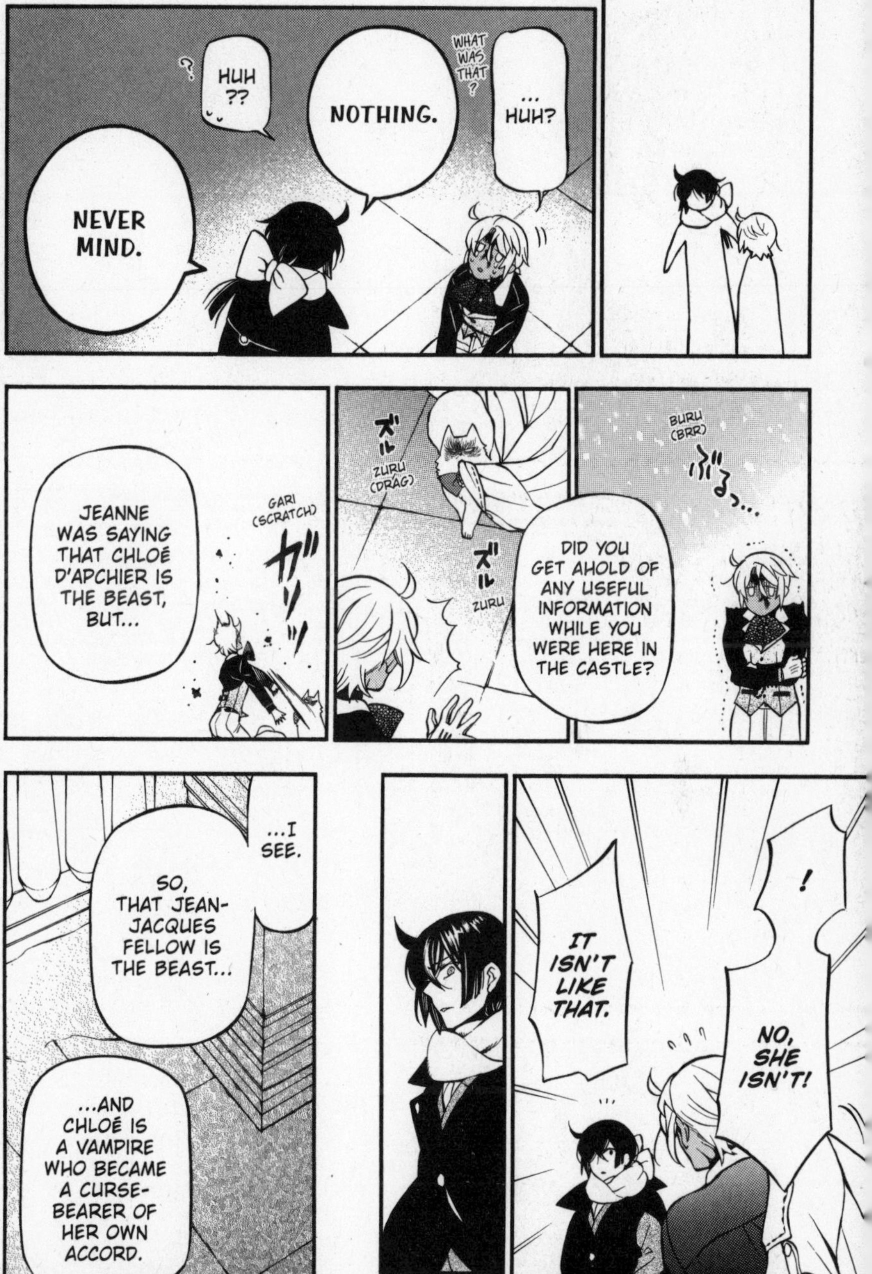
WHAT WAS THAT?
...HUH?
NOTHING.
HUH??
NEVER MIND.
BURU (BRR)
ぶるっ…
DID YOU GET AHOLD OF ANY USEFUL INFORMATION WHILE YOU WERE HERE IN THE CASTLE?
ズル
ZURU (DRAG)
ズル
ZURU
GARI (SCRATCH)
ガッ
JEANNE WAS SAYING THAT CHLOÉ D'APCHIER IS THE BEAST, BUT...
NO, SHE ISN'T!
IT ISN'T LIKE THAT.
...I SEE.
SO, THAT JEAN-JACQUES FELLOW IS THE BEAST...
...AND CHLOÉ IS A VAMPIRE WHO BECAME A CURSE-BEARER OF HER OWN ACCORD.

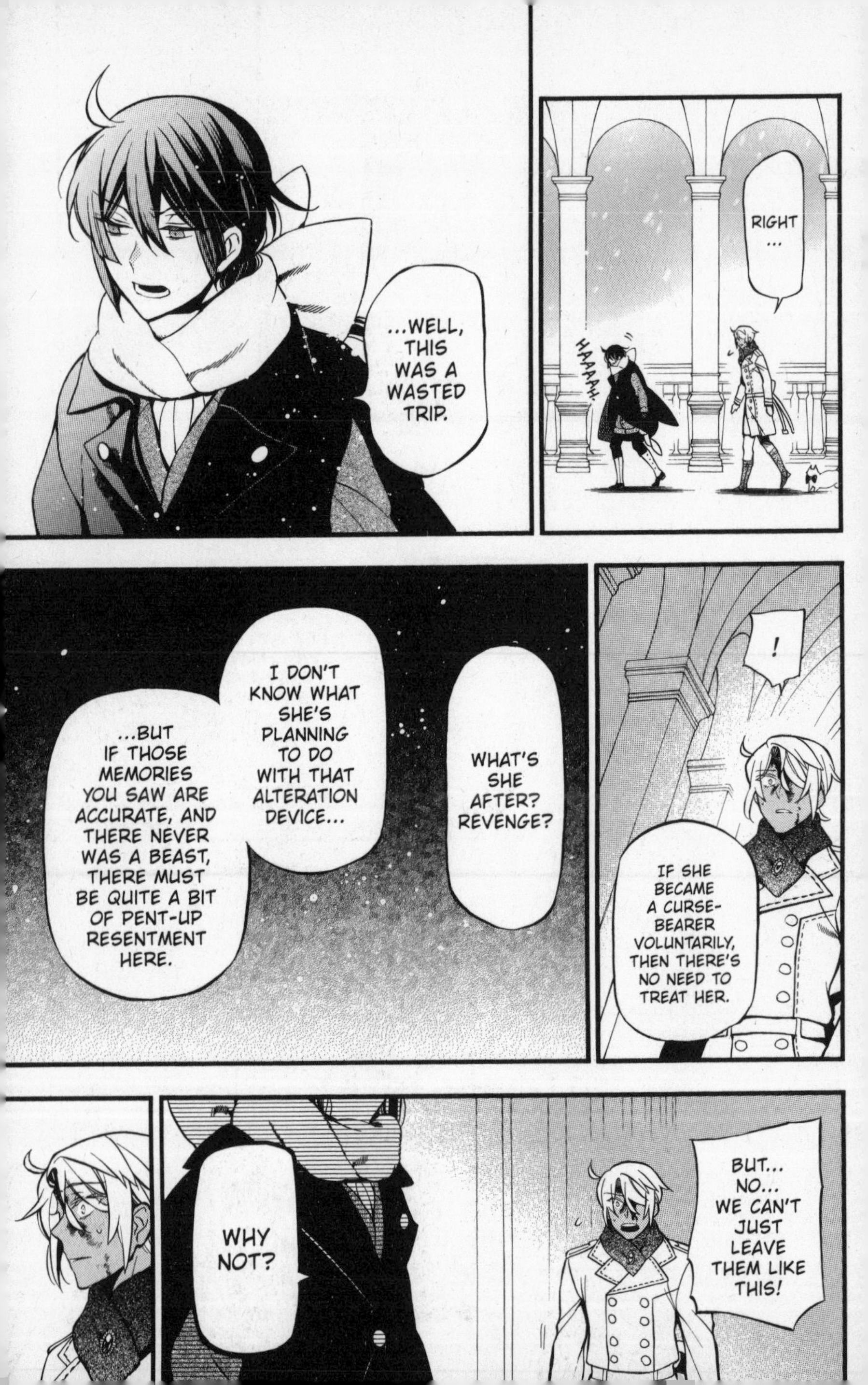
RIGHT...
HAAAAH.
...WELL, THIS WAS A WASTED TRIP.
!
IF SHE BECAME A CURSE-BEARER VOLUNTARILY, THEN THERE'S NO NEED TO TREAT HER.
WHAT'S SHE AFTER? REVENGE?
I DON'T KNOW WHAT SHE'S PLANNING TO DO WITH THAT ALTERATION DEVICE...
...BUT IF THOSE MEMORIES YOU SAW ARE ACCURATE, AND THERE NEVER WAS A BEAST, THERE MUST BE QUITE A BIT OF PENT-UP RESENTMENT HERE.
BUT... NO... WE CAN'T JUST LEAVE THEM LIKE THIS!
WHY NOT?

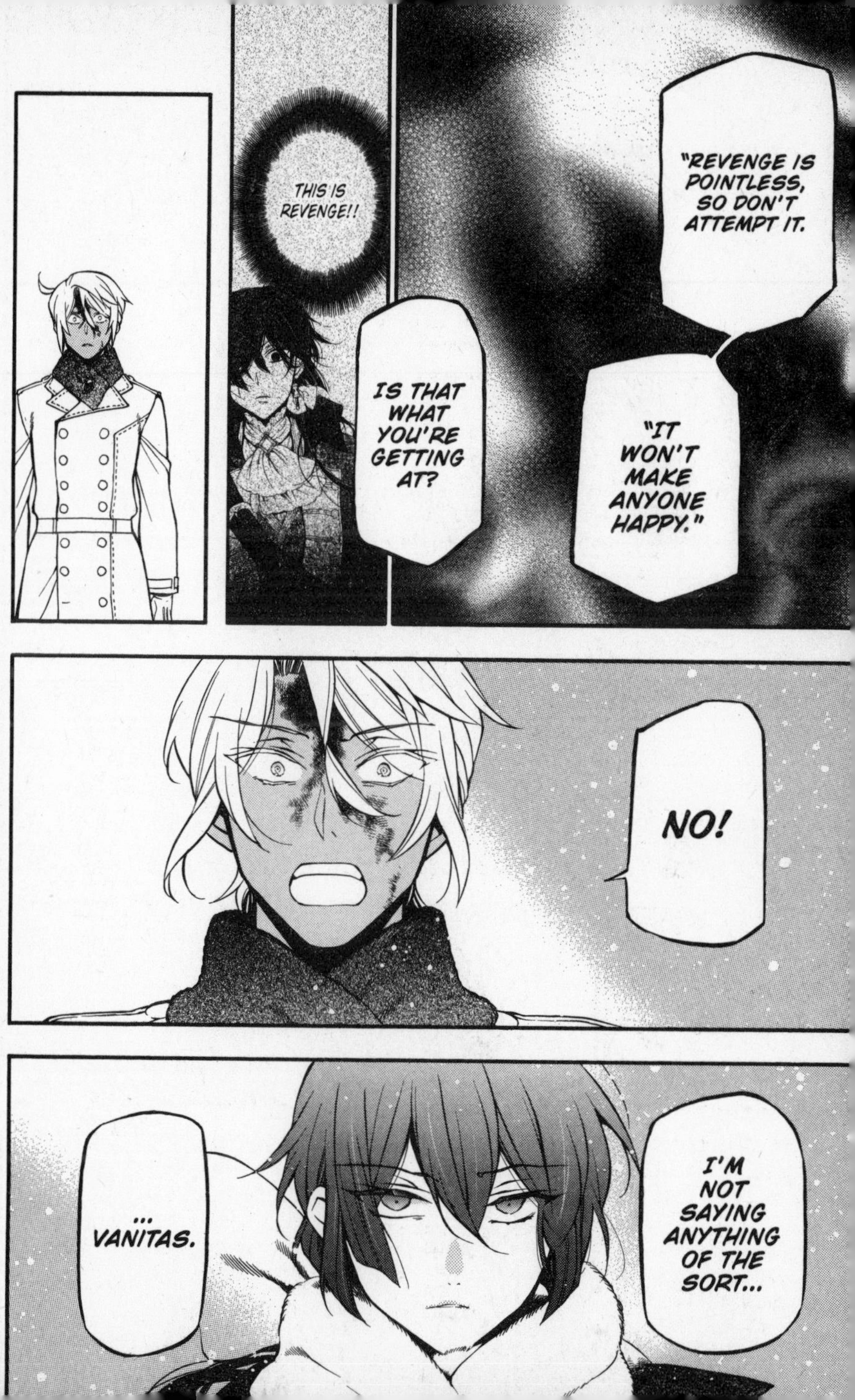
"REVENGE IS POINTLESS, SO DON'T ATTEMPT IT.
"IT WON'T MAKE ANYONE HAPPY."
THIS IS REVENGE!!
IS THAT WHAT YOU'RE GETTING AT?
NO!
I'M NOT SAYING ANYTHING OF THE SORT...
...VANITAS.

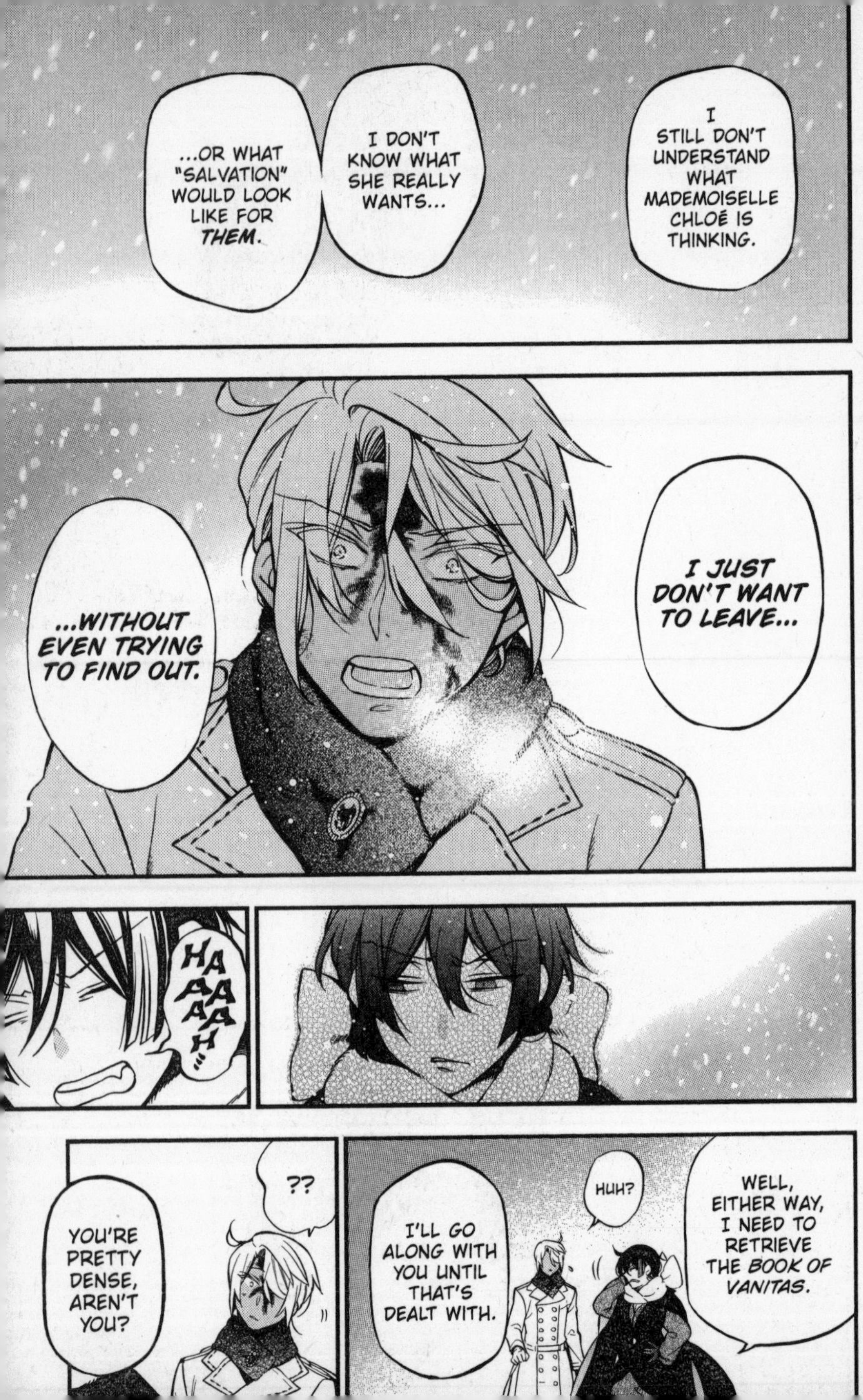
I STILL DON'T UNDERSTAND WHAT MADEMOISELLE CHLOÉ IS THINKING.
I DON'T KNOW WHAT SHE REALLY WANTS...
...OR WHAT "SALVATION" WOULD LOOK LIKE FOR *THEM*.
I JUST DON'T WANT TO LEAVE...
...WITHOUT EVEN TRYING TO FIND OUT.
HAAAAH!!
WELL, EITHER WAY, I NEED TO RETRIEVE THE *BOOK OF VANITAS*.
HUH?
I'LL GO ALONG WITH YOU UNTIL THAT'S DEALT WITH.
??
YOU'RE PRETTY DENSE, AREN'T YOU?

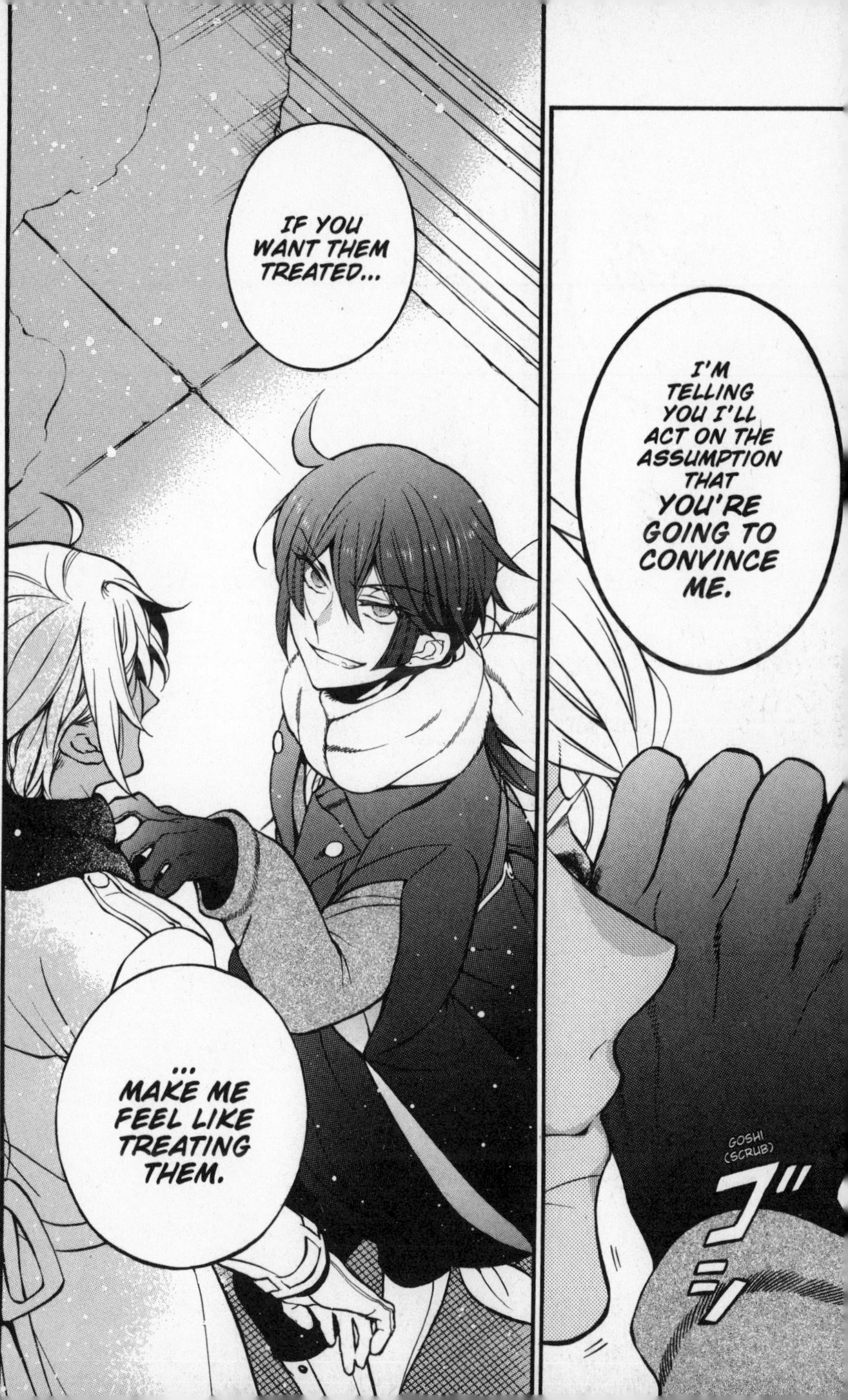
I'M TELLING YOU I'LL ACT ON THE ASSUMPTION THAT YOU'RE GOING TO CONVINCE ME.
GOSHI (SCRUB)
ゴシ
IF YOU WANT THEM TREATED...
...MAKE ME FEEL LIKE TREATING THEM.

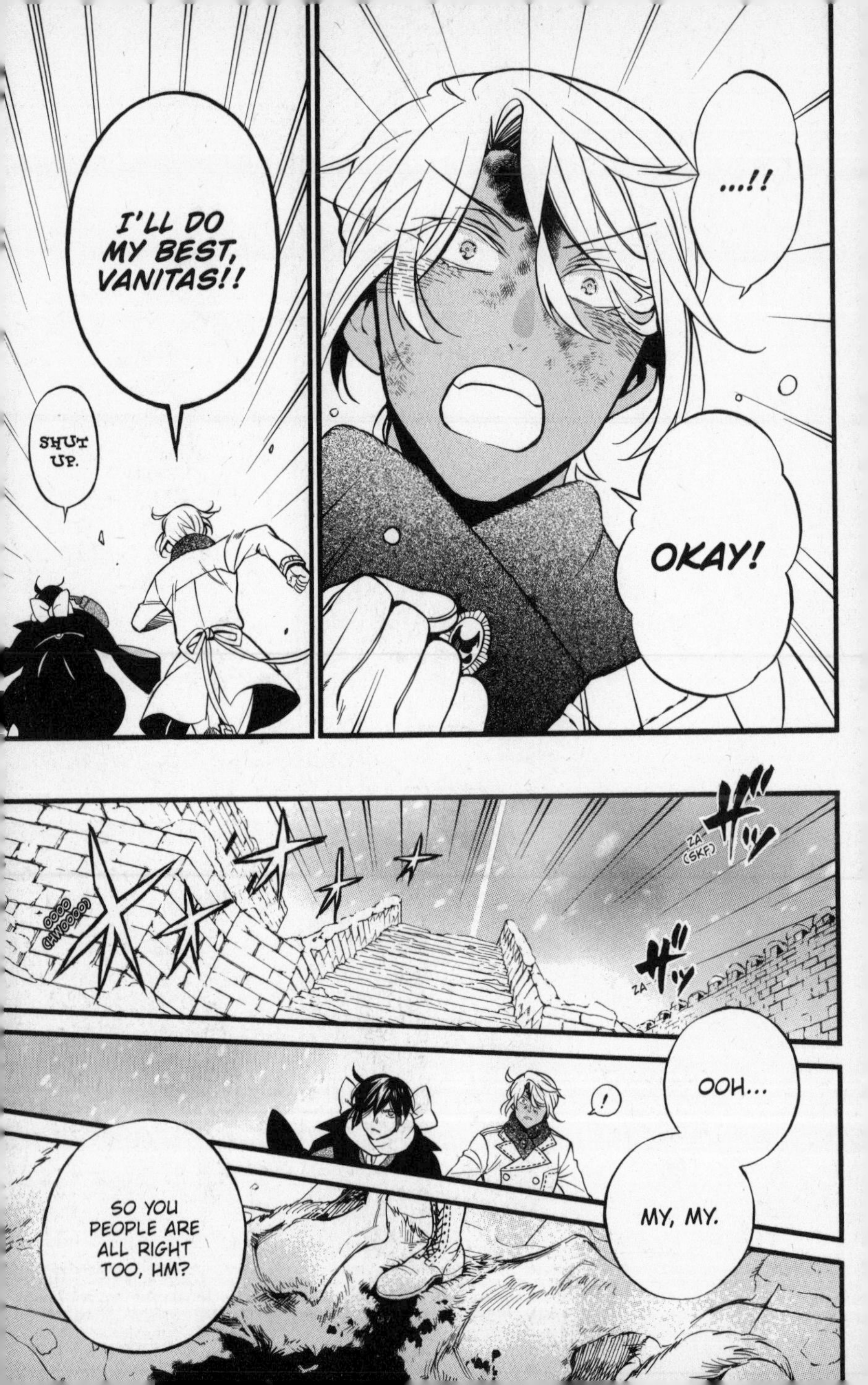
...!!
OKAY!
I'LL DO MY BEST, VANITAS!!
SHUT UP.
ZA (SKF)
ZA
OOOO (WHOOOO)
OOH...
MY, MY.
!
SO YOU PEOPLE ARE ALL RIGHT TOO, HM?

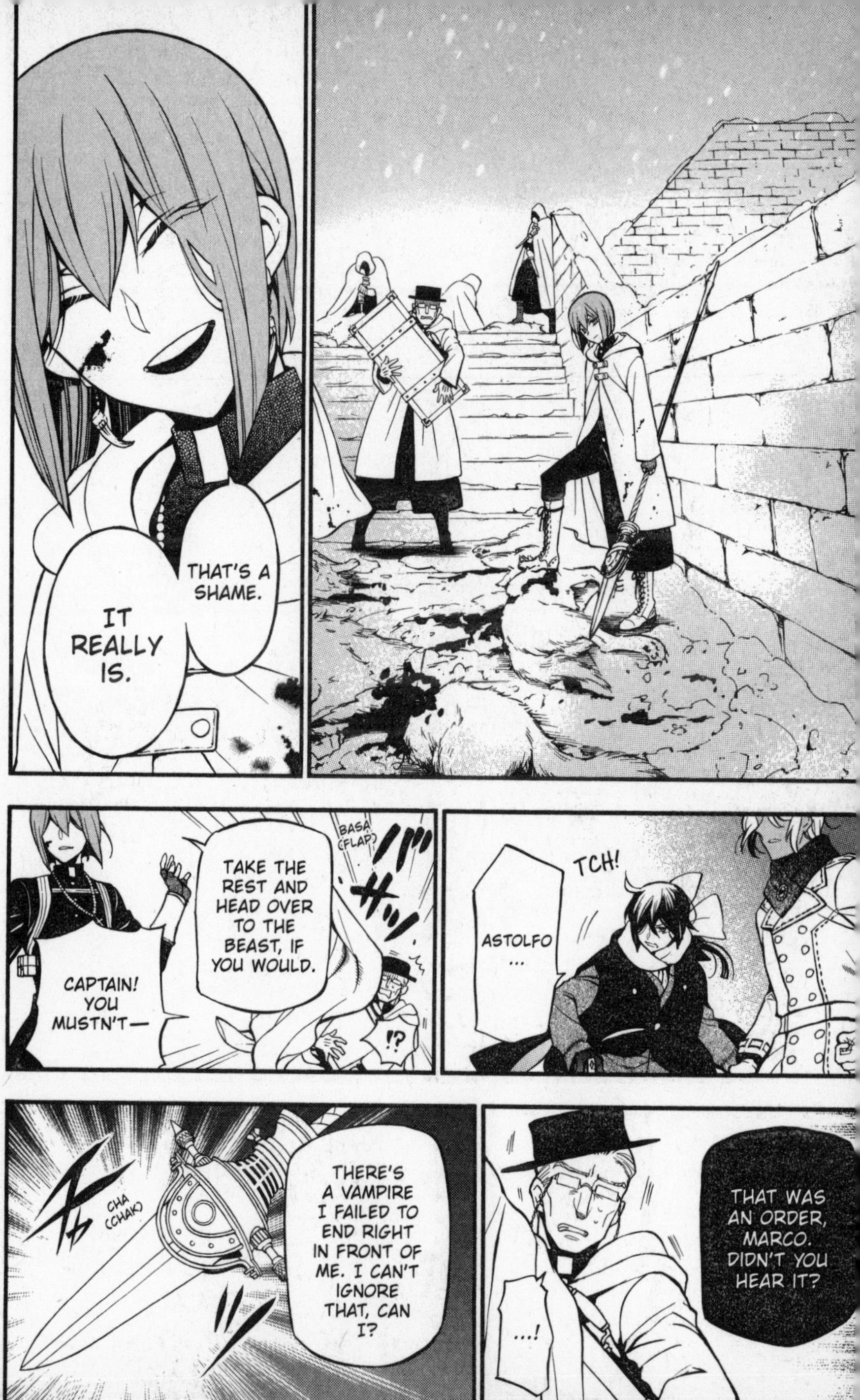
THAT'S A SHAME.
IT REALLY IS.
TCH!
ASTOLFO...
BASA (FLAP)
TAKE THE REST AND HEAD OVER TO THE BEAST, IF YOU WOULD.
!?
CAPTAIN! YOU MUSTN'T—
THAT WAS AN ORDER, MARCO. DIDN'T YOU HEAR IT?
...!
THERE'S A VAMPIRE I FAILED TO END RIGHT IN FRONT OF ME. I CAN'T IGNORE THAT, CAN I?
CHA (CHAK)

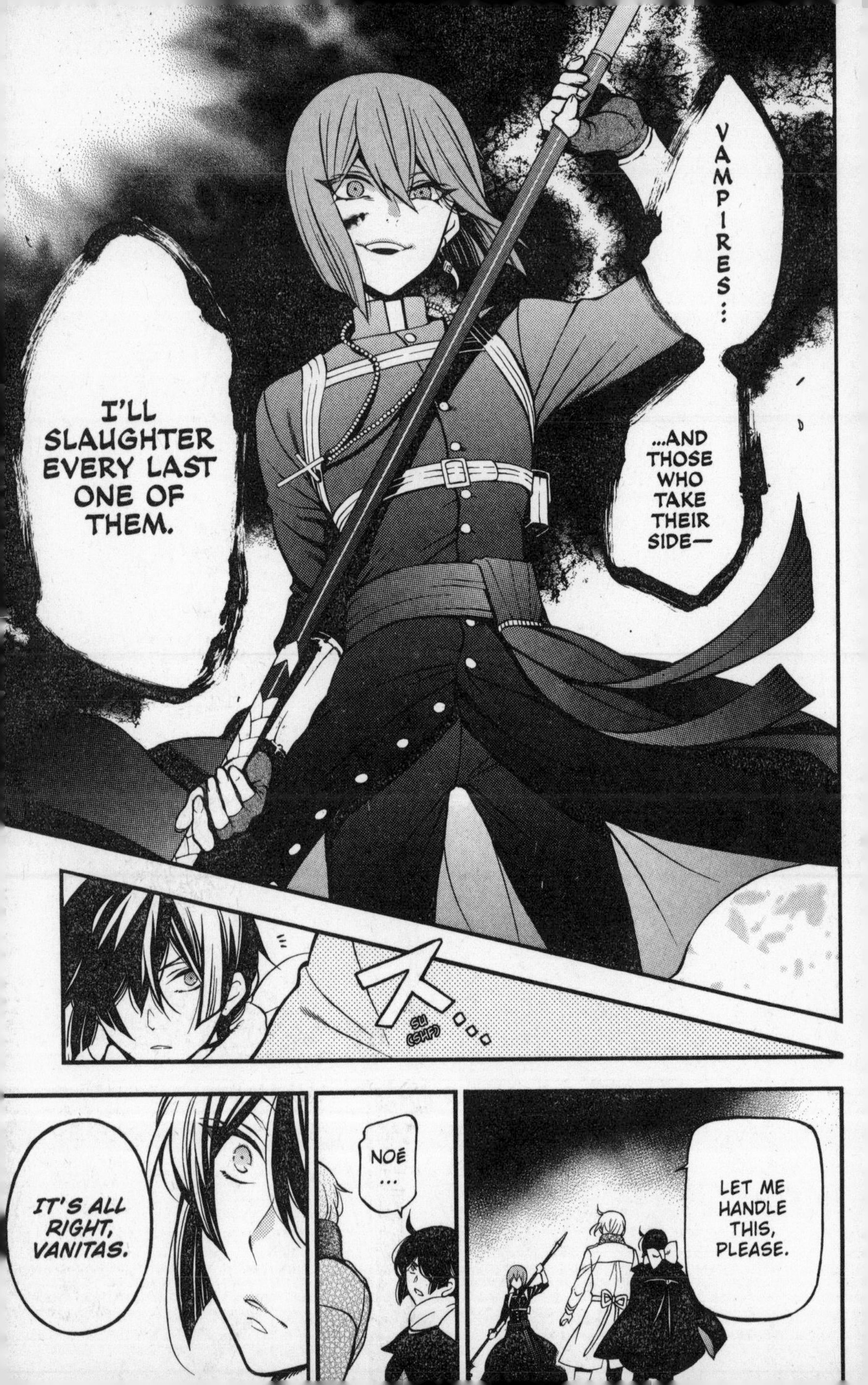
VAMPIRES...
...AND THOSE WHO TAKE THEIR SIDE—
I'LL SLAUGHTER EVERY LAST ONE OF THEM.
SU (SHF)
LET ME HANDLE THIS, PLEASE.
NOÉ ...
IT'S ALL RIGHT, VANITAS.

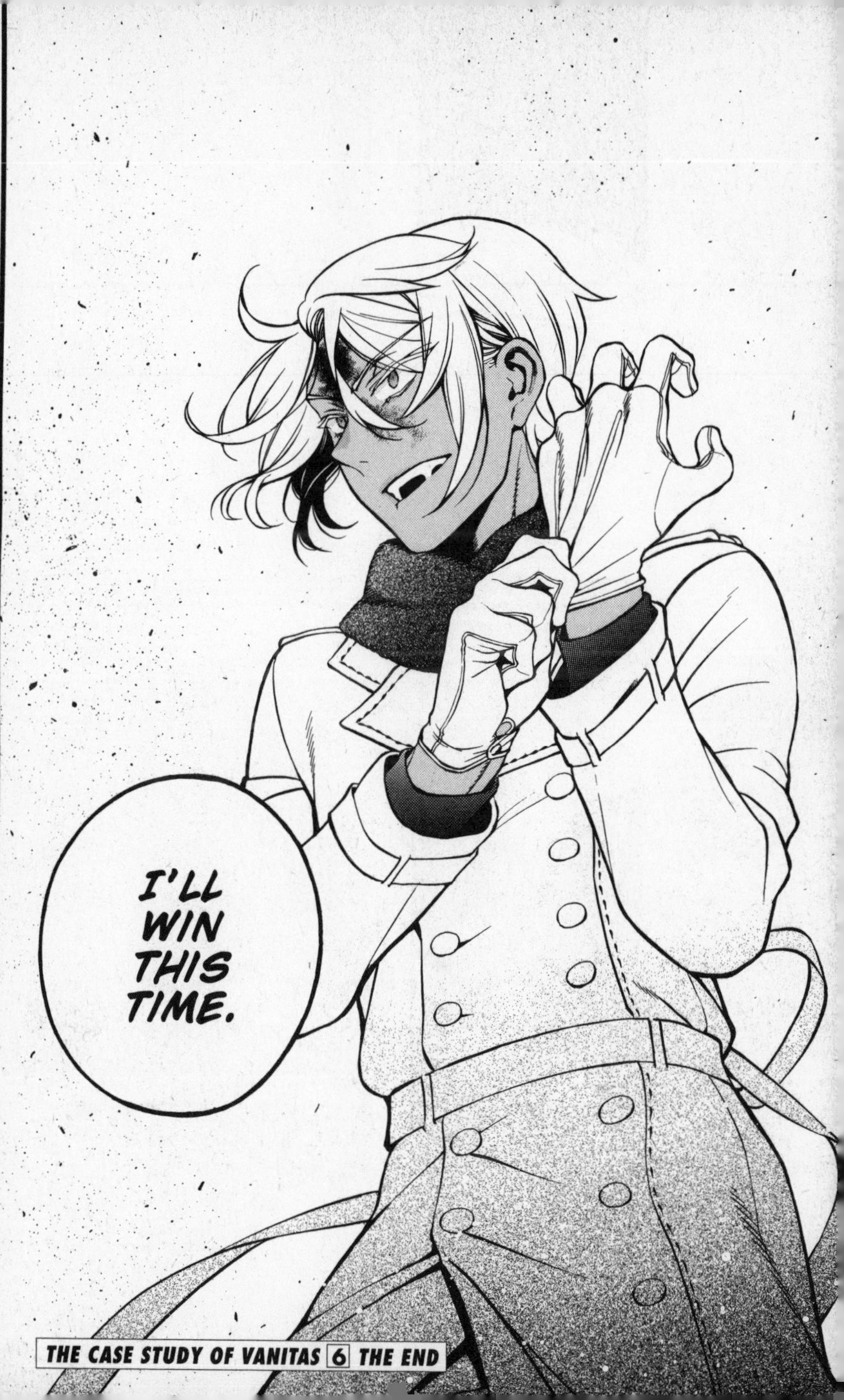
I'LL WIN THIS TIME.
THE CASE STUDY OF VANITAS 6 THE END